maran

illustrated

Piano

BOOK BONUS!

Visit www.maran.com/piano to download MP3 files you can listen to and play along with for all the chords, scales, exercises and practice pieces in the book.

COURSE TECHNOLOGY
CENGAGE Learning™

Australia • Brazil • Japan • Korea • Mexico • Singapore • Spain • United Kingdom • United States

COURSE TECHNOLOGY
CENGAGE Learning™

Maran Illustrated Piano
maranGraphics Development Group

Publisher and General Manager, Course Technology PTR:
Stacy L. Hiquet

Associate Director of Marketing, Course Technology PTR:
Sarah Panella

National Sales Manager, Course Technology PTR:
Amy Merrill

Manager of Editorial Services, Course Technology PTR:
Heather Talbot

Author:
maranGraphics Development Group

Content Architects:
Ruth Maran and Kelleigh Johnson

Technical Consultant:
Frank Horvat BMus, ARCT, RMT

Project Manager:
Judy Maran

Copy Development Director:
Jill Maran Dutfield

Copy Developers:
Adam Giles, Raquel Scott, and Michael B. Kelly

Editor:
Adam Giles

Electronic Creation of Music Examples:
Tim Martin

Layout Designer:
Richard Hung

Front Cover Image and Overview Designer:
Russ Marini

Photographic Retouching:
Russ Marini and Richard Hung

Indexer:
Kelleigh Johnson

Photography and Post Production:
Robert Maran

Printed in the United States of America
8 9 10 11 12 11

Library of Congress Catalog Card Number: 2005921014
ISBN-13: 978-1-59200-864-3
ISBN-10: 1-59200-864-X

maranGraphics Inc.
5755 Coopers Avenue
Mississauga, Ontario
L4Z 1R9

Course Technology
20 Channel Center Street
Boston, MA 02210

Cengage Learning is a leading provider of customized learning solutions with office locations around the globe, including Singapore, the United Kingdom, Australia, Mexico, Brazil, and Japan. Locate your local office at: **international. cengage.com/region**

Cengage Learning products are represented in Canada by Nelson Education, Ltd.

For your lifelong learning solutions, visit **courseptr.com**

Visit our corporate website at **cengage.com**

maranGraphics is a family-run business

At **maranGraphics**, we believe in producing great consumer books–one book at a time.

Each maranGraphics book uses the award-winning communication process that we have been developing over the last 30 years. Using this process, we organize photographs and text in a way that makes it easy for you to learn new concepts and tasks.

We spend hours deciding the best way to perform each task, so you don't have to! Our clear, easy-to-follow photographs and instructions walk you through each task from beginning to end.

We want to thank you for purchasing what we feel are the best books money can buy. We hope you enjoy using this book as much as we enjoyed creating it!

Sincerely,

The Maran Family

We would love to hear from you! Send your comments and feedback about our books to family@maran.com

To sign up for sneak peeks and news about our upcoming books, send an e-mail to newbooks@maran.com

Please visit us on the Web at:

www.maran.com

ACKNOWLEDGMENTS

Thanks to the dedicated staff of maranGraphics, including Adam Giles, Richard Hung, Kelleigh Johnson, Wanda Lawrie, Jill Maran Dutfield, Judy Maran, Robert Maran, Ruth Maran, Russ Marini and Raquel Scott.

Finally, to Richard Maran who originated the easy-to-use graphic format of this guide. Thank you for your inspiration and guidance.

ABOUT THE TECHNICAL CONSULTANT...

Frank Horvat

Composer, performer and teacher, Frank Horvat began his musical studies at the age of five. He has ventured into many areas of music and has received many awards and scholarships along the way. He holds an ARCT Diploma with Honours in Piano Teaching from the Royal Conservatory of Music. He also holds a Bachelor of Music Degree, majoring in Composition at the Faculty of Music, University of Toronto.

Frank has been an active piano and theory teacher for many years. He has also worked closely with music teaching colleagues in the Ontario Registered Music Teachers' Association where he has been an active member and President of the Central Toronto Branch.

He has also performed, directed and arranged many styles of music, including Classical, Blues, Rock, Jazz and Pop both in ensembles and as a soloist.

Frank began writing music at the age of eleven. His portfolio consists of chamber, pop, electronic, musical theatre, film and large ensemble works. His work has been performed on many occasions in a variety of live venues and on television networks like the CBC and Bravo.

Frank maintains a private teaching studio along with being a member of the College of Examiners for the Royal Conservatory of Music. Additionally, he conducts workshops and authors articles on a variety of topics related to music education. Along with making concert appearances as a performer, he also continues work on a variety of compositions from his home studio for live concert and film genres.

SPECIAL THANKS...

Thank you to the following companies for allowing us to show photographs of their equipment in our book:

Baldwin Pianos-Gibson Guitar Corp.
www.baldwinpiano.com

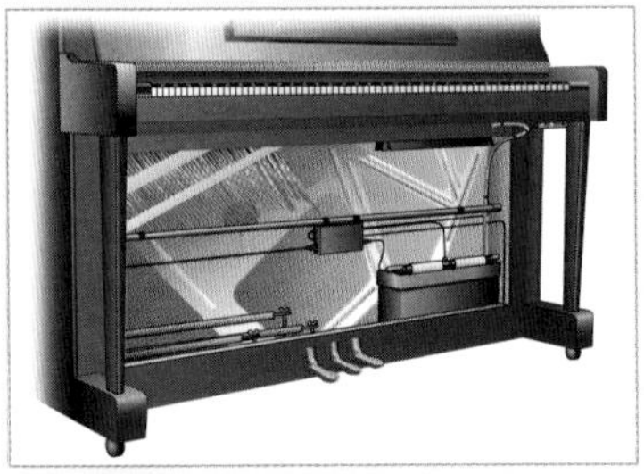

Dampp-Chaser© Corp.
www.dampp-chaser.com

Paul L. Jansen & Son, Inc.
www.pljansen.com

Roland Corporation, U.S.
www.rolandus.com

Claviers Baroques
www.claviersbaroques.com

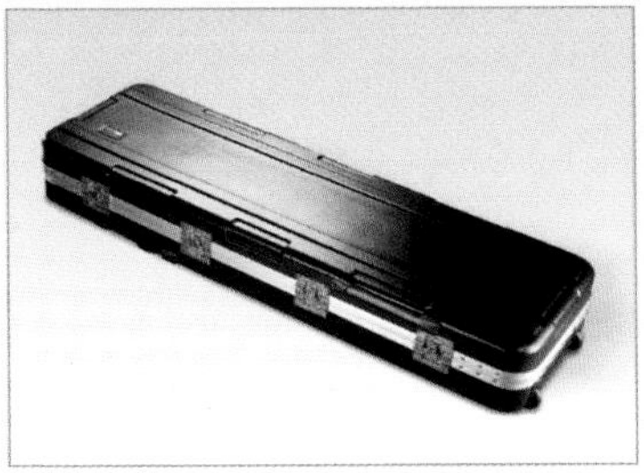

Gator Cases
www.gatorcases.com

Table of Contents

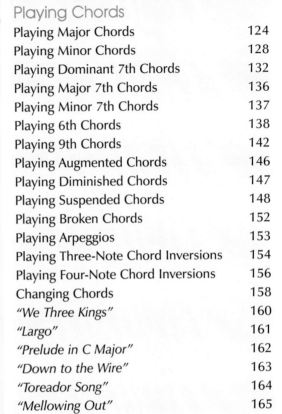

CHAPTER 5 Playing Chords

CHAPTER 6 Beyond the Basics of Reading Music

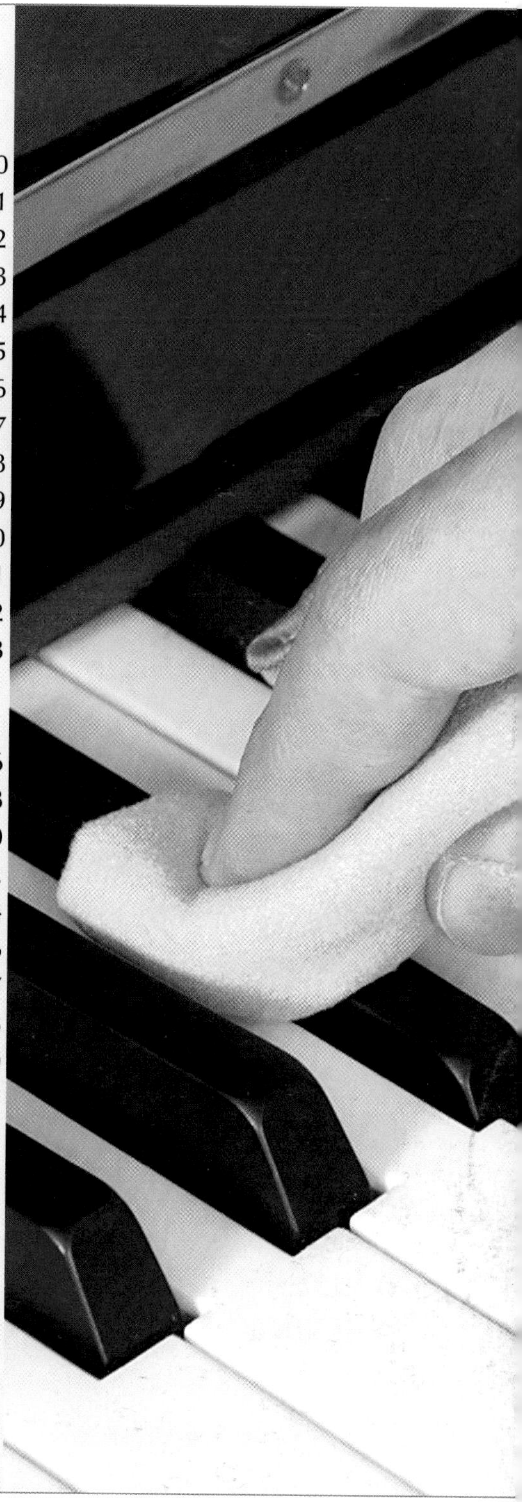

Chapter 1

For hundreds of years, people have been playing the piano to express themselves musically. This chapter will introduce you to the basics of the piano and will help get you started on your musical journey. You will learn about the different types of pianos and printed music, as well as how to name the keys on the keyboard and properly sit at the piano. You will also find an overview of the history of the piano as well as information on famous composers and pianists.

Piano Basics

In this Chapter...

- Why Play the Piano?
- Commonly Asked Questions
- Types of Pianos
- Inside an Acoustic Piano
- How to Sit at the Piano
- Naming Keys on the Keyboard
- Types of Printed Music
- Famous Composers
- Famous Pianists
- The History of the Piano

why play the piano?

There are many reasons to play the piano. Benefits of playing the piano include developing a greater appreciation for music, promoting self-discipline, increasing your self-confidence and more.

Provide Entertainment

Even a beginner can play the piano to entertain friends and family. You may want to play a popular song and have everyone sing along.

Develop an Appreciation for Music

Playing the piano gives you a greater appreciation for music. When you hear your favorite song on the radio, you will better appreciate the skill, dedication and creativity needed to compose and play the music.

Soothe Your Soul

If you are feeling stressed at the end of a long day, you may find that playing the piano helps you relax and gives you an overall sense of well-being. Playing the piano also offers a powerful way to express your emotions through the music you play.

Promote Self-Discipline

When learning to play the piano, you need to practice on a regular basis. The self-discipline required to set and stick to a regular practice schedule can benefit many other areas of your life. Practicing the piano on a regular basis also helps children develop good study habits, which will benefit them throughout their schooling.

Increase Your Self-Confidence

The sense of accomplishment you will feel when you are finally able to play a musical piece well after practicing the piece for hours, days or weeks will build your self-confidence and help you feel good about yourself. Playing the piano can be challenging and requires hard work, but the ability to play a piece well after much dedication and effort is a great reward.

Improve Your Coordination

Playing the piano is an excellent way to strengthen your hand-eye coordination and improve your fine motor skills. When playing the piano, you need to read music and instantly translate the information you see into using your fingers to press the correct keys on the keyboard.

Exercise Your Mind

Playing the piano exercises the mind and benefits people of all ages. Studies have shown that children who study music, such as playing the piano, perform better in school, particularly in subjects such as math and science. Adults who play the piano keep mentally active, which can reduce the chance of developing Alzheimer's disease.

Commonly asked questions

You may have some questions before you begin learning how to play the piano, such as how to fit playing the piano into your busy lifestyle. Here is a list of commonly asked questions that are posed to piano teaching professionals.

I do not have time to practice playing the piano, but I want to learn. What should I do?

As a beginner piano player, all you need is 10 to 15 minutes each day to practice and develop good piano playing skills. Try to schedule a short practice session each day at the same time, such as when you get home from work or school.

I cannot afford to buy a piano. What should I do?

If you cannot afford to buy a piano, you can buy an electronic keyboard to begin learning how to play. Electronic keyboards are less expensive than pianos. You can even rent a piano for a month or two before making a larger investment.

How long will it take me to become good at playing the piano?

The length of time required depends on your natural ability, your goals and the amount of time you dedicate to practicing and playing. If you practice regularly, you will need about six months to a year to play basic piano music well. It may take you about three to five years to play at an intermediate level.

I have experience with another musical instrument. Will I learn to play the piano faster?

If you play another musical instrument, you will likely have experience with reading music. You will also already have been introduced to important musical concepts, such as keeping a beat, which will help you when learning how to play the piano.

Am I too old to start playing the piano?

You are never too old to learn how to play the piano. Adults have some advantages over children when it comes to learning to play the piano—adults have better concentration, have more developed motor skills and are usually motivated by their own desire to play the piano.

When should my child start to learn how to play the piano?

If your child has some music experience, the child can begin taking piano lessons as early as four to six years old. If your child does not have any prior music experience, a good time to start is between the ages of six and eight. By this age, a child will have developed the motor skills and coordination needed to play the piano.

types of pianos

Pianos are available in different sizes, shapes and types. You can play an acoustic piano or an electronic keyboard or piano. The main difference between acoustic pianos and electronic keyboards and pianos is how each creates sound.

Acoustic pianos, which include upright and grand pianos, contain strings that vibrate to produce sound waves when struck by hammers. The sound waves create authentic sounds without the need for electricity. Electronic keyboards and pianos, also known as digital keyboards and pianos, use prerecorded sound samples stored on memory chips to simulate authentic sounds. The simulated sounds produced by electronic keyboards and pianos cannot match the superior sound quality of acoustic pianos. In addition to producing high-quality sound, acoustic pianos have weighted keys, which give acoustic pianos a unique feel when played.

The advantage of electronic keyboards and pianos is that they provide a less expensive way to learn how to play the piano. If you do not want to spend the money to buy an acoustic piano or if you have limited space and do not want to disturb your neighbors, consider using an electronic keyboard or piano. If you have the money and space, consider investing in an acoustic piano.

Acoustic Pianos

- Acoustic pianos do not require electricity and include upright and grand pianos. Acoustic pianos offer better sound quality and a more traditional appearance than electronic keyboards and pianos. Acoustic pianos also have weighted keys, which give acoustic pianos a unique feel when played.

Upright Pianos

- Upright pianos are usually placed against a wall, so they require less room than grand pianos. Most upright pianos are less expensive than grand pianos.

Grand Pianos

- Grand pianos produce a richer, louder sound and have a more distinct appearance than upright pianos. Grand pianos also have more sensitive keys so you have greater control over the volume when you press lightly or firmly on the keys.
- When you open the lid of a grand piano, the piano produces an even richer, louder sound that fills the room.

Tip

What are synthesizers?

Synthesizers are similar to electronic keyboards except synthesizers feature more advanced capabilities, such as the ability to manipulate sounds. These advanced features help professional musicians record music and perform on stage. Synthesizers, which need to be hooked up to an amplifier since they do not include built-in speakers, produce excellent sound, but weigh more and cost more than electronic keyboards. With synthesizers, you can also usually add more sound samples that imitate different instruments by inserting electronic cards into the synthesizer.

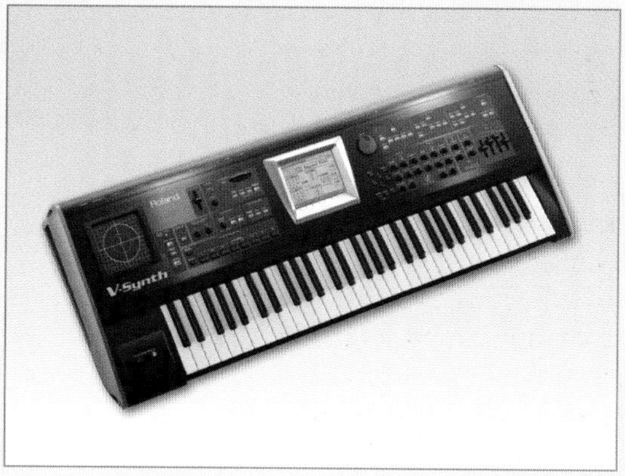

Electronic Keyboards and Pianos

- Electronic keyboards and pianos are significantly less expensive and are lighter and easier to move than acoustic pianos. Electronic keyboards and pianos also do not require regular tunings.

Electronic Keyboards

- Electronic keyboards provide an inexpensive way to begin learning how to play the piano. Electronic keyboards do not have weighted keys and have fewer keys than electronic and acoustic pianos.

Electronic Pianos

- Electronic pianos imitate the sound and feel of acoustic pianos. Electronic pianos are more expensive than electronic keyboards, but offer better sound quality, more keys and the keys are weighted.

- Electronic keyboards and pianos also provide a wide range of additional features such as the ability to imitate other instruments and provide a background beat for your music.

inside an acoustic piano

Acoustic pianos, which include upright and grand pianos, consist of numerous moving parts that work together to produce sound without the need for electricity. You can lift the lid of your acoustic piano, press a key and watch how the parts inside the piano work. Not only will knowing the main parts inside your acoustic piano give you a better understanding of how your piano generates sound, it will help you determine what needs to be fixed if something goes wrong with your piano.

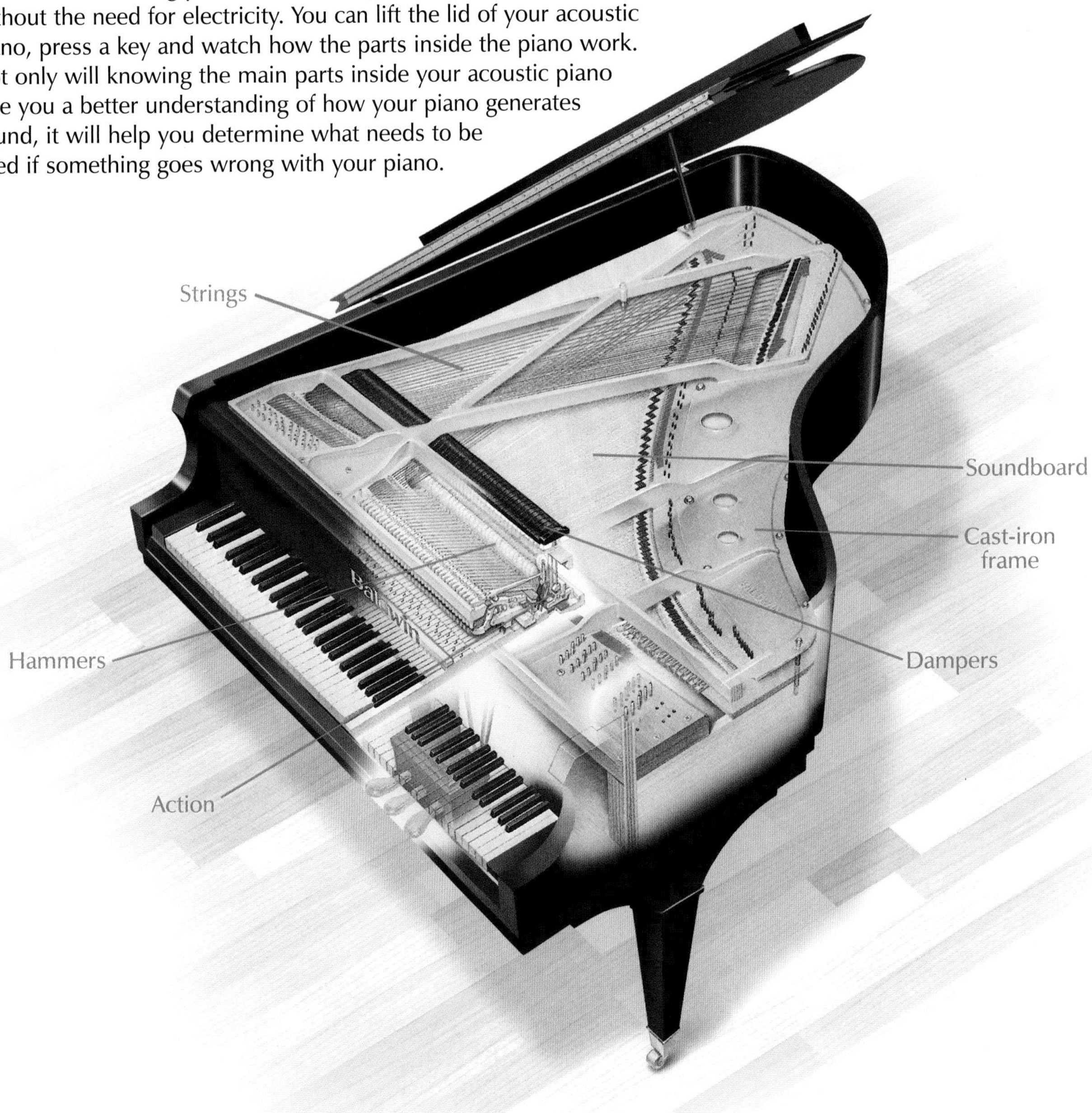

Action

The action consists of all the moving parts that work together to produce a sound when you press a key. The action also refers to how the keys on a specific piano feel, which can be a light or heavy weight. The heavier the action, the heavier the keys and the more force you need to use to press the keys.

Cast-Iron Frame

The strings in a piano are attached to a cast-iron frame. The cast-iron frame helps maintain the tension of the strings so the strings stay in tune for a longer period of time.

Dampers

When you press a key, a damper lifts off the strings for the key you pressed so the strings can vibrate and make a sound. When you release the key, the damper once again rests on the strings to stop the strings from vibrating and making a sound. Dampers are usually made of wood and the part of the damper that rests on the strings is covered with felt.

Hammers

Each key is connected to a hammer. When you press a key, a hammer strikes the strings for the key you pressed, which causes the strings to vibrate and make a sound. Hammers are usually made of wood and the part of the hammer that strikes the strings is covered with felt.

Soundboard

The soundboard consists of a large piece of wood that amplifies the sound produced by the piano. On a grand piano, the soundboard is the entire piece of wood at the bottom of the piano. On an upright piano, the soundboard is the entire piece of wood at the back of the piano.

Strings

Each key on a piano has one, two or three strings. Keys that produce lower sounds have fewer strings than keys that produce higher sounds. The strings for lower-sounding keys are also longer and thicker than the strings for higher-sounding keys. Strings are all made of metal, but the strings for lower-sounding keys are wrapped with copper wire.

how to sit at the piano

You should position yourself properly at the piano so you can comfortably and efficiently reach the keys you want to play.

When you sit at the piano, relax the muscles in your shoulders and keep your back straight. If you slouch or hunch over, you limit the ability of your arms to move up and down the keyboard, which means you lose access to keys that should be within reach.

Proper positioning prevents cramping in your hands and tension in your neck, shoulders, back and forearms. Improper positioning can lead to repetitive strain injuries, such as tendonitis or carpal tunnel syndrome. If you experience pain while playing the piano, you should contact your doctor.

Proper positioning also involves holding your hands correctly. When you place your hands on the keyboard, your fingers should curve as if you are holding a tennis ball in each hand. Your fingertips should make contact with the keys. To ensure your fingertips make proper contact with the keys, keep your fingernails short.

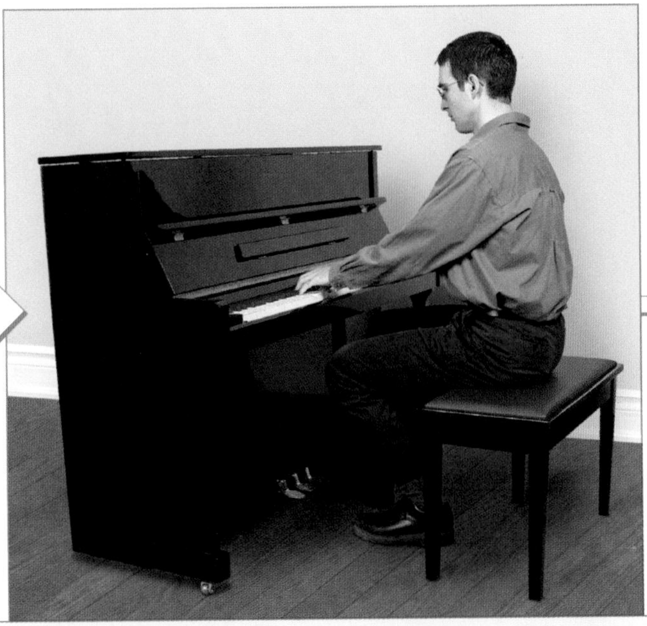

- When sitting at the piano, sit on the front part of the bench and rest your feet flat on the floor. Rest your right foot beside the right pedal.
- Keep your back straight and your shoulders squarely facing the keyboard.
- Lean forward slightly to move some of your body weight into your fingers to give them more strength.
- Keep your shoulders relaxed and down, with your elbows close to the sides of your body.
- To ensure you are sitting at the correct height, your forearms should be parallel to the floor and your wrists should be straight.
- For children, place a cushion or phone book on the piano bench to raise them to the correct height. You may also need to provide a footstool to rest their feet on.
- To ensure you are sitting at the correct distance from the keyboard, place your arms straight in front of you and touch the backs of the keys. If you cannot reach the backs of the keys, you are too far away from the keyboard. If your elbows are bent, you are too close.

How can I ensure that I sit properly when playing an electronic keyboard?

You should sit in front of an electronic keyboard the same way you sit in front of a piano. The keyboard should be positioned between 27 and 32 inches from the floor. If the keyboard is too high, you will have to angle your forearms and bend your wrists to reach the keys, which can lead to a strain injury. If you have a table or desk at the correct height, you can position the electronic keyboard on the edge of the table or desk. You can also buy an adjustable stand for your electronic keyboard.

Can I play the piano standing up?

No. If you play the piano standing up, you will end up hunched over and bending your wrists to reach the keyboard, which places unnecessary tension on your back and wrists. In addition, since you are not sitting in front of the piano, you will not be able to properly hear the sound the piano produces.

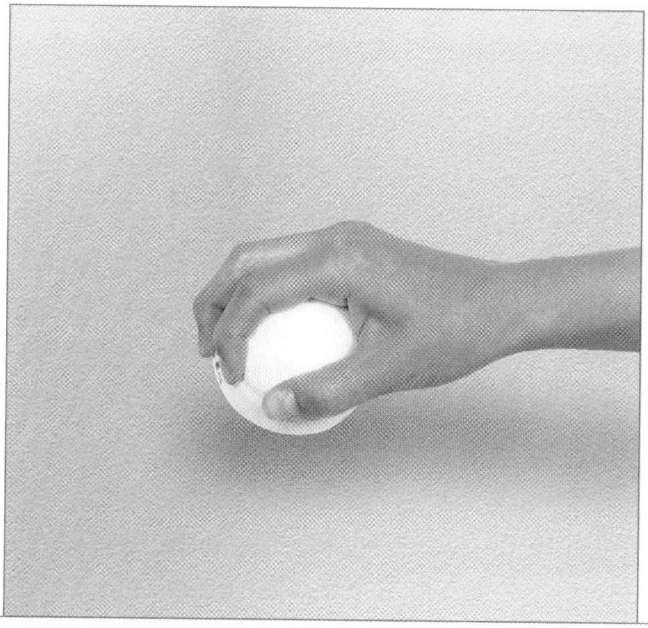

- When you place your hands on the keyboard, your fingers should be curved as if you are holding a tennis ball in each hand.
- Allow your fingertips to make contact with the keys and curve your thumbs slightly toward your hands to make better contact with the keys.

Common Mistakes

- When playing the piano, adults often raise their wrists and curve their fingers too much.
- When playing the piano, children often lower their wrists and rest their palms on the edge of the keyboard. Also, children often do not curve their fingers enough.
- Always make sure you keep your wrists straight and properly curve your fingers when playing the piano.

naming keys on the keyboard

The piano keyboard consists of black keys and white keys, each representing a specific note. The keys are arranged in a repeated pattern of five black keys surrounded by seven white keys.

The white piano keys are named using the letters A, B, C, D, E, F and G. These key names repeat as you move across the keyboard. You can use the raised black keys to help identify the white keys. For example, the white key directly to the left of a group of two black keys is the C note.

The C key closest to the middle of the keyboard is called middle C, which is the most basic keyboard note. On 88-key pianos, middle C is the fourth C from the left side of the keyboard.

A black key can have one of two names depending on the white key to its left or right. A black key to the right of a white key is called a "sharp" of that white key. A black key to the left of a white key is called a "flat" of that white key.

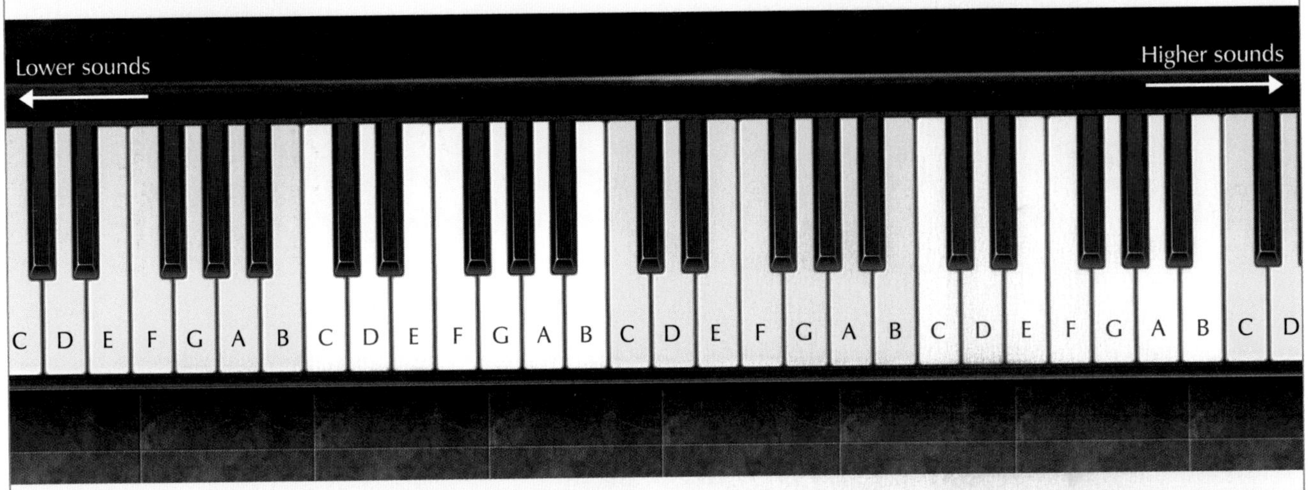

The Basic Keyboard Layout

- The keyboard consists of white keys and black keys. The raised black keys are in groups of twos and threes.
- A group of 5 black keys and their neighboring 7 white keys form a pattern of 12 keys that repeat several times across the keyboard.
- As you move down the keyboard, which means to the left, the sound produced by the keys becomes lower. As you move up the keyboard, which means to the right, the sound produced by the keys becomes higher.

Naming the White Keys

- The white piano keys are named using the first seven letters of the alphabet (A, B, C, D, E, F and G). These key names repeat as you move across the keyboard.
- The black keys can help you quickly identify the white keys. For example, the white key directly to the left of a group of two black keys is the note C.

Tip

How can I learn to quickly identify keys on the keyboard?

You can perform the following exercises:

Exercise 1: Play every C key on the keyboard. Then repeat for the D, E, F, G, A and B keys.

Exercise 2: Name the notes of each key on the keyboard from left to right, starting with the first key on the left. Notice how you are saying the letters in alphabetical order. Then name the notes from right to left, starting with the first key on the right side. Notice how you are saying the letters in reverse alphabetical order.

Exercise 3: Press random white keys and try to quickly name them as you play.

Exercise 4: Press a random white key and try to quickly name it as you play. Then play the black key to the right (if applicable) and name it as a sharp of that white key, such as G-sharp. Then play the black key to the left (if applicable) and name it as a flat of that white key, such as G-flat.

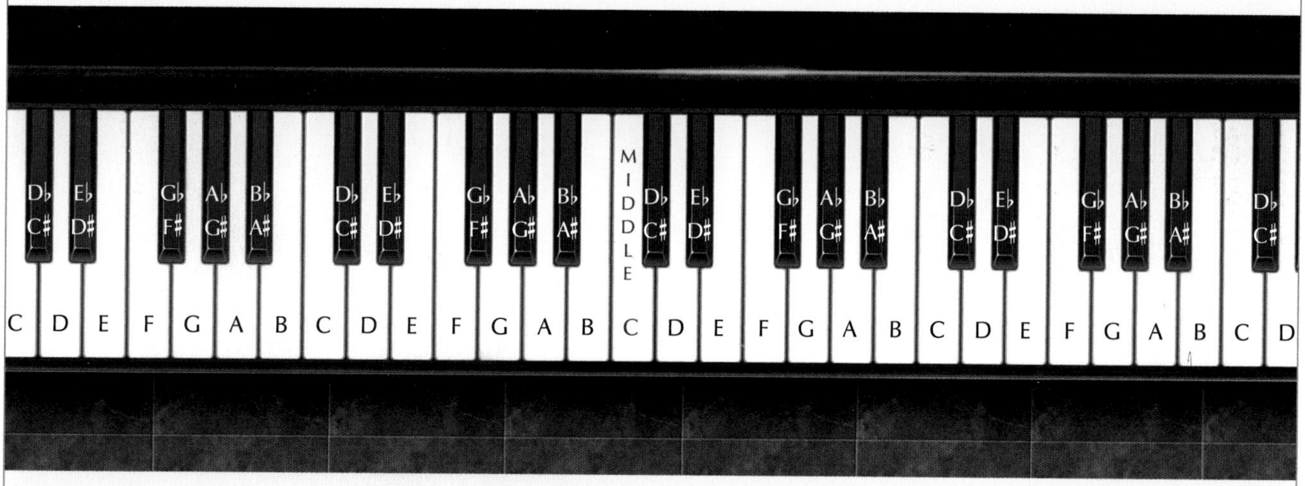

Middle C

- The C key closest to the middle of the keyboard is known as middle C, which is the most basic keyboard note. Most beginner piano music is written around middle C.
- On pianos that have 88 keys, middle C is the fourth C from the left side of the keyboard.
- Some electronic keyboards will mark middle C to help you quickly find the key.

Naming the Black Keys

- Each black key is named according to the white key to its left or right.
- A black key to the right of a white key is called a "sharp" of that white key. For example, the black key to the right of C is C-sharp (C♯).
- A black key to the left of a white key is called a "flat" of that white key. For example, the black key to the left of D is D-flat (D♭).

Note: Since each black key sits between two white keys, each black key has two names. For example, the black key between C and D is C-sharp and D-flat.

types of printed music

There are three types of printed music available for piano players—sheet music, folios and lead sheets.

Sheet music consists of a single song printed on pages that are folded or stapled together. In addition to displaying the grand staff, which shows the notes for both hands, sheet music may also provide song lyrics and chord names. Some sheet music also displays an additional staff, which shows the notes that a singer would sing.

A folio, or collection of musical pieces sold in a book format, can contain a few pieces or over a hundred pieces. The songs in a folio usually have a certain theme, such as songs written by a specific artist or the best-selling songs from a particular year.

Lead sheets provide only an outline of the essential elements of a song, leaving a pianist free to improvise. Improvising allows experienced pianists to creatively modify the music as they play. Lead sheets, which can also be used by musicians that play other instruments, are often used to play rock, jazz and country music. Classical music is not usually available in lead sheet form.

Sheet music, folios and lead sheets are available at music stores and on the Internet.

Sheet Music

- Sheet music is one song printed on a few pages, which are folded or stapled together. You can usually obtain sheet music for popular songs you want to play.
- Sheet music displays the grand staff, which shows the notes for the left and right hands. Sheet music may also provide the lyrics for a song, the names of the chords you play and an additional staff, which shows the notes that a singer would sing.

Folios

- Folios are collections of musical pieces sold in a book format. Folios can contain a few pieces or over a hundred pieces and usually contain pieces with a certain theme, such as pieces written by a specific artist or the best-selling songs from a particular year.
- Buying a folio is less expensive than buying the same musical pieces individually as sheet music.
- The musical pieces in a folio use the same format as pieces available in sheet music.

Tip

Is printed music available for different skill levels?

Yes. Publishers of written music have editors that can take an original piece of music and arrange it to make the music suitable for piano players of different skill levels. For example, a piece of music can be simplified to make the music easier for a beginner to play. Music editors can also take a song that was not originally written for the piano and arrange it so that it can be played on the piano.

Can sheet music be used like lead sheets?

You can use sheet music as lead sheets so you can improvise the music as you play. If you have sheet music that displays the chord names as well as an additional staff showing the notes a singer would sing, you can use the chord names as a basis for the chords and the vocal notes as a basis for the melody. Ignore everything else on the sheet music.

Is there another way I can obtain written music?

Yes. You can also purchase a CD-ROM of written music, which can contain hundreds of songs. As you browse through the CD-ROM, you can print out the written music for the pieces you like.

Lead Sheets

- A lead sheet is a piece of written music that provides only an outline of a musical piece, which gives pianists the freedom to modify the music as they play, which is known as improvising. Lead sheets are also called music charts.
- To use a lead sheet, you should be very familiar with chords and have the creative ability to improvise.
- A lead sheet provides a melody, or tune, written on a treble clef (𝄞) staff, with chord names written above the staff. A lead sheet may also provide the lyrics for a musical piece.

Note: For more information on improvising using lead sheets, see page 226.

- When using a lead sheet, the right hand usually plays the melody and the left hand usually plays chords. The location of the chord names indicates when you should play the chords in the music.
- Most musical pieces in lead sheet form are printed on one page or less.
- Lead sheets are usually organized into collections and sold in a book format, called a fake book. Fake books can contain music for one or many styles of music, such as Broadway tunes, country, jazz or rock music.

famous composers

In the history of the piano, there are many composers who stand out as exceptional. Each composer had a particular style and creativity that has helped their music stand the test of time. The following is just a sampling of the truly talented composers of the last several centuries.

Johann Sebastian Bach (1685-1750)

One of the true genius composers in the history of music, Bach was regarded by his peers as little more than a common church musician. The music he created, however, is anything but common. Composed during the Baroque period of the 17th and early-18th centuries, Bach's music was complex, ornate and almost mathematical. Bach was responsible for having perfected the contrapuntal technique of music composition. In the contrapuntal technique, different melodies of equal importance are played at the same time. One of his most famous compositions is *Musette in D major*.

Béla Bartók (1881-1945)

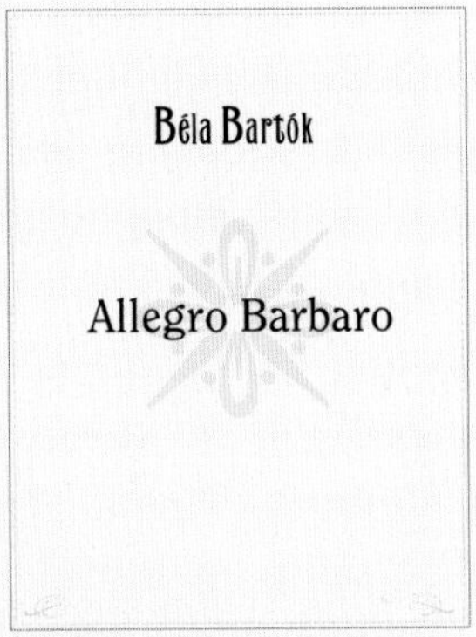

An important composer of the Contemporary period, the Hungarian-born Bartók combined the folk musical traditions of his eastern European roots with the more technically challenging rhythms of 20th-century composition. This kind of blended composition was a development of the Contemporary period, which permitted harsh sounds and the combination of distinct musical styles. Bartók's most well-known work is *Allegro Barbaro*.

Ludwig van Beethoven (1770-1827)

Beethoven composed during the Classical period. Music from this period often had a clean and objective sound. Beethoven's music, however, included a flair for the dramatic with violent mood swings that mirrored his own personal and emotional highs and lows. In fact, some of his more creative and interesting pieces came later in life as he gradually lost his hearing. Two of his most famous pieces are *Für Elise* and *Moonlight Sonata*.

Johannes Brahms (1833-1897)

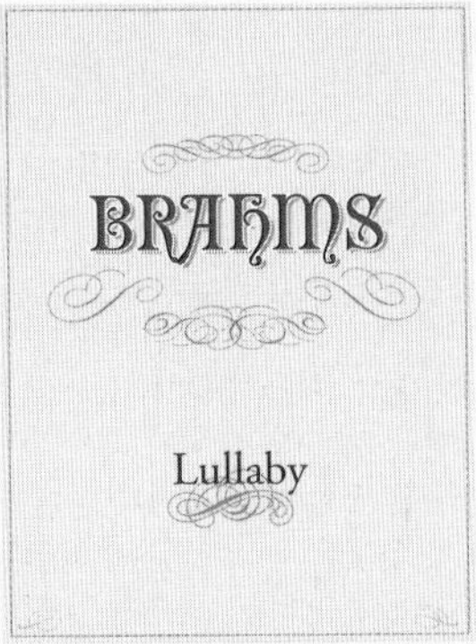

Well known for his musical orchestrations, Brahms blended the sounds from a variety of musical instruments with very creative results. Although traditional in structure, Brahms's music is very expressive and emotional, reflecting the tone of the 19th-century Romantic period. Brahms's most well known piano composition is *Lullaby*.

Frédéric Chopin (1810-1849)

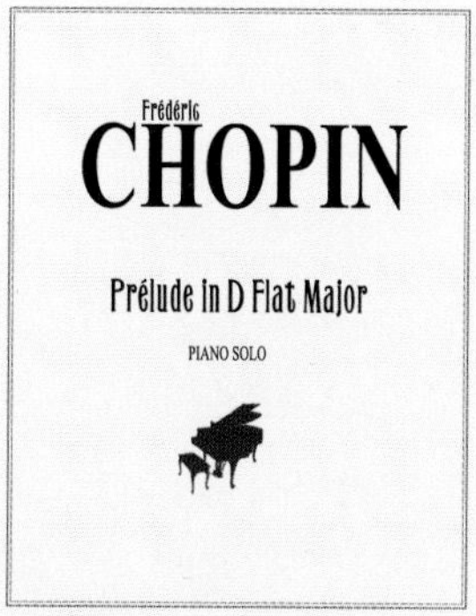

A celebrated composer of the Romantic period, Chopin wrote music almost exclusively for the piano. His piano compositions were revolutionary in his day. Chopin was one of the first composers to incorporate all 88 piano keys into his compositions. He also relied heavily on a technique known as rubato. Rubato uses different tempos, or speeds of music, to create more expressiveness within a piece. The Polish-born Chopin used many traditional folk pieces from his homeland as inspiration for his own music. One of Chopin's most famous pieces is *Prelude in D flat major*.

Claude Debussy (1862-1918)

Debussy is considered the father of Impressionist music. The Impressionist period of the late-19th and early-20th centuries is known for its unconventional musical principles. The dreamy pieces of this period ignored traditional rules of composition in favor of flowing and shifting music without a focused central beat. Debussy incorporated influences from the Middle Ages and non-Western influences into his compositions to create a unique sound. Debussy's most famous composition is *Clair de Lune*.

George Gershwin (1898-1937)

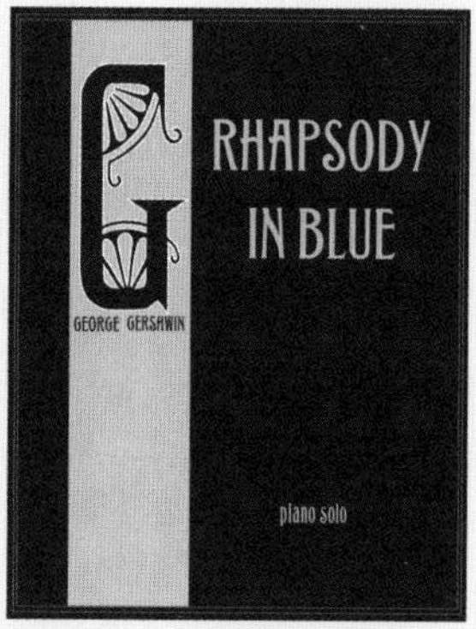

The American-born Gershwin was one of the first composers to combine elements of jazz and Classical music. Composing music during the 20th-century Contemporary period, Gershwin was influenced by the experimental style of the period. While Gershwin's most famous composition is *Rhapsody in Blue*, he is also well known for writing Broadway scores with his brother Ira in the 1920s and 1930s.

Franz Joseph Haydn (1732-1809)

Haydn composed during the Classical period, which extended from the mid-18th to the early-19th centuries. As one of the first notable composers of this period, Haydn established many of the period's main characteristics. His work was highly structured, featured memorable melodies and included light accompaniment, all hallmark elements of the Classical period. A royal musician for most of his life, Haydn's set of *Piano Sonatas* stands as a very important contribution to the piano repertoire.

CONTINUED...

famous composers *(continued)*

Scott Joplin (1868-1917)

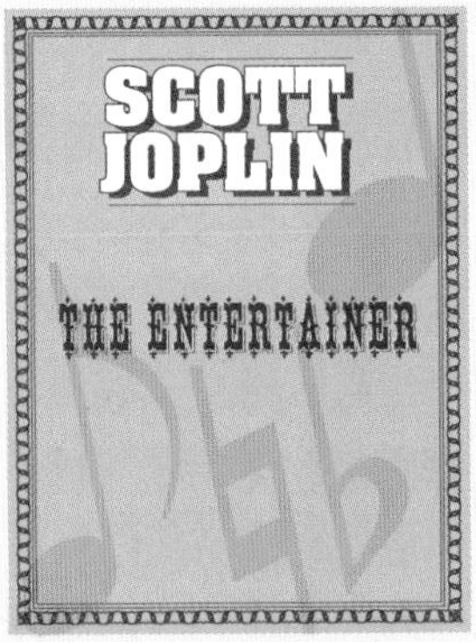

The American-born Joplin was the innovator of the ragtime style, a precursor to jazz, and is referred to as the "King of Ragtime." Although now famous, Joplin knew little success during his lifetime and was not recognized as a serious composer until more than 50 years after his death. In fact, some of his most famous pieces were originally performed in brothels. Joplin's most famous piece, *The Entertainer*, was featured in the Academy Award winning score of the 1973 film *The Sting*.

Franz Liszt (1811-1886)

Liszt is most famous for his ability to play the piano with a technical genius that had never been seen before. Liszt's theatrical and awe-inspiring concerts brought him celebrity status across Europe. Liszt composed during the 19th-century's Romantic period, which emphasized emotion over tradition and an equal respect for melody and accompaniment. His most famous composition is *Hungarian Rhapsody #2*.

Wolfgang Amadeus Mozart (1756-1791)

A child prodigy who composed his first piece at age 5, Mozart composed during the Classical period of the mid-18th to early-19th centuries. His piano compositions feature singing-like melodies and elegant expression. The Austrian-born Mozart was instructed by his father Leopold, who was a respected musician and composer. Mozart was well known early in his career and gave performances across Europe as a youngster. One of Mozart's most famous piano pieces is *Turkish Rondo*.

Sergei Prokofiev (1891-1953)

Prokofiev's compositions illustrate the Contemporary period characteristics of experimentation and integration of multiple musical styles. His music combined elements of traditional Romanticism with more modern rhythmic and harmonic ideas. Prokofiev was one of the first musicians to compose for the then new medium of motion pictures. His most famous composition is *Piano Concerto No. 2 in G minor*.

Sergei Rachmaninoff (1873-1943)

Rachmaninoff was a talented composer and pianist of the Romantic period, which was characterized by emotionally-charged music. Forced by political turmoil to flee his native Russia, Rachmaninoff moved to the United States where he enjoyed a successful performing career. Rachmaninoff became famous for his concerts in which he played dramatic interpretations of Romantic compositions, including his own. His *Piano Concerto No. 3* is considered by many pianists to be one of the most difficult piano concertos to perform.

Maurice Ravel (1875-1937)

Although he composed during the latter stages of the Impressionist period in the early-20th century, Ravel's music was influenced by many sources. His melodic compositions combined elements of Impressionist music, Spanish folk music and more Classical styles. Ravel was also influenced by the jazz he heard in the Parisian clubs he would frequent when insomnia prevented him from sleeping. Ravel's most famous piano work is *Pavane pour une Infante Défunte*.

Franz Schubert (1797-1828)

Schubert's compositions helped bridge the gap between the Classical period, which focused on structure and elegance, and the Romantic period, which focused on emotion and melody. The Austrian-born Schubert was a prolific composer, writing hundreds of songs for both voice and piano. Schubert was very poor and would often sell a song for the price of a meal. Schubert's most famous piano composition is *Impromptu #2 in E flat major*.

Robert Schumann (1810-1856)

A composer of the Romantic period, Schumann is best known for pushing the expressive and dramatic boundaries of this period's music. When Schumann was stricken with a variety of physical and mental ailments, his wife Clara promoted and performed his work. Clara was a talented performer and composer in her own right. The German-born Schumann's most famous work is *Träumerei*.

famous pianists

There are many exceptional piano players who stand out for their unique talent and creativity. The following is just a sampling of some very talented pianists.

Tori Amos (1963-)

Born Myra Ellen Amos, this American rock/pop pianist and vocalist is known for her emotion-filled piano playing and singing. A child prodigy, Amos was accepted to a prestigious conservatory at age five, only to be kicked out years later for wanting to play by ear. She turned her creative attention to popular music and began playing in clubs at age 13.

Vladimir Ashkenazy (1937-)

Unlike other performers who tend to specialize in one particular style of music, this Russian-born pianist has recorded works from all the major periods in musical history. In fact, Ashkenazy has performed just about every major work in the piano repertoire, from Bach to Prokofiev. Ashkenazy is also very active as a conductor with many of the top orchestras in the world.

Dave Brubeck (1920-)

An American jazz pianist, Brubeck's *Take Five* was the first jazz single to sell more than a million copies. Brubeck's compositions are known in musical circles as creative hybrids of jazz and non-western rhythms, such as rhythms that have five or seven beats per bar. In addition to piano composition, Brubeck has also composed for other musical genres including ballet and choral music.

Van Cliburn (1934-)

At the age of 23, Cliburn burst onto the worldwide musical stage when he won the first Tchaikovsky International Piano Competition in Moscow. To this day, he remains one of the great interpreters of Tchaikovsky. A longtime supporter of young pianists, Cliburn hosts the Van Cliburn International Piano Competition every four years. The competition features up-and-coming performers from around the world.

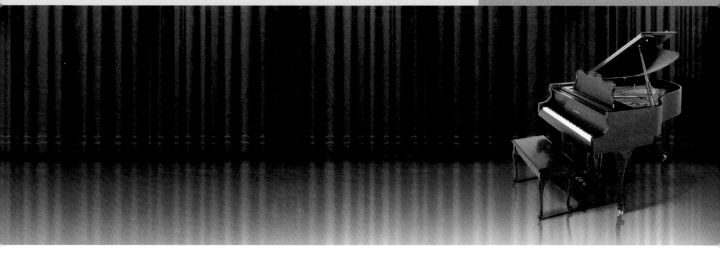

Harry Connick Jr. (1967-)

One of today's most talented jazz pianists, the Grammy Award winner is also well known as a vocalist, big band leader and actor. His early résumé is a tribute to the musical heritage of his hometown of New Orleans. Connick Jr. studied under master jazz pianists James Booker and Ellis Marsalis, attended the New Orleans Center for the Creative Arts and became a regular performer in the city's jazz club and festival scene.

Floyd Cramer (1933-1997)

Cramer started out as a session player for artists such as Elvis Presley, Patsy Cline and Roy Orbison. He later became famous for his own recordings of relaxing and melodious piano pieces. Cramer popularized the technique known as "slip note," in which the main melody notes of a piece are adorned with a quick flick of another note.

Duke Ellington (1899-1974)

Legendary pianist and big band leader Duke Ellington, born Edward Kennedy Ellington, was the first great composer of jazz music. His arrangements of big band music were renowned for their unique style and level of complexity. Even though he was a gifted piano player, he never let his own virtuosity overshadow the sound of his band, the Duke Ellington Orchestra.

Glenn Gould (1932-1982)

The Canadian-born Gould is famous for being a gifted interpreter of Bach's music. Gould began playing at age three and at age 14 was the youngest person ever to graduate from the Royal Conservatory of Music in Toronto. Gould is also remembered for his eccentric and reclusive behavior, which included singing along to his own playing and abruptly ending his career as a live performer in 1964.

Vladimir Horowitz (1903-1989)

The Russian-born Horowitz was renowned for his interpretation of Chopin's music. A multiple Grammy Award winner, Horowitz had one of the most spectacular musical careers of the 20th century. The highlights of that career range from playing 70 sold-out concerts in a single year at the young age of 21 to making repeated successful professional comebacks from a variety of mental and physical ailments.

CONTINUED...

famous pianists *(continued)*

Keith Jarrett (1945-)

American pianist Jarrett's first live performance—at just six years of age—included two of his own compositions. Although a battle with Chronic Fatigue Syndrome temporarily suspended his recording and performing, Jarrett now has a very active musical career. Jarrett is well known for his virtuosity as both a jazz and a classical pianist.

Billy Joel (1949-)

Fittingly, Joel's first big hit was titled *Piano Man*. The rock/pop pianist and vocalist has gone on to record many more hit songs and continues to sell out concerts around the world. His music chronicles the day-to-day challenges and rewards of working-class family life. In this way, Joel is considered the Bruce Springsteen of piano players. Joel's piano playing is characterized by intricate rhythmic patterns that beautifully accompany his singing.

Elton John (1947-)

Born Reginald Kenneth Dwight, Elton John has been writing and performing rock/pop music for over 30 years. The British performer is as well known for his flamboyant and energetic stage presence as he is for his catchy melodies. His piano playing reflects a traditional music education that was accompanied by an early interest in rock and rhythm and blues. John has also written music for stage and film, winning a Best Original Song Oscar for *Circle of Life* from *The Lion King*.

Evgeny Kissin (1971-)

The Russian-born Kissin is the most exciting pianist on the classical music scene today. The excitement surrounding his career is generated as much by his speed—he plays with a lightning-fast technique—as by his concert showmanship. Kissin began playing at the age of six and by the age of twelve, had already begun his recording career.

Thelonious Monk (1917-1982)

An American jazz pianist, Monk creatively bridged the gap between the traditional way of playing jazz and the more avant-garde approach. This contribution to jazz's musical heritage is exemplified in his creation of bop, a new and complex form of jazz. Monk had a very unorthodox way of playing, incorporating odd hand positions and unusual body movements into his piano playing.

Jelly Roll Morton (1890-1941)

Morton was one of the first jazz musicians to write down his compositions in music notation. Born Ferdinand Joseph Lamothe, Morton helped facilitate the transition from the ragtime style to the jazz style of piano playing. Like many other jazz artists, Morton found it difficult to make a living playing the piano. He subsidized his income as a gambler, pool shark and vaudeville comedian.

Oscar Peterson (1925-)

A Canadian jazz pianist, Peterson has addressed socially conscious issues in some of his work. For example, his *Hymn to Freedom* became an anthem for the Civil Rights Movement of the 1960s. Peterson is well regarded for his technical yet soulful improvisations that also display gospel influences. A prolific performer and recording artist—even in his 70s—Peterson has shared the spotlight with many jazz greats, including Charlie Parker, Dizzy Gillespie and Ella Fitzgerald.

Little Richard (1932-)

Born Richard Wayne Penniman, this pianist and vocalist is considered one of the founding fathers of rock and roll. In fact, Little Richard is one of the 10 original inductees into the Rock and Roll Hall of Fame. An aggressive instrumentalist, Little Richard is known for hammering out chords while standing and dancing at the piano. The first big hit for the American performer was *Tutti Frutti*.

Arthur Rubinstein (1887-1982)

The Polish-born Rubinstein performed a wide range of genres throughout his long career. His performance repertoire was just as likely to feature music from the Romantic period of the 19th-century as 20th-century new music. Pushing the limits of technique, Rubinstein's focus was on the emotion of each piece. He willingly took chances, even making mistakes with precise note-playing to fully convey his interpretation of works.

Stevie Wonder (1950-)

Signing his first recording contract at age 10, Stevie Wonder displayed a prodigy level talent for singing and piano playing despite being blind. Born Steveland Judkins Moore, this immensely popular rock, pop and rhythm-and-blues artist has deftly combined musical technologies—including electronic keyboards and pianos—to create unique soulful sounds. He was inducted into the Rock and Roll Hall of Fame in 1989.

the history of the piano

The instrument we know today as a piano has a long history, ranging as far back as the 15th century, when musicians first conceived of attaching a keyboard to a harp and having the harp's strings be plucked by a device instead of the musician's fingers. Over hundreds of years, the piano evolved into one of today's most popular instruments.

BEFORE THE PIANO

The two main precursors to the piano were the clavichord and the harpsichord. These keyboard instruments produced sound by having their strings struck or plucked. The mechanics and construction of the clavichord and the harpsichord did not allow either instrument to produce sounds at different volumes, which limited the expressiveness that musicians could achieve in their playing.

The Clavichord

The clavichord, first documented in the early 1400s, was similar to today's pianos in that the strings of the clavichord were struck to produce sound. However, the clavichord produced a soft sound that could not be amplified. As a result, the clavichord was not suitable for large performances. While early clavichords had only two octaves of keys, later versions of the instrument featured more keys.

The Harpsichord

Unlike today's pianos, in which hammers strike the strings inside the instrument to produce sound, harpsichords had small hooks, known as quills, which plucked the strings when a musician pressed the keys on the harpsichord. While today's pianos can produce louder or softer sounds, depending on how hard or soft the keys are played, harpsichords were not capable of producing different volumes. Harpsichords also had only four octaves of keys—much fewer than today's pianos. Many composers and pianists of the Baroque period (1600s to 1750s) played their music on the harpsichord.

THE FIRST PIANO

The first piano was invented in Florence, Italy, in the early 1700s by Bartolomeo Cristofori. Cristofori, a harpsichord maker, based the design of his instrument on the harpsichord. The way the instrument produced sound, however, was more like that of the clavichord.

The first piano had small hammers that struck the strings to produce sound. The hammers in this new instrument retracted instantly so the strings were able to vibrate. This meant that the new instrument was capable of playing at different volumes. The harder the musician pressed a key, the harder the hammer hit the string and the louder the sound that was produced. Because the instrument was capable of playing softly and loudly, the instrument was aptly named pianoforte, which means "soft loud" in Italian. The name pianoforte was eventually shortened to piano.

Cristofori's pianoforte, which featured four octaves of keys, did not become popular until an article spread word about it throughout Europe.

THE NEXT GENERATION OF THE PIANO

In the 1730s, a German organ builder named Gottfried Silbermann was inspired by the article about Cristofori's pianoforte and tried to duplicate the instrument. Silbermann also added his own invention to Cristofori's design—an early version of what later became known as the damper pedal, which allowed a musician to have notes continue to sound after the keys were released. From that point on, almost all piano manufacturers incorporated Silbermann's invention into their pianos.

With the start of the Seven Years War in 1756, several piano makers moved from Germany to England to continue work on their instruments. By the late 1700s, the piano was becoming more popular among musicians and composers and piano making boomed. However, the piano was generally an instrument only for the upper classes and the aristocracy, as most families could not afford to buy a piano.

CONTINUED...

the history of the piano *(continued)*

PERIOD OF CHANGE—THE 19TH CENTURY

Between the late 1700s and the late 1800s, musicians and composers alike wanted a stronger and more resonant sound from the piano. This desire sparked the continuing evolution of the piano. The Industrial Revolution also allowed manufacturers to produce components with better-quality materials.

The following are some of the changes the piano underwent during this period.

- The number of octaves of keys expanded to more than seven.
- With the invention of cross stringing in the early to mid 1800s, the strings inside the piano were allowed to spread out over a wider area of the soundboard. Spacing out the strings gave each string more room to vibrate and produce sound.
- Double escapement action, introduced in the early to mid 1800s, allowed pianists to repeat a note without having to let the key rise all the way back up after pressing it. This helped pianists play much faster.
- In the mid-1800s, manufacturers began covering hammers with felt to ensure good tone quality when the hammers struck the strings.
- Heavier strings that produced a stronger and more resonant sound were introduced.
- The heavier strings required a stronger piano frame, so manufacturers started constructing piano frames out of iron rather than wood. In the mid 1800s, an iron frame was used for the first time.
- In the mid 1800s, the sostenuto pedal, also called the sustain pedal, was invented. When the sostenuto pedal is pressed, the notes played at the same time as the pedal is pressed will continue to sound after the pianist's fingers lift off the keys.
- The piano grew more important as more and more European and North American families were able to afford pianos. Pianos also became common in public institutions, such as schools and hotels.

THE MODERN PIANO

By the early-20th century, the piano had more or less evolved into the instrument we know today. However, following the invention of several new forms of entertainment, such as the radio and phonograph, the popularity of the piano began to decline. This, coupled with the Great Depression of the 1930s, caused piano sales to plummet and bankrupted several manufacturers.

Recreational piano playing suffered again with the widely-popular invention of the electronic keyboard in the late 20th century. Many musicians preferred the electronic keyboard for performing popular music. Despite these setbacks, the piano still serves as an important instrument in many homes today.

Modern Piano Manufacturers

Worldwide, piano manufacturers build pianos of all types and price ranges every day. Many of these manufacturers still hand-craft important parts of the pianos they build, while other companies build pianos mostly by machine. You can visit the Web sites of some of the most popular piano manufacturers for information on the pianos they create.

Manufacturer	Web Site
Baldwin	www.baldwinpiano.com
Bösendorfer	www.bosendorfer.com/_english_version
Kawai	www.kawaius.com
Pleyel Paris	www.pleyel.fr
Schimmel	www.schimmel-piano.de
Steinway & Sons	www.steinway.com
Yamaha Pianos	www.yamaha.com
Young Chang	www.youngchang.com

Chapter 2

You will often need to be able to read music in order to play your favorite pieces on the piano. This chapter will introduce you to the basics of reading music. You will find information on how to name the notes on the musical staff, how to identify note values and what many of the symbols you find in written music mean. When you complete this chapter, you will be ready to play some songs to practice your new music-reading skills.

The Basics of Reading Music

In this Chapter...

Understanding the Staff and Clefs
Naming Notes on the Staff
Naming Notes Below or Above the Staff
Using the Correct Fingers
Note Values
Measures
Rests
Dotted Notes
Tied Notes
Time Signatures
Sharps and Flats
Key Signatures
Double Notes
Repetition Markers
Incomplete Measures
"Mary Had a Little Lamb"
"Are You Sleeping"
"When the Saints Go Marching In"
"Ode to Joy"

understanding the staff and clefs

Written music, also called music notation, covers many important aspects of playing a particular song. For example, music notation instructs you on what notes to play and how long to play the notes. Music is written on the staff, which consists of five lines and the four spaces between the lines. Circular symbols placed on the lines and spaces of the staff represent the specific notes that you need to play. The position of the note on a staff determines if the pitch is high or low. The higher a note is on the staff, the higher the sound of the note.

At the beginning of every staff appears a symbol called a clef. Clefs tell you which hand you should use to play the notes on the staff. The treble clef, also called the G clef, refers to the higher sounding notes, usually played with your right hand. The bass clef, also called the F clef, refers to the lower sounding notes, usually played with your left hand. The grand staff consists of a treble clef and a bass clef joined together by a brace, indicating that you use both hands to play the music.

The Staff

The Clef and Treble Clef

- Music is written on the staff, which consists of five lines and the four spaces between the lines.
- Each line and space on the staff represents a specific note, which corresponds to a specific key on the keyboard.
- Notes are represented by circular symbols placed on the staff. The higher a note appears on the staff, the higher the sound of the note.
- The clef is a symbol that appears at the beginning of the staff. The clef indicates which hand you use to play the notes on the staff—the left or right hand.
- The treble clef (𝄞), also called the G clef, indicates the higher-sounding notes that you play with your right hand.
- The treble clef includes notes which represent keys located on the right section of your keyboard.

Tip

Can different clefs appear on the grand staff in written music?

In most piano music, the top staff shows the treble clef (𝄞) and the bottom staff shows the bass clef (𝄢). However, this can change as it is possible to have two of the same clefs appear on both staffs. For example, the bottom staff can also show a treble clef (𝄞). In this case, both hands play the higher notes on the keyboard. Conversely, the top staff can also show a bass clef (𝄢). In this case, both hands play the lower notes on the keyboard.

The Bass Clef

The Grand Staff

Excerpt from "Jingle Bells"
by Pierpont

- The bass clef (𝄢), also called the F clef, indicates the lower-sounding notes that you play with your left hand.

  Note: Bass is pronounced "base."

- The bass clef includes notes which represent keys located on the left section of your keyboard.

- The grand staff shows the treble and bass staves joined together with a brace. The grand staff allows you to read the notes for both hands at the same time.

Note: "Staves" is the plural form of "staff."

naming notes on the staff

In written music, each line and space on a staff represents a different note on the keyboard. Notes on the keyboard are named using the first seven letters of the alphabet (A through G). In order to read music, you must memorize the letter names of the notes assigned to the lines and spaces on the staff.

However, it is important to remember that the lines and spaces correspond to different note letters in the treble clef and the bass clef. As a result, you must treat treble clefs and bass clefs individually when figuring out the note names on the staves.

If you find it difficult to remember all of the note names, you can create a word or phrase using the letter names as a helpful reminder. For example, the note names of the lines on the treble clef staff, from bottom to top, are E, G, B, D and F. To help you remember the note names, you can use a phrase such as "Every Good Boy Does Fine." With practice, you will be able to identify notes automatically.

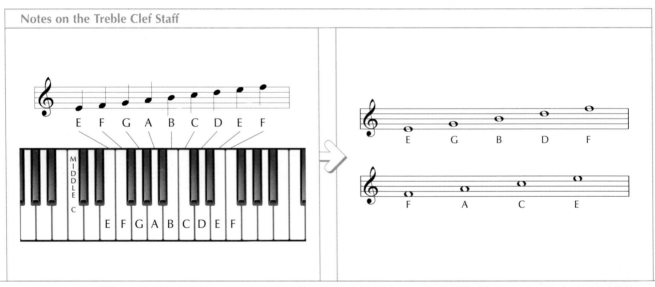

Notes on the Treble Clef Staff

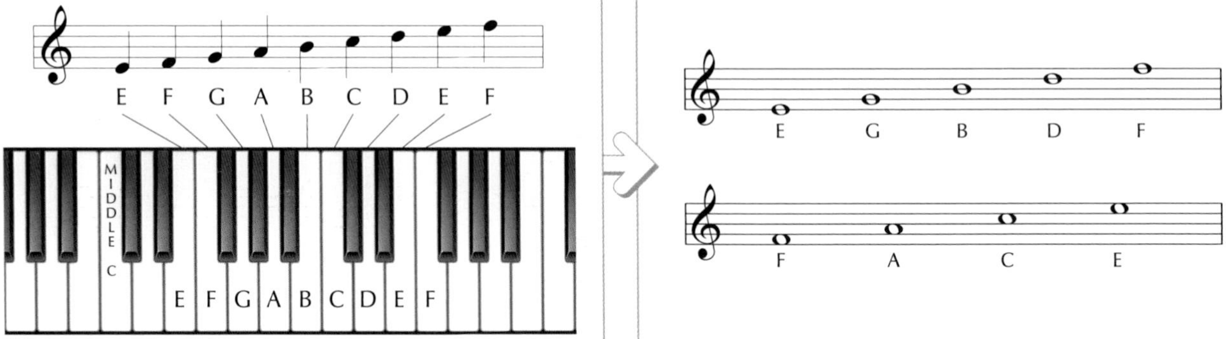

- The treble clef (𝄞) indicates the higher-sounding notes that you play with your right hand.
- Each line and space on the staff represents a specific key on your keyboard. As the notes go upward on the staff, you play keys going to the right on your keyboard.
- The lines and spaces on the staff are named using the first seven letters in the alphabet (A, B, C, D, E, F and G), just like the white keys on the keyboard.
- The bottom line on the staff represents the note E. The keyboard has several E notes, but the bottom line represents the first E note above middle C. Middle C is the C key closest to the middle of the keyboard.
- On the treble clef staff, the note names for the lines from bottom to top are E, G, B, D and F. To help you remember the note names, you can use a phrase such as "Every Good Boy Does Fine."
- The note names for the spaces from bottom to top are F, A, C and E. To help you remember the note names, notice how the letters spell the word "FACE."

Tip

Is there another way to identify the notes on the staff?

Yes. If you look at the treble clef symbol (𝄞), you will notice that it circles the second line from the bottom of the staff, which represents the G note above middle C. Middle C is the C key closest to the middle of the keyboard. Using the G line as a reference point, you can then identify other notes on the staff. For example, one step below the G line is the F space and one step below the F space is the E line.

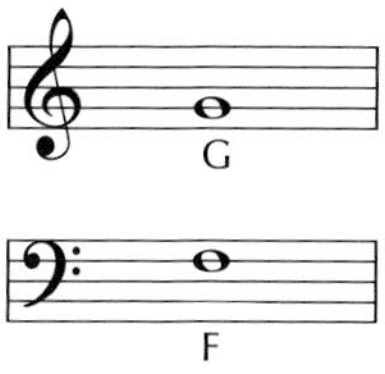

Similarly, the bass clef (𝄢) symbol has two dots that are positioned above and below the fourth line on the staff, which represents the F note below middle C. Using the F line as a reference point, you can then identify the other notes on the staff. For example, one step above the F line is the G space and one step below the F line is the E space.

Notes on the Bass Clef Staff

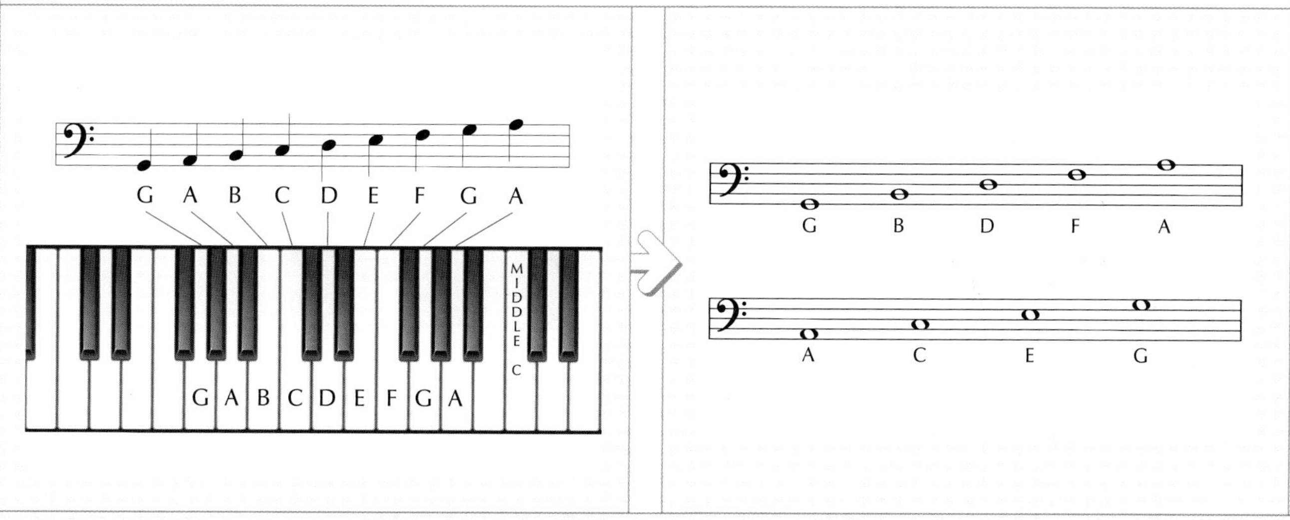

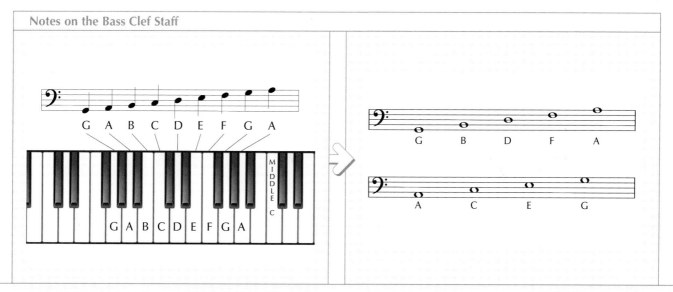

- The bass clef (𝄢) indicates the lower-sounding notes that you play with your left hand.
- Each line and space on the staff represents a specific key on your keyboard. As the notes go upward on the staff, you play keys going to the right on your keyboard.
- The lines and spaces on the staff are named using the first seven letters in the alphabet (A, B, C, D, E, F and G), just like the white keys on the keyboard.
- The top line on the staff represents the note A. The keyboard has several A notes, but the top line represents the first A note below middle C. Middle C is the C key closest to the middle of the keyboard.
- On the bass clef staff, the note names for the lines from bottom to top are G, B, D, F and A. To help you remember the note names, you can use a phrase such as "Good Bikes Don't Fall Apart."
- The note names for the spaces from bottom to top are A, C, E and G. To help you remember the note names, you can use a phrase such as "All Cows Eat Grass."

naming notes below or above the staff

In written music, not all notes appear within the lines and spaces of the staff. Often, music will use lower notes, which appear below the staff, and higher notes, which appear above the staff. Composers are able to extend the staff downward and upward by adding ledger lines (—) below and above the staff. Notes that progress farther below and above the staff represent keys that are farther left and right on the keyboard.

Since ledger lines continue the staff's pattern of lines and spaces, the letter names of notes below and above the staff progress alphabetically from the letter names on the staff, using the letters A through G. For example, since the highest line of the treble clef staff is F, the first space that sits on top of the line is G and the ledger line above the space is A. At the bottom of the treble clef, the lowest line is E, so the space underneath the line is D and the ledger line below the space is C.

Notes Below or Above the Treble Clef Staff

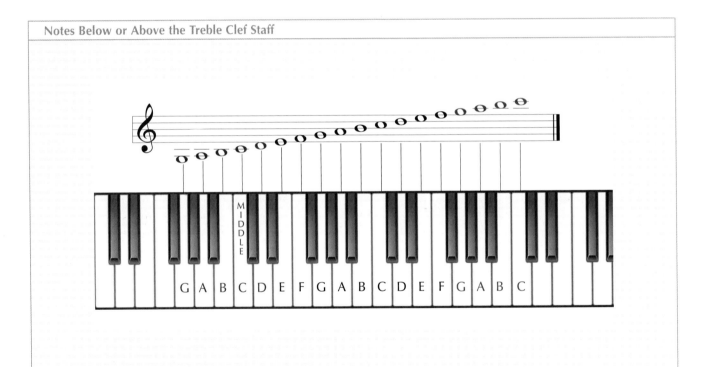

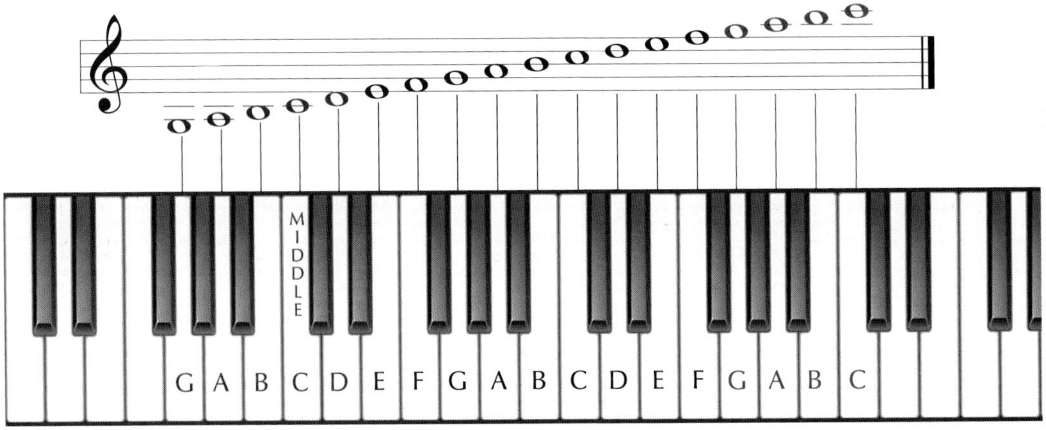

- The treble clef (𝄞) indicates the higher-sounding notes that you play with your right hand.
- Notes that are below or above the five lines on the staff are written with ledger lines (—). The names of the notes progress alphabetically from A to G, just like the notes on the staff and the keys on the keyboard.
- As the notes go upward on the staff, you play keys going to the right on your keyboard.

Where is middle C on the staff?

Middle C is the most basic keyboard note. Most beginner piano music is written around middle C, so it is important that you can identify middle C on both the keyboard and the staff. Middle C is the C key closest to the middle of the keyboard and can be played with either hand, depending on how the written music is arranged.

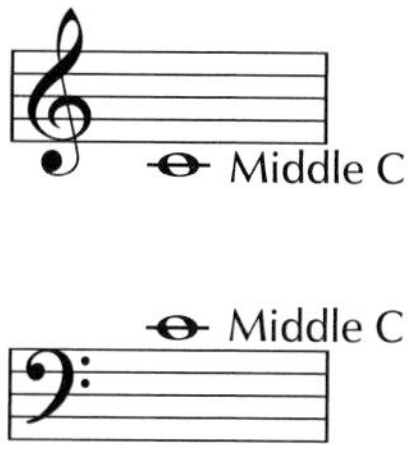

Since you can play middle C with your right hand or your left hand, middle C appears on both the treble clef staff and the bass clef staff. On the treble clef staff, middle C is located on the first ledger line below the staff. On the bass clef staff, middle C is located on the first ledger line above the staff.

Notes Below or Above the Bass Clef Staff

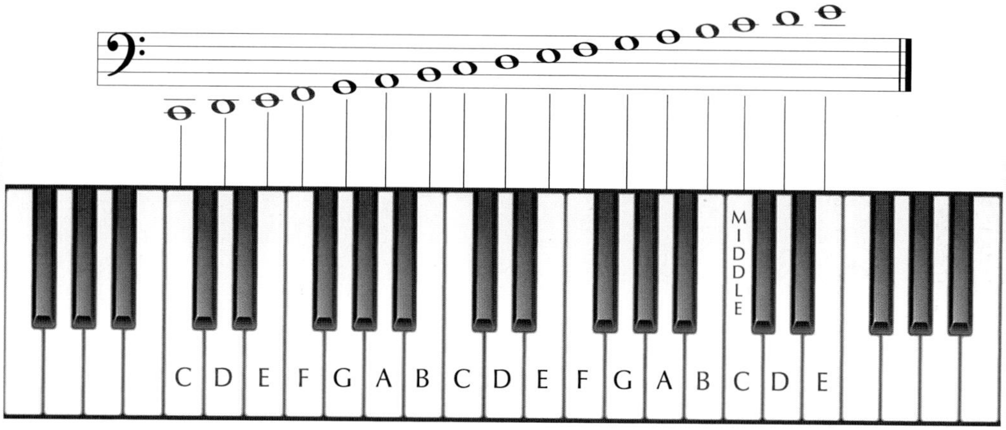

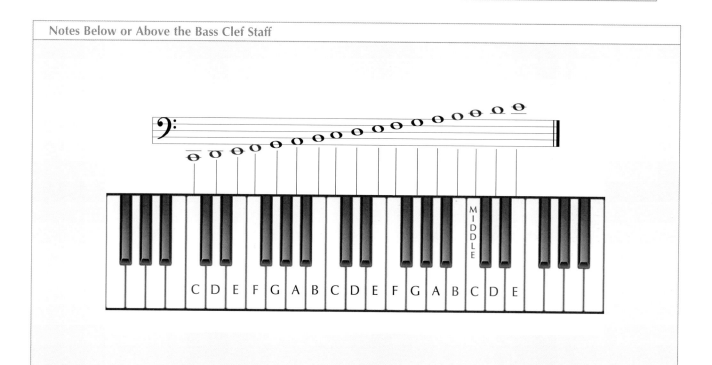

- The bass clef (𝄢) indicates the lower-sounding notes that you play with your left hand.
- Notes that are below or above the five lines on the staff are written with ledger lines (—). The names of the notes progress alphabetically from A to G, just like the notes on the staff and the keys on the keyboard.
- As the notes go upward on the staff, you play keys going to the right on your keyboard.

using the correct fingers

Learning correct fingering is essential to playing the piano well. Correct fingering involves knowing the best finger to use to efficiently and comfortably play each note of a piece. Playing a piece is easier when you use correct fingering, as this helps ensure your hands are always in the proper position to move to upcoming notes without having to twist your fingers or disrupt the rhythm of the piece.

The fingering system numbers the fingers of each hand from 1 to 5, starting with the thumb. In some written music, you will see the numbers for the correct fingers above the notes or below the notes.

To make it easier for you to learn a piece, make sure you always use the correct fingering. Music written for beginners usually includes fingering information, but more advanced pieces usually do not. If there is no fingering information for a piece, you can figure out the fingering and write it in for reference. Writing in the fingering is especially helpful for learning tricky spots in a piece.

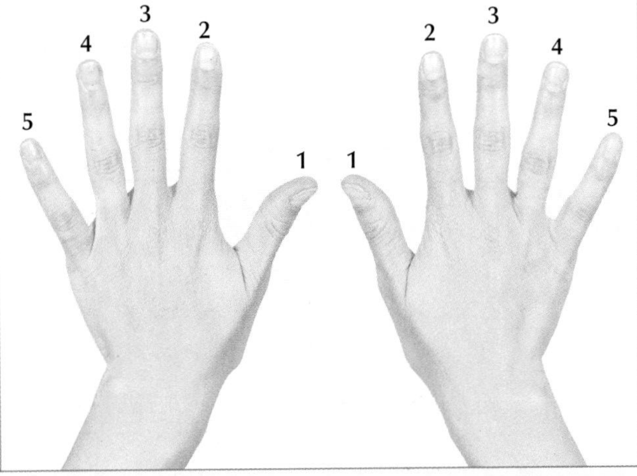

Excerpt from "Mary Had a Little Lamb"
by Hale

- When playing the piano, you need to use the correct fingering, which means you need to use the best fingers to play each note in a piece. Using the correct fingering helps you to set up your hands for the next notes in a piece.

- To know which fingers to use when playing a piece, the fingers on your left and right hand are numbered from 1 to 5, starting with your thumb.

  1 Thumb
  2 Index finger
  3 Middle finger
  4 Ring finger
  5 Pinky finger

- In some written music, especially beginner music, the suggested fingering appears above or below the notes to help you determine which fingers to use.

note values

Every note you play in music lasts for a certain amount of time, which is measured in beats. The amount of time, or number of beats, you should play a note is determined by the note value.

A note may last one or more beats or a fraction of a beat. A whole note is the largest note value. All other types of notes, such as half notes, are fractions of the whole. Keep in mind, however, that the note value is not the only indicator of the number of beats a note receives. The number of beats a note receives also depends on the time signature. For information on time signatures, see page 54.

The direction for the stem on a note depends on its position on the staff. The stem for a note points upward when it appears below the third line on the staff. The stem for a note above the third line points downward. The stem for a note on the third line may point up or down.

Note Symbol	Note Name	Number of Beats in 4/4 Time
𝅝	whole note	4
𝅗𝅥	half note	2
♩	quarter note	1
♪	eighth note	1/2
𝅘𝅥𝅯	sixteenth note	1/4

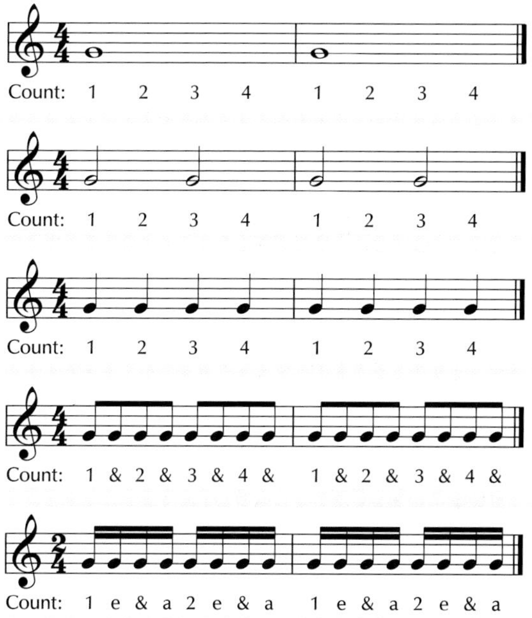

- In written music, every note you play lasts for a certain amount of time, which is measured in beats.
- The type of note symbol displayed in written music indicates the number of beats you play a note.
- 1 whole note is equal to 2 half notes, 4 quarter notes, 8 eighth notes and 16 sixteenth notes.

Note: When two or more eighth (♪) or sixteenth (𝅘𝅥𝅯) notes appear in a row, the notes are usually joined with a beam (♫ or ♬).

- This example of written music contains notes of various values. To practice how long to play each note, clap your hands or tap your foot as you count the beats out loud. Clap or tap only once for each note.
- When a note appears below the third line on the staff, the stem of the note goes up (♩). When a note appears above the third line on the staff, the stem of the note goes down ( ).

measures

The vertical lines on the music staff, called barlines, help to break down the staff into units of time that are smaller and easier to manage. These units of time are called bars or measures.

In each measure, there is a specific number of beats—usually four. In most cases, the number of beats in each measure is the same throughout a song. Measures help you easily keep track of your place in a musical piece and give you the feel of the beat, which is important since some beats in a measure are stronger than others. For example, in most styles of music, the first beat of a measure is emphasized slightly more than subsequent beats.

On the staff, each measure is separated by a single vertical line. A double barline with two thin lines marks the end of a section, such as a verse or chorus, and the introduction of a new musical theme or idea. A double barline with one thin line and one thick line at the end of a staff indicates the end of a piece.

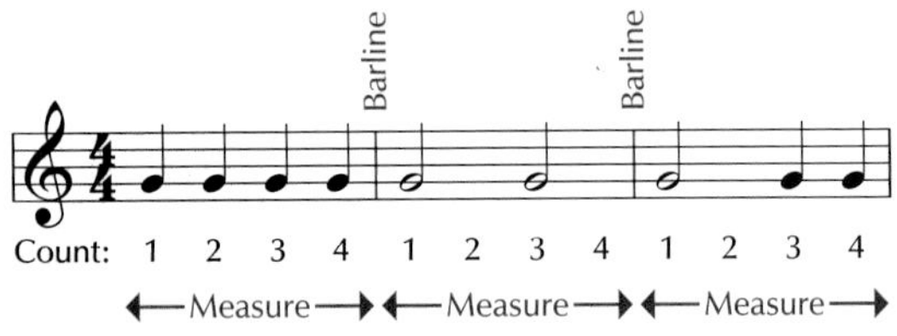

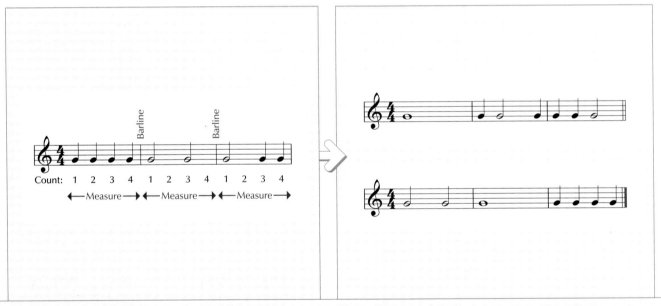

- Written music is divided into sections of equal duration, called measures or bars. Each measure or bar is separated by a single vertical line called a barline (|).
- In each measure, all the note values add up to the same number of beats. Most commonly, each measure has a total of 4 beats.
- Grouping the beats into measures helps you easily feel the beat of the music, since certain beats in each measure are usually emphasized. For example, in most styles of music, the first beat in each measure is slightly emphasized.
- A double barline with two thin lines (‖) indicates the end of a section. The new section will be different in some way, such as introducing new lyrics.
- A double barline with one thin and one thick line (‖) at the end of the staff indicates the end of the music.

rests

In written music, rest symbols indicate moments of silence. Moments of silence are as important to the rhythm and structure of a musical piece as sounded notes. Many people consider the combination of notes and moments of silence to be what makes music interesting.

Rest values work the same as note values. For example, a quarter rest and a quarter note both have a value of one beat. Rest values are important because rests allow you to continue counting beats even when you do not play a note. The value of a rest symbol may change depending on the bottom number of the time signature, which indicates the type of note or rest that receives one beat. For information on time signatures, see page 54.

The total value of all the notes and rests in a measure must equal the number of beats per measure, which is determined by the top number of the time signature. When a whole rest appears alone in a measure, a composer wants silence for the entire measure. For example, in 4/4 time, a whole rest receives four beats, whereas in 3/4 time, a whole rest receives three beats.

Rest Symbol	Rest Name	Number of Beats in 4/4 Time	Corresponding Note
	whole rest	4	
	half rest	2	
	quarter rest	1	
	eighth rest	1/2	
	sixteenth rest	1/4	

- In written music, rest symbols indicate moments of silence.
- The rest symbol displayed in written music indicates the number of beats you should not play.
- During a rest, you should keep your fingers on the keyboard, ready to play the next set of notes.
- These examples of written music contain rest symbols. Clap your hands or tap your foot as you count the beats out loud. When you see a rest symbol, open your hands or lift your foot as you continue to count the beats.

dotted notes

In written music, a note followed by a dot is known as a dotted note. When you see a dotted note, you add half of the value of the note to the note. For example, a half note (𝅗𝅥) equals 2 beats, so a dotted half note (𝅗𝅥.) equals 3 beats.

Dotted notes are necessary since a note that is equal to 3, 1 1/2 or 3/4 beats does not exist. Any note can be a dotted note, but dotted half notes and dotted quarter notes are the most common.

Dots are also used to change the number of beats of rest symbols, which indicate moments of silence. Treat dotted rests the same as dotted notes, adding half the value of the rest to the rest.

The number of beats of a dotted note or rest may change depending on the time signature, which describes the number of beats in every measure. For information on time signatures, see page 54.

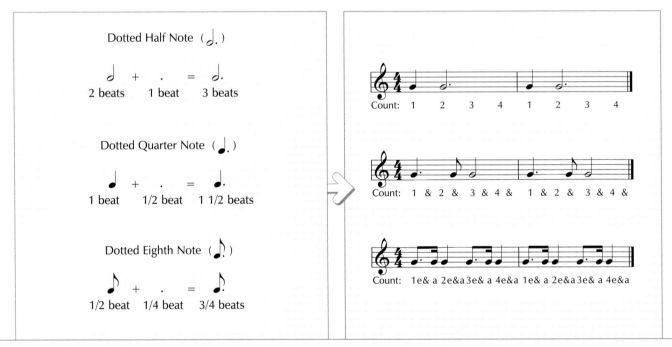

Dotted Half Note (𝅗𝅥.)

𝅗𝅥	+	.	=	𝅗𝅥.
2 beats		1 beat		3 beats

Dotted Quarter Note (♩.)

♩	+	.	=	♩.
1 beat		1/2 beat		1 1/2 beats

Dotted Eighth Note (♪.)

♪	+	.	=	♪.
1/2 beat		1/4 beat		3/4 beats

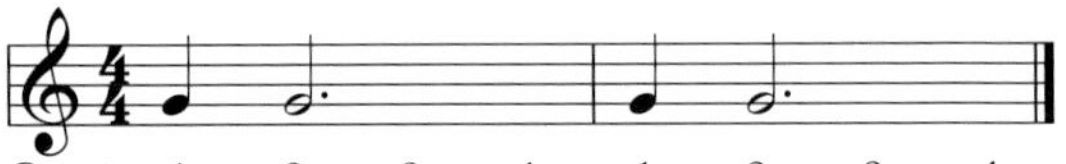

Count: 1 2 3 4 1 2 3 4

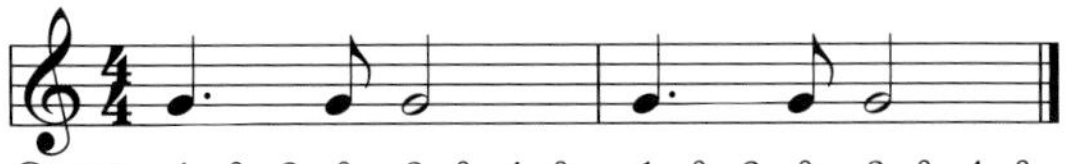

Count: 1 & 2 & 3 & 4 & 1 & 2 & 3 & 4 &

Count: 1e& a 2e&a 3e& a 4e&a 1e& a 2e&a 3e& a 4e&a

- In written music, a note followed by a dot is known as a dotted note.
- The dotted note symbol displayed in written music indicates the number of beats you play the note.
- When you see a dotted note, you need to increase the amount of time you hold the note by half of its original value. For example, a half note (𝅗𝅥) equals 2 beats, so a dotted half note (𝅗𝅥.) equals 3 beats.
- This example of written music contains dotted notes of various values. To practice how long to hold each note, clap your hands or tap your foot as you count the beats out loud. Clap only once for each note.

Note: When two or more eighth (♪) or sixteenth (𝅘𝅥𝅯) notes appear in a row, the notes are usually joined with a beam (♫ or ♬).

tied notes

A tie is a curved line that joins two notes that have the same pitch, which means the notes appear on the same line or space on the staff. A tie indicates that you should add the value of the second note to the first note and not play the second note. In other words, the first note should be held for the combined value of the two notes. For example, if a quarter note is tied to another quarter note, you play the note for a duration of two beats.

Ties can be used to join notes within a measure to combine notes that could not be expressed as a single note. A measure is a section of music between two vertical lines on the staff. However, a more common use for ties is to join a note at the end of one measure with a note in the following measure. This indicates that you should hold the note into the next measure. Ties can also be used to join more than two notes. In this case, the notes are usually tied over two or more measures.

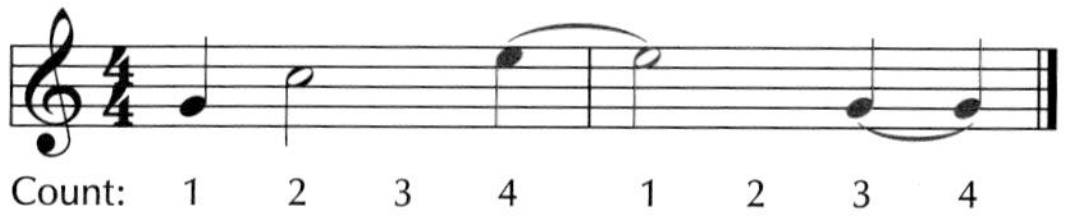

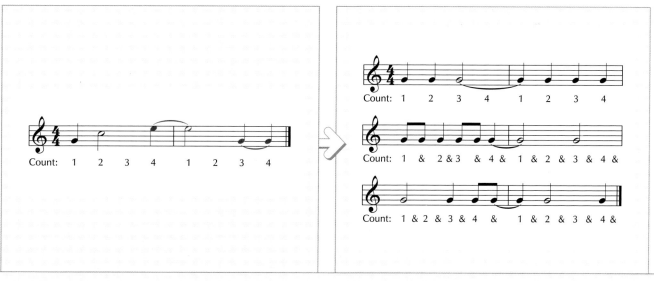

- In written music, a tie is a curved line that joins two identical notes together to increase the amount of time you play a note.
- When a tie appears between two notes, you play only the first note and hold the note for the combined value of both notes.

- Ties are often used across barlines to extend the duration of the last note in a measure. For example, if a note played on the fourth beat must last more than 1 beat, a tie can be used to extend the duration of the note.

Note: Written music is broken down into units of time called measures, with each measure separated by a vertical line called a barline.

- This example of written music contains ties between various notes. To practice how long to play each note, clap your hands or tap your foot as you count the beats out loud. When you see two notes tied together, only clap or tap for the first tied note.

time signatures

At the beginning of a musical piece is a time signature that provides information about the beats in every measure of a piece. A measure is a section of music between two vertical lines on the staff.

A time signature is made up of two numbers, one on top of the other. The top number indicates the number of beats in each measure. The bottom number indicates the type of note that receives one beat. For example, the most common bottom number is 4, which means a quarter note (♩) receives one beat.

The most common time signatures are 4/4 and 3/4, but 2/4, 6/8 and 2/2 are also frequently used. The 4/4 time signature, which specifies that each measure has four beats and each quarter note (♩) receives one beat, is considered "common time" and may be indicated by 𝄴 instead of 4/4. The 2/2 time signature is commonly referred to as "cut common time" and is often indicated by 𝄵 on the staff. In cut common time, each measure has two beats and each half note (𝅗𝅥) receives one beat.

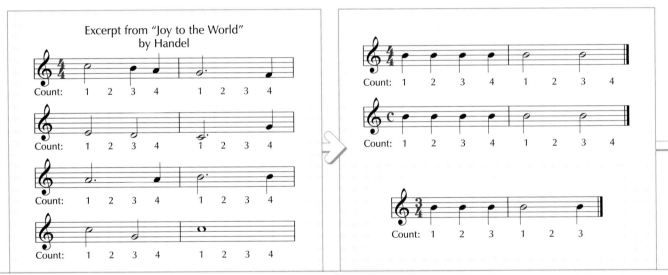

Excerpt from "Joy to the World"
by Handel

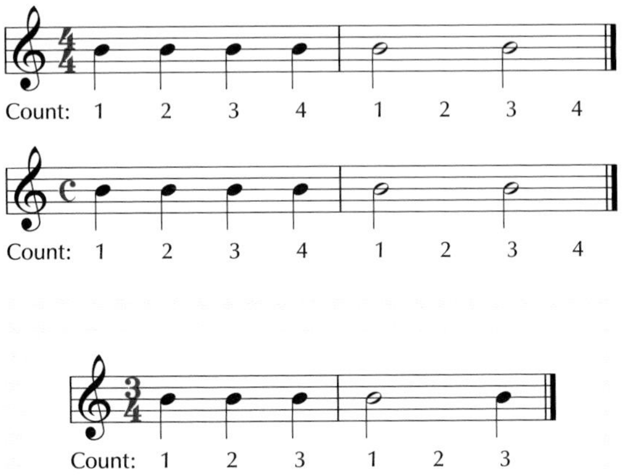

- In written music, the time signature appears at the beginning of a musical piece.
- The time signature is made up of two numbers, one on top of the other, that describe the beats in every measure.
- The top number of the time signature indicates the number of beats in each measure. The bottom number indicates the type of note that receives one beat, such as 4 for a quarter note (♩), 2 for a half note (𝅗𝅥) or 8 for an eighth note (♪).
- The most common time signature is 4/4, which specifies that each measure has 4 beats and each quarter note (♩) receives one beat. Traditionally, the first beat in each measure is emphasized and the third beat is slightly emphasized while the second and fourth beats are weak. Since the 4/4 time signature is also known as "common time," you may also see the 4/4 time signature indicated by 𝄴 .
- The 3/4 time signature is also quite common. In the 3/4 time signature, each measure has 3 beats and each quarter note (♩) receives one beat. Traditionally, the first beat in each measure is emphasized, which makes this time signature ideal for waltzes.

Tip

Can there be more than one time signature in a musical piece?

Yes. A musical piece can change time signatures partway through the piece. For example, a piece that starts in 4/4 time may later change to 3/4 time. Whenever there is a time signature change, you will see a new time signature on the staff. Time signature changes are often used to change the mood of a piece.

How can I make learning different time signatures easier?

Before you play a piece of music, determine the number of beats each note value would receive in the given time signature. Then write out the beats on the printed music, matching up the beats with the appropriate notes. For example, if the time signature is 4/4 and you have four quarter notes in a measure, write the numbers "1, 2, 3, 4" under the notes. Then play the piece slowly (even if it is a fast piece), saying the beats out loud as you play.

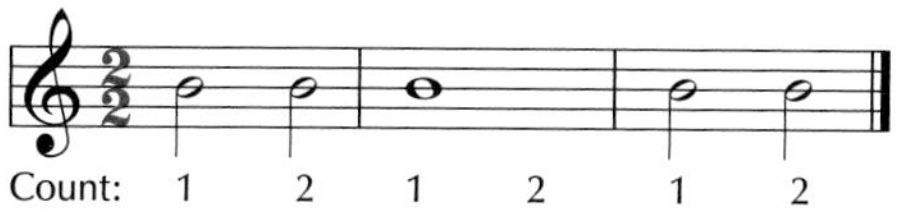

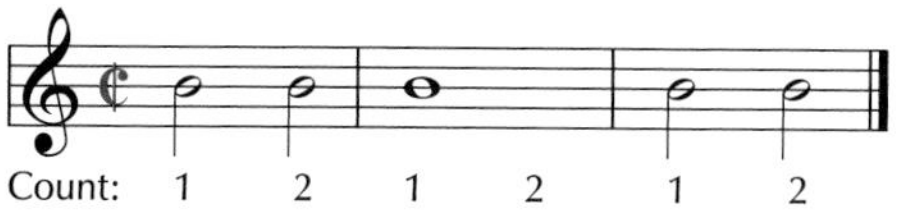

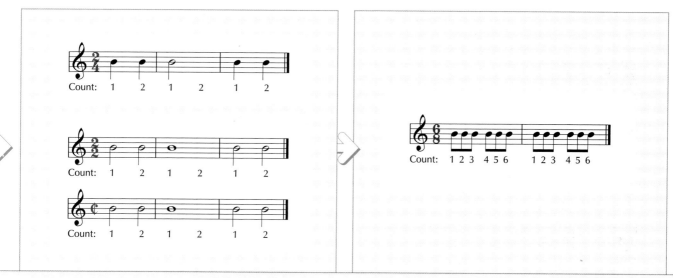

- In the 2/4 time signature, each measure has 2 beats and each quarter note (♩) receives one beat. Traditionally, the first beat in each measure is emphasized. This time signature produces lively music and is often used in polkas and marches.

- In the 2/2 time signature, each measure has 2 beats and each half note (𝅗𝅥) receives one beat. Traditionally, the first beat in each measure is emphasized. Since the 2/2 time signature is also known as "cut common time," you may also see the 2/2 time signature indicated by ¢.

- In the 6/8 time signature, each measure has 6 beats and each eighth note (♪) receives one beat. Traditionally, the first and fourth beats in each measure are emphasized, which makes this time signature ideal for music such as 1950s rock ballads and jigs in folk music.

Note: When two or more eighth (♪) notes appear in a row, the notes are usually joined with a beam (♫).

sharps and flats

While the white keys on the piano are named after letters, the black keys are referred to with a letter along with sharp or flat symbols.

To indicate that a note is a sharp or flat, a symbol, called an accidental, appears in front of the note on the staff. The ♯ symbol represents a sharp and the ♭ symbol represents a flat. When a sharp symbol appears before a note, you play the black key directly to the right of the corresponding white key. When a flat symbol appears before a note, you play the black key directly to the left of the corresponding white key.

When a note is marked as sharp or flat, all the subsequent occurrences of that note in the same measure will also be sharp or flat. If an occurrence of the note within the same measure is meant to revert back to a white key, you will see a natural sign (♮) before the note, canceling the sharp or flat. When you need to play the sharp or flat note in another measure, the note will be rewritten with a sharp or flat in the new measure.

The Sharp Symbol (♯)

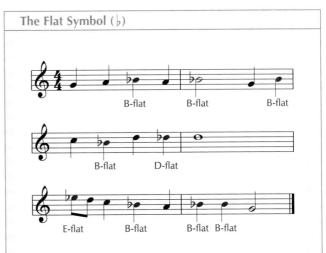

The Flat Symbol (♭)

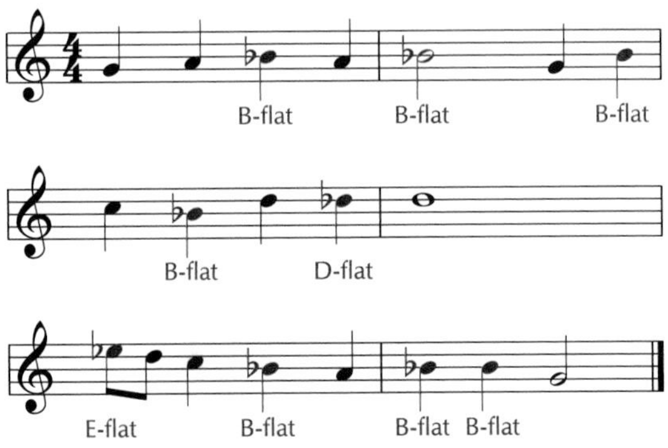

- In written music, each line and space on the staff represents a specific white key on your keyboard.
- When you see a sharp symbol (♯) before a note, play the black key directly to the right of the corresponding white key. For example, when you see ♯ before an F note, play the black key directly to the right of the F key.
- When you see a sharp symbol before a note, you must play the rest of the notes on the same line or space in the same measure as sharps. For example, when you see ♯ before an F note, you must play all the F notes on the same line or space in the same measure as F-sharp.

Note: A measure is a section of music between two vertical lines on the staff.

- When you see a flat symbol (♭) before a note, play the black key directly to the left of the corresponding white key. For example, when you see ♭ before a B note, play the black key directly to the left of the B key.
- When you see a flat symbol before a note, you must play the rest of the notes on the same line or space in the same measure as flats. For example, when you see ♭ before a B note, you must play all the B notes on the same line or space in the same measure as B-flat.

Are there other types of sharps and flats?

In advanced piano music, you may see double-sharps and double-flats.

Double-sharps are written as the letter name of a note followed by 𝄪, such as A𝄪. On the staff, the symbol appears before the note, such as 𝄪♩. When a double-sharp appears in a piece, you play two keys to the right of the note, counting black and white keys. For an A double-sharp, you play the B key.

A double-sharp (A𝄪) = B

A double-flat (A𝄫) = G

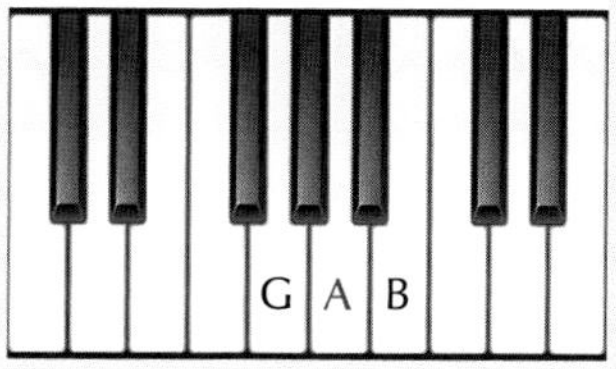

Double-flats are written as the letter name of a note followed by two flat symbols (𝄫), such as A𝄫. On the staff, the symbol appears before the note, such as 𝄫♩. When you see a double-flat next to a note, you play two keys to the left of that note, counting black and white keys. For an A double-flat, you play the G key.

Override a Sharp or Flat

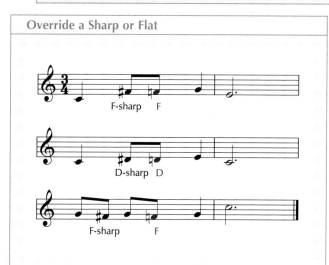

Practice

Excerpt from "Für Elise"
by Beethoven

- If a composer does not want you to play the same note in the same measure as a sharp or flat, a natural sign (♮) will appear before the note.
- For example, if a measure contains the F-sharp note, a natural sign before the next F note in the same measure indicates you should play F instead of F-sharp.
- In this example of written music, play the notes as shown, making sure to sharp or flat the appropriate notes.

key signatures

In written music, you may notice sharp symbols (♯) or flat symbols (♭) on lines or spaces of the staff immediately following the clef. These sharps or flats are called a key signature and indicate the notes in the song that you must play as sharps or flats. For example, if there is a sharp symbol on the top (F) line of the staff, you must play all the F notes in the song as F-sharps. The sharps or flats specified in the key signature apply to every note with the same letter name anywhere on the staff. The key signature prevents the staff from becoming cluttered with sharp and flat symbols next to notes throughout the song.

A composer can, however, override the key signature by placing a natural sign (♮) in front of specific notes that should not be played as sharps or flats. For example, if the key signature indicates that all F notes are sharps, there may be F notes that should not be played as sharps. When you see a natural sign, you should play the note and the rest of the notes on the same line or space in that measure as natural notes.

Understanding Key Signatures

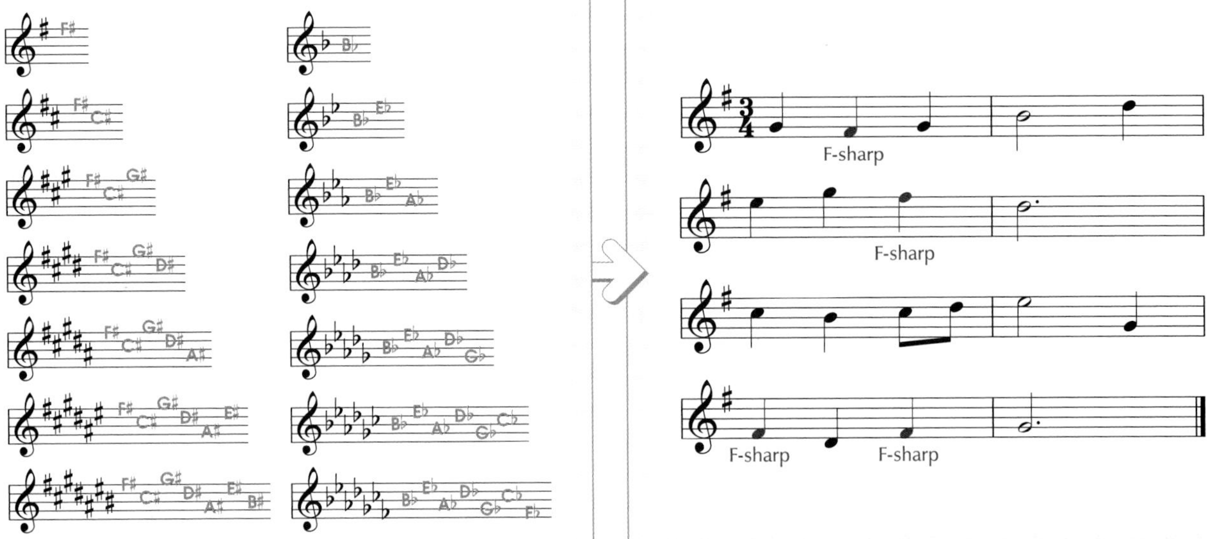

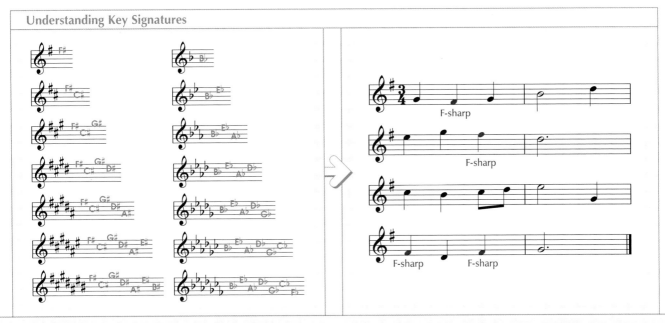

- In written music, sharps (♯) or flats (♭) can appear just after the clef on a staff. These sharps or flats are called a key signature and indicate the notes in the song that you need to play as sharps or flats.
- Each line and space on the staff represents a specific white key on your keyboard. The sharp symbol (♯) indicates that you need to play the black key directly to the right of the corresponding white key. The flat symbol (♭) indicates that you need to play the black key directly to the left of the corresponding white key.
- When a key signature indicates that you must play a certain note as a sharp or flat, you must play every note with the same letter name throughout the entire song as a sharp or flat.
- For example, if the key signature contains an F-sharp, you must play every F note on the keyboard as F-sharp throughout the entire song.
- Key signatures prevent composers from having to write symbols before every sharp or flat in a song, which keeps the symbols from cluttering the music.

Tip

Do all sharps and flats refer to black keys?

Most sharps and flats in a key signature refer to the black keys on the keyboard. However, in more advanced music, you may need to play a white key as a sharp or flat. This can occur when there is not a black key between two white keys. For example, there is not a black key between the B and C white keys. As a result, you play B♯ with the white C key and you play C♭ with the white B key.

Can a key signature change in a song?

Yes. If a key signature changes partway through a song, a new key signature appears at the point of the change.

How can I keep track of sharps and flats?

If you find it hard to remember which notes to play as sharps and flats, you can circle all the notes that need to be played as sharps or flats throughout the song as a reminder.

Override a Sharp or Flat

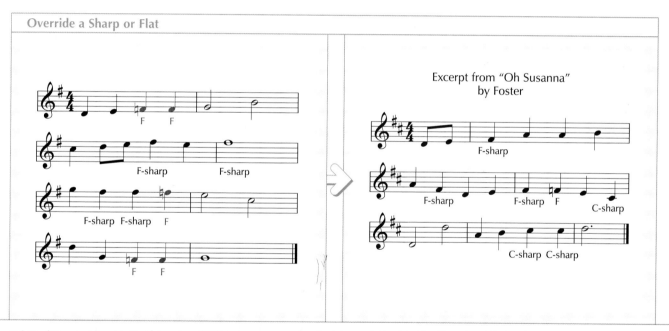

Excerpt from "Oh Susanna"
by Foster

- In written music, a natural sign (♮) appears before a note to specify that you do not play the note as a sharp or flat as indicated in the key signature.
- For example, if the key signature contains an F-sharp, a natural sign before an F note indicates you should play F instead of F-sharp.
- When you see a natural sign before a note, you also do not play the rest of the notes on the same line or space in the same measure as sharps or flats.

Note: A measure is a section of music between two vertical lines on the staff.

- In this example of written music, play the notes as shown, making sure to sharp or flat the appropriate notes.

double notes

You will often play two notes at the same time, which is known as playing double notes. Playing double notes falls between playing a single note and playing a chord. A chord is usually made up of three or more notes. Melodies using double notes sound richer than melodies using single notes.

The distance between two notes is measured in intervals. Intervals help you determine how far your hand needs to span to play both notes. The smaller the distance between notes, the smaller the interval. Double notes with smaller intervals are easier to play since the keys are closer together.

To determine the interval between two notes, count the two notes plus the number of notes in between. For example, the notes A and B are two notes apart, so they form the interval of a second. The notes A and C are three notes apart, so they form the interval of a third.

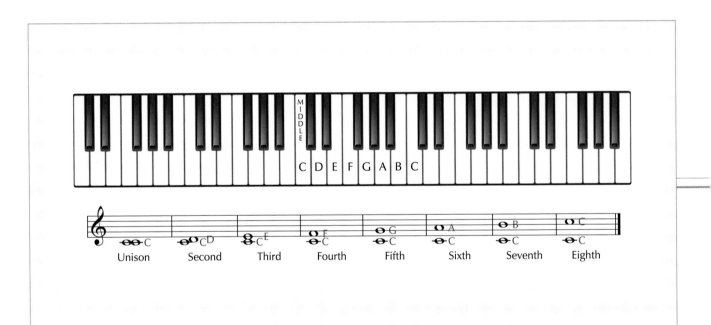

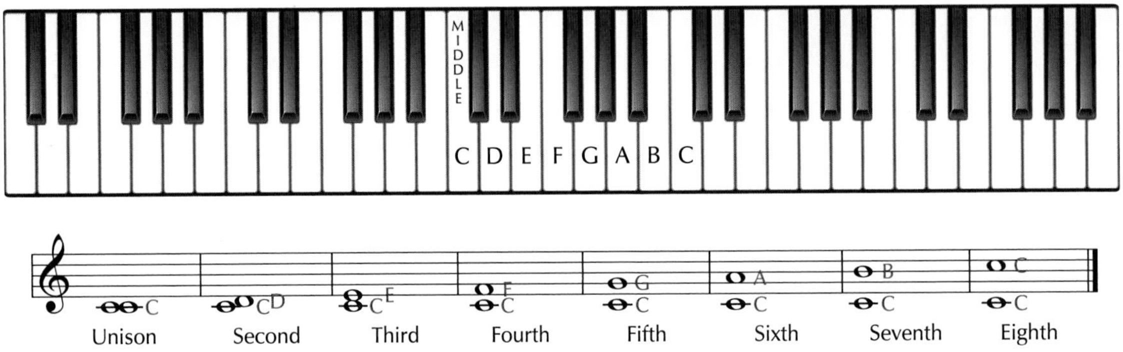

- You will often play two notes at the same time, which is known as playing double notes.
- In written music, double notes are shown as two notes stacked on top of each other on the staff.
- The distance between two notes is measured in intervals. The smaller the distance between two notes, the smaller the interval.
- When playing double notes, recognizing the interval between two notes on the staff helps you to quickly determine the distance between the notes on the keyboard so you can more quickly play the notes.
- To determine the interval between two notes, count the two notes plus each line and space between the notes on the staff.
- The smallest interval is the interval of a unison, which is the distance between two identical notes. The interval of a unison is also called an interval of a first.
- The largest commonly used interval is the interval of an eighth, which is the distance between two notes with the same letter name, eight notes apart. An interval of an eighth is also called an octave.

Tip

I cannot reach an interval of an eighth. What should I do?

If you have small hands or cannot stretch your thumb and pinky finger to reach an interval of an eighth, you can compensate by playing the low note first and then quickly shifting to play the high note. This will not sound like a true double note, but it will be close.

Are there different types of intervals?

Yes. There are two different types of intervals—harmonic and melodic. Harmonic intervals involve playing two notes at the same time. Melodic intervals involve playing two notes individually, one right after another.

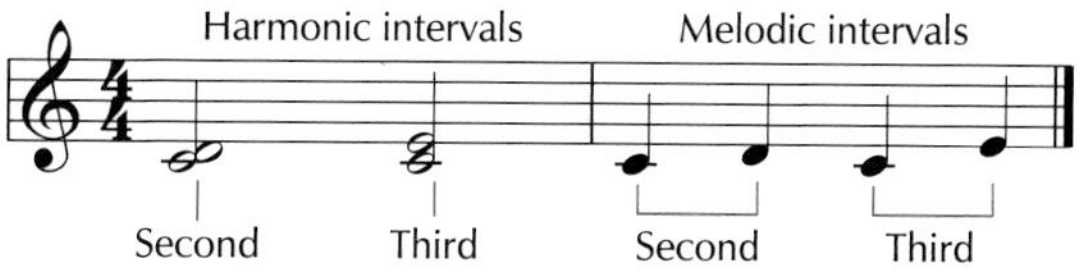

- When playing double notes, make sure you press the keys for the notes at the same time and lift the keys at the same time.
- When playing double notes with larger intervals, you will need to stretch the fingers of your hand to reach the notes. For example, to play the interval of an eighth, you will need to stretch your thumb and pinky finger to play the notes.
- In this example, play the notes as shown to practice playing double notes.
- Make sure you observe the numbers above the notes to help you determine which finger to use for each note. Your fingers are numbered from 1 to 5—thumb (1), index (2), middle (3), ring (4) and pinky (5) finger.

repetition markers

Musical pieces are often structured around repetition. Just think of any popular song on the radio—the chorus is usually repeated after every verse. For this reason, you will often find symbols in music telling you to repeat certain sections. These symbols may seem confusing at first, but once you learn what they mean, you will be able to easily navigate through written music.

Two repeat symbols commonly found in written music are the start repeat marker (𝄆) and the end repeat marker (𝄇). When you reach the end repeat marker, you return to the start repeat marker and play the music between the two markers again.

If you do not see a start repeat marker, you return to the beginning of the piece.

When music has more than one ending, a number and horizontal bracket will appear above the staff for each ending. The first time you play the music, you play the first ending. You then return to the start repeat marker (𝄆) and play the music again, finishing with the next ending.

When you see *D.C. al Fine* in written music, you return to the beginning of the music and play the music again until you see *Fine*. When you see *D.S.* in written music, you return to 𝄋 and play the music again.

Repeat Markers

Multiple Endings

- In written music, repeat markers indicate that you should repeat the section of music that appears between the start repeat marker (𝄆) and the end repeat marker (𝄇).
- When you first see a start repeat marker in music, ignore the marker. When you see the end repeat marker, return to the start repeat marker and play the music between the markers again.
- If music does not contain a start repeat marker, when you see the end repeat marker, return to the beginning of the music and play the music again.
- If written music has multiple endings, a number and horizontal bracket will appear above the staff to indicate each ending.
- When you see multiple endings, play the first ending the first time you play the music. You then return to the start repeat marker (𝄆) and play the music again, ignoring the first ending and finishing with the next ending. If the music does not contain a start repeat marker, return to the beginning of the music and play the music again.

Tip

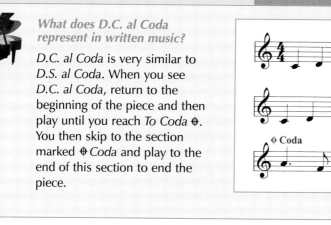

What does D.C. al Coda represent in written music?

D.C. al Coda is very similar to *D.S. al Coda*. When you see *D.C. al Coda*, return to the beginning of the piece and then play until you reach *To Coda* 𝄌. You then skip to the section marked 𝄌 *Coda* and play to the end of this section to end the piece.

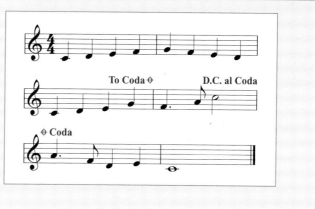

D.C. (from the beginning)

D.S. (from the sign)

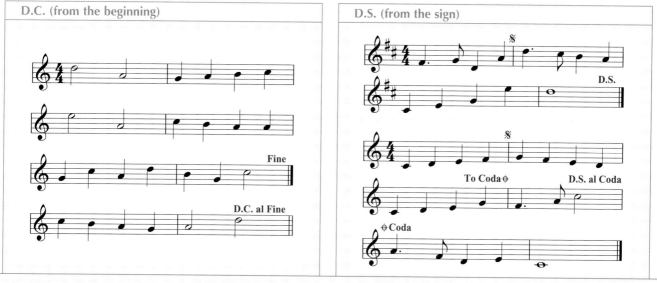

- When you see *D.C. al Fine* in written music, return to the beginning of the music, then play the music again until you see *Fine* and end the music in this location. Make sure you ignore *Fine* the first time you play the music.

Note: D.C. is short for the Italian term Da Capo, which means "from the beginning." Al Fine is the Italian term for "to the end." Fine is the Italian term for "end."

- When you see *D.S.* in written music, return to 𝄋 and play the music again, ignoring *D.S.* the second time you play the music.

Note: D.S. is short for the Italian term Dal Segno, which means "from the sign."

- When you see *D.S. al Coda*, return to 𝄋 and then play until you reach *To Coda* 𝄌. You then skip to the section marked 𝄌 *Coda* and play to the end of this section to end the song. The 𝄌 *Coda* section is usually a separate section of music at the end of a song.

incomplete measures

There are some cases when a measure does not have the complete number of beats required by the time signature. These instances are called incomplete measures and occur when a musical piece does not start on the first beat of a measure. Omitting the often-emphasized first beat of the measure allows composers to start with a weaker beat and lead into a stronger beat in the next measure.

Notes that appear in an incomplete measure at the beginning of a song are called pickup notes. If a piece begins with pickup notes, the last measure of the piece will also usually have an incomplete number of beats. When you add the number of beats in the first and last measure, they usually equal the total number of beats required in a complete measure.

When you play a piece with an incomplete measure, count out the missing beats in the first measure to establish a steady tempo before you begin playing. For example, in 4/4 time, if there is one quarter note in the first measure, it would be treated as beat number four, so remember to first count beats one, two and three before starting the piece.

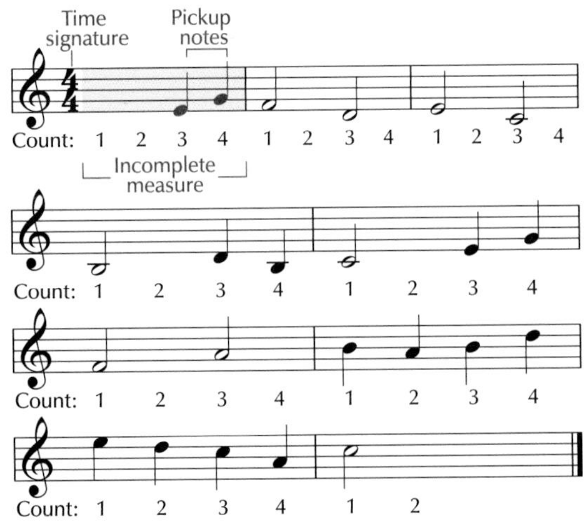

Excerpt from "When the Saints Go Marching In"

- A measure is a section of music between two vertical lines on the staff. In some written music, the first measure does not contain the number of beats required by the time signature. In this case, the first measure is known as an incomplete measure and the notes in the measure are known as pickup notes.

Note: The top number of the time signature indicates the number of beats in each measure. For example, in the 4/4 time signature, each measure contains 4 beats. An incomplete measure may have only 1, 2 or 3 beats.

- You should treat the notes in an incomplete measure as the last beats in a complete measure. For example, if two quarter notes (♩) appear in an incomplete measure, before you start playing the music, count "one, two" and then count the quarter notes as "three, four."

- This example of written music contains an incomplete measure. Make sure you count the missing beats in the first measure before you begin playing the music.

Note: When a curved line, known as a tie, appears between two identical notes, you play only the first note and hold the note for the combined value of both notes. For more information on tied notes, see page 53.

- If a musical piece begins with an incomplete measure, the last measure will also usually be an incomplete measure. When you add the beats in the first and last measures, the total number of beats will usually equal the number of beats in a complete measure.

songs for practice

Mary Had a Little Lamb

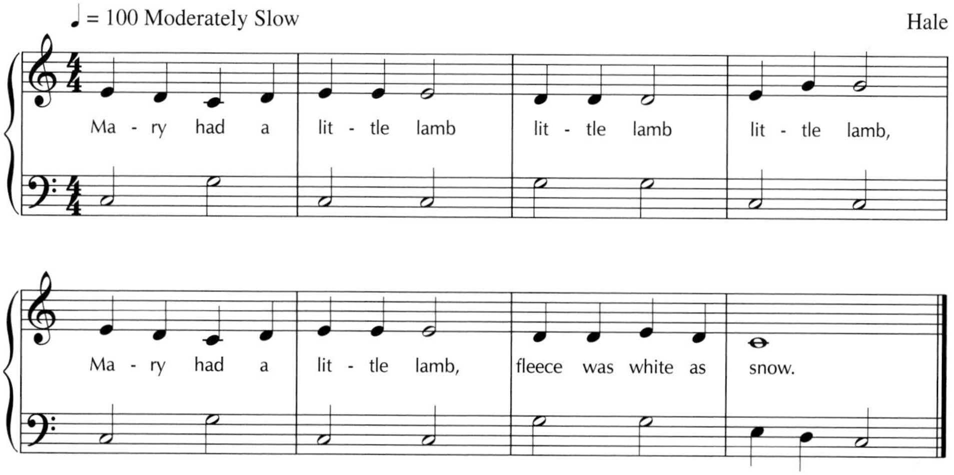

Are You Sleeping

When the Saints Go Marching In

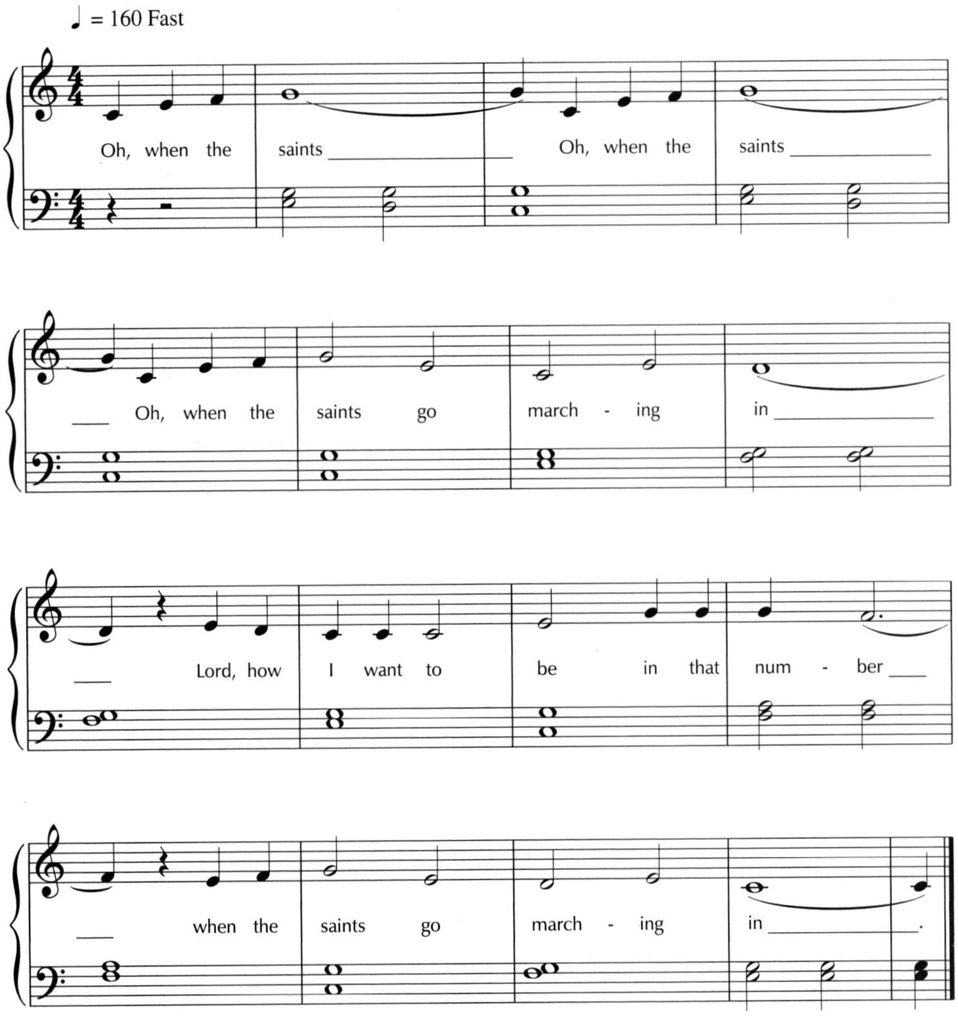

Ode to Joy

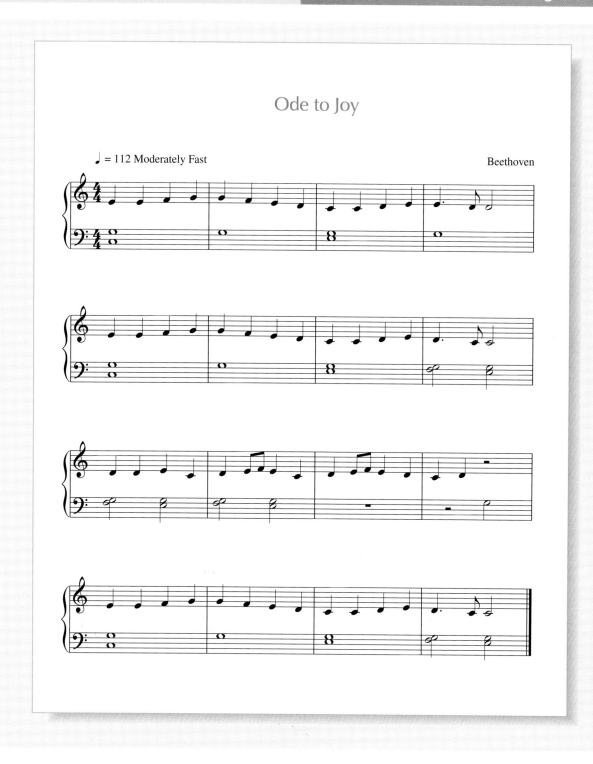

Chapter 3

Many beginner pieces that you will play on the piano require you to place your hands in specific locations, or positions, on the keyboard. This chapter will introduce to you three of the most basic hand positions—C, Middle C and G. You will also learn handy tips for playing the piano with both hands and how to change from one hand position to another within a piece.

Basic Hand Positions

In this Chapter...

place your right hand in C position

Before you play a musical piece, your hands must be in a position for your fingers to access the correct notes. In many beginner pieces, your right hand starts in C position, which allows you to easily play middle C and the four keys to the right of middle C (D, E, F and G). Middle C is the C key in the middle of the keyboard.

To place your right hand in C position, rest your right thumb on middle C and your right index, middle, ring and pinky fingers on the next four white keys. Your fingertips make contact with the keys, so your wrist should be straight and your fingers should be curved as if you are holding a tennis ball.

Since many pieces require you to play more than the five notes of C position with your right hand, you can stretch your thumb one white key to the left to play the B key below middle C. You can also stretch your pinky finger one white key to the right to play the A key.

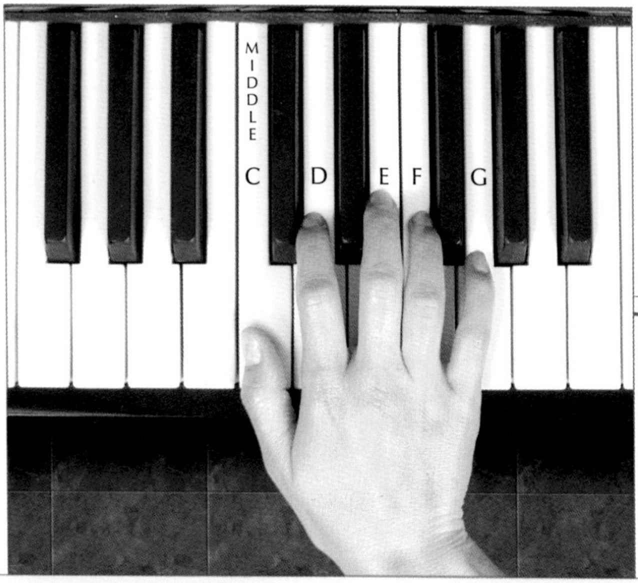

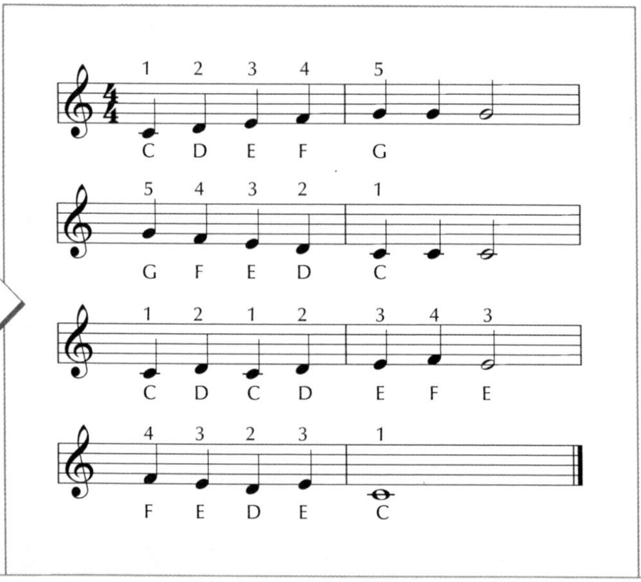

- Many beginner pieces begin with the right hand in C position. C position allows you to easily play middle C and the four keys to the right of middle C (D, E, F and G).

  Note: Middle C is the C key in the middle of the keyboard.

1 To place your right hand in C position, rest your right thumb on middle C and your right index, middle, ring and pinky fingers on the next four white keys (D, E, F and G).

- To play this example, position your right hand in C position and play the notes as shown.
- Make sure you observe the numbers above the notes to help you determine which finger to use for each note. Your fingers are numbered from 1 to 5—thumb (1), index (2), middle (3), ring (4) and pinky (5) finger.

- As the notes go upward on the staff, you play keys going to the right on your keyboard.

Tip

How do I know if my right hand is in C position?

In some written music, especially beginner music, the suggested fingering for your right hand appears above or below the notes on the treble clef staff to help you determine which fingers to use. For information on fingering, see page 48. Before you begin playing, place the suggested finger on the first note. If your right thumb falls on the middle C key, your right hand is in C position.

When my right hand is in C position, what notes can I play?

When your right hand is in C position, you can play the notes B, middle C, D, E, F, G and A.

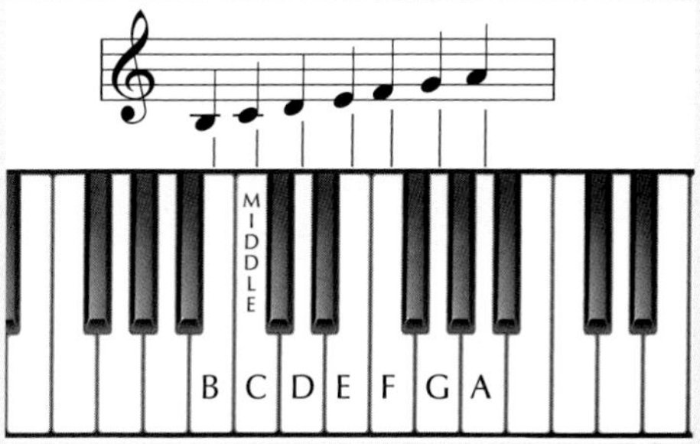

Play More Notes in C Position

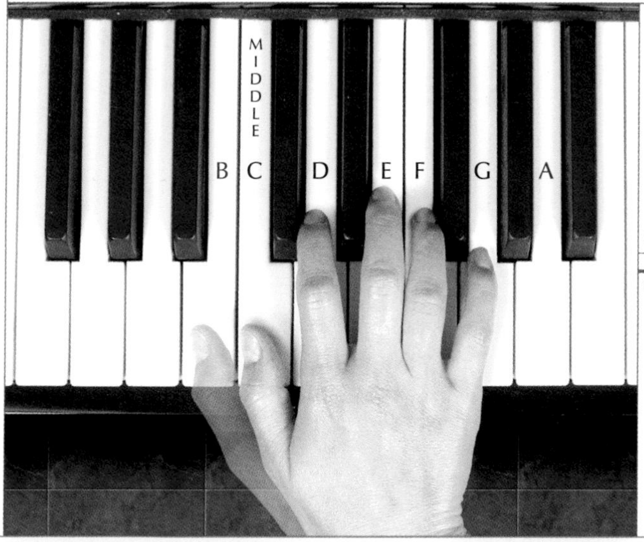

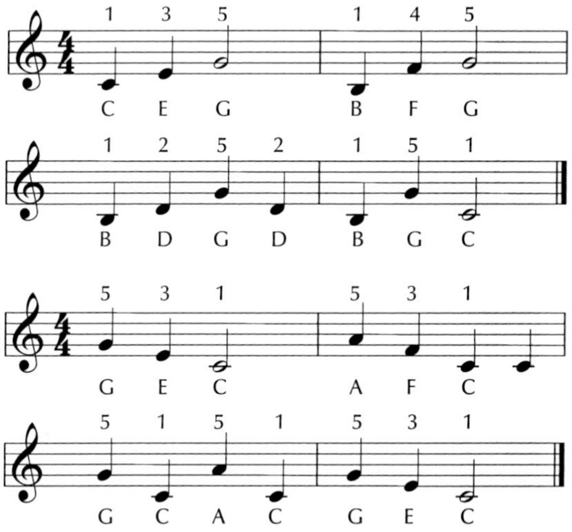

- In pieces that begin in C position, you may need to stretch your thumb and/or pinky finger to reach other notes.

1 When your right hand is in C position, you can stretch your thumb one white key to the left to play the B key below middle C. Make sure your other fingers remain in the same position when stretching your thumb.

2 When your right hand is in C position, you can also leave your thumb on middle C and shift each of your remaining fingers one white key to the right to allow your pinky finger to reach and play the A key.

- To play the first example, position your right hand in C position and play the notes as shown, stretching your thumb to play the B key when needed.
- Make sure you observe the numbers above the notes to help you determine which finger to use for each note. Your fingers are numbered from 1 to 5—thumb (1), index (2), middle (3), ring (4) and pinky (5) finger.
- To play the second example, position your right hand in C position and play the notes as shown, shifting your index, middle, ring and pinky fingers to allow your pinky finger to play the A key when needed.

place your left hand in C position

Before playing a musical piece, you need to position your hands so that your fingers can access the correct notes. In many beginner pieces, your left hand starts in C position, which allows you to easily play the C key below middle C and the four keys to the right of the C key (D, E, F and G). Middle C is the C key in the middle of the keyboard.

To place your left hand in C position, rest your left pinky finger on the C key below middle C and your left ring finger, middle finger, index finger and thumb on the next four white keys. Your fingertips make contact with the keys, so your wrist should be straight and your fingers should be curved as if you are holding a tennis ball.

Since many pieces require you to play more than the five notes of C position with your left hand, you can stretch your pinky finger one white key to the left to play the B key. You can also stretch your thumb one white key to the right to play the A key.

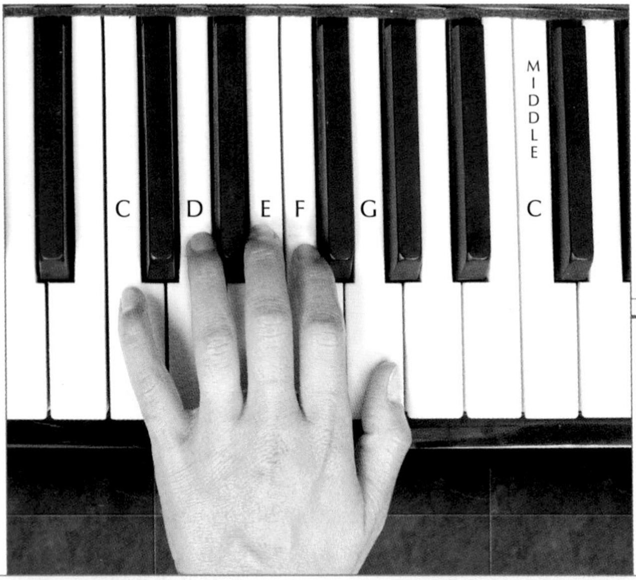

- Many beginner pieces begin with the left hand in C position. C position allows you to easily play the C key below middle C and the four keys to the right of the C key (D, E, F and G).

Note: Middle C is the C key in the middle of the keyboard.

1 To place your left hand in C position, rest your left pinky finger on the C key below middle C and your left ring finger, middle finger, index finger and thumb on the next four white keys (D, E, F and G).

- To play this example, position your left hand in C position and play the notes as shown.
- Make sure you observe the numbers below the notes to help you determine which finger to use for each note. Your fingers are numbered from 1 to 5—thumb (1), index (2), middle (3), ring (4) and pinky (5) finger.

- As the notes go upward on the staff, you play keys going to the right on your keyboard.

Tip

How do I know if my left hand is in C position?

In some written music, especially beginner music, the suggested fingering for your left hand appears above or below the notes on the bass clef staff to help you determine which fingers to use. For information on fingering, see page 48. Before you begin playing, place the suggested finger on the first note. If your left pinky finger falls on the C key below middle C, your left hand is in C position. Middle C is the C key in the middle of the keyboard.

When my left hand is in C position, what notes can I play?

When your left hand is in C position, you can play the notes B, C, D, E, F, G and A, which appear right below middle C.

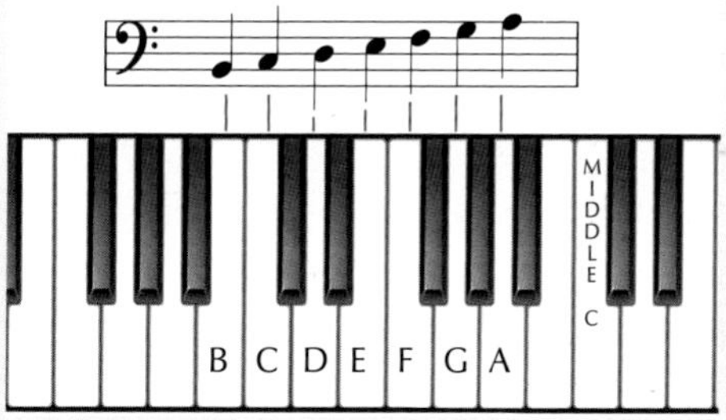

Play More Notes in C Position

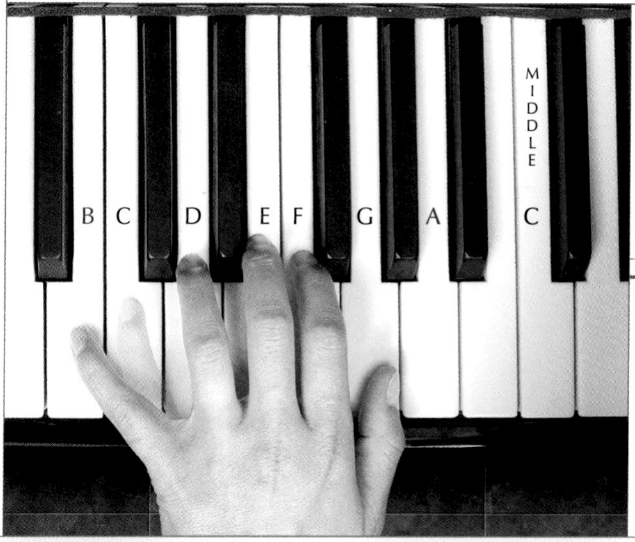

- In pieces that begin in C position, you may need to stretch your pinky finger and/or thumb to reach other notes.

1 When your left hand is in C position, you can stretch your pinky finger one white key to the left to play the B key. Make sure your other fingers remain in the same position when stretching your pinky finger.

2 When your left hand is in C position, you can also stretch your thumb one white key to the right to play the A key. Make sure your other fingers remain in the same position when stretching your thumb.

- To play the first example, position your left hand in C position and play the notes as shown, stretching your pinky finger to play the B key when needed.
- Make sure you observe the numbers below the notes to help you determine which finger to use for each note. Your fingers are numbered from 1 to 5—thumb (1), index (2), middle (3), ring (4) and pinky (5) finger.
- To play the second example, position your left hand in C position and play the notes as shown, stretching your thumb to play the A key when needed.

place your right hand in G position

Before you play a piece of music, you need to start in the proper position so you will be able to easily access the notes in the piece. For many beginner pieces, you will start with your right hand in G position.

To position your right hand in G position, place your right thumb on the G key above middle C and allow your right index, middle, ring and pinky fingers to rest on the next four white keys (A, B, C and D).

As you play, keep your wrist straight with your fingers curved so that only your fingertips make contact with the keys.

Some pieces that begin in G position require additional notes. With your right hand in G position, you can stretch your thumb or pinky finger to the left or right to play the required notes. For example, you can extend your thumb to the left to play F-sharp or extend your pinky finger to the right to play E.

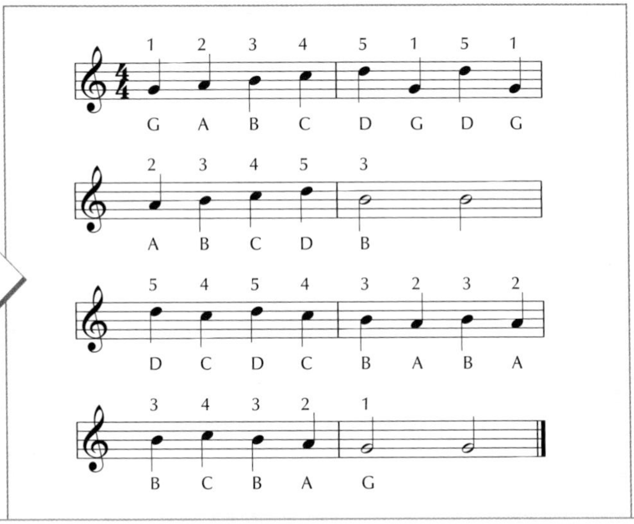

- Many beginner pieces begin with the right hand in G position. G position allows you to easily play the G key above middle C and the four keys to the right of the G key (A, B, C and D).

  Note: Middle C is the C key in the middle of the keyboard.

1 To place your right hand in G position, rest your right thumb on the G key above middle C and your right index, middle, ring and pinky fingers on the next four white keys (A, B, C and D).

- In this example, position your right hand in G position and play the notes as shown.
- Make sure you observe the numbers above the notes to help you determine which finger to use for each note. Your fingers are numbered from 1 to 5—thumb (1), index (2), middle (3), ring (4) and pinky (5) finger.
- As the notes go upward on the staff, you play keys going to the right on your keyboard.

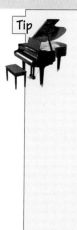

Tip

How do I know if my right hand is in G position?

In some written music, especially beginner music, the suggested fingering for your right hand appears above or below the notes on the treble clef staff to help you determine which fingers to use. For information on fingering, see page 48. Before you begin playing, place the suggested finger on the first note. If your right thumb falls on the G key above middle C, your right hand is in G position.

When my right hand is in G position, what notes can I play?

With your right hand in G position, you can play the notes F♯, G, A, B, C, D and E.

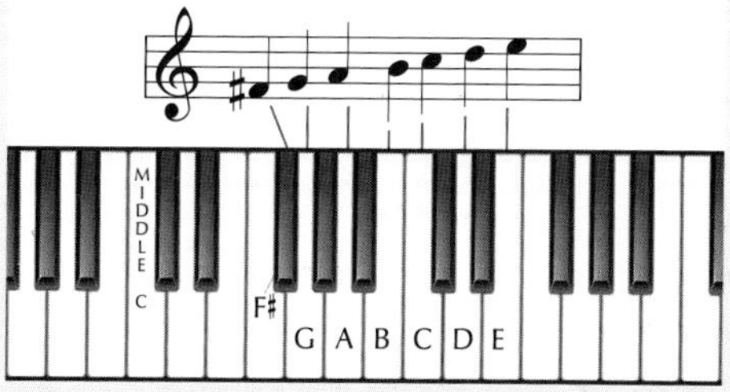

Play More Notes in G Position

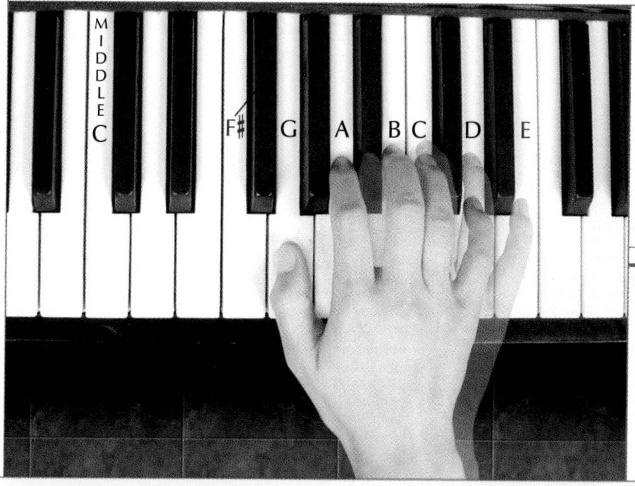

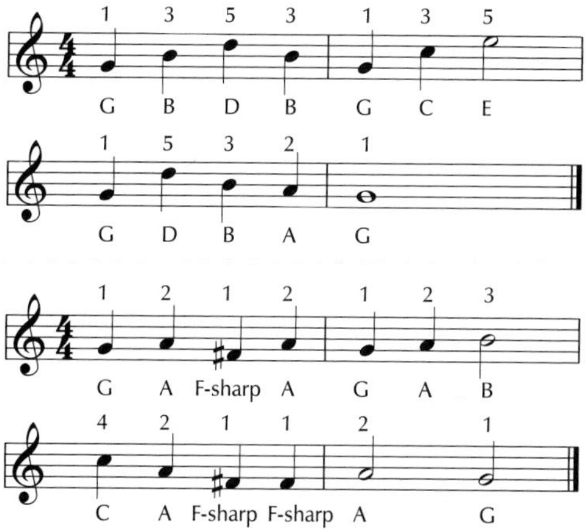

- In pieces that begin in G position, you may need to use your thumb and/or pinky finger to reach other notes.

1 When your right hand is in G position, you can leave your thumb on the G key and shift each of your remaining fingers one white key to the right to allow your pinky finger to reach and play the E key.

2 When your right hand is in G position, you can stretch your thumb one black key to the left to play the F-sharp (F♯) key. Make sure your other fingers remain in the same position when stretching your thumb.

Note: When your right hand is in G position, you will play the F-sharp key more often than the F key.

- In the first example, position your right hand in G position and play the notes as shown, shifting your index, middle, ring and pinky fingers to allow your pinky finger to play the E key when needed.

- Make sure you observe the numbers above the notes to help you determine which finger to use for each note. Your fingers are numbered from 1 to 5—thumb (1), index (2), middle (3), ring (4) and pinky (5) finger.

- In the second example, position your right hand in G position and play the notes as shown, stretching your thumb to play the F-sharp key when needed.

place your left hand in G position

Before you play a piece of music, you need to start in the proper position so you will be able to easily access the notes in the piece. Many beginner pieces start with your left hand in G position.

There are two commonly used G positions for the left hand. You can place your pinky finger on the first G key below middle C or further to the left on the second G key below middle C. In either case, you then rest your ring, middle, index finger and thumb on the next four white keys (A, B, C and D).

As you play, keep your wrist straight with your fingers curved so that only your fingertips make contact with the keys.

If the piece you are playing requires additional notes, you can stretch your thumb or pinky finger to the left or right to play the required notes without moving your left hand out of G position. For example, you can extend your thumb to the right to play E or extend your pinky finger to the left to play F-sharp.

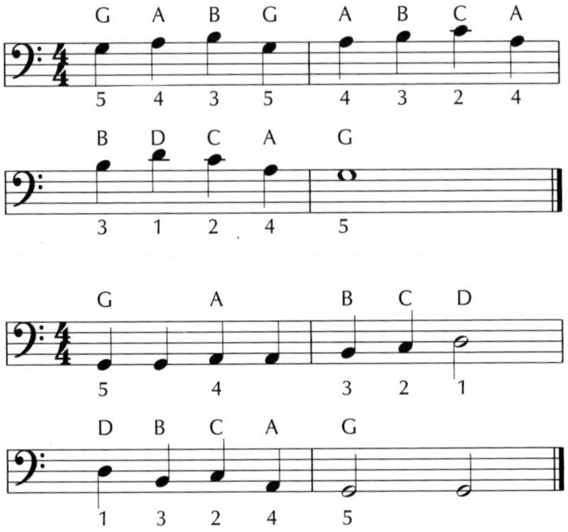

- Many beginner pieces begin with the left hand in G position. G position allows you to easily play the G key and the four keys to the right of the G key (A, B, C and D).

1 To place your left hand in the high G position, rest your left pinky finger on the first G key below middle C and your left ring finger, middle finger, index finger and thumb on the next four white keys (A, B, C and D).

Note: Middle C is the C key in the middle of the keyboard.

2 To place your left hand in the low G position, rest your left pinky finger on the second G key below middle C and your left ring finger, middle finger, index finger and thumb on the next four white keys (A, B, C and D).

- In the first example, position your left hand in the high G position and play the notes as shown.
- Make sure you observe the numbers below the notes to help you determine which finger to use for each note. Your fingers are numbered from 1 to 5—thumb (1), index (2), middle (3), ring (4) and pinky (5) finger.

- In the second example, position your left hand in the low G position and play the notes as shown.
- As the notes go upward on the staff, you play keys going to the right on your keyboard.

Tip

How do I know if my left hand is in G position?

In some written music, especially beginner music, the suggested fingering appears below the notes on the bass clef staff to help you determine which finger to use to play each note. Your fingers are numbered from 1 to 5—thumb (1), index (2), middle (3), ring (4) and pinky (5) finger. Before you begin playing a piece, place the suggested finger on the first note. If your left pinky finger rests on the G key, your left hand is in G position.

When my left hand is in G position, what notes can I play?

With your left hand in G position, you can play the notes F-sharp, G, A, B, C, D and E.

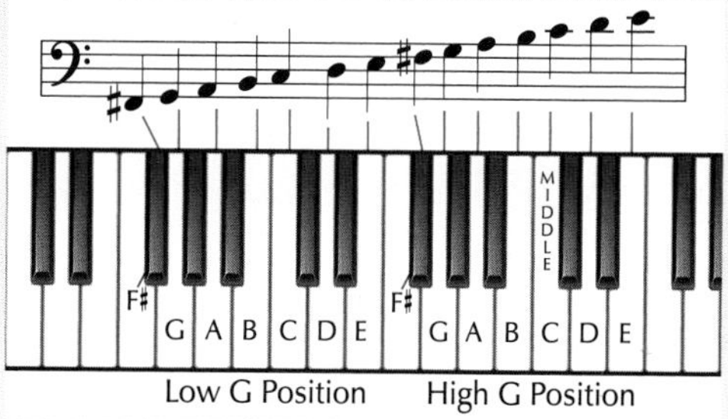

Play More Notes in G Position

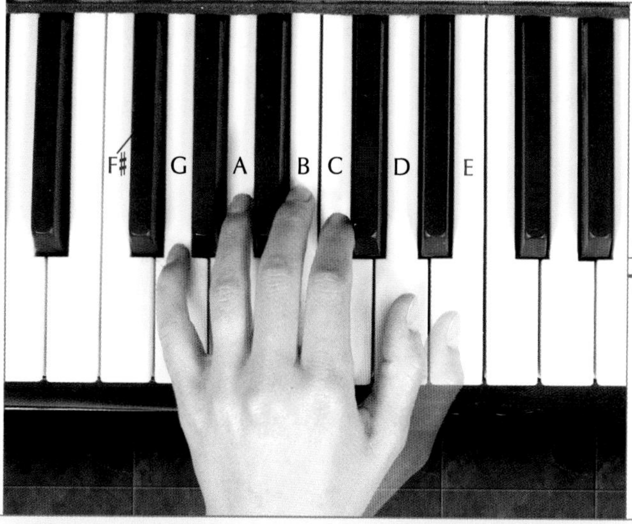

- In pieces that begin in G position, you may need to use your thumb and/or pinky finger to reach other notes.

1 When your left hand is in G position, you can stretch your thumb one white key to the right to play the E key. Make sure your other fingers remain in the same position when stretching your thumb.

2 When your left hand is in G position, you can stretch your pinky finger one black key to the left to play the F-sharp (F♯) key. Make sure your other fingers remain in the same position when stretching your pinky finger.

Note: When your left hand is in G position, you will play the F-sharp key more often than the F key.

- In the first example, position your left hand in the high G position and play the notes as shown. When needed, stretch your thumb to play the E key and your pinky finger to play the F-sharp key.
- Make sure you observe the numbers below the notes to help you determine which finger to use for each note. Your fingers are numbered from 1 to 5—thumb (1), index (2), middle (3), ring (4) and pinky (5) finger.
- In the second example, position your left hand in the low G position and play the notes as shown.

basics of playing with both hands

Once you are comfortable playing notes with either hand, you can expand your range by using both hands at the same time to play a piece.

Coordinating both hands to play different notes at the same time can be challenging. Your right hand is usually dominant, playing the melody while your left hand plays accompaniment.

The grand staff allows you to read notes for both hands at the same time. The treble clef (𝄞) staff shows the right hand notes. The bass clef (𝄢) staff shows the left hand notes. Notes that appear directly above or below each other on the staff are played at the same time. You should pay special attention to which staff displays a note so you can use the appropriate hand to play the note.

To get started playing a piece with both hands, play the piece first with just your right hand and then with just your left hand. When you feel comfortable with the notes, you can use both hands. You should concentrate on playing the correct notes at a slow, steady pace. As you become more confident, you can work towards playing at a faster speed.

- The grand staff allows you to read notes for both hands at the same time. The treble clef (𝄞) staff shows the notes you play with your right hand. The bass clef (𝄢) staff shows the notes you play with your left hand.
- When reading music on the grand staff, notes that appear above or below each other on the staff are played at the same time.
- When playing a musical piece with both hands, make sure you look at the written music, not at your hands.
- Before trying to play a musical piece with both hands, play the left and right hand parts separately. When your left and right hands can play the notes well, you are ready to play the musical piece with both hands at the same time.
- When you first play a musical piece with both hands, play slowly. As you become more comfortable with the music, you can gradually work toward playing at the appropriate speed. Playing the correct notes with both hands is more important than playing at the correct speed.

place both hands in C position

Many beginner pieces start with both hands in C position. When you place both hands in C position, the position of your hands is the same as when you place just your left or right hand in C position.

To place your right hand in C position, rest your right thumb on middle C and your right index, middle, ring and pinky fingers on the next four white keys. Middle C is the C key in the middle of the keyboard. To place your left hand in C position, rest your left pinky finger on the C key below middle C and your left ring finger, middle finger, index finger and thumb on the next four white keys.

To play additional notes in C position, you can stretch your left pinky finger and right thumb one white key to the left to play the B key. You can also stretch your left thumb and right pinky finger one white key to the right to play the A key.

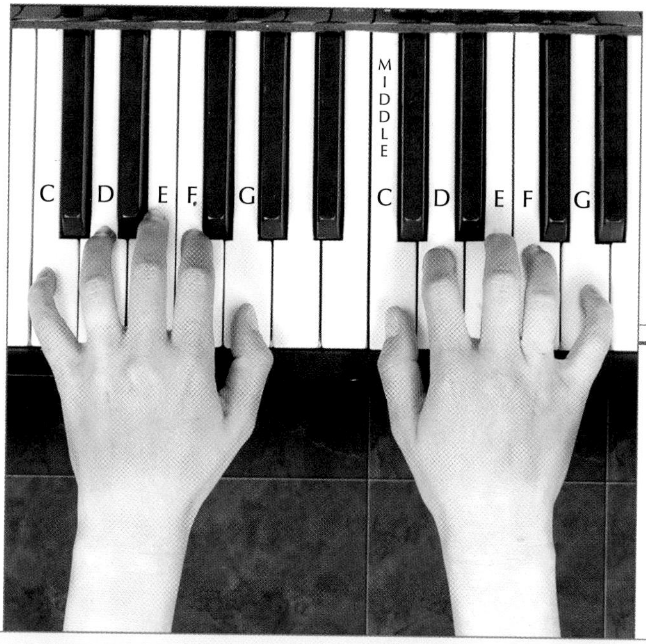

- Many beginner pieces start with both hands in C position.

1 To place your right hand in C position, rest your right thumb on middle C and your right index, middle, ring and pinky fingers on the next four white keys (D, E, F and G).

Note: Middle C is the C key in the middle of the keyboard.

2 To place your left hand in C position, rest your left pinky finger on the C key below middle C and your left ring finger, middle finger, index finger and thumb on the next four white keys (D, E, F and G).

- In this example of written music, position both hands in C position and play the notes as shown.

- Make sure you observe the numbers above or below the notes to help you determine which finger to use for each note. Your fingers are numbered from 1 to 5—thumb (1), index (2), middle (3), ring (4) and pinky (5) finger.

place both hands in middle C position

Many beginner pieces start with both hands in middle C position. When you place both hands in middle C position, your right thumb and your left thumb share middle C. Middle C is the C key in the middle of the keyboard.

To place your right hand in middle C position, rest your right thumb on middle C and your right index, middle, ring and pinky fingers on the next four white keys. To place your left hand in middle C position, rest your left pinky finger on the F key directly below middle C and your left ring finger, middle finger, index finger and thumb on the next four white keys.

When playing in middle C position, both of your thumbs rest on middle C. You should play middle C with your right thumb if middle C appears in the treble clef staff. You should play middle C with your left thumb if middle C appears in the bass clef staff. When you play middle C with one thumb, your other thumb should lift slightly out of the way.

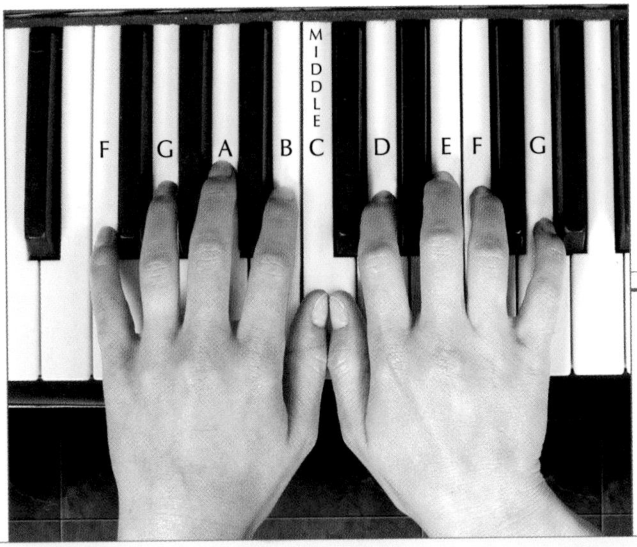

- Many beginner pieces start with both hands in middle C position.

1 To place your right hand in middle C position, rest your right thumb on middle C and your right index, middle, ring and pinky fingers on the next four white keys (D, E, F and G).

Note: Middle C is the C key in the middle of the keyboard.

2 To place your left hand in middle C position, rest your left pinky finger on the F key directly below middle C and your left ring finger, middle finger, index finger and thumb on the next four white keys (G, A, B and middle C).

- Both thumbs rest on middle C.

- In this example of written music, position both hands in middle C position and play the notes as shown.
- Make sure you observe the numbers above or below the notes to help you determine which finger to use for each note. Your fingers are numbered from 1 to 5—thumb (1), index (2), middle (3), ring (4) and pinky (5) finger.

- If middle C appears in the treble clef (𝄞) staff, play middle C with your right hand. If middle C appears in the bass clef (𝄢) staff, play middle C with your left hand.

place both hands in G position

Starting in the proper position when playing a piece of music allows you to easily reach the notes in the piece. Many beginner pieces start with both hands in G position.

The position of both hands in G position is the same as when you place just the left or right hand in G position. To position your left hand in G position, you place your pinky finger on the first or second G key below middle C. Then you rest your left ring, middle, index finger and thumb on the next four white keys (A, B, C and D). To position your right hand, place your right thumb on the first G key above middle C and rest your right index, middle, ring and pinky fingers on the next four white keys (A, B, C and D).

If the piece you are playing requires additional notes, you can stretch the thumb or pinky finger of either hand to the left or right to play the required notes without moving your hands out of G position. For example, you can use your left thumb or right pinky finger to play the E key.

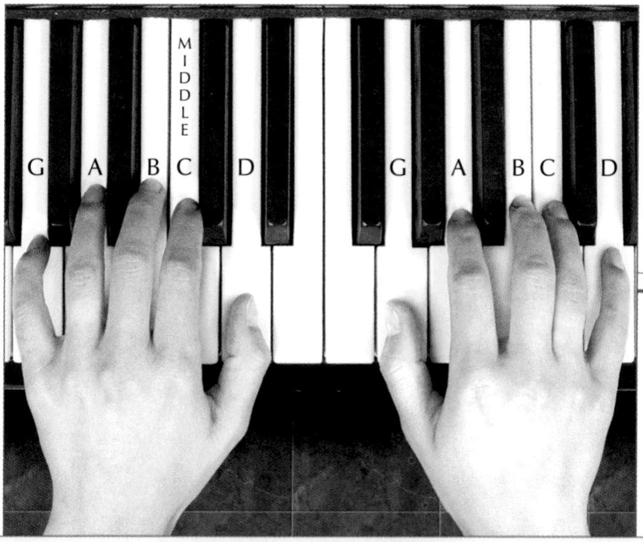

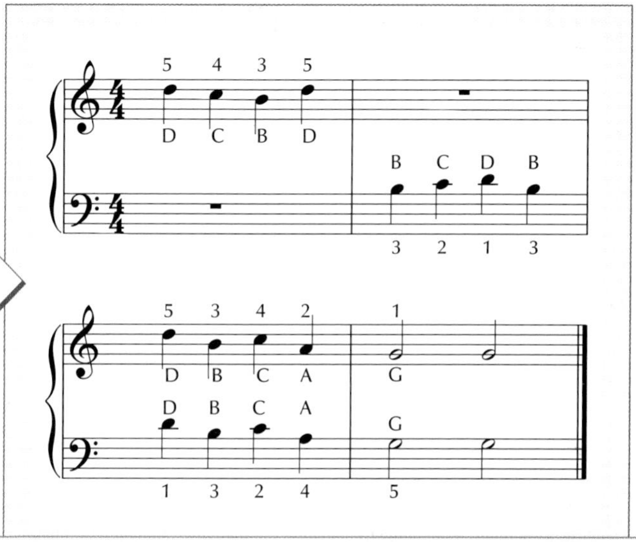

- Many beginner pieces begin with both hands in G position.

1 To place your right hand in G position, rest your right thumb on the first G key above middle C and your right index, middle, ring and pinky fingers on the next four white keys (A, B, C and D).

Note: Middle C is the C key in the middle of the keyboard.

2 To place your left hand in G position, rest your left pinky finger on the first or second G key below middle C and your left ring finger, middle finger, index finger and thumb on the next four white keys (A, B, C and D).

- In this example of written music, position both hands in G position and play the notes as shown.

Note: In this example, the left pinky finger is on the first G key below middle C.

- Make sure you observe the numbers above or below the notes to help you determine which finger to use for each note. Your fingers are numbered from 1 to 5—thumb (1), index (2), middle (3), ring (4) and pinky (5) finger.

Changing positions on the keyboard

When playing a piece of music, you will often need to move your hands to different positions on the keyboard in order to play all the notes in the piece. Using a variety of positions allows you to play a wider range of notes in a piece.

Changing from one position to another in the middle of a piece can be challenging, but you can master the skill with practice. You should try to anticipate the change in positions ahead of time and move your hand as soon as you get a chance. To ensure a smooth transition in the music, do not wait until the last second to change positions. Beginner pieces usually include rests to give you an opportunity to shift hand positions.

You will most often switch between C, middle C and G positions. When moving one hand to a new position, you can quickly glance at the keyboard to make sure your hand is moving to the correct position while your other hand continues to play.

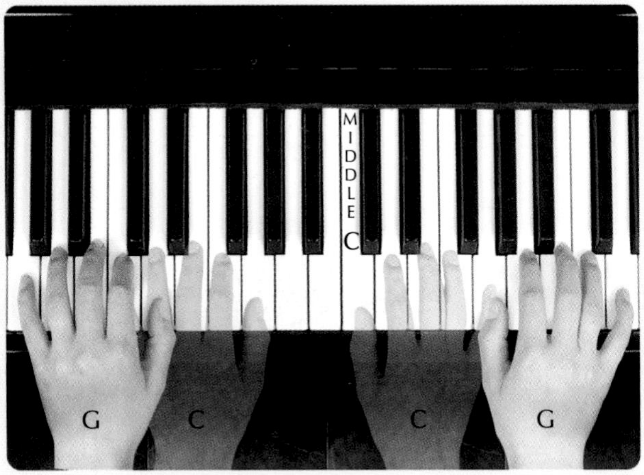

- When playing a musical piece, you will often need to move your hands to different positions on the keyboard. Moving your hands to different positions allows you to play all the notes in a piece.
- You will commonly switch between C, middle C and G positions. For more information on C, middle C and G positions, see pages 70 to 81.
- In this example of written music, play the notes as shown, moving your hands to new positions when needed.
- When the next series of notes requires one of your hands to move to a different position, beginner music will usually include a rest symbol to give you time to move your hand. A rest symbol, such as 𝄽, indicates a moment of silence.

songs for practice

Row Row Row Your Boat

♩ = 144 Fast
Row row row your boat, gent - ly down the stream.
Merri - ly merri - ly merri - ly merri - ly life is but a dream.
Row row row your boat, gent - ly down the stream.
Merri - ly merri - ly merri - ly merri - ly life is but a dream.

Auld Lang Syne

♩ = 72 Slow

words by Robert Burns

Should auld ac - quaint - ance be for - got and_ nev - er brought to
mind? Should auld ac - quaint - ance be for - got and_ days of Auld Lang
Syne For Auld___ Lang___ Syne my dear for Auld___ Lang___
Syne we'll take a cup of kind - ness yet For__ Auld___ Lang___ Syne

Lavender's Blue

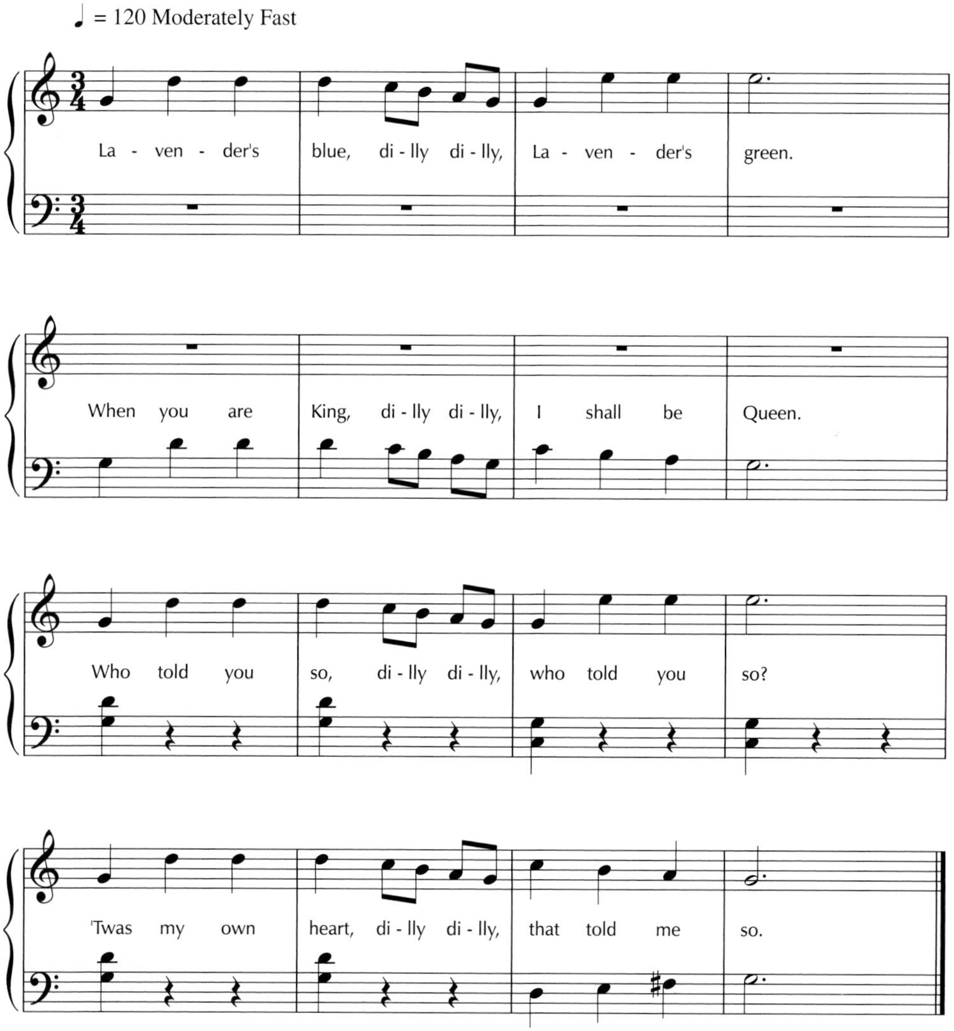
♩ = 120 Moderately Fast
La - ven - der's blue, di - lly di - lly, La - ven - der's green.
When you are King, di - lly di - lly, I shall be Queen.
Who told you so, di - lly di - lly, who told you so?
'Twas my own heart, di - lly di - lly, that told me so.

Chapter 4

Most musical pieces are based on the notes of a particular scale. This chapter will teach you about the scales used in piano music, including major, minor, pentatonic and blues scales. You will also learn about an ancient form of scales, called modes, that are also used in music today. Once you have an understanding of scales, you can play many different scales during your practice sessions to help exercise and train your fingers.

Playing Scales

In this Chapter...

- Introduction to Scales
- Playing Major Scales
- Playing Minor Scales
- Playing Pentatonic Scales
- Playing Chromatic Scales
- Playing Blues Scales
- Playing Modes

introduction to scales

A scale is a series of notes that you play in ascending and/or descending order. Composers use the notes of a scale to create melodies. A simple melody often contains the notes from just one scale. A more complex melody may use the notes from more than one scale.

Scales consist of notes that are close in proximity to each other on the keyboard. You can measure the distances, or intervals, between the keys on the keyboard in whole steps and half steps. Two keys that are separated by another key, whether white or black, are a whole step apart. Two keys that are side by side, whether white or black, are a half step apart. Each type of scale has a specific pattern of whole steps and half steps between the notes in the scale.

Most scales have more than five different notes. For example, major scales and minor scales, the most common types of scales, contain seven different notes. Since we only have five fingers, you must cross your fingers in order to play the notes that go beyond the span of five notes. You can cross your fingers in two different ways—over and under.

Understanding Scales

C Major Scale

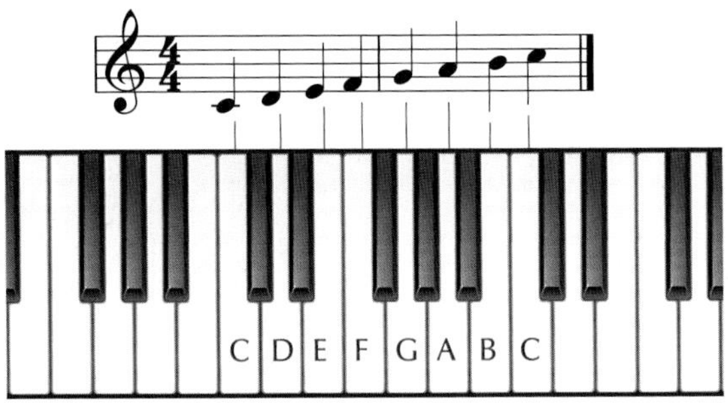

- A scale is a series of notes that you play in ascending and/or descending order.
- The major and minor scales are the most common types of scales. Major and minor scales contain seven different notes.
- When you play a scale, you repeat the first note again one octave higher. For example, to play the C major scale, you would play the C, D, E, F, G, A, B notes and then play the C note again, one octave higher.

Note: An octave refers to the distance between two notes with the same letter name on the keyboard.

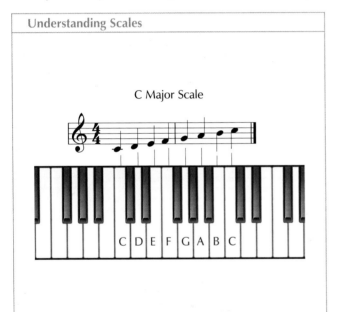

Reasons for Playing Scales

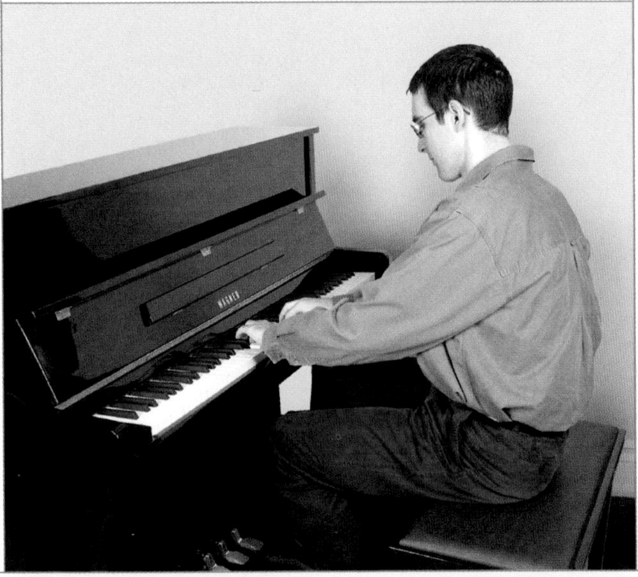

- Playing scales is a great way to warm up your fingers before playing. Just like an athlete needs to stretch before playing a sport, you should play scales to enhance the flexibility and strength in your fingers before playing music.
- Playing scales helps train your fingers to move in specific patterns, which can help you learn musical pieces more quickly.

Tip

How often should I practice scales?

You should make practicing scales a part of your daily routine. Before playing a piece of music, you should play scales for at least five minutes a day.

How fast should I play scales?

When you first start playing scales, play slowly and with a steady beat. Do not pause when performing finger crosses. As you become more familiar with scales, you can attempt to play them faster.

What are the most commonly used notes in a scale?

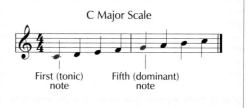

In classical and popular music, the first (tonic) and fifth (dominant) notes in a scale are the most commonly used notes.

C Major Scale

Whole Steps and Half Steps

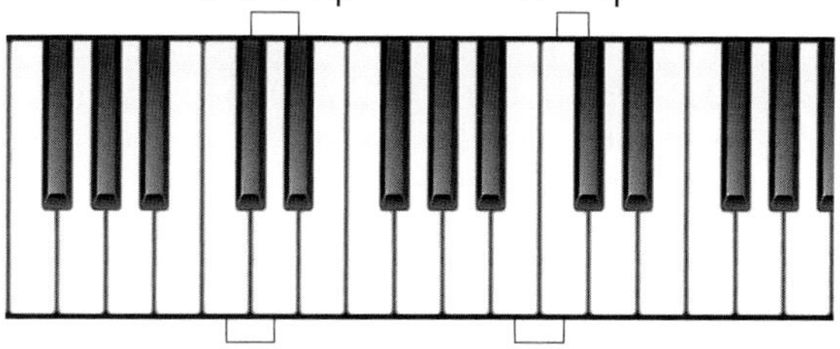

- You can measure the distances, or intervals, between the keys on the keyboard in whole steps and half steps.

  Note: Whole steps and half steps are also known as tones and semi-tones.

- Two keys that are separated by another key, whether white or black, are a whole step apart. Two keys that are side by side, whether white or black, are a half step apart.

- Each type of scale has a specific pattern of whole steps and half steps between the notes in the scale.

Cross Over

Cross Under

- When you play a scale, you will need to cross your fingers to play certain notes in the scale. You can cross your fingers in two different ways—over and under.

- You will commonly need to cross your index, middle or ring finger OVER your thumb to play a note. You will commonly need to cross your thumb UNDER your index, middle or ring finger to play a note.

- When crossing your fingers, make sure you keep your wrist straight and you do not stick out your elbow.

playing major scales

Most happy sounding musical pieces, such as "Jingle Bells," use notes from a major scale. A major scale contains seven different notes plus the first note repeated at the next higher location on the keyboard. For example, to play the C major scale, you would play the C, D, E, F, G, A, B notes and the next C note one key higher.

A major scale is named after the first (tonic) note of the scale. For example, if the first note in a major scale is C, the name of the scale is C major. Music that uses the notes from a scale is said to be in the key of that scale, so a song using the C major scale is in the key of C.

There are 12 major scales, including the C, C♯ (also known as D♭), D, E♭, E, F, F♯ (also known as G♭), G, A♭, A, B♭ and B major scales. Major scales sound different from other types of scales because of their specific pattern of whole steps and half steps between the notes. The step pattern for every major scale is whole, whole, half, whole, whole, whole, half step. You can start on any key, apply this pattern and create a major scale.

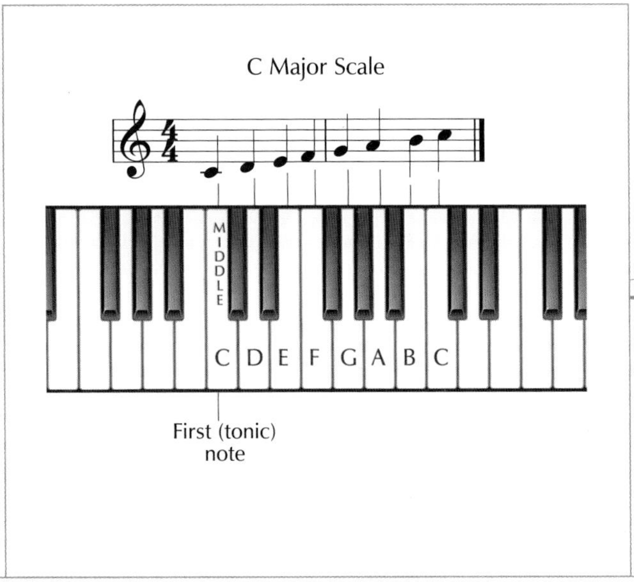

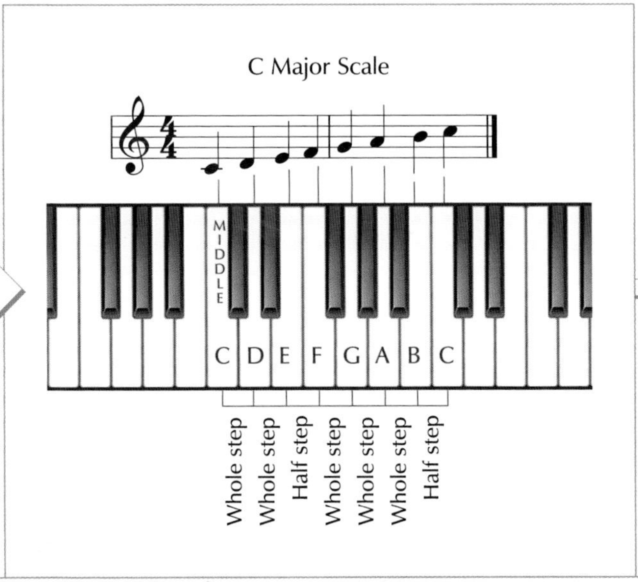

- Major scales are happy sounding scales. There are 12 major scales.
- Each major scale contains seven different notes. When you play a major scale, you repeat the first note again one octave higher. For example, to play the C major scale, you would play the C, D, E, F, G, A, B notes and then play the C note again, one octave higher.

Note: An octave refers to the distance between two notes with the same letter name on the keyboard.

- Major scales are named after the first (tonic) note of the scale. For example, if the first note in a major scale is C, the name of the scale is C major.
- Every major scale has the same pattern of whole steps and half steps between the notes in the scale. The specific pattern used by every major scale is whole, whole, half, whole, whole, whole, half step. For information on whole steps and half steps, see page 89.
- For example, you can play a C major scale by starting on any C key on the keyboard and applying the pattern of whole steps and half steps all the way to the next C key.

Tip

Which keys are used to play scales?

Every major scale consists of a different combination of white and black keys. The only major scale played strictly with white keys is the C major scale.

How are scales normally played?

You will normally play the eight notes in a scale going up the keyboard and then play the same eight notes going down the keyboard. To help train your fingers to play musical pieces, scales are played going up and down the keyboard since note patterns will go up and down in music.

How can I make playing scales more challenging?

When you begin playing scales, play one hand at a time. When you are more comfortable with the note and fingering patterns, you can play scales with both hands at the same time.

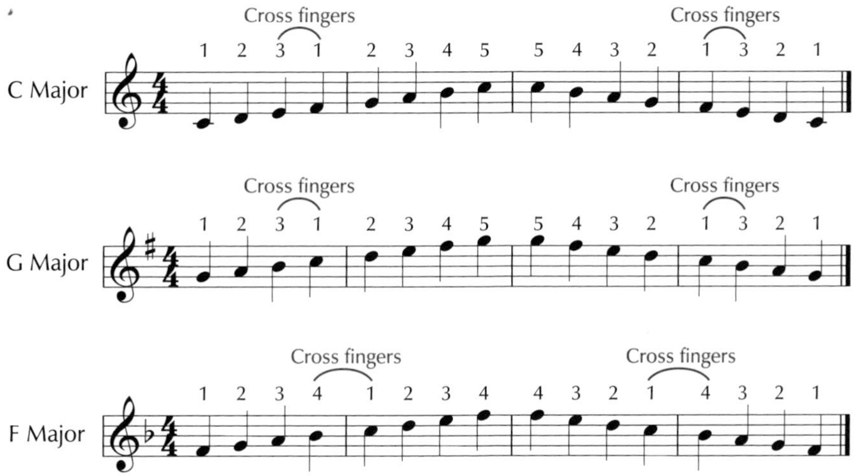

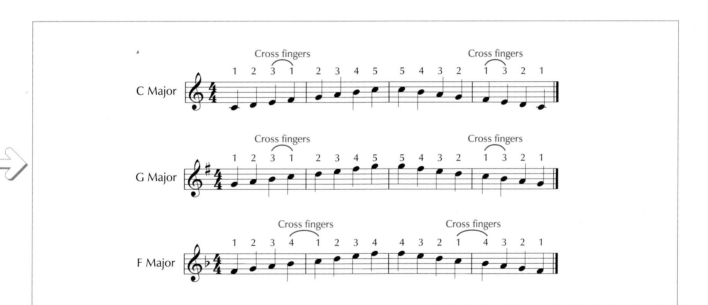

- These examples show the notes in the C, G and F major scales for the right hand. Play the notes as shown, crossing your fingers over or under when needed. For information on finger crosses, see page 89.

- Make sure you observe the numbers above the notes to help you determine which finger to use for each note. Your fingers are numbered from 1 to 5—thumb (1), index (2), middle (3), ring (4) and pinky (5) finger.

- Make sure you also observe any sharps (♯) or flats (♭) that appear at the beginning of a staff. The sharps or flats at the beginning of a staff are called a key signature and indicate the notes in the scale that you need to play as sharps or flats. For more information on key signatures, see page 58.

playing major scales

C Major

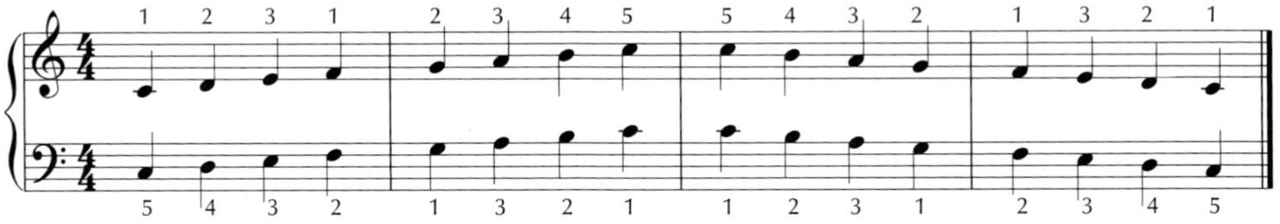

C♯ Major
Also known as D♭ Major

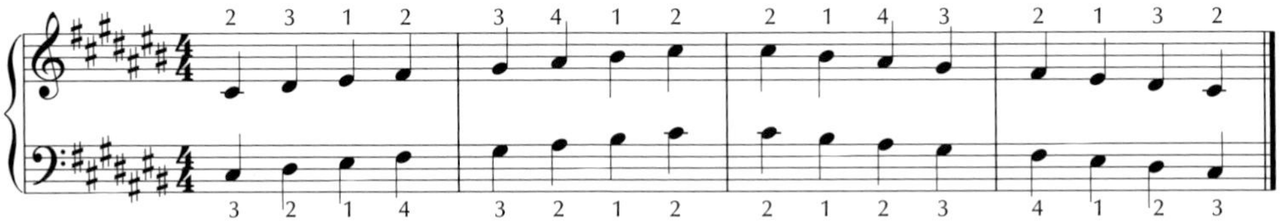

D Major

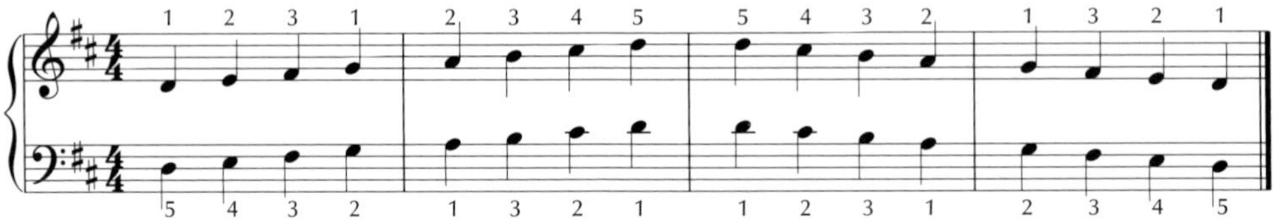

E♭ Major

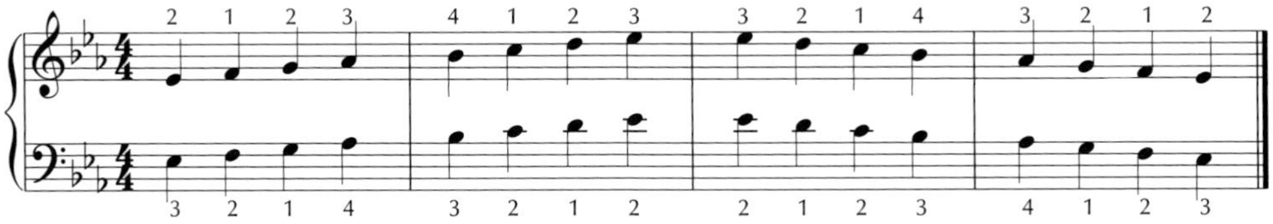

E Major

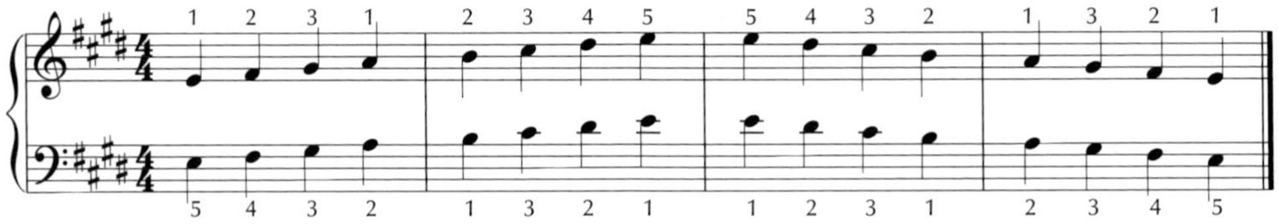

F Major

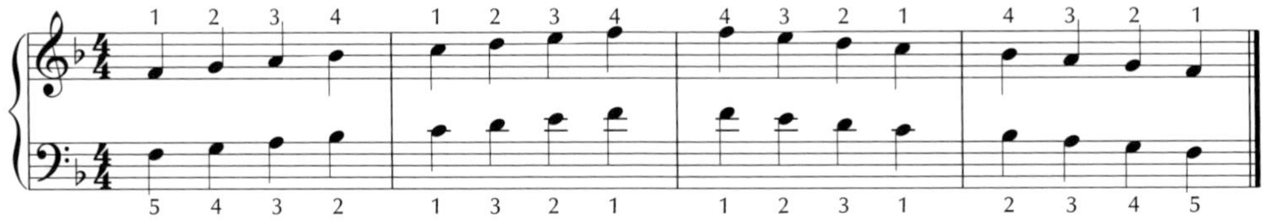

F♯ Major
Also known as G♭ Major

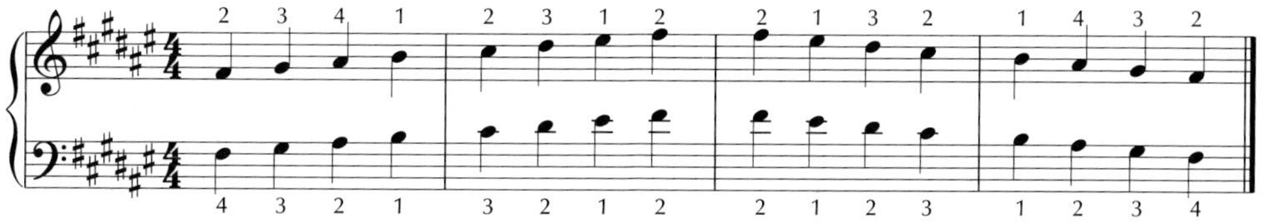

G Major

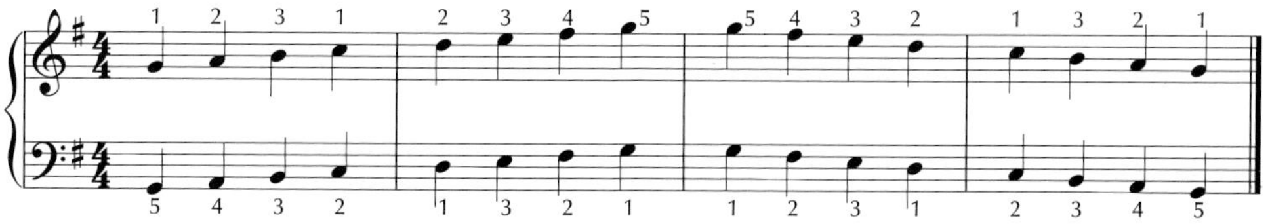

A♭ Major

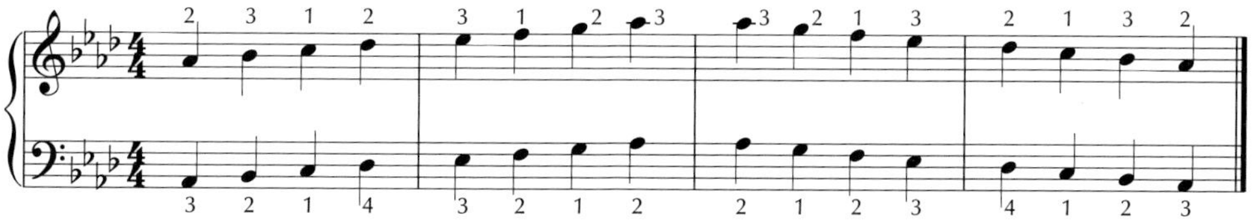

A Major

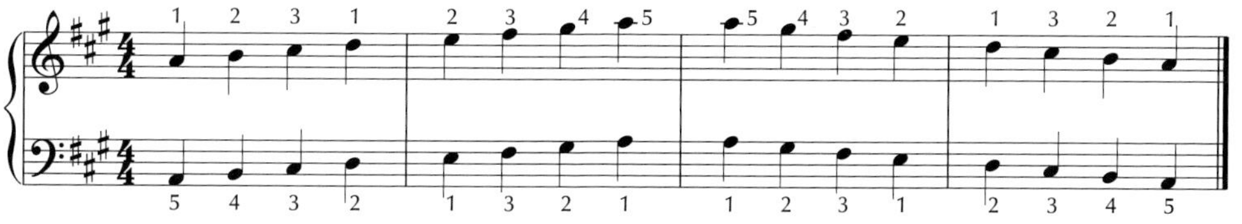

B♭ Major

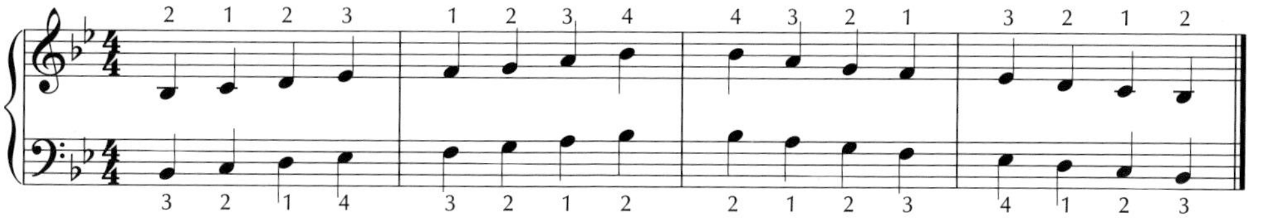

B Major

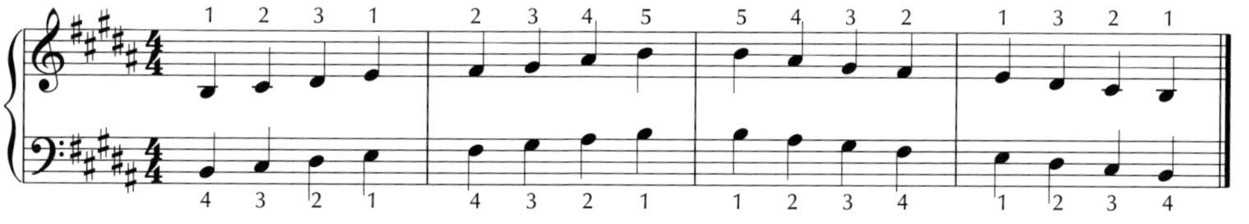

playing minor scales

Minor scales are serious, sad sounding scales. You will find notes from minor scales used in songs, such as "Scarborough Fair" and "House of the Rising Sun."

You can play three different types of minor scales—natural, harmonic and melodic minor scales. In music, there are 12 minor scales, including A, B♭, B, C, C♯, D, E♭ (also known as D♯), E, F, F♯, G and G♯ (also known as A♭). Every minor scale uses a different combination of sharp and flat notes, which means each scale involves a different set of white and black keys. Music that uses the notes from a scale is said to be in the key of that scale, so a song using the A minor scale is in the key of A minor.

Natural minor scales are all structured with the same pattern of whole steps and half steps between notes. The step pattern for natural minor scales from low to high notes is whole, half, whole, whole, half, whole, whole step. You can start on any key, apply this pattern and create a natural minor scale.

Minor Scales

A Natural Minor Scale

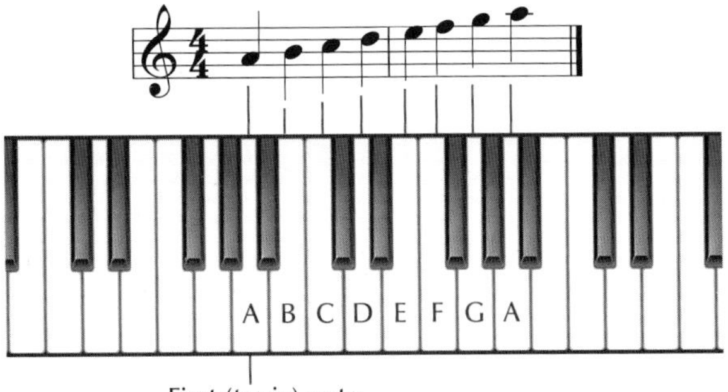

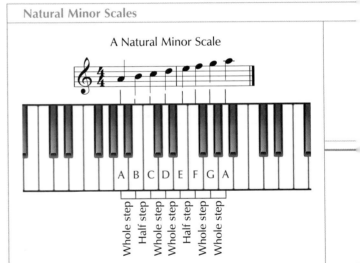

- Minor scales are serious, sad sounding scales.
- There are three different types of minor scales—natural, harmonic and melodic minor scales.
- Each minor scale contains seven different notes. When you play a minor scale, you repeat the first note again one octave higher. For example, to play the A natural minor scale, you would play the A, B, C, D, E, F, G notes and then play the A note again, one octave higher.

Note: An octave refers to the distance between two notes with the same letter name on the keyboard.

- Minor scales are named after the first (tonic) note in the scale. For example, if the first note in a natural minor scale is A, the name of the scale is A natural minor.

Natural Minor Scales

A Natural Minor Scale

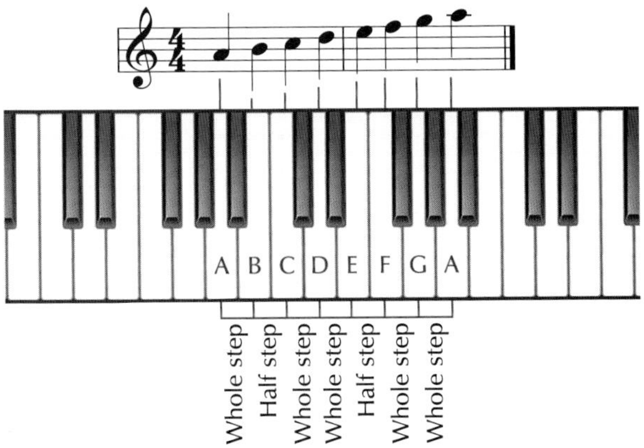

- The notes in natural minor scales are often used in jazz and pop music. There are 12 natural minor scales.
- Every natural minor scale has the same pattern of whole steps and half steps between the notes in the scale. The specific pattern used by every natural minor scale is whole, half, whole, whole, half, whole, whole step. For information on whole steps and half steps, see page 89.
- For example, you can play the A natural minor scale by starting on any A key on the keyboard and applying the pattern of whole steps and half steps all the way to the next A key.

Tip

How can I practice playing minor scales?

You will normally play the eight notes in a scale going up the keyboard and then play the same eight notes going down the keyboard. To help train your fingers to play music, play scales going up and down the keyboard since notes will go up and down the keyboard in music.

Is there a difference in sound between a major scale and a minor scale?

There is a distinct difference between the sound of a major scale compared to a minor scale. Major scales produce happy sounds while minor scales produce sad sounds. Composers will use notes from major scales or minor scales, depending on the type of sound they want to produce. To hear the difference between a major and minor scale, you can play the C major scale and then the C natural minor scale.

C Major Scale

C Natural Minor Scale

A Natural Minor Scale

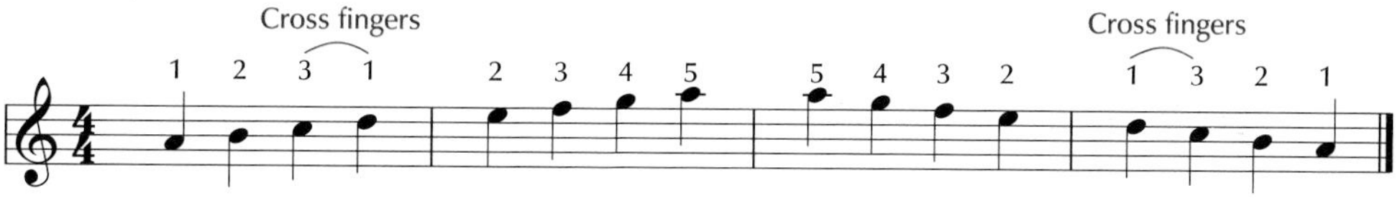

D Natural Minor Scale

E Natural Minor Scale

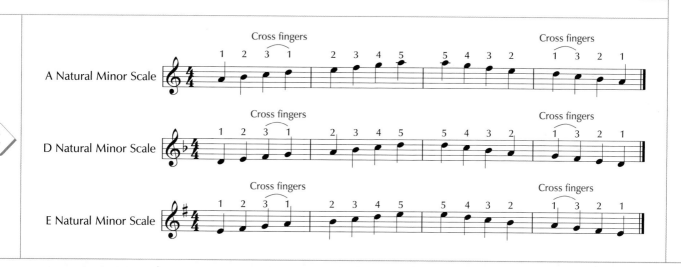

- These examples show the notes in the A, D and E natural minor scales for the right hand. Play the notes as shown, crossing your fingers over or under when needed. For information on crossing your fingers, see page 89.
- Make sure you observe the numbers above the notes to help you determine which finger to use for each note. Your fingers are numbered from 1 to 5—thumb (1), index (2), middle (3), ring (4) and pinky (5) finger.
- Make sure you also observe any sharps (♯) or flats (♭) that appear at the beginning of a staff. The sharps or flats at the beginning of a staff are called a key signature and indicate the notes in the scale that you need to play as sharps or flats. For more information on key signatures, see page 58.

CONTINUED...

playing minor scales *(continued)*

Harmonic minor scales are very similar to natural minor scales. The difference is that in harmonic minor scales, the seventh note of the scale is played one half step higher.

To play a harmonic minor scale, play a natural minor scale, but raise the seventh note by half a step. For example, if the seventh note was originally a natural note, play it as a sharp note. If the seventh note was originally a flat note, play it as a natural note. The seventh note remains raised by one half step regardless of whether you play the scale going up or down the keyboard.

Melodic minor scales have the same notes as a natural minor scale, except the sixth and seventh notes of the scale are each played one half step higher when you play the scale moving up the keyboard. The sixth and seventh notes are not raised when you play the scale moving down the keyboard. As a result, when you play a melodic minor scale in reverse order on the keyboard, the notes that make up the scale are exactly the same as the natural minor scale.

Harmonic Minor Scales

A Harmonic Minor Scale

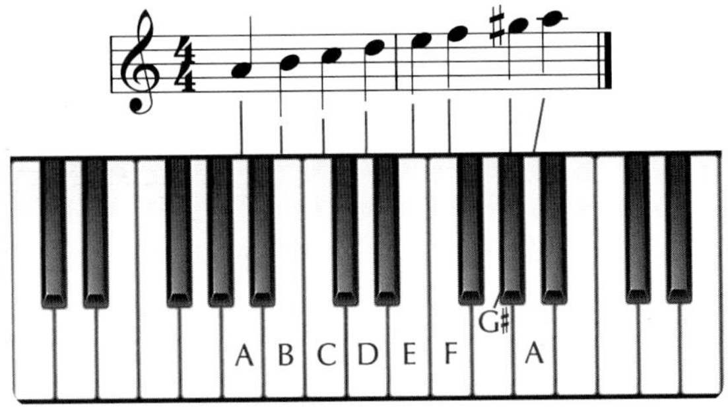

Melodic Minor Scales

A Melodic Minor Scale

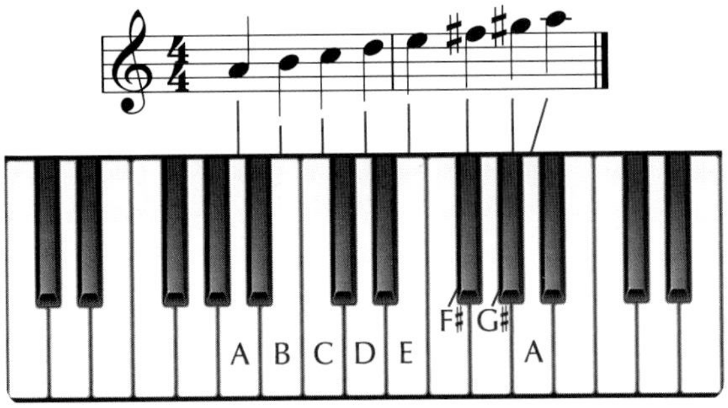

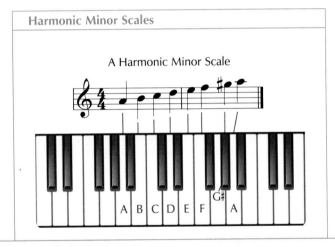

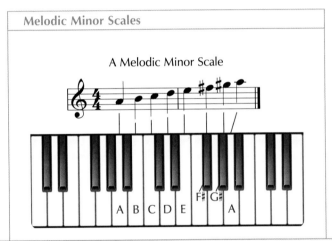

- The notes in harmonic minor scales are often used in classical music. There are 12 harmonic minor scales.
- A harmonic minor scale has the same notes as a natural minor scale, except the seventh note of the scale is raised by one half step. For information on half steps, see page 89.
- For example, the A harmonic minor scale has the same notes as the A natural minor scale, except the seventh note of the natural minor scale (G) is raised by one half step (G♯).
- The notes in melodic minor scales are often used in classical music. There are 12 melodic minor scales.
- A melodic minor scale has the same notes as a natural minor scale, except the sixth and seventh notes of the scale are each raised by one half step when you play the scale moving up the keyboard. When you play the scale moving down the keyboard, the sixth and seventh notes are not raised.
- For example, the A melodic minor scale has the same notes as the A natural minor scale, except the sixth and seventh notes of the natural minor scale (F and G) are raised by one half step (F♯ and G♯) when you play the scale moving up the keyboard. When you play the scale moving down the keyboard, the sixth and seventh notes (F and G) are not raised.

Tip

Do the minor scales relate to the major scales?

Yes. Every minor scale, whether it is a natural, harmonic or melodic scale, is related to a corresponding major scale. A minor scale contains the same notes as its relative major scale.

A Natural Minor Scale

C Major Scale

To determine a minor scale's relative major scale, find the minor scale's first note on the keyboard and then count three half steps up on the keyboard. The name of the key you reach is the name of the major scale that corresponds to the minor scale.

For example, to find the relative major scale for the A minor scale, count three half steps up from the A key and you reach the C key, which means the C major scale is related to the A minor scale.

Knowing the relationships between minor scales and major scales is useful since many composers will change from a major scale to a relative minor scale in the middle of a piece of music.

A Natural Minor Scale

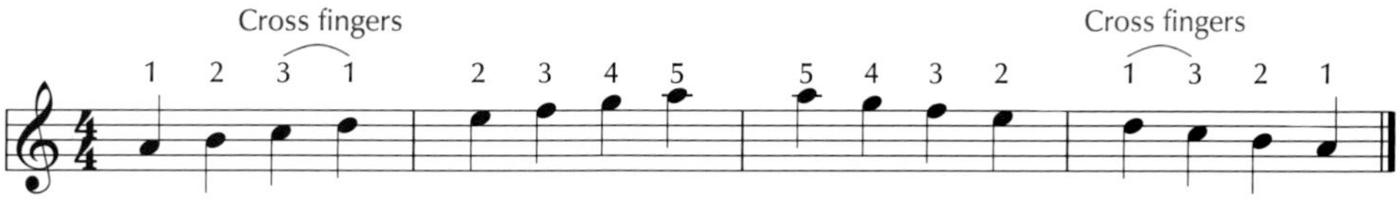

A Harmonic Minor Scale

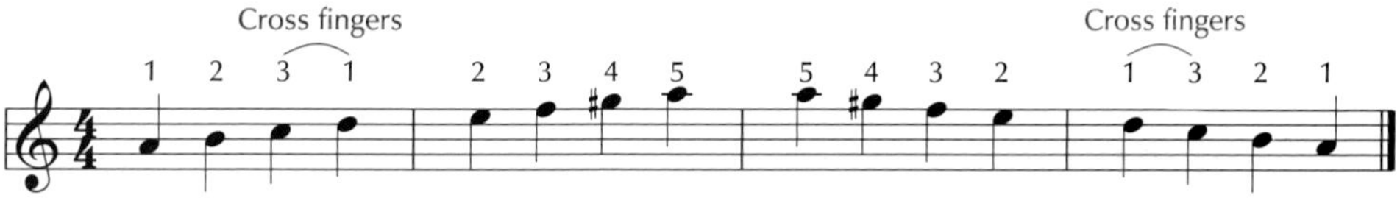

A Melodic Minor Scale

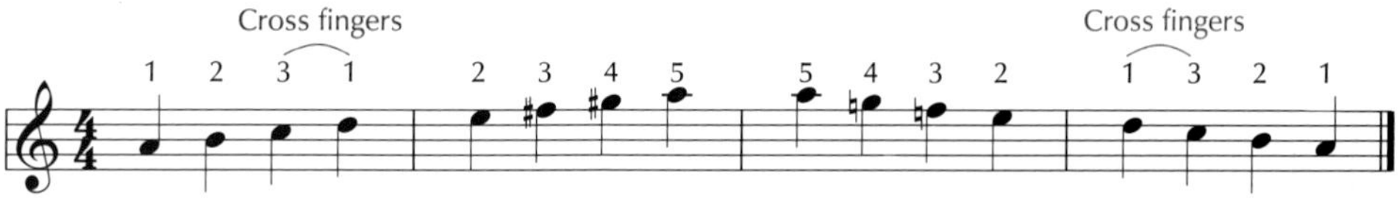

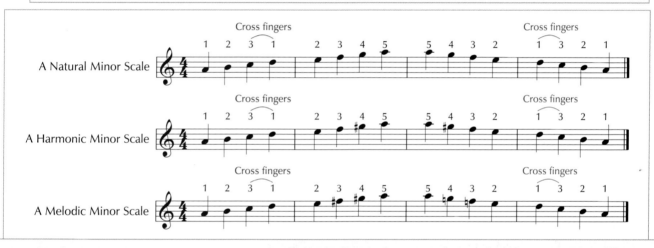

- These examples show the notes in the A natural, harmonic and melodic minor scales for the right hand. Play the notes as shown, crossing your fingers over or under when needed. For information on crossing your fingers, see page 89.

Note: Notes that display a natural sign (♮) are played as white keys, not as sharps or flats.

- Make sure you observe the numbers above the notes to help you determine which finger to use for each note. Your fingers are numbered from 1 to 5—thumb (1), index (2), middle (3), ring (4) and pinky (5) finger.

playing minor scales

A Natural Minor

A Harmonic Minor

A Melodic Minor

B♭ Natural Minor

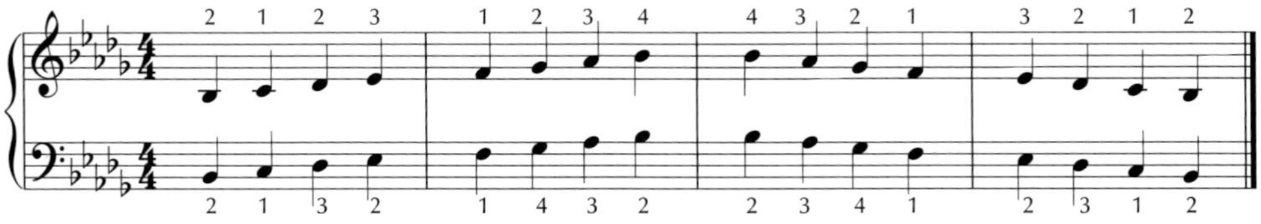

B♭ Harmonic Minor

B♭ Melodic Minor

B Natural Minor

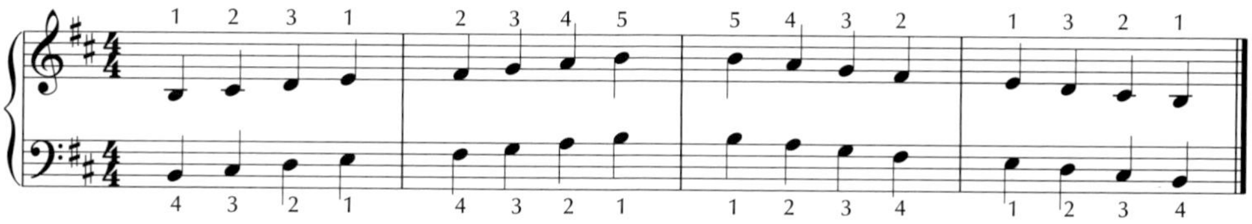

B Harmonic Minor

B Melodic Minor

C Natural Minor

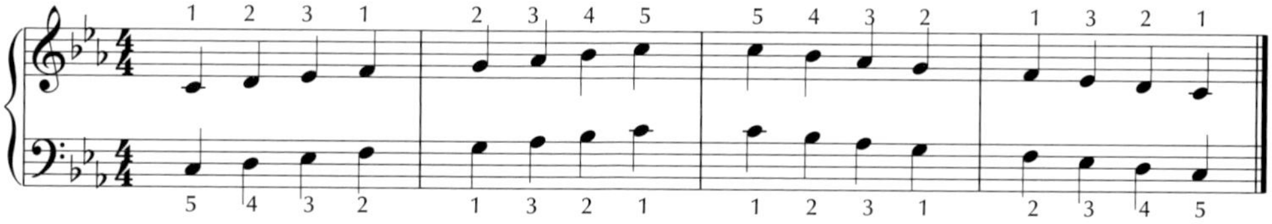

C Harmonic Minor

C Melodic Minor

playing minor scales

C♯ Natural Minor

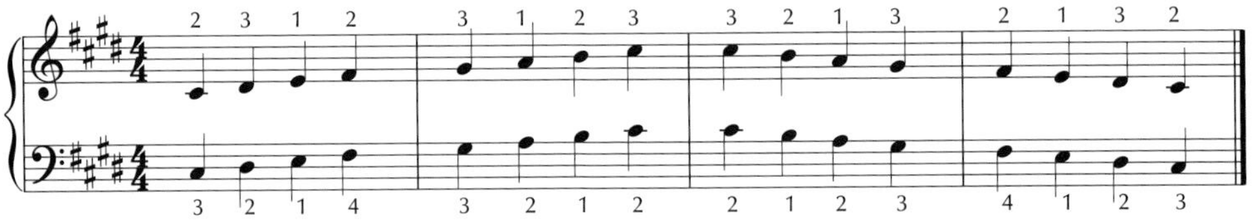

C♯ Harmonic Minor

C♯ Melodic Minor

D Natural Minor

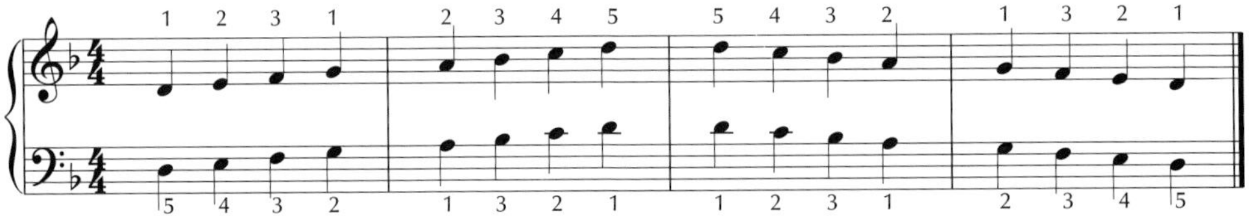

D Harmonic Minor

D Melodic Minor

E♭ Natural Minor

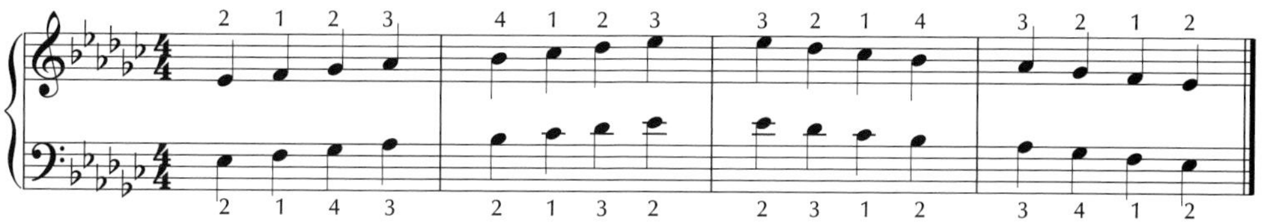

E♭ Harmonic Minor

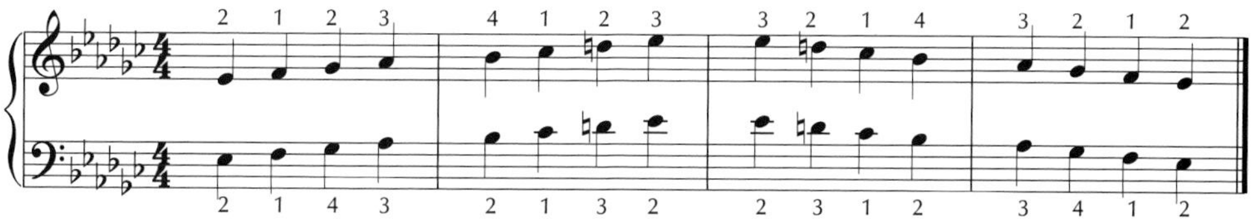

E♭ Melodic Minor

E Natural Minor

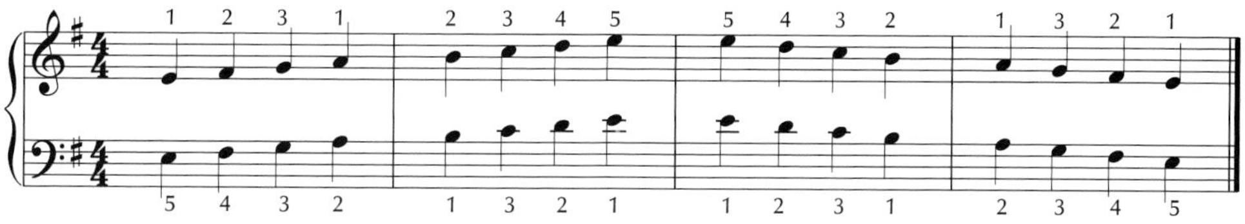

E Harmonic Minor

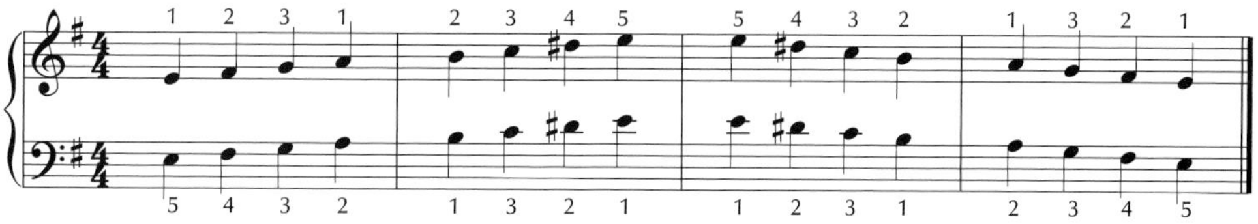

E Melodic Minor

playing minor scales

F Natural Minor

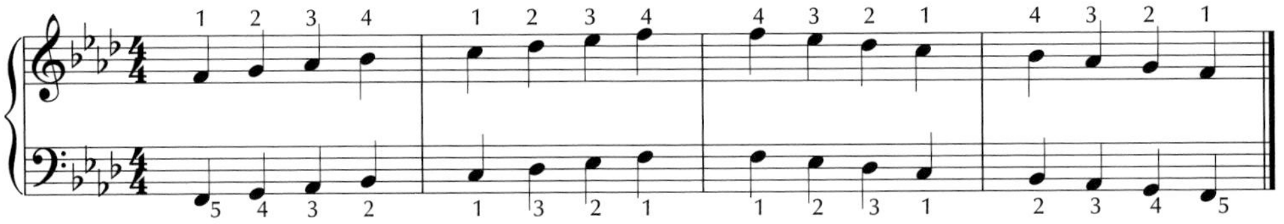

F Harmonic Minor

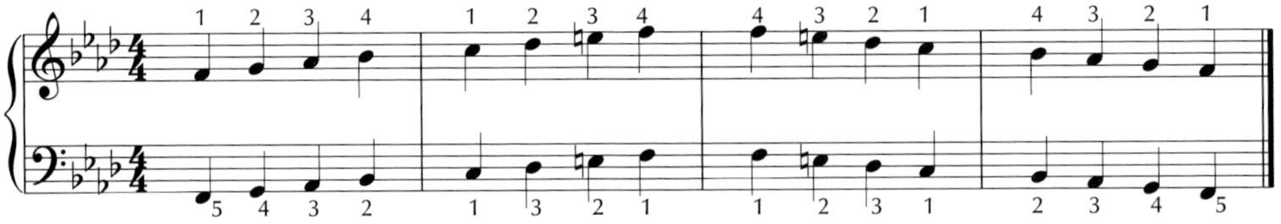

F Melodic Minor

F♯ Natural Minor

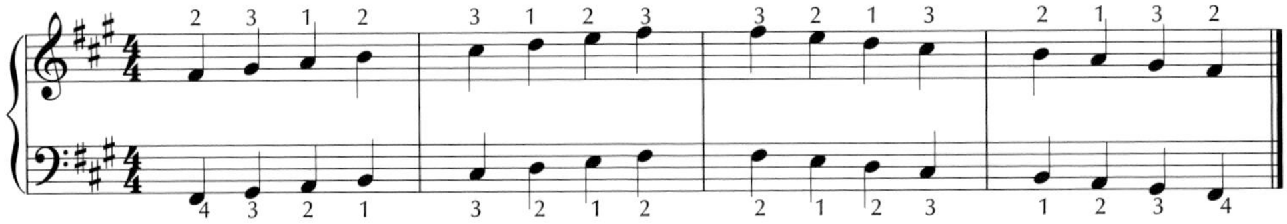

F♯ Harmonic Minor

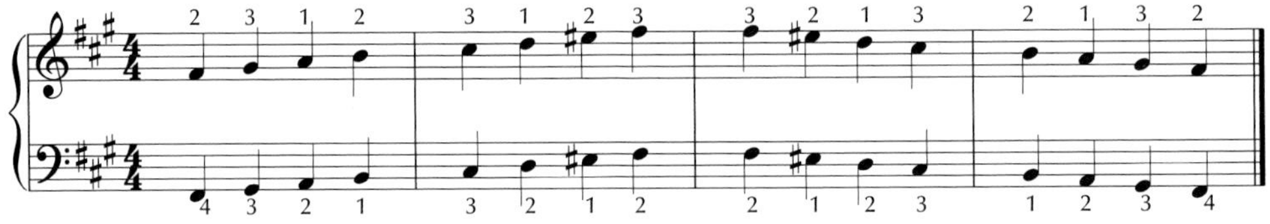

F♯ Melodic Minor

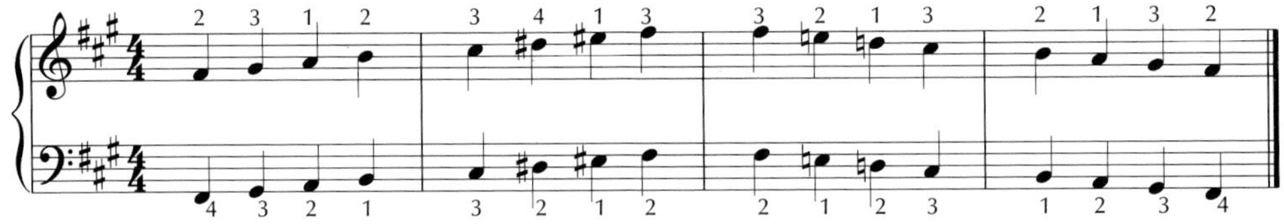

G Natural Minor

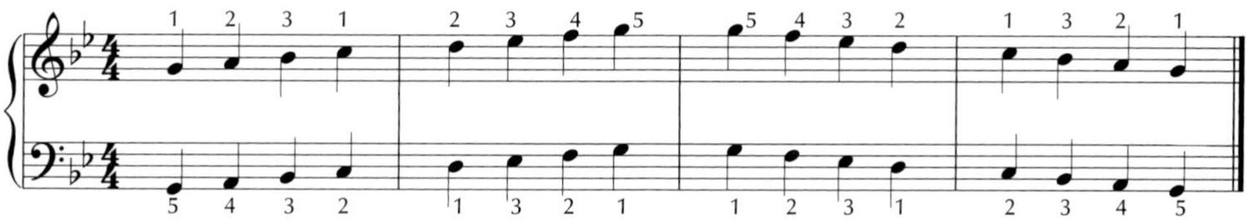

G Harmonic Minor

G Melodic Minor

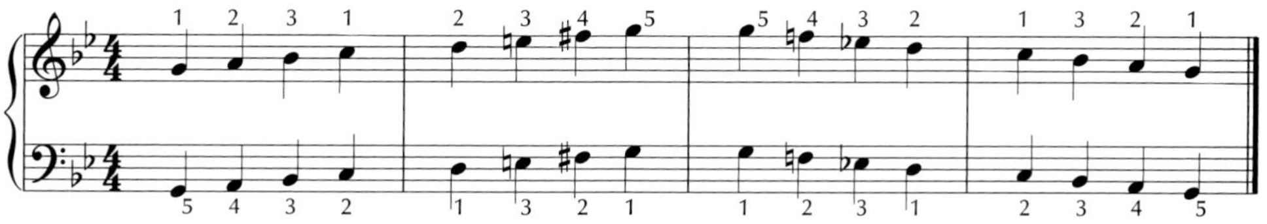

G♯ Natural Minor

G♯ Harmonic Minor

G♯ Melodic Minor

playing pentatonic scales

A pentatonic scale is a scale that consists of five different notes. The notes in pentatonic scales create unique melodies in many types of music, including jazz, blues, rock, folk and country music. In Western music, there are three main types of pentatonic scales—major, major (flat3) and minor pentatonic scales.

Major pentatonic scales consist of the same notes as major scales, except the fourth and seventh notes of the major scale are omitted. For example, the C major pentatonic scale omits the fourth (F) and seventh (B) notes of the C major scale.

Major (flat3) pentatonic scales consist of the same notes as major pentatonic scales, except the third note of the major pentatonic scale is lowered by one half step. For example, the C major (flat3) pentatonic scale lowers the third note of the major pentatonic scale by one half step from E to E♭.

Minor pentatonic scales consist of the same notes as natural minor scales, except the second and sixth notes of the natural minor scale are omitted. For example, the C minor pentatonic scale omits the second (D) and sixth (A♭) notes of the C natural minor scale.

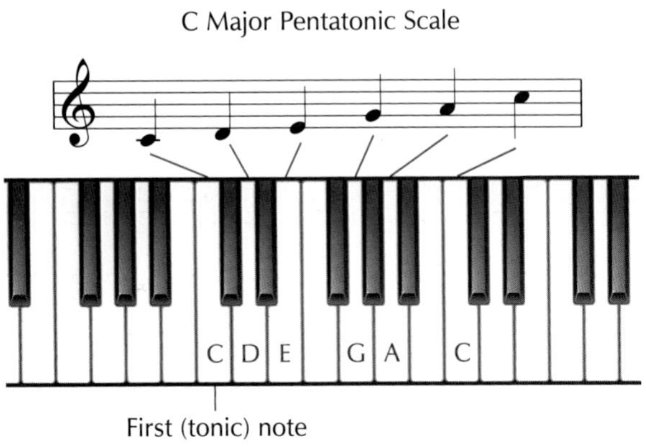

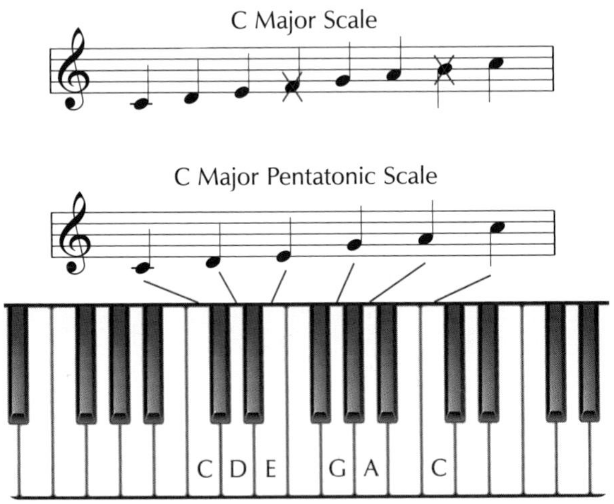

- There are three main types of pentatonic scales used in jazz, blues, rock, folk and country music—the major, major (flat3) and minor pentatonic scales.
- Each pentatonic scale contains five different notes. When you play a pentatonic scale, you repeat the first note again one octave higher. For example, to play the C major pentatonic scale, you play the C, D, E, G and A notes and then play the C note again one octave higher.

Note: An octave refers to the distance between two notes with the same letter name on the keyboard.

- Pentatonic scales are named after the first (tonic) note in the scale. For example, if the first note in a major pentatonic scale is C, the name of the scale is C major pentatonic.

Major Pentatonic Scales

- There are 12 major pentatonic scales—the C, C♯, D, E♭, E, F, F♯, G, A♭, A, B♭ and B major pentatonic scales.
- A major pentatonic scale has the same notes as a major scale, except the fourth and seventh notes of the major scale are left out. For information on major scales, see page 90.
- For example, the C major pentatonic scale has the same notes as the C major scale, except the fourth (F) and seventh (B) notes of the major scale are left out.

Tip

How many different pentatonic scales are there?

There are thousands of pentatonic scales. You can create a pentatonic scale by simply playing any five different notes within an octave on the piano. An octave refers to the distance between a note and the next note with the same letter name on the keyboard. For example, you can play any five white or black keys on your keyboard and create a pentatonic scale, as long as none of the keys are the same note. You can remember that pentatonic scales consist of five different notes by thinking of the word penta, which is Greek for "five."

Should I practice playing pentatonic scales?

Yes. You should practice playing pentatonic scales before you play music that uses these scales. Not only does practicing scales help you warm up your fingers before playing music, it trains your fingers to move in specific patterns, which can help you learn musical pieces more quickly. To see the notes in the three main types of pentatonic scales, see pages 106 to 109.

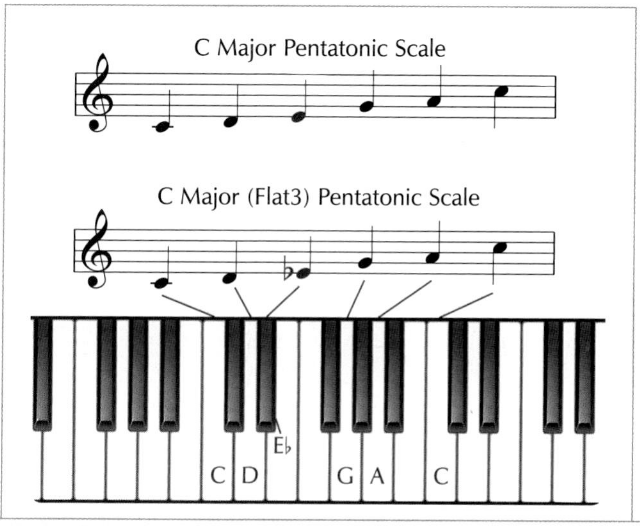

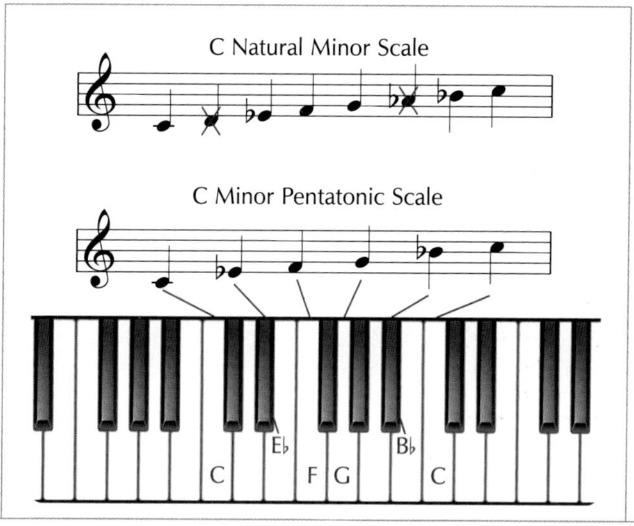

Major (Flat3) Pentatonic Scales

- There are 12 major (flat3) pentatonic scales—the C, C♯, D, E♭, E, F, F♯, G, A♭, A, B♭ and B major (flat3) pentatonic scales.
- A major (flat3) pentatonic scale has the same notes as a major pentatonic scale, except the third note of the major pentatonic scale is lowered by one half step.

Note: When you lower a note by one half step, you play the white or black key directly to the left.

- For example, the C major (flat3) pentatonic scale has the same notes as the C major pentatonic scale, except the third note of the major pentatonic scale (E) is lowered by one half step (E♭).

Minor Pentatonic Scales

- There are 12 minor pentatonic scales—the C, C♯, D, E♭, E, F, F♯, G, G♯, A, B♭ and B minor pentatonic scales.
- A minor pentatonic scale has the same notes as a natural minor scale, except the second and sixth notes of the natural minor scale are left out. For information on natural minor scales, see page 94.
- For example, the C minor pentatonic scale has the same notes as the C natural minor scale, except the second (D) and sixth (A♭) notes of the natural minor scale are left out.

playing pentatonic scales

C Major Pentatonic

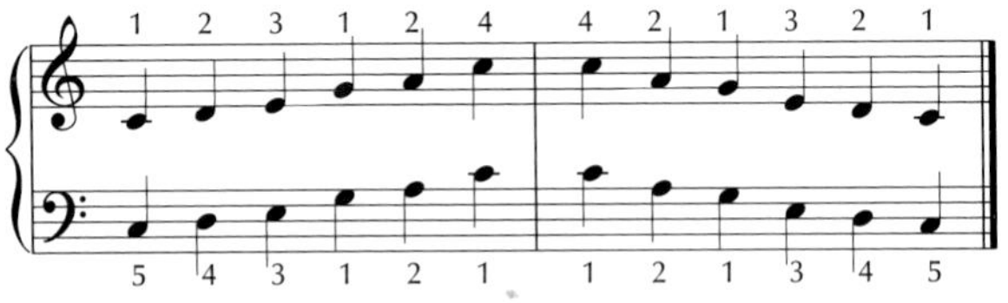

C Major (flat3) Pentatonic

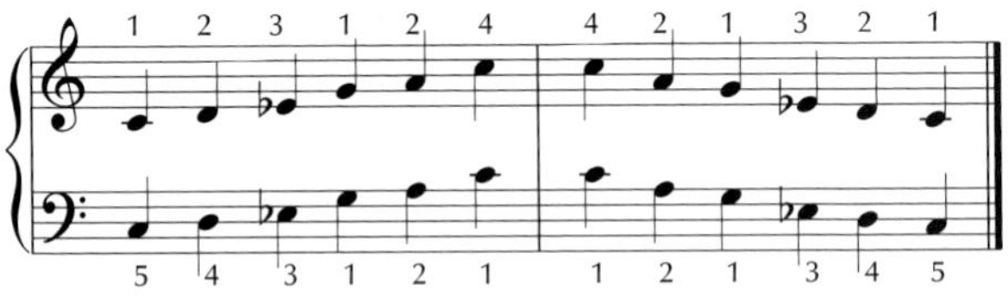

C Minor Pentatonic

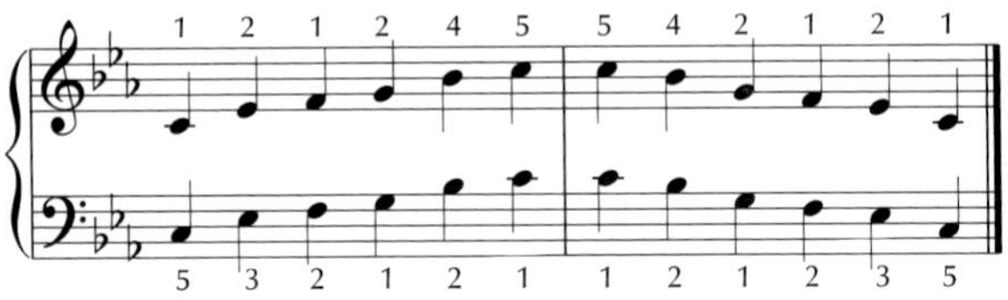

C♯ Major Pentatonic

Also known as D♭ Major Pentatonic

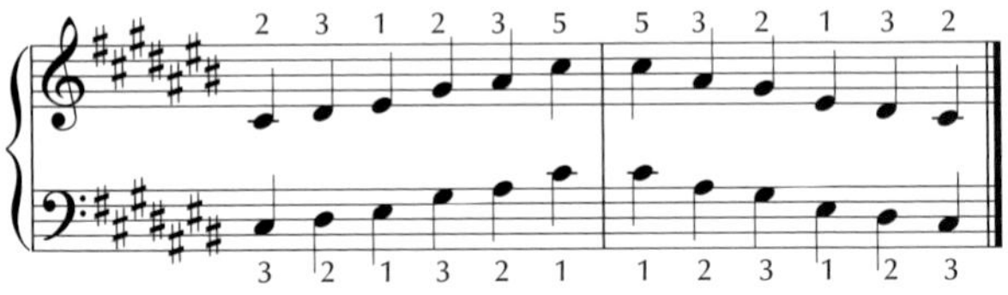

C♯ Major (flat3) Pentatonic

Also known as D♭ Major (flat3) Pentatonic

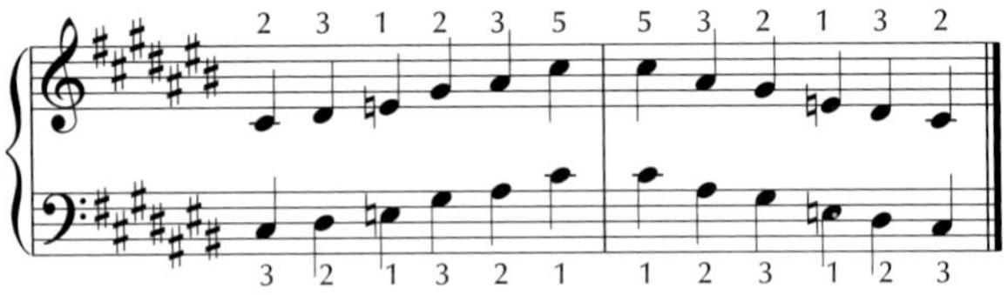

C♯ Minor Pentatonic

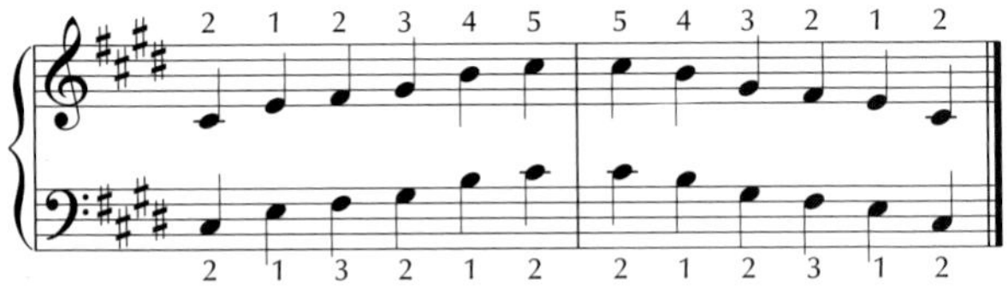

D Major Pentatonic

D Major (flat3) Pentatonic

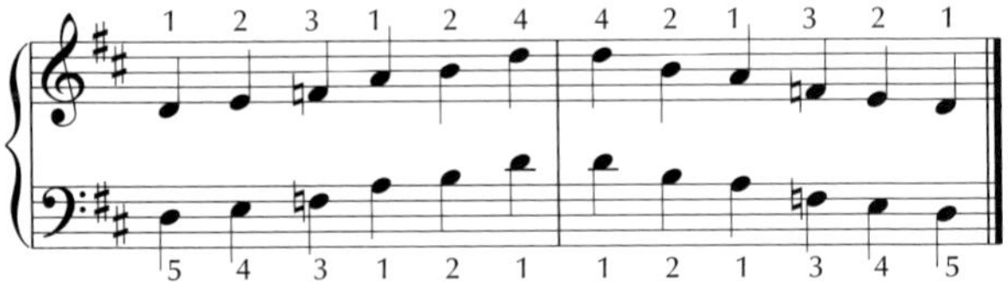

D Minor Pentatonic

E♭ Major Pentatonic

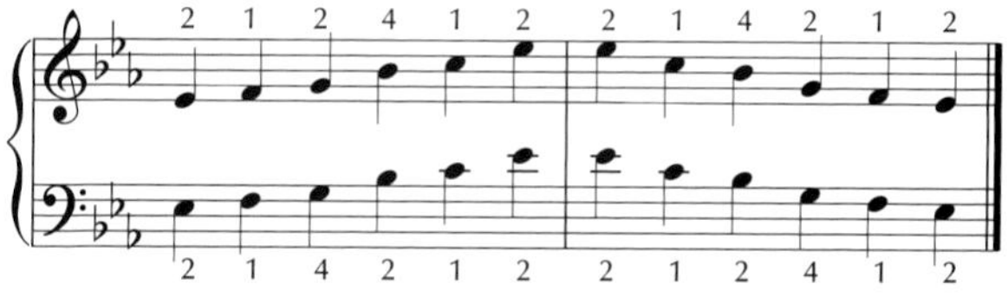

E♭ Major (flat3) Pentatonic

E♭ Minor Pentatonic

E Major Pentatonic

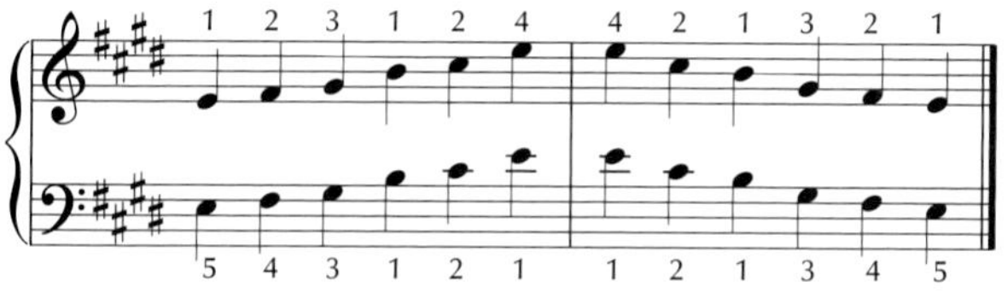

E Major (flat3) Pentatonic

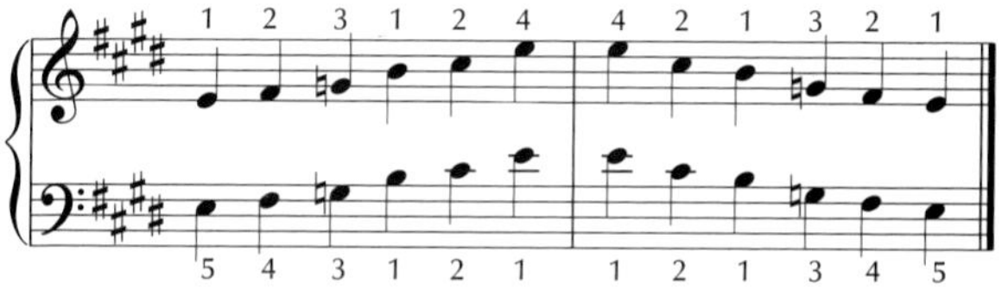

E Minor Pentatonic

F Major Pentatonic

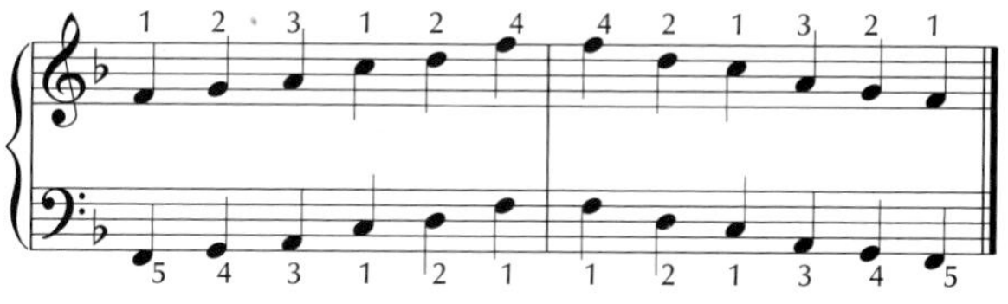

F Major (flat3) Pentatonic

F Minor Pentatonic

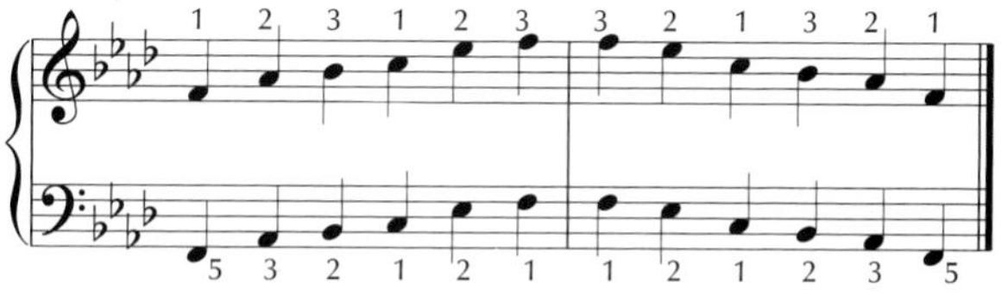

CONTINUED...

playing pentatonic scales *(continued)*

F♯ Major Pentatonic
Also known as G♭ Major Pentatonic

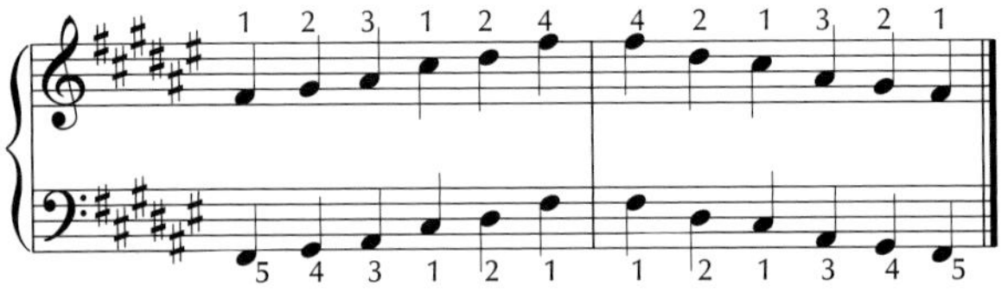

F♯ Major (flat3) Pentatonic
Also known as G♭ Major (flat3) Pentatonic

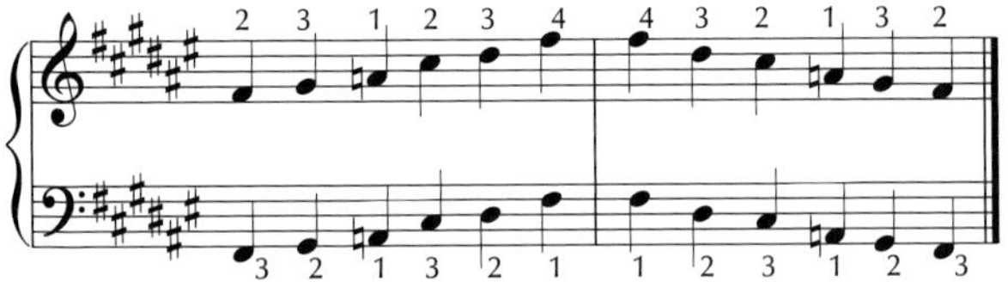

F♯ Minor Pentatonic

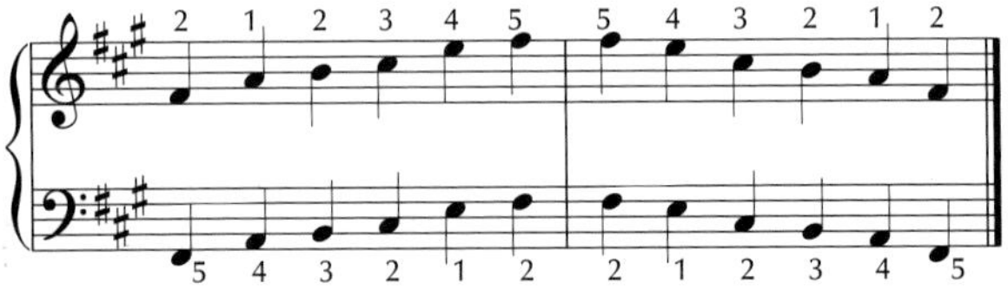

G Major Pentatonic

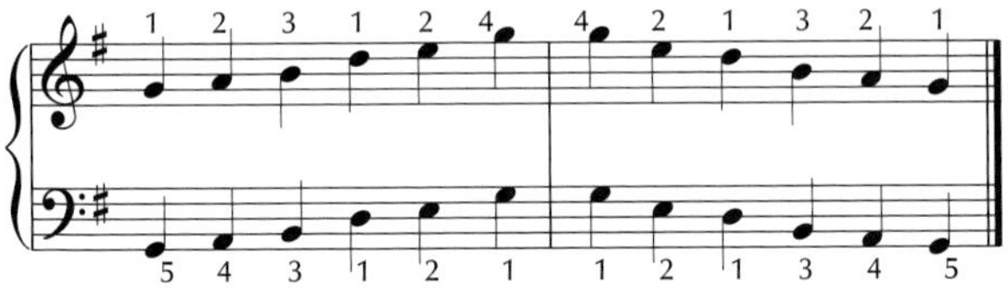

G Major (flat3) Pentatonic

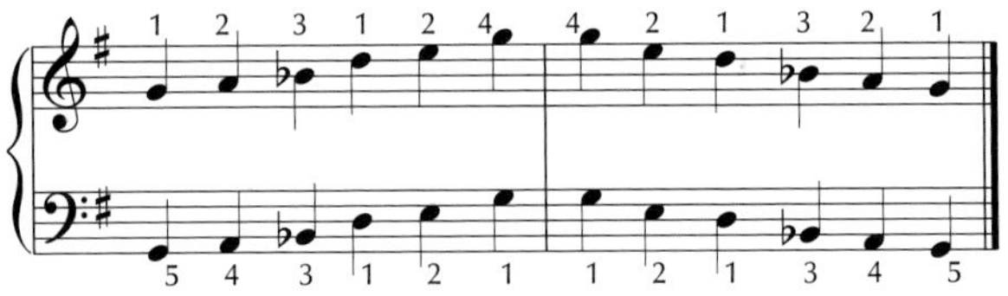

G Minor Pentatonic

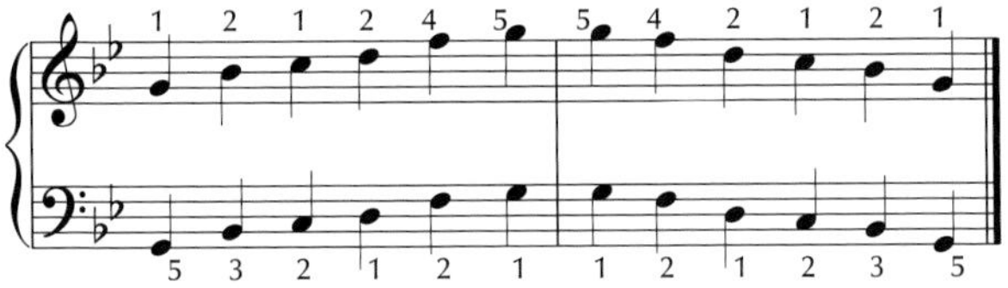

A♭ Major Pentatonic

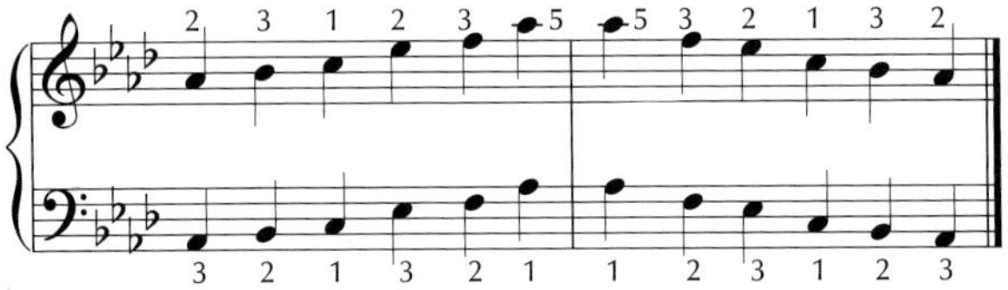

A♭ Major (flat3) Pentatonic

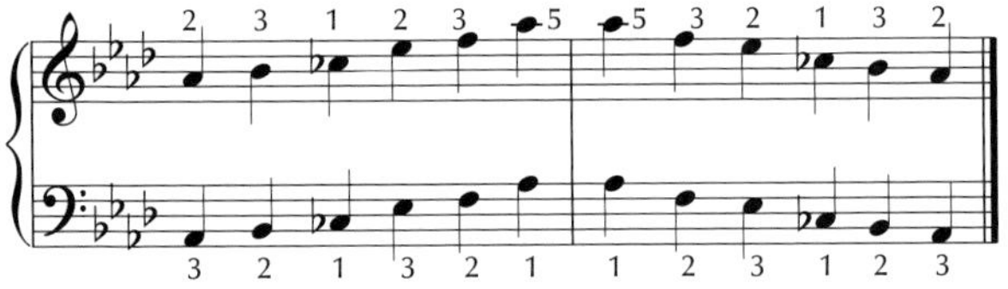

G♯ Minor Pentatonic
Also known as A♭ Minor Pentatonic

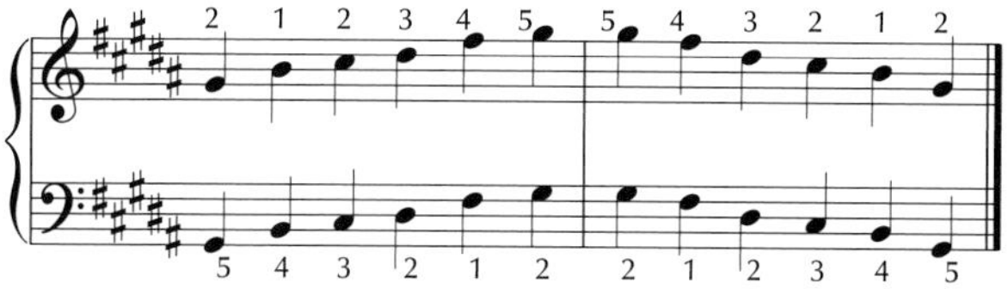

A Major Pentatonic

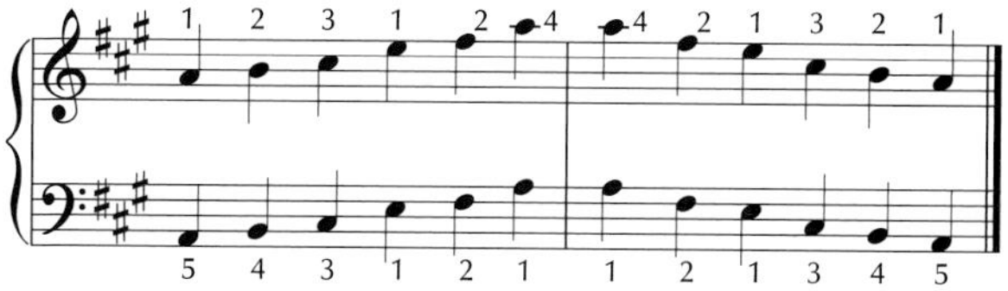

A Major (flat3) Pentatonic

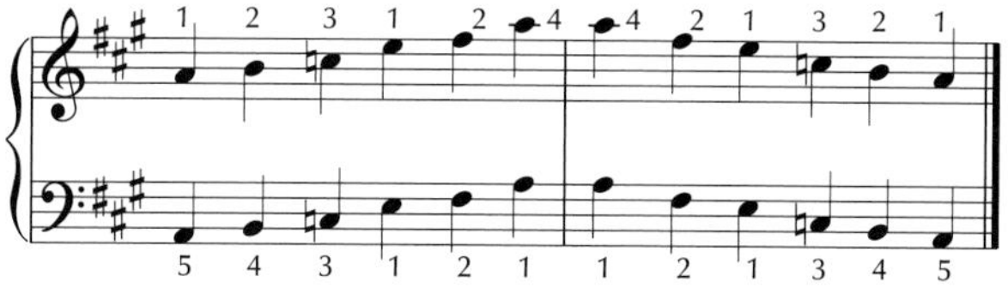

A Minor Pentatonic

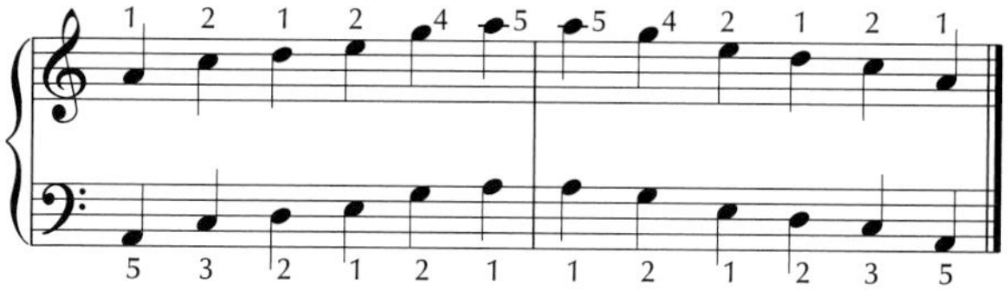

B♭ Major Pentatonic

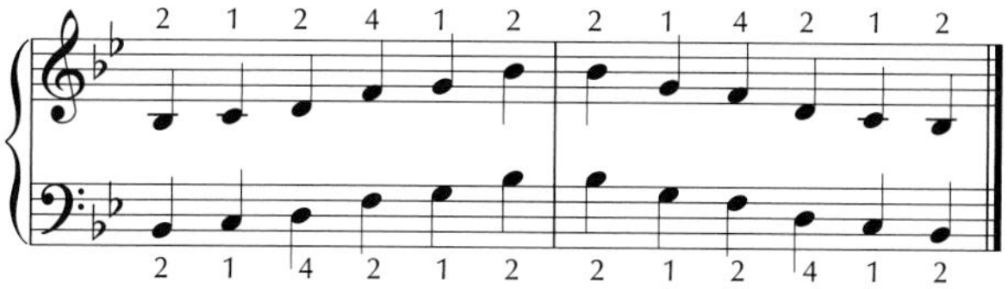

B♭ Major (flat3) Pentatonic

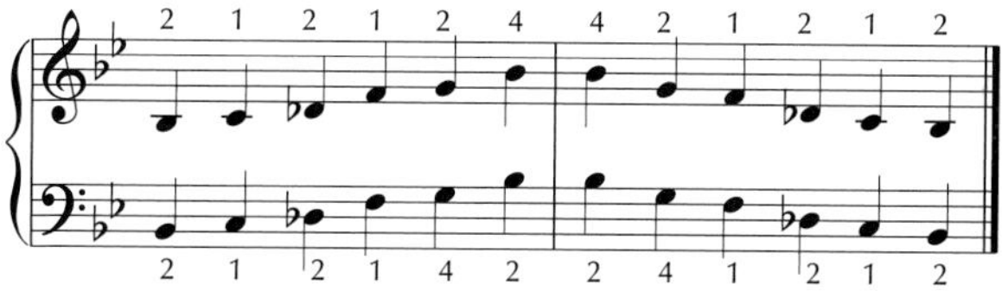

B♭ Minor Pentatonic

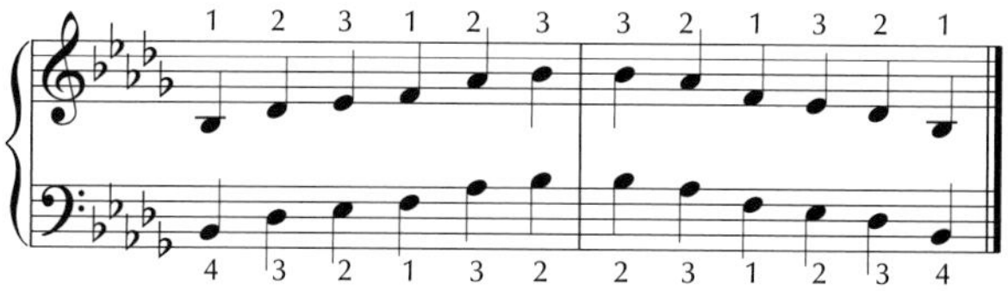

B Major Pentatonic

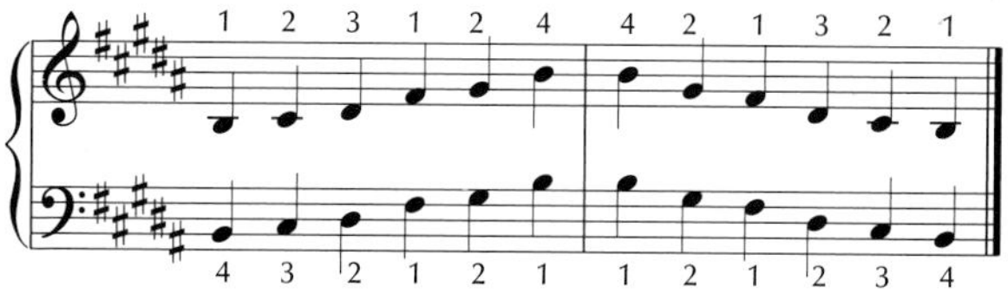

B Major (flat3) Pentatonic

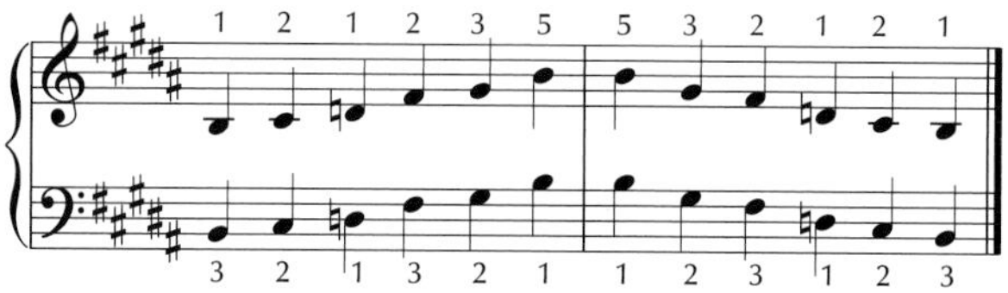

B Minor Pentatonic

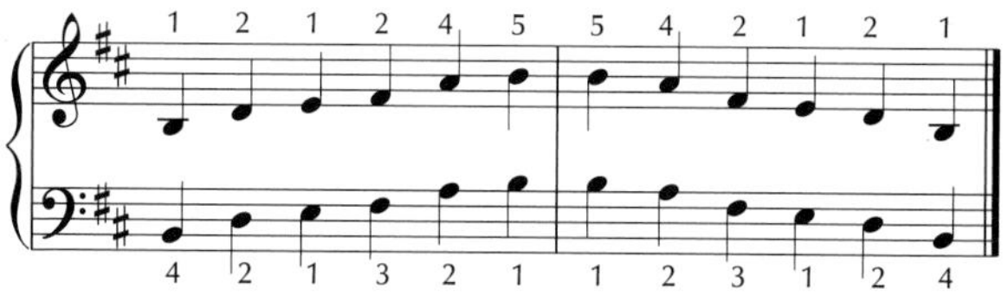

playing chromatic scales

Chromatic scales can be used to generate excitement in many styles of music. Musical pieces may use an entire chromatic scale or a portion of a chromatic scale.

There are 12 chromatic scales—the C, C♯, D, D♯, E, F, F♯, G, G♯, A, A♯ and B chromatic scales. Each chromatic scale contains the same 12 notes, which consist of all the white and black keys in one octave. An octave refers to the distance between two notes with the same letter name on the keyboard. To play a chromatic scale, start with any note on the keyboard and play every white and black key until you repeat the first note of the scale at the next higher location on the keyboard.

Intermediate to advanced players should regularly practice chromatic scales. Not only does playing scales help warm up your fingers before playing music, it also trains your fingers to move in specific patterns, which can help you learn musical pieces more quickly. When practicing chromatic scales, you should play the 12 notes in each scale going up the keyboard and then play the same 12 notes going down the keyboard.

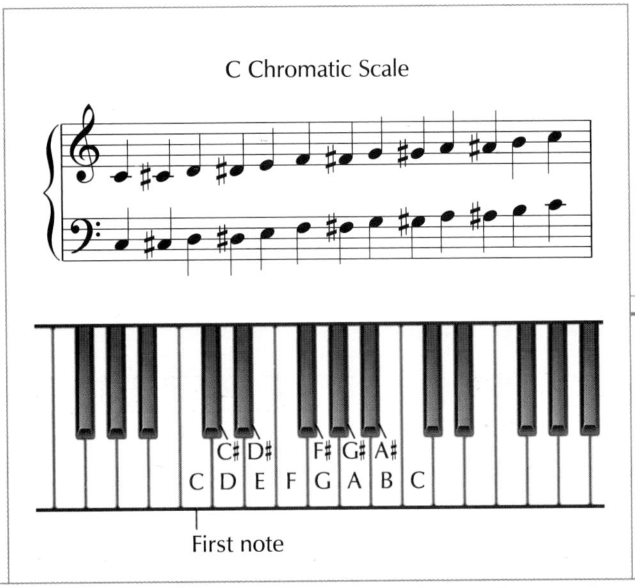

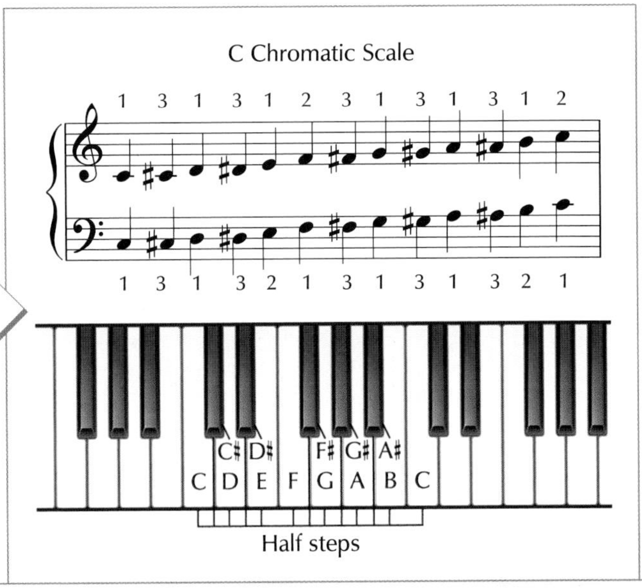

- There are 12 chromatic scales. Each chromatic scale contains the same 12 notes, which consist of all the white and black keys in one octave.

Note: An octave refers to the distance between two notes with the same letter name on the keyboard.

- When you play a chromatic scale, you repeat the first note again one octave higher. For example, to play the C chromatic scale, you play the C, C♯, D, D♯, E, F, F♯, G, G♯, A, A♯ and B notes and then play the C note again, one octave higher.
- Chromatic scales are named after the first note in the scale. For example, if the first note in a chromatic scale is C, the name of the scale is the C chromatic scale.
- Every chromatic scale has a half step between each note in the scale. A half step is the distance from one key to the next, whether the keys are white or black.
- For example, you can play a C chromatic scale by starting on any C key on the keyboard and moving up one half step at a time until you reach the next C key.
- When playing a chromatic scale with your right or left hand, use your middle finger (3) to play all the black keys and use your thumb (1) to play the white keys. When playing two white keys in a row, use your thumb and index (2) finger.

playing blues scales

Blues scales are sad sounding scales often used in jazz, blues, rock and country music. There are 12 blues scales—the C, C♯, D, E♭, E, F, F♯, G, G♯, A, B♭ and B blues scales.

Each blues scale contains six different notes plus the first note of the scale repeated at the next higher location on the keyboard. For example, to play the C blues scale, you would play the C, E♭, F, G♭, G and B♭ notes and the next higher C note on the keyboard.

Blues scales consist of the same notes as minor pentatonic scales, except you add one note between the third and fourth notes of the minor pentatonic scale. The new note is one half step higher than the third note of the minor pentatonic scale. For example, the C blues scale adds a note (G♭) between the third (F) note and fourth (G) note of the C minor pentatonic scale.

You should practice playing blues scales before you play music that uses these scales. Not only does playing scales help warm up your fingers before playing music, it also trains your fingers to move in specific patterns, which can help you learn musical pieces more quickly.

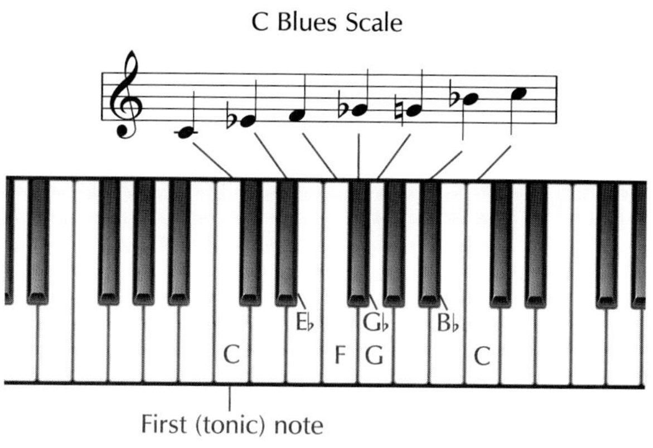

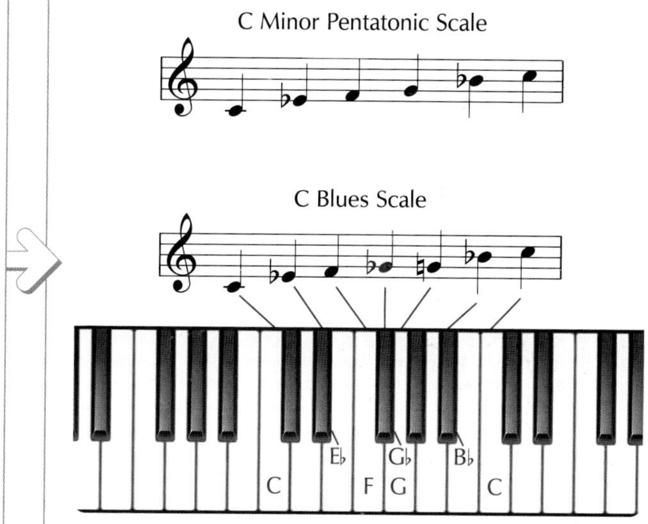

- Blues scales are sad sounding scales. There are 12 blues scales.
- Each blues scale contains six different notes. When you play a blues scale, you repeat the first note again one octave higher. For example, to play the C blues scale, you play the C, E♭, F, G♭, G and B♭ notes and then play the C note again one octave higher.

Note: An octave refers to the distance between two notes with the same letter name on the keyboard.

- Blues scales are named after the first (tonic) note in the scale. For example, if the first note in a blues scale is C, the name of the scale is the C blues scale.

- A blues scale has the same notes as a minor pentatonic scale, except a note is added between the 3rd and 4th notes of the minor pentatonic scale. The new note is one half step higher than the 3rd note of the minor pentatonic scale.

Note: When you raise a note by one half step, you play the white or black key directly to the right.

- For example, the C blues scale has the same notes as the C minor pentatonic scale, except a note (G♭) is added between the 3rd and 4th notes.

playing blues scales

C Blues

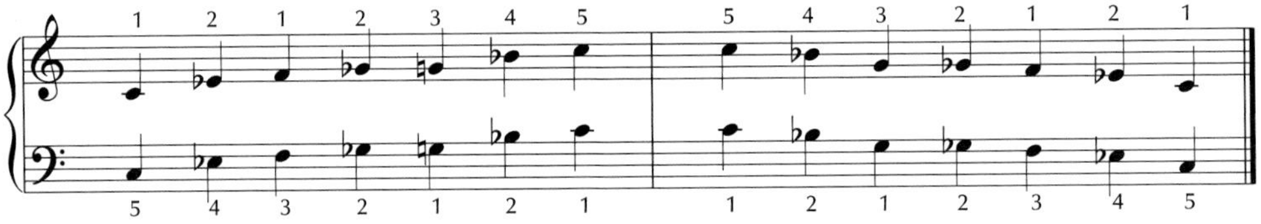

C♯ Blues

D Blues

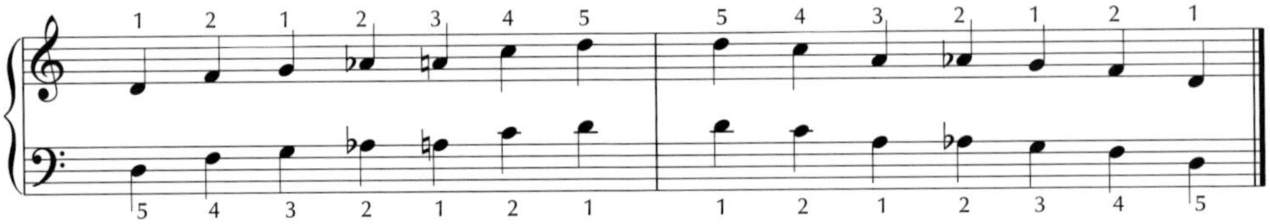

E♭ Blues

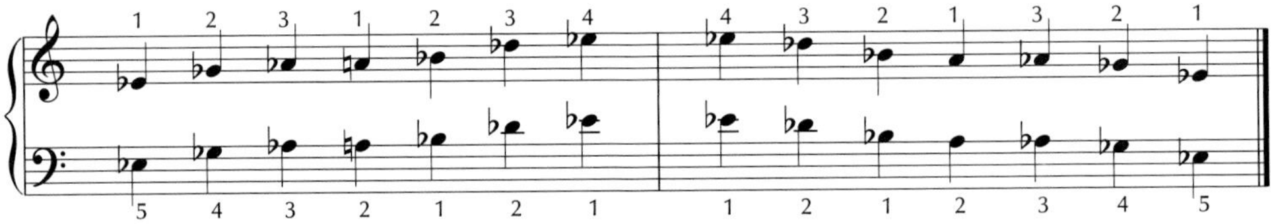

E Blues

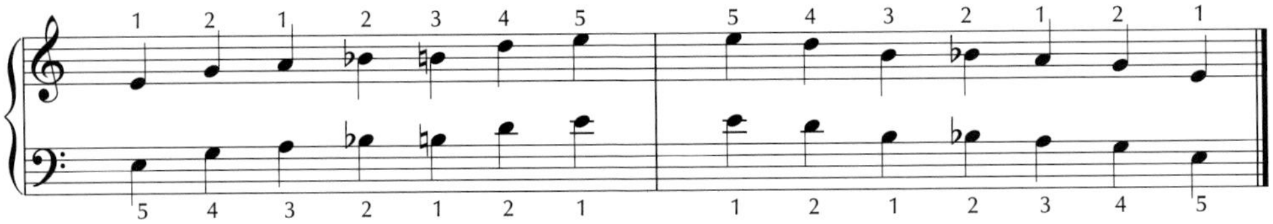

F Blues

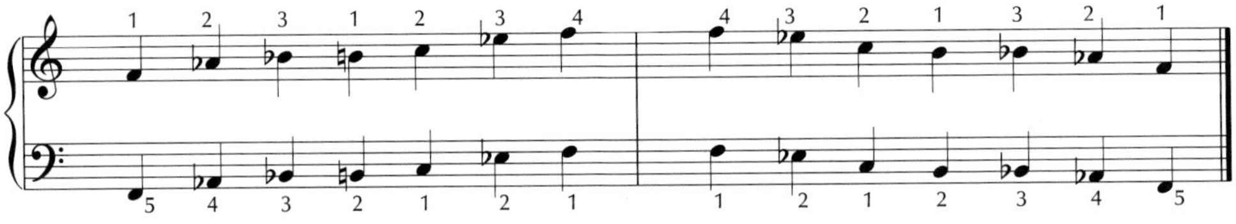

F♯ Blues

G Blues

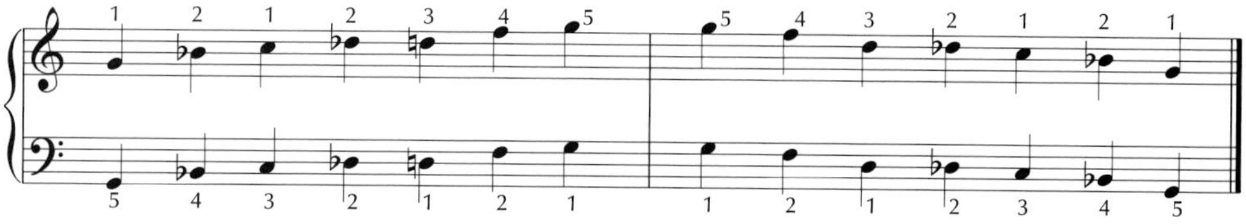

G♯ Blues

A Blues

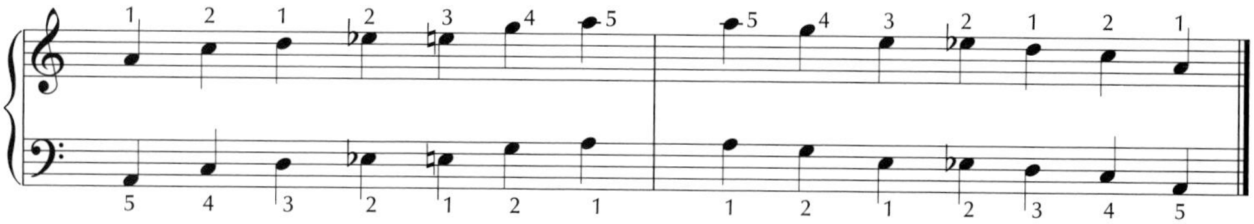

B♭ Blues

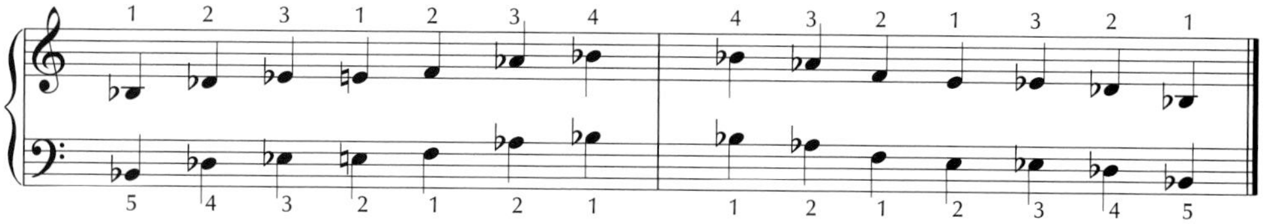

B Blues

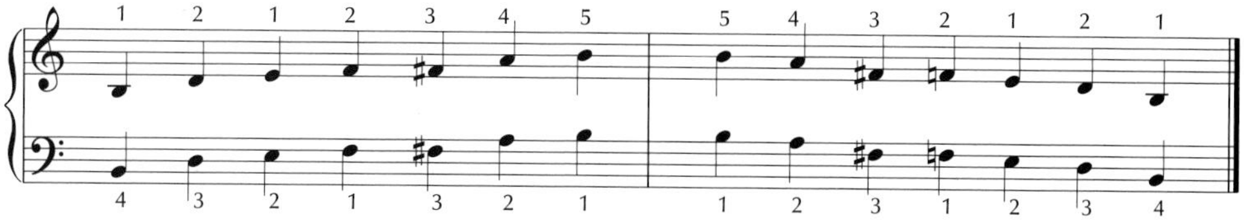

playing modes

Modes are ancient scales that became the basis for today's major and minor scales. Prevalent in the middle ages, modes gave way to major and minor scales from the 1600s to the end of the 1800s. By the late 1800s, some composers returned to using modes and in the 1940s, jazz musicians began incorporating modes into their music. Today, modes are used in many styles of music, such as jazz and rock.

There are seven main types of modes, three of which—the dorian, mixolydian and lydian modes—are used in jazz and some rock music. The remaining types of modes include the ionian mode, which is now known as the major scale and the aeolin mode, which is now known as the natural minor scale. The phyrygian and locrian modes are not as common in popular music.

You should practice playing modes before you play music that is based on modes, especially jazz. Not only does practicing modes help you warm up your fingers before playing music, it trains your fingers to move in specific patterns, which can help you learn musical pieces more quickly.

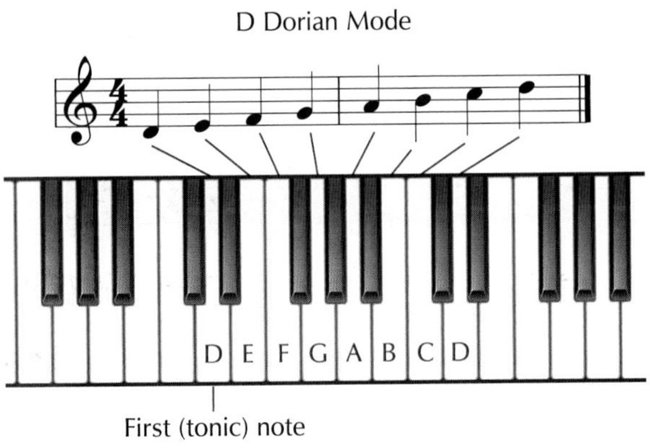

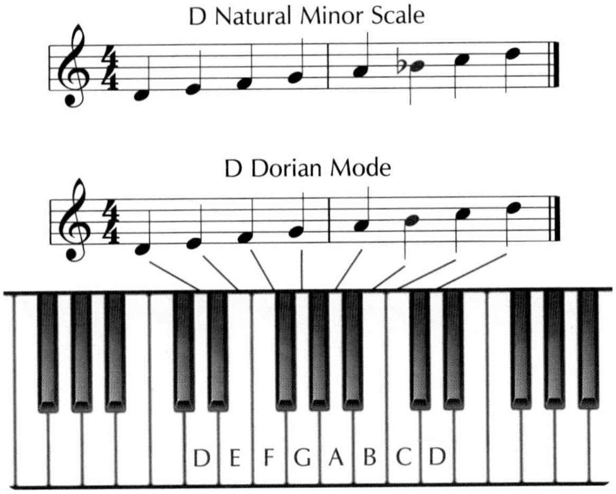

- Modes are scales that have been around for centuries. There are three commonly used modes found in jazz and rock music today—the dorian, mixolydian and lydian modes.
- Each mode contains seven different notes. When you play a mode, you repeat the first note again one octave higher. For example, to play the D dorian mode, you play the D, E, F, G, A, B and C notes and then play the D note again one octave higher.

Note: An octave refers to the distance between two notes with the same letter name on the keyboard.

- Modes are named after the first (tonic) note in the mode. For example, if the first note in a dorian mode is D, the name of the mode is the D dorian mode.

Dorian Modes

- There are 12 dorian modes—the C, C♯, D, E♭, E, F, F♯, G, G♯, A, B♭ and B dorian modes.
- A dorian mode has the same notes as a natural minor scale, except the sixth note of the natural minor scale is raised by one half step. For information on natural minor scales, see page 94.

Note: When you raise a note by one half step, you play the white or black key directly to the right.

- For example, the D dorian mode has the same notes as the D natural minor scale, except the sixth note of the natural minor scale (B♭) is raised by one half step (B).

Tip

Can I determine the notes in a mode by using a pattern of whole steps and half steps?

Yes. The dorian, mixolydian and lydian modes each have a unique pattern of whole steps and half steps between the notes. For information on whole steps and half steps, see page 89.

Dorian mode: whole, half, whole, whole, whole, half, whole step.

Mixolydian mode: whole, whole, half, whole, whole, half, whole step.

Lydian mode: whole, whole, whole, half, whole, whole, half step.

Is there another way to determine the notes in the dorian, mixolydian and lydian modes?

For a dorian mode, play a major scale starting on the scale's second note. For example, if you play the C major scale starting on the scale's second note (D), you play the D dorian mode.

For a mixolydian mode, play a dorian mode, but raise the third note by one half step. For example, to play the D mixolydian mode, play the D dorian mode but raise the third note (F) by one half step (F♯).

For a lydian mode, play a major scale starting on the scale's fourth note. For example, if you play the A major scale starting on the scale's fourth note (D), you play the D lydian mode.

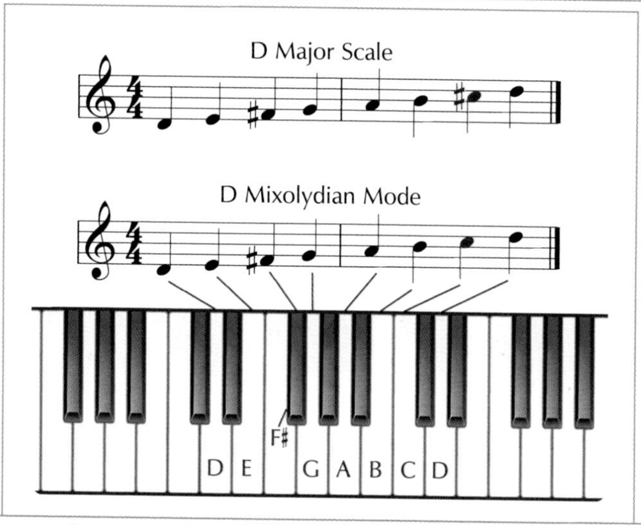

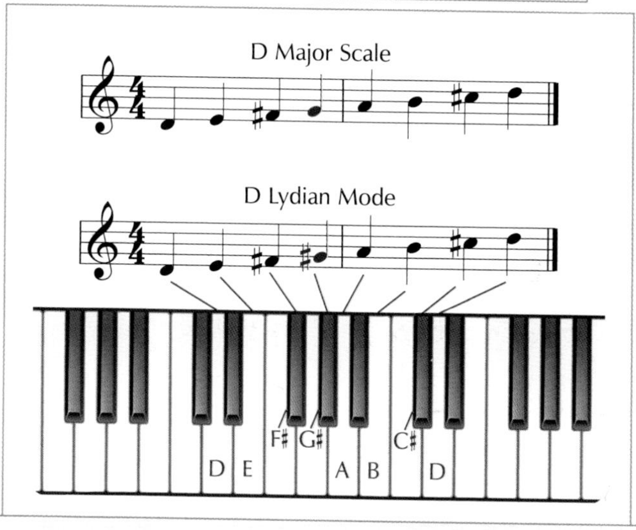

Mixolydian Modes

- There are 12 mixolydian modes—the C, C♯, D, E♭, E, F, F♯, G, A♭, A, B♭ and B mixolydian modes.
- A mixolydian mode has the same notes as a major scale, except the seventh note of the major scale is lowered by one half step. For information on major scales, see page 90.

Note: When you lower a note by one half step, you play the white or black key directly to the left.

- For example, the D mixolydian mode has the same notes as the D major scale, except the seventh note of the major scale (C♯) is lowered by one half step (C).

Lydian Modes

- There are 12 lydian modes—the C, C♯, D, E♭, E, F, F♯, G, A♭, A, B♭ and B lydian modes.
- A lydian mode has the same notes as a major scale, except the fourth note of the major scale is raised by one half step. For information on major scales, see page 90.

Note: When you raise a note by one half step, you play the white or black key directly to the right.

- For example, the D lydian mode has the same notes as the D major scale, except the fourth note of the major scale (G) is raised by one half step (G♯).

playing modes

C Dorian

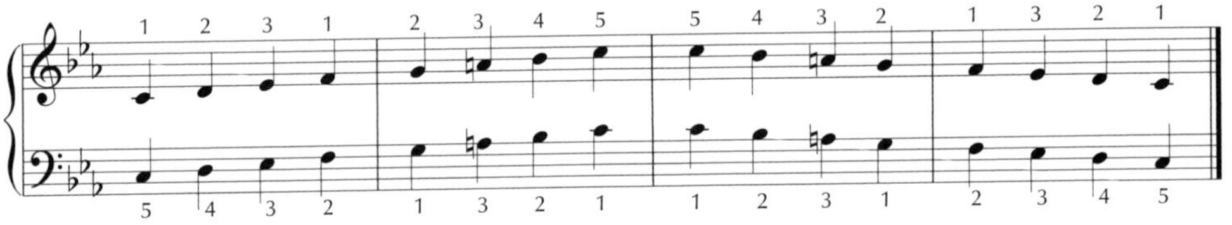

C Mixolydian

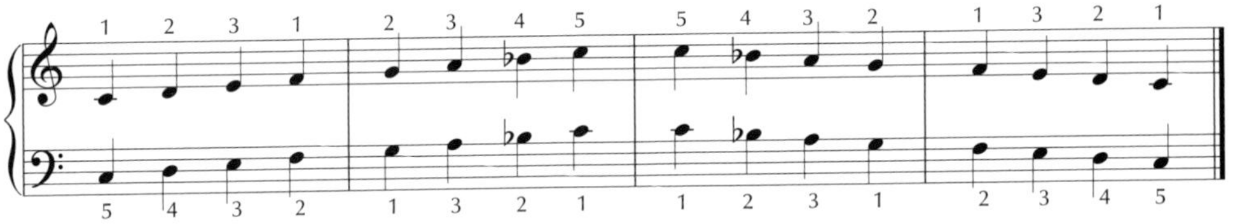

C Lydian

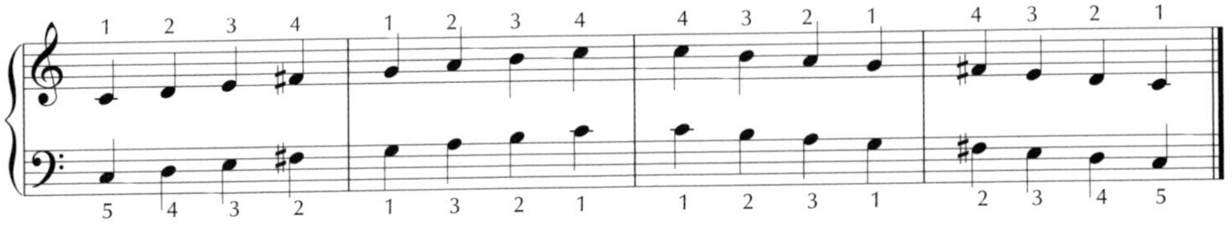

C♯ Dorian

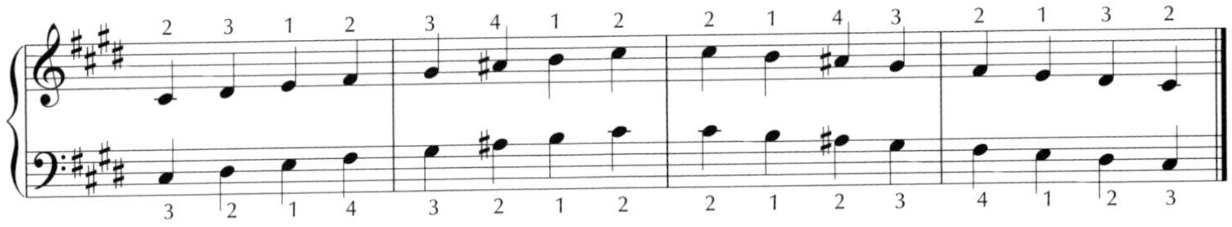

C♯ Mixolydian

C♯ Lydian

D Dorian

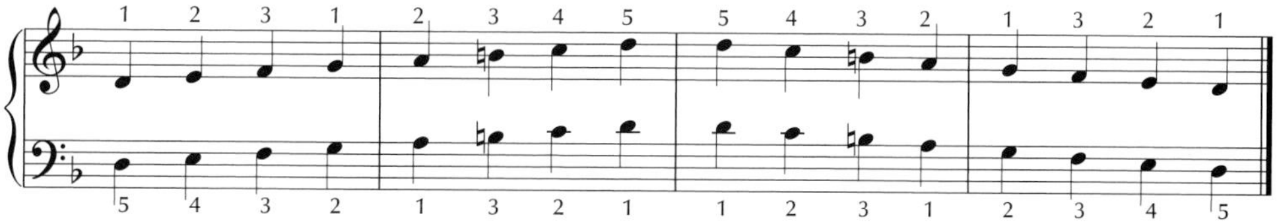

D Mixolydian

D Lydian

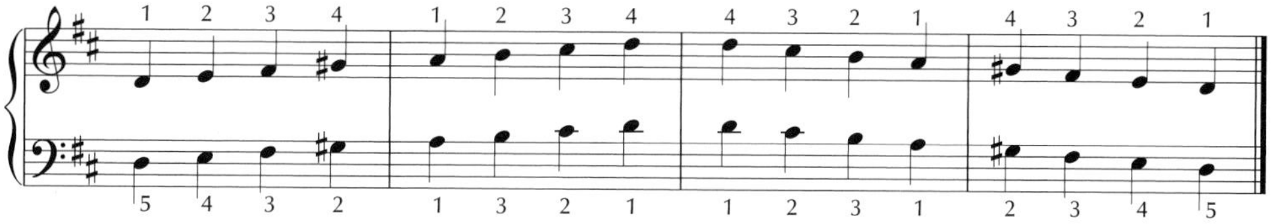

E♭ Dorian

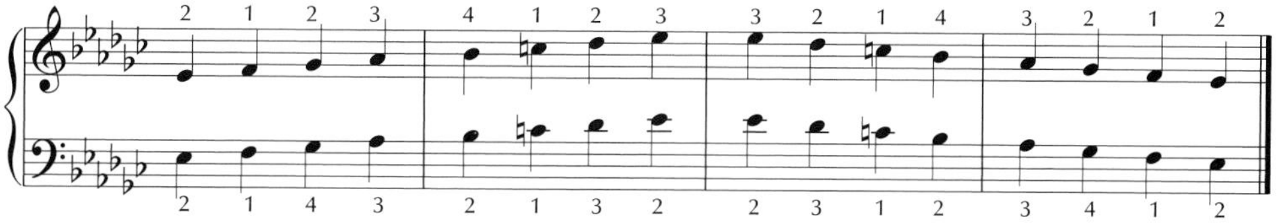

E♭ Mixolydian

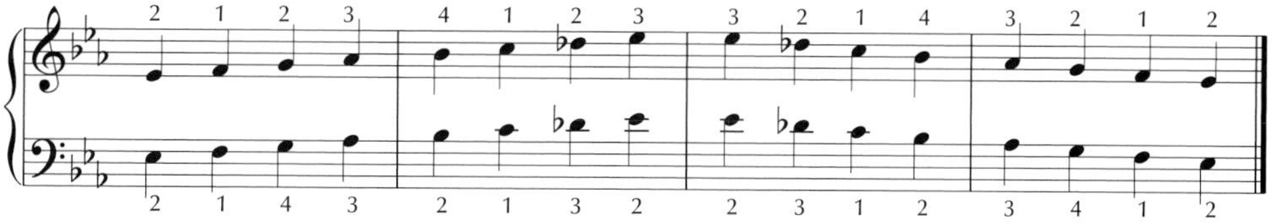

E♭ Lydian

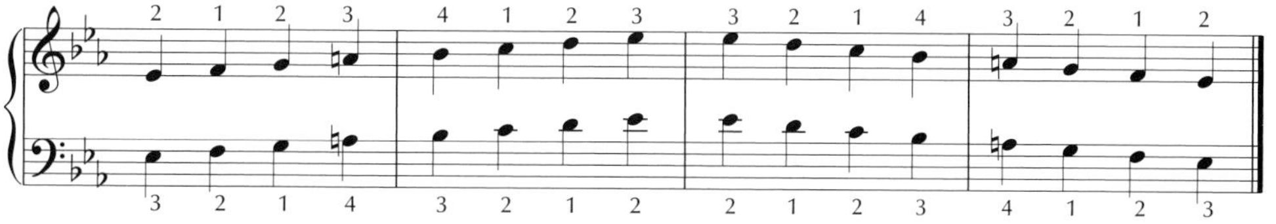

CONTINUED...

playing modes *(continued)*

E Dorian

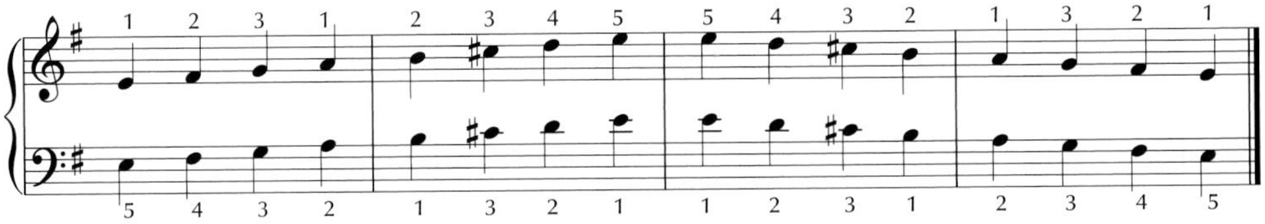

E Mixolydian

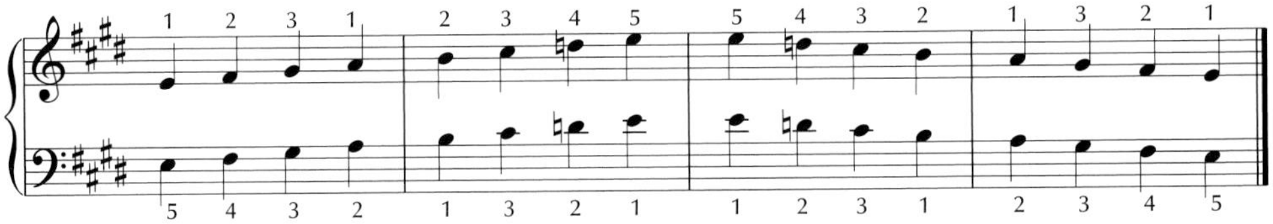

E Lydian

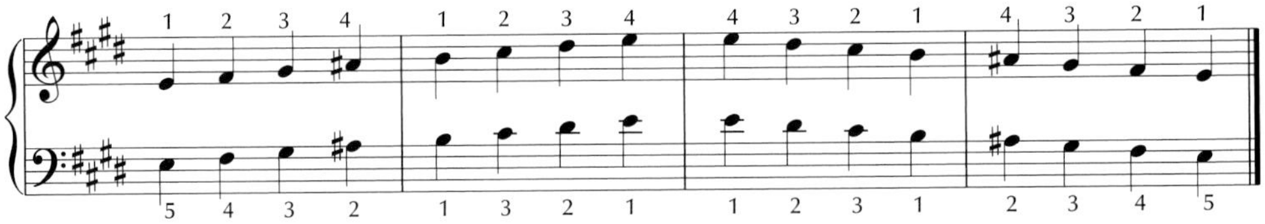

F Dorian

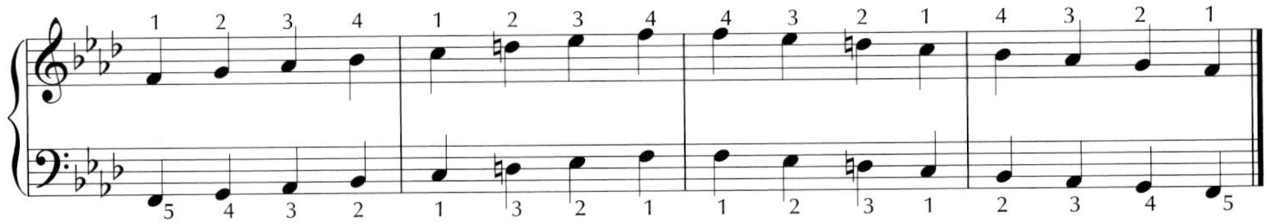

F Mixolydian

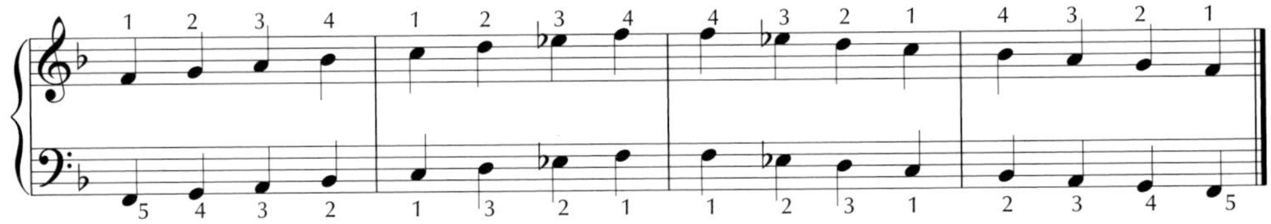

F Lydian

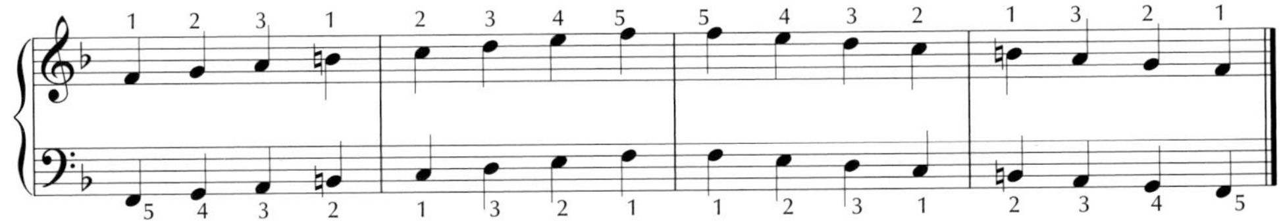

F♯ Dorian

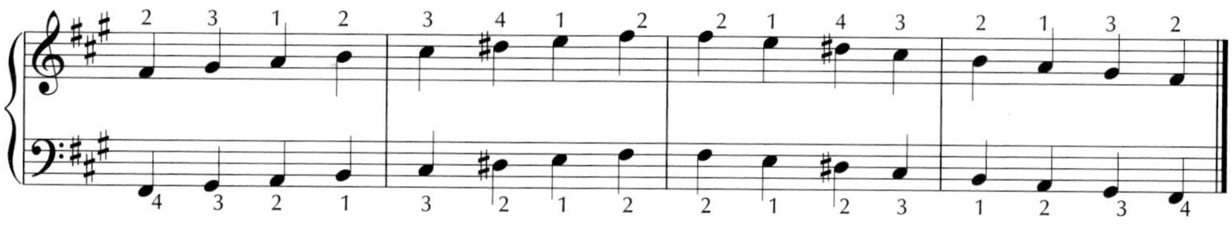

F♯ Mixolydian

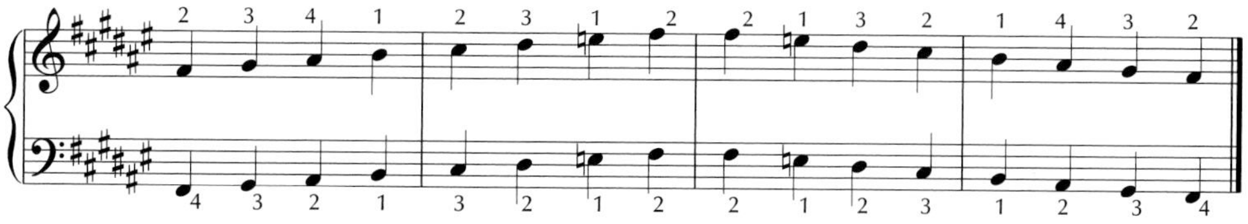

F♯ Lydian

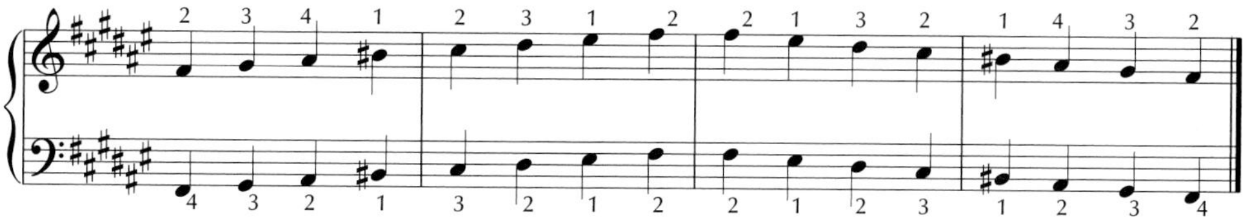

G Dorian

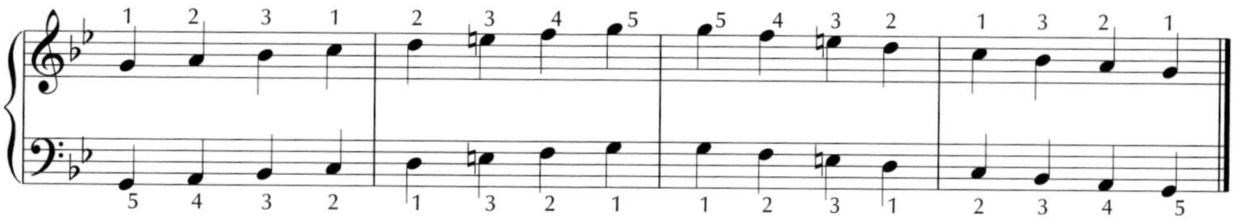

G Mixolydian

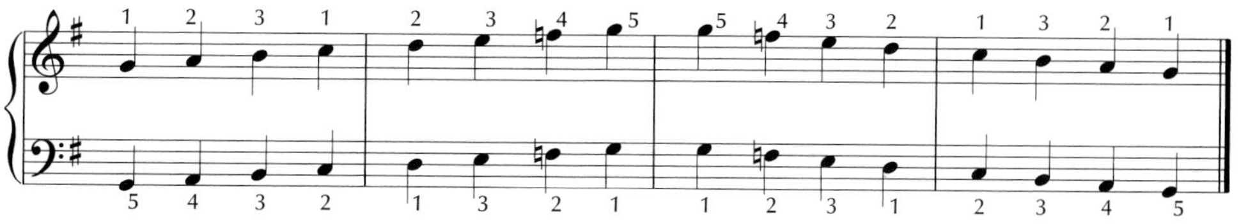

G Lydian

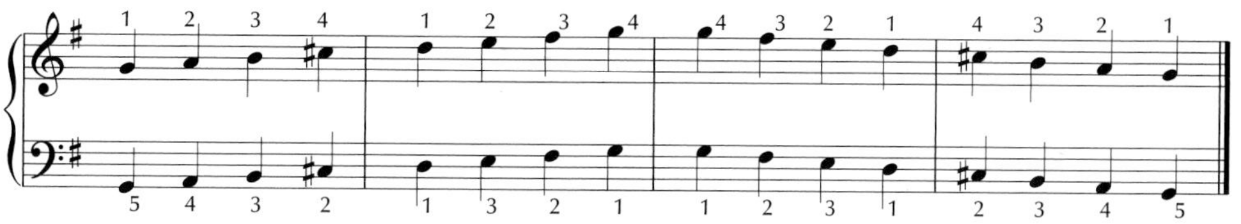

CONTINUED...

G♯ Dorian

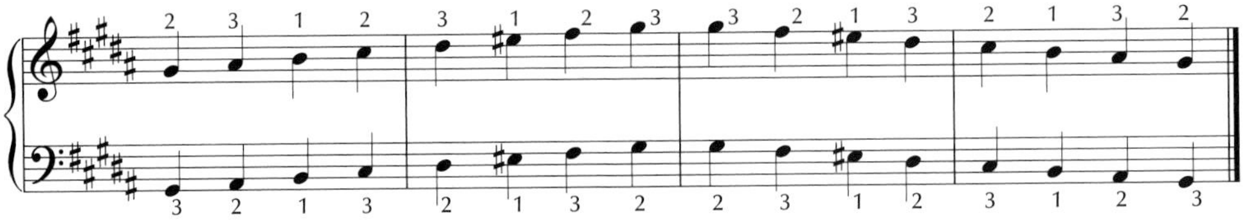

A♭ Mixolydian

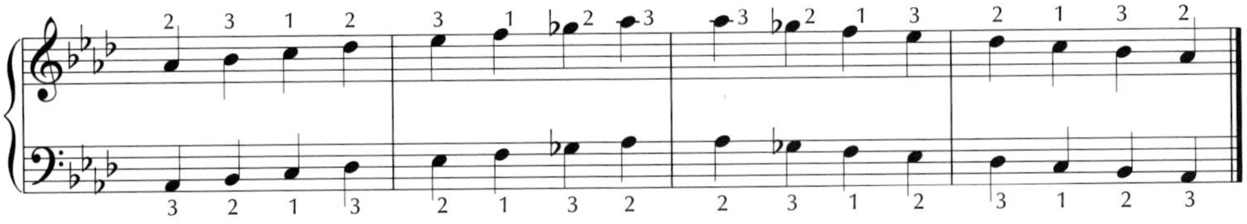

A♭ Lydian

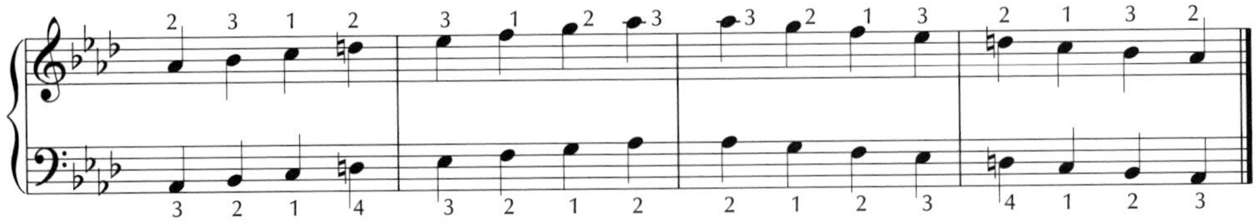

A Dorian

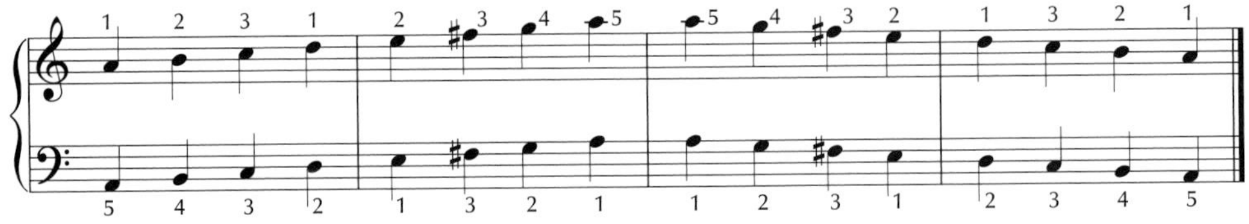

A Mixolydian

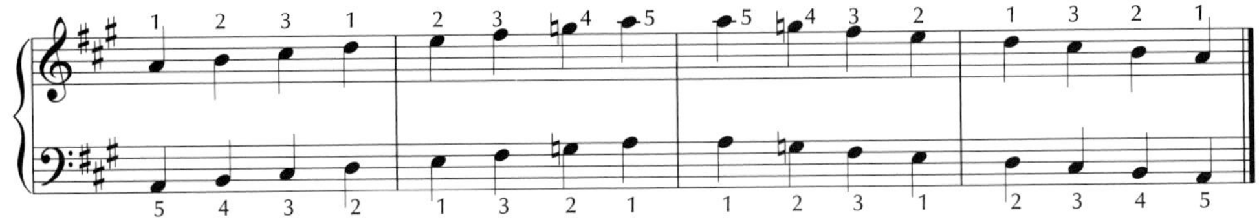

A Lydian

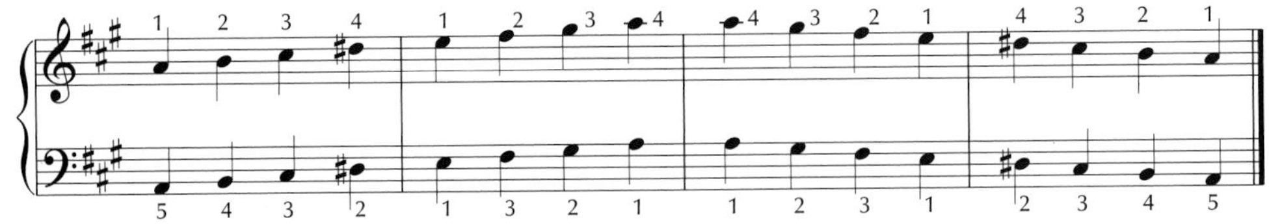

B♭ Dorian

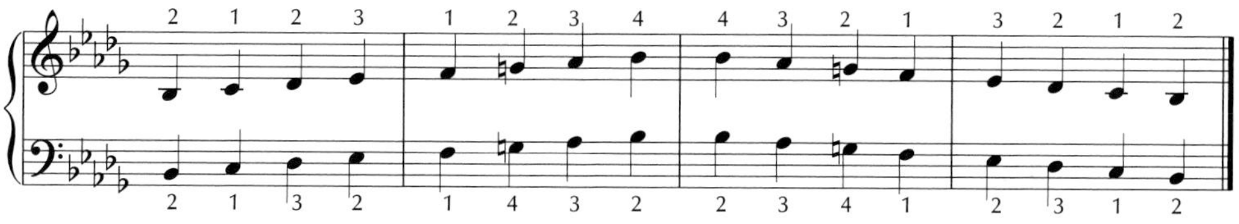

B♭ Mixolydian

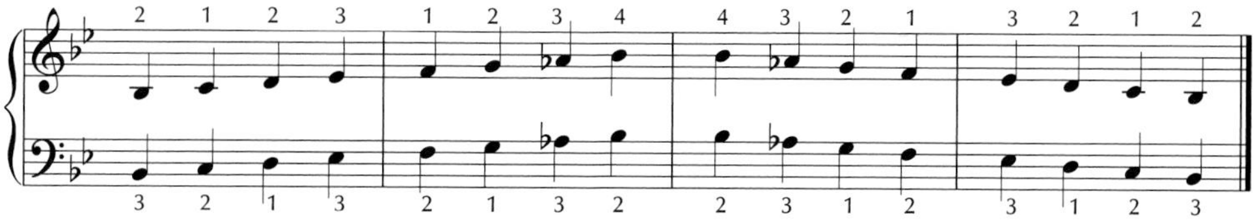

B♭ Lydian

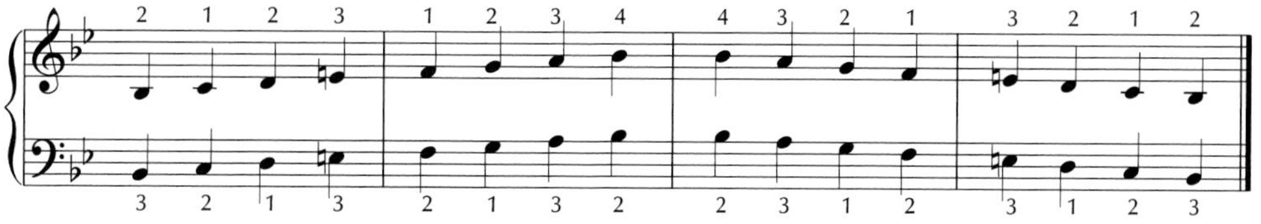

B Dorian

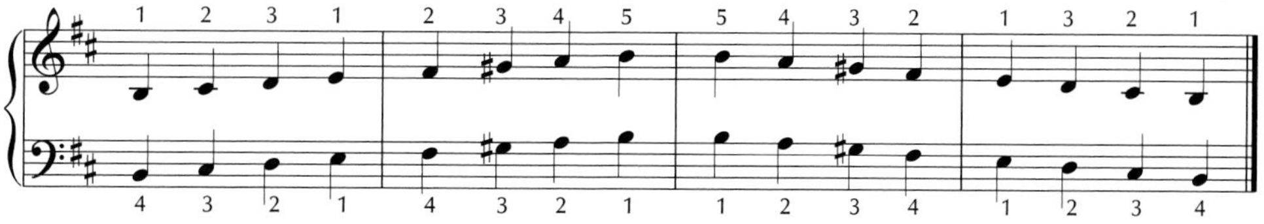

B Mixolydian

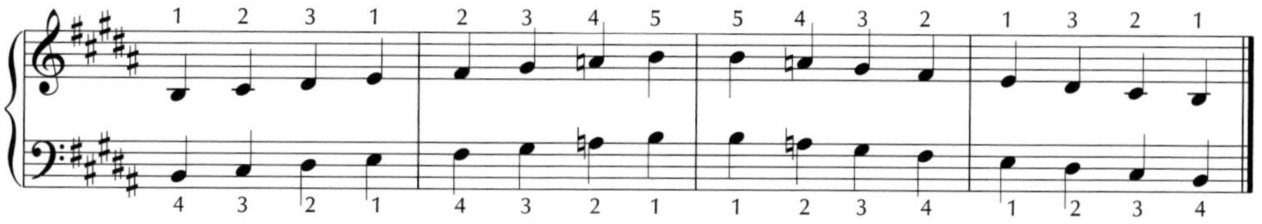

B Lydian

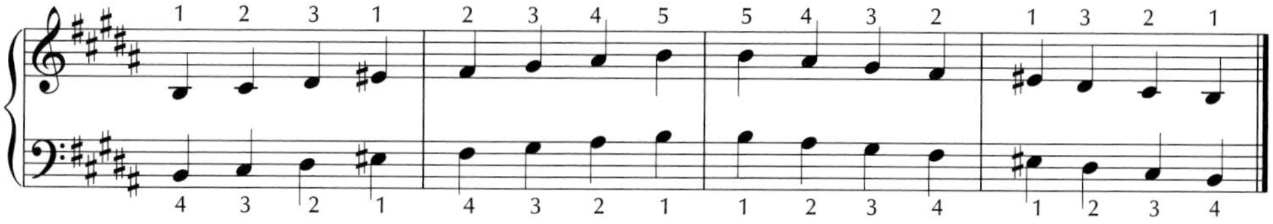

Chapter 5

Musical pieces often include chords to fill out the sound of the music. This chapter introduces you to the chords you will most commonly find in piano music, including major, minor, 7th, diminished and suspended chords. You will also learn how to change the order of the notes in chords to change between chords more easily when playing a piece.

Playing Chords

In this Chapter...

Playing Major Chords
Playing Minor Chords
Playing Dominant 7th Chords
Playing Major 7th Chords
Playing Minor 7th Chords
Playing 6th Chords
Playing 9th Chords
Playing Augmented Chords
Playing Diminished Chords
Playing Suspended Chords
Playing Broken Chords
Playing Arpeggios
Playing Three-Note Chord Inversions
Playing Four-Note Chord Inversions
Changing Chords
"We Three Kings"
"Largo"
"Prelude in C Major"
"Down to the Wire"
"Toreador Song"
"Mellowing Out"

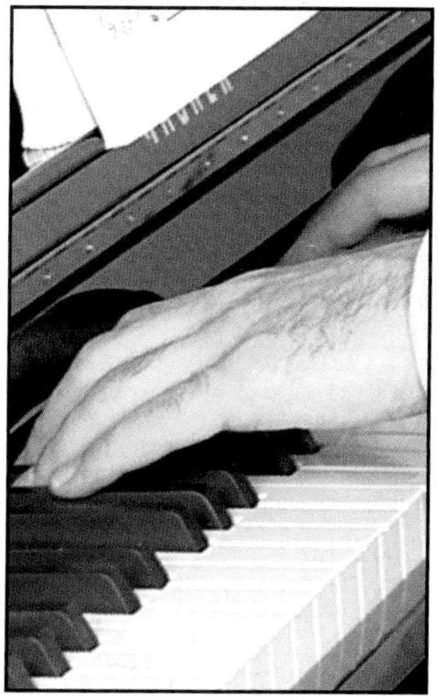

playing major chords

Major chords are the most commonly used chords in music and produce uplifting, happy sounds. Major chords are usually written as a capital letter name, such as C, or as a capital letter name followed by M or maj, such as CM or Cmaj.

A major chord consists of three notes—the first (root), third and fifth notes of a major scale. A major scale is a group of related notes arranged in order of pitch. To play a major chord, start with the first note of the chord's major scale and then add the third and fifth notes from the same scale. For example, to play the C major chord, you play the first (C), third (E) and fifth (G) notes from the C major scale together. The name of the major chord is the same as the letter name of the lowest note in the chord.

The notes of a major chord appear in many locations on the keyboard. Where you play a chord depends on how high or low you want the chord to sound.

You usually use your pinky finger, middle finger and thumb to play major chords. When using your left hand, your pinky finger plays the root note. When using your right hand, your thumb plays the root note.

Understanding Major Chords

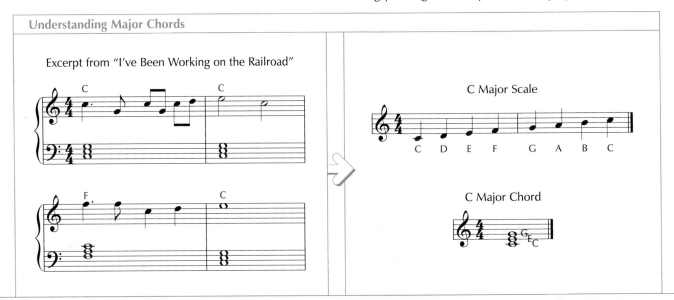

Excerpt from "I've Been Working on the Railroad"

C Major Scale

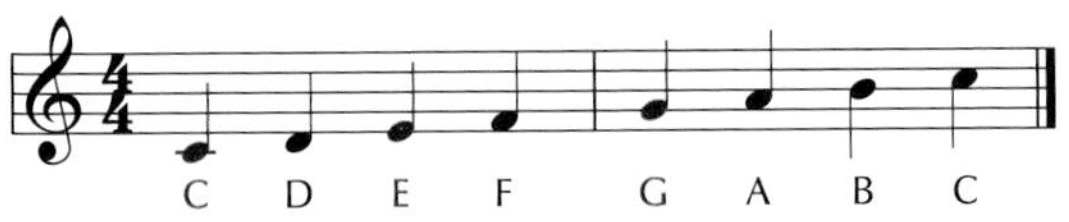

C Major Chord

- A major chord consists of three notes that you play at the same time to produce a happy sound.
- In written music, a major chord is usually indicated as three notes stacked on top of each other on the staff.
- Major chords are usually written as a letter name, such as C, or a letter name followed by M or maj, such as CM or Cmaj.
- A major chord consists of the first (root), third and fifth notes of a major scale.

Note: A scale is a series of notes that you play in a specific order. For more information on major scales, see page 90.

- For example, the C major chord consists of the first (C), third (E) and fifth (G) notes of the C major scale.

Tip

How can I practice playing major chords?

You can start on the C major chord and then, keeping your fingers in the same formation, move all of your fingers up the keyboard, a half step at a time. The first half step is the D♭ major chord, followed by the D major chord, and so on. This exercise lets you see that the distances between each of the notes in all of the major chords are exactly the same.

Why do I need to know the notes that make up each chord?

In some written music, you are only provided with the name of the chord and not given the actual notes to play. In these instances, the name of the chord the composer wants you to play often appears above the treble clef. In order to play the music, you need to know how to find the notes that make up each chord. It is a good idea to practice your chords often.

Play a Major Chord With Your Right Hand

- You can play a major chord at any location on the keyboard, since the notes that make up a chord can be found in many locations. Where you play a chord depends on the sound you want to produce.

1. To play a major chord with your right hand, rest your thumb on the key for the first (root) note of the chord you want to play.
2. Rest your middle finger on the key for the middle note of the chord.
3. Rest your pinky finger on the key for the top note of the chord.
4. Press down on all three keys at the same time to play the chord.

Play a Major Chord With Your Left Hand

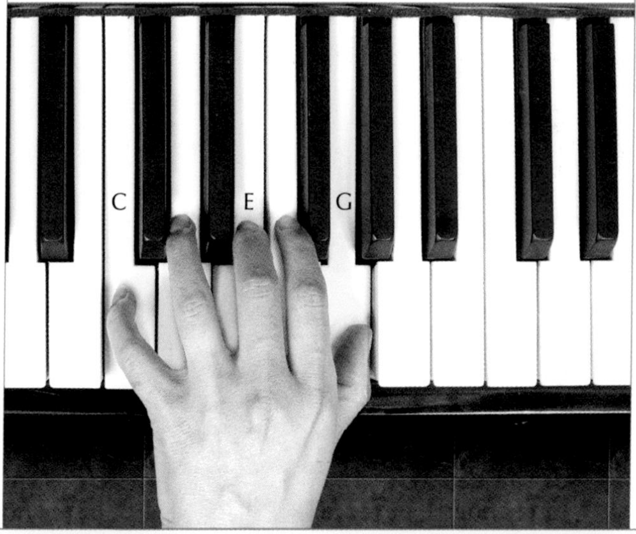

- When your right hand is playing a melody, you can play major chords with your left hand to provide accompaniment.

1. To play a major chord with your left hand, rest your pinky finger on the key for the first (root) note of the chord you want to play.
2. Rest your middle finger on the key for the middle note of the chord.
3. Rest your thumb on the key for the top note of the chord.
4. Press down on all three keys at the same time to play the chord.

playing major chords

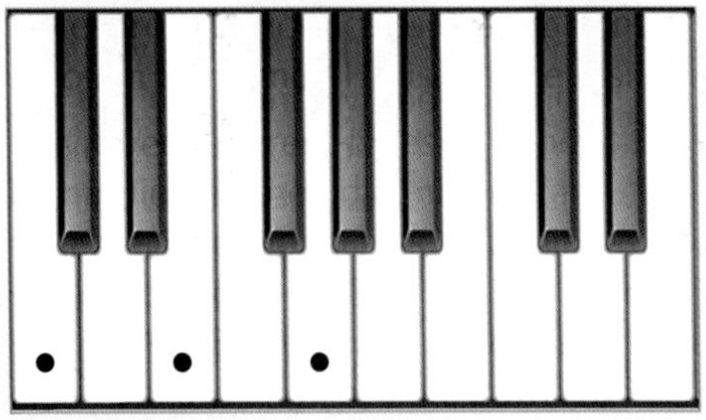

C Major Chord

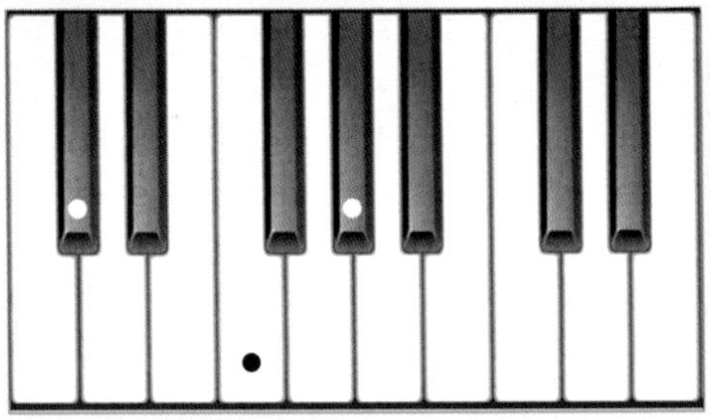

D♭ Major Chord
Also known as C♯ Major Chord

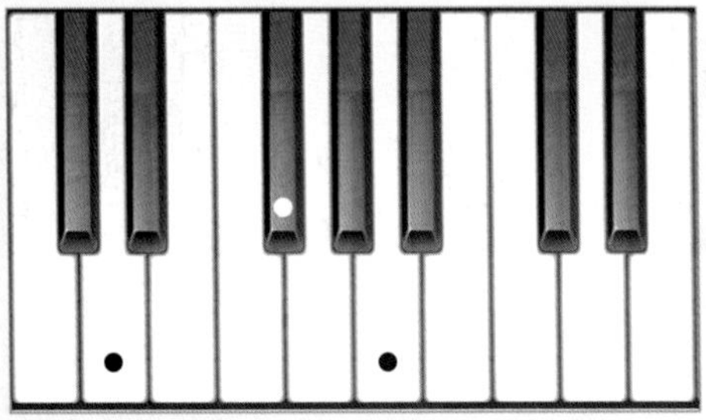

D Major Chord

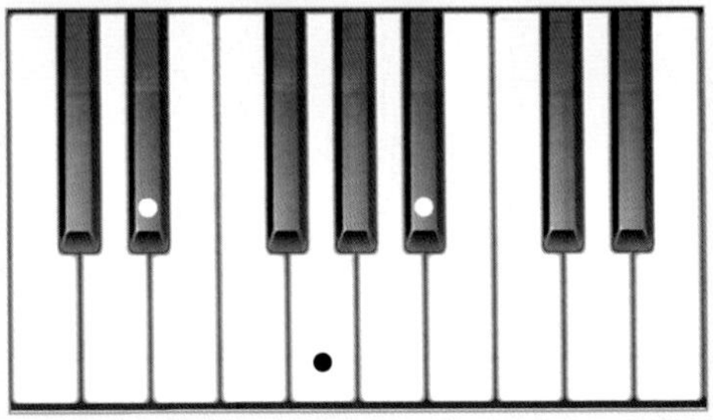

E♭ Major Chord

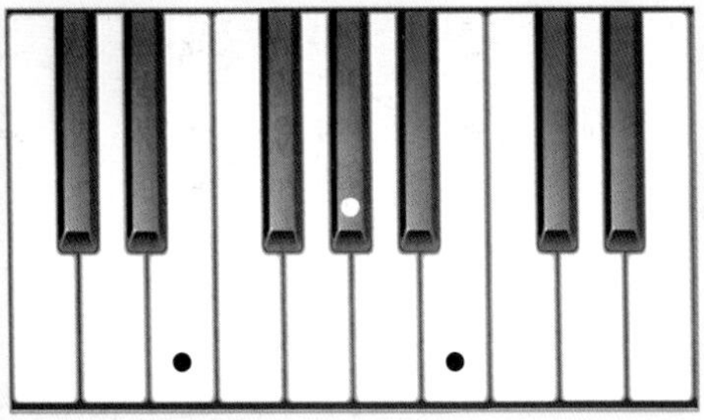

E Major Chord

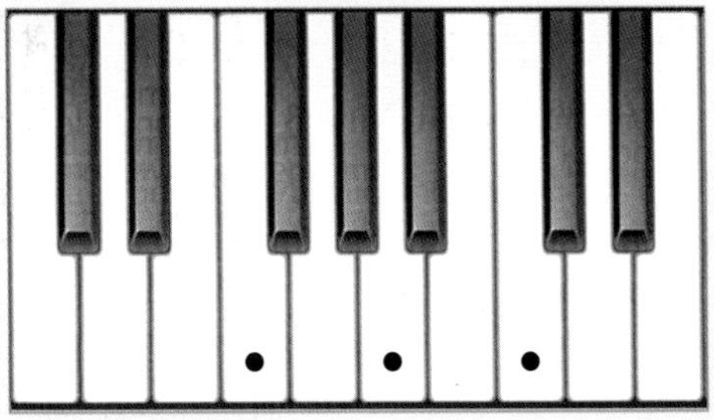

F Major Chord

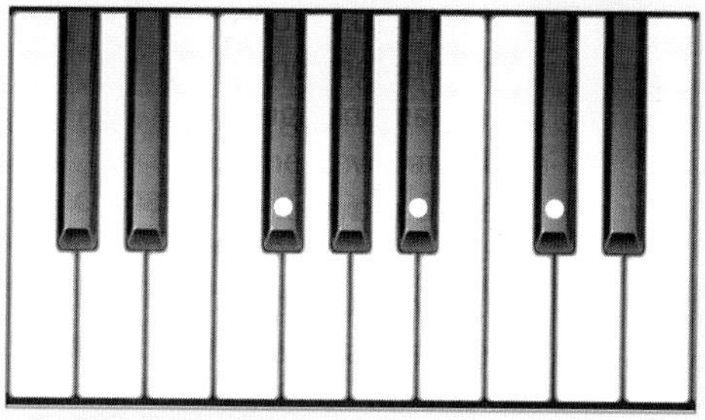

F♯ Major Chord
Also known as G♭ Major Chord

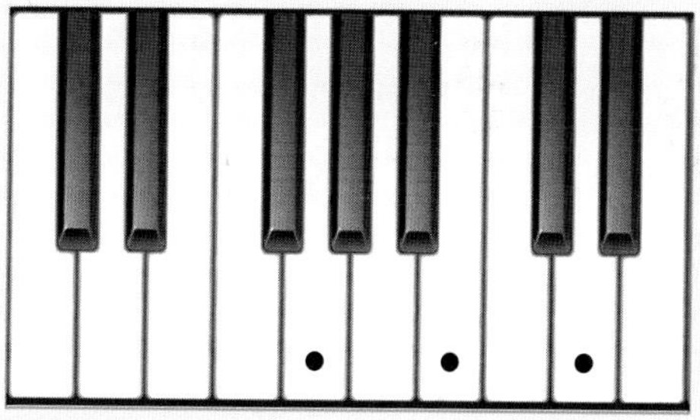

G Major Chord

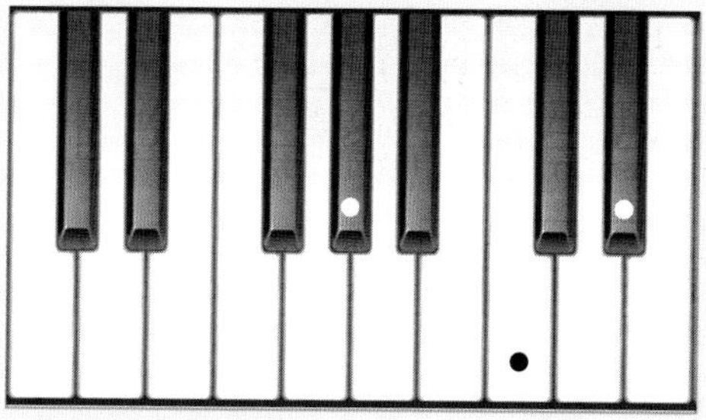

A♭ Major Chord

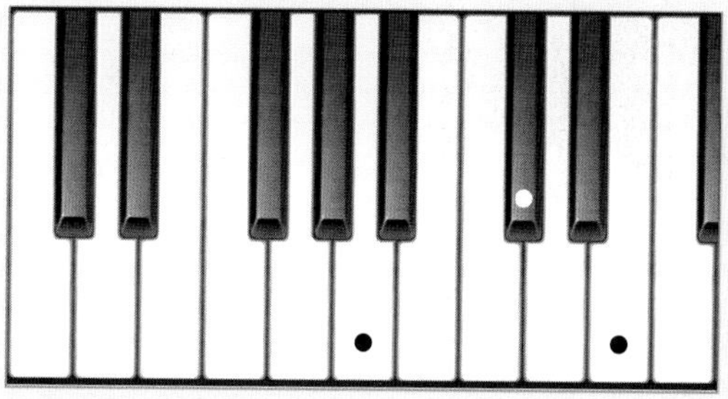

A Major Chord

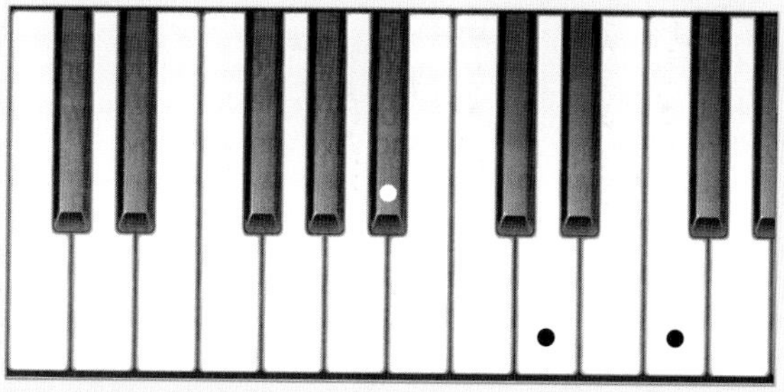

B♭ Major Chord

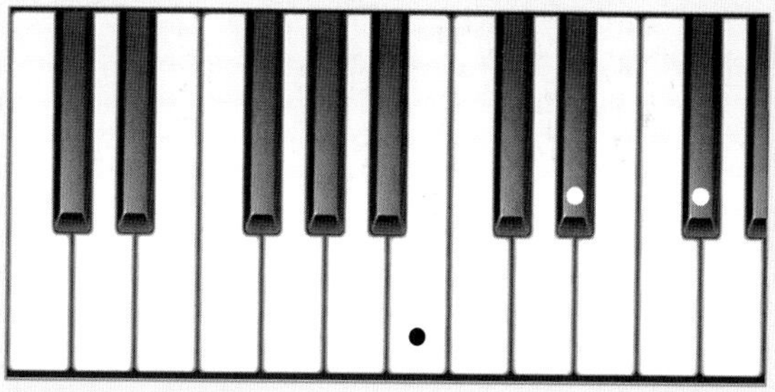

B Major Chord

playing minor chords

Minor chords are characterized by the dark, sad sounds they produce. To differentiate minor chords from major chords, minor chords are labelled with an "m" or "min" beside their letter name, such as Em or Emin.

A minor chord consists of three notes—the first, third and fifth notes of a minor scale. A minor scale is a series of related notes arranged in order of pitch. For information on minor scales, see page 94.

To play a minor chord, start with the root (first) note of the chord's minor scale and then add the third and fifth notes from the same scale. For example, to play the A minor chord, you play the first (A), third (C) and fifth (E) notes from the A minor scale together.

The notes of a minor chord can be found in many locations on the keyboard. Where you play a chord depends on how high or low you want the chord to sound.

You usually use your pinky, middle finger and thumb to play minor chords. When using your left hand, the pinky finger plays the root note. When using your right hand, the thumb plays the root note.

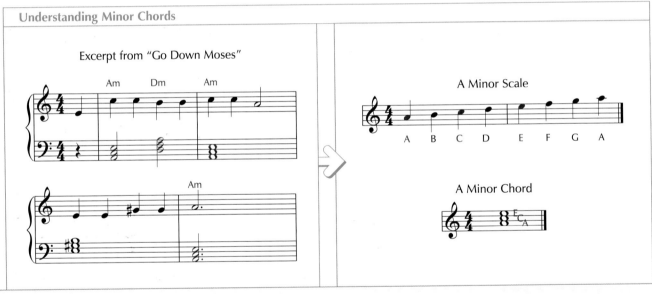

Understanding Minor Chords

Excerpt from "Go Down Moses"

A Minor Scale

A Minor Chord

- A minor chord consists of three notes that you play at the same time to produce a sad sound.
- In written music, a minor chord is usually indicated as three notes stacked on top of each other on the staff.

- Minor chords are usually labelled with an "m" or "min" beside their letter name, such as Am or Amin.

- A minor chord consists of the first (root), third and fifth notes of a minor scale.

Note: A scale is a series of notes that you play in a specific order. For more information on minor scales, see page 94.

- For example, the A minor chord (Am) consists of the first (A), third (C) and fifth (E) notes of the A minor scale.

Is there another way to figure out the notes of a minor chord?

If you compare a major and minor chord of the same letter name, only one note is different between the chords. In a minor chord, the middle note is a half step lower than the middle note in the corresponding major chord. You can play a minor chord by playing the corresponding major chord, but lower the middle note by one half step. For example, the C major chord uses the C, E and G notes, so to make the C minor chord, lower the middle note (E) by one half step (E♭). The C minor chord uses notes C, E♭ and G.

How can I tell the difference between a minor and a major chord?

To hear the difference between a minor chord, such as Em, and a major chord, such as E, you can play the chords back to back. To play the E major chord, press the E, G♯ and B keys together. To play the E minor chord, press the E, G, and B keys together. For more information on playing major chords, see page 124.

Play a Minor Chord With Your Right Hand

- You can play a minor chord at any location on the keyboard, since the notes that make up a chord can be found in many locations. Where you play a chord depends on how high or low you want the chord to sound.

1 To play a minor chord with your right hand, rest your thumb on the key for the first (root) note of the chord you want to play.

2 Rest your middle finger on the key for the middle note of the chord.

3 Rest your pinky finger on the key for the top note of the chord.

4 Press all three keys at the same time to play the chord.

Play a Minor Chord With Your Left Hand

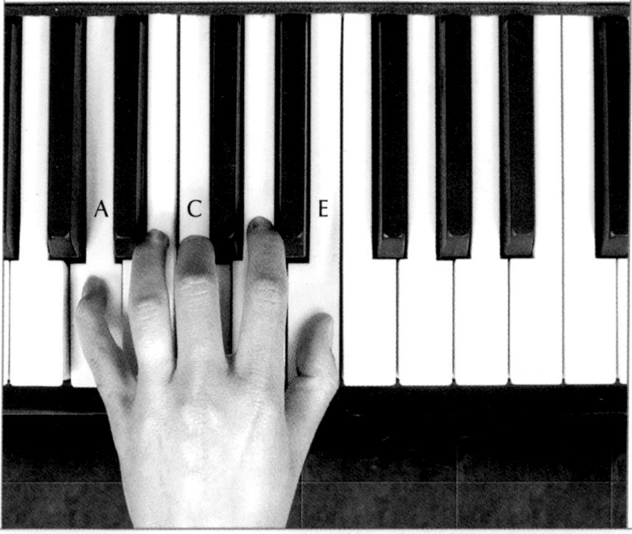

- When your right hand is playing a melody, you can play minor chords with your left hand to provide accompaniment.

1 To play a minor chord with your left hand, rest your pinky finger on the key for the first (root) note of the chord you want to play.

2 Rest your middle finger on the key for the middle note of the chord.

3 Rest your thumb on the key for the top note of the chord.

4 Press all three keys at the same time to play the chord.

playing minor chords

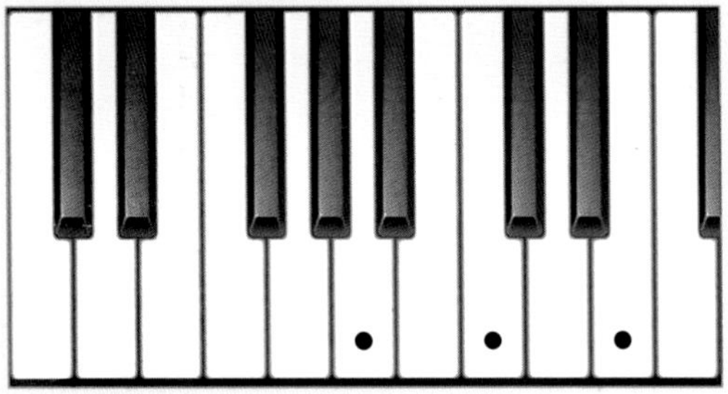

A Minor Chord

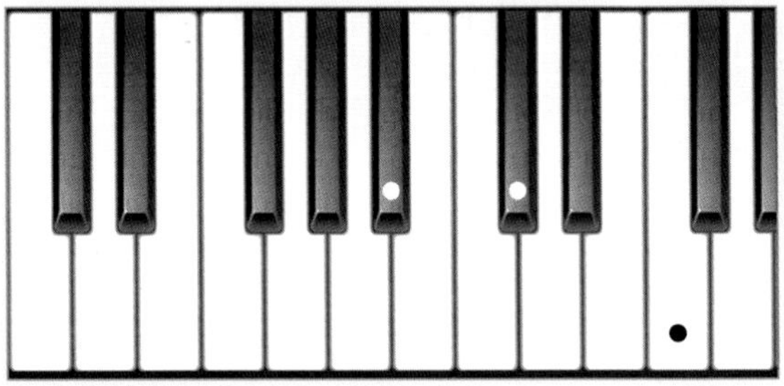

B♭ Minor Chord
Also known as A♯ Minor Chord

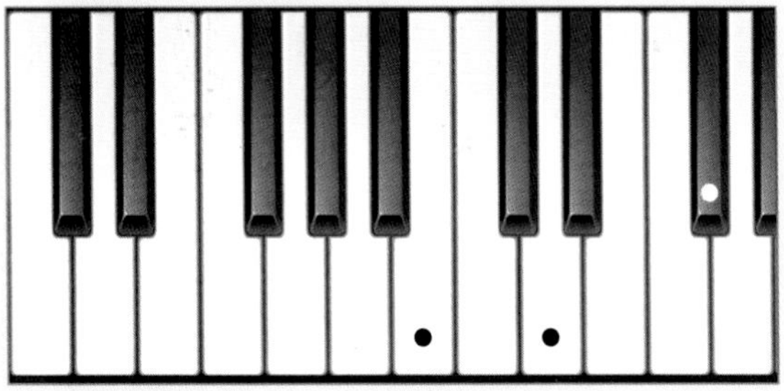

B Minor Chord

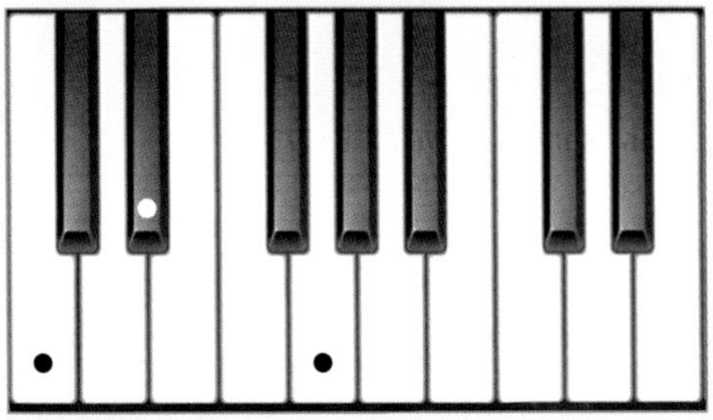

C Minor Chord

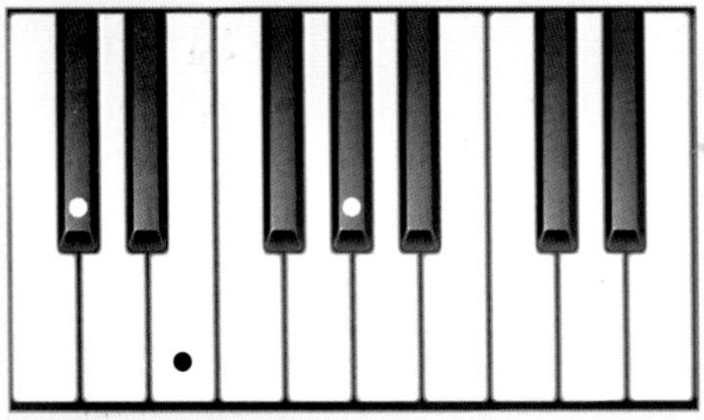

C♯ Minor Chord

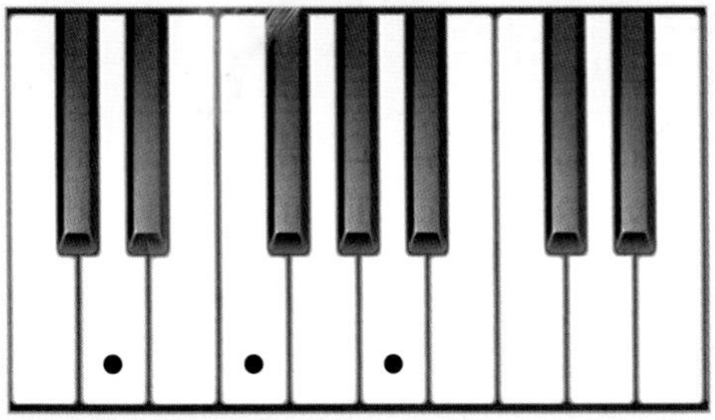

D Minor Chord

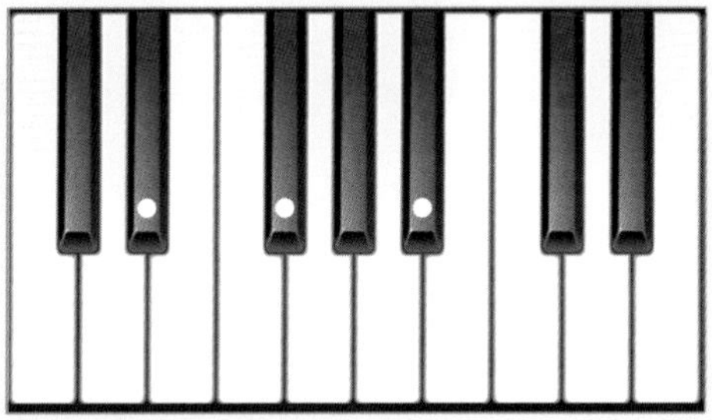

E♭ Minor Chord
Also known as D♯ Minor Chord

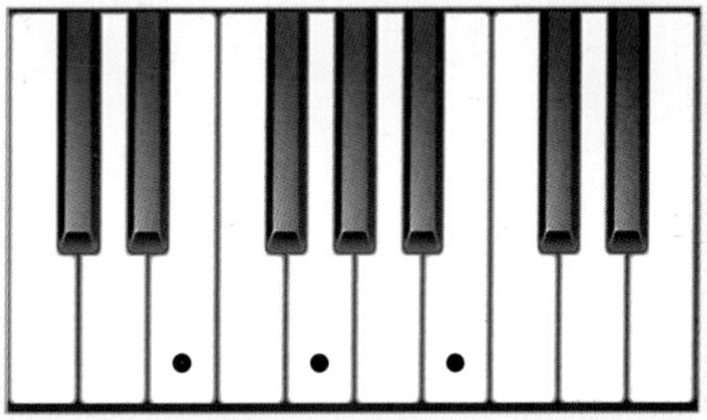

E Minor Chord

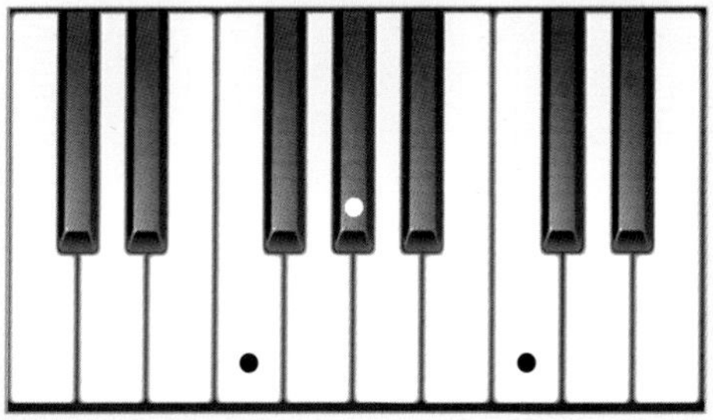

F Minor Chord

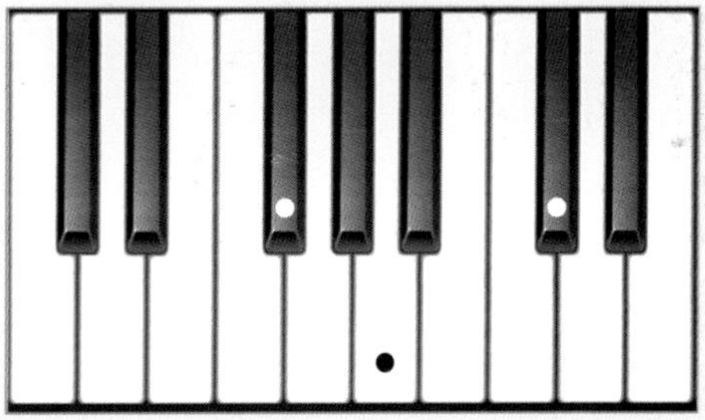

F♯ Minor Chord

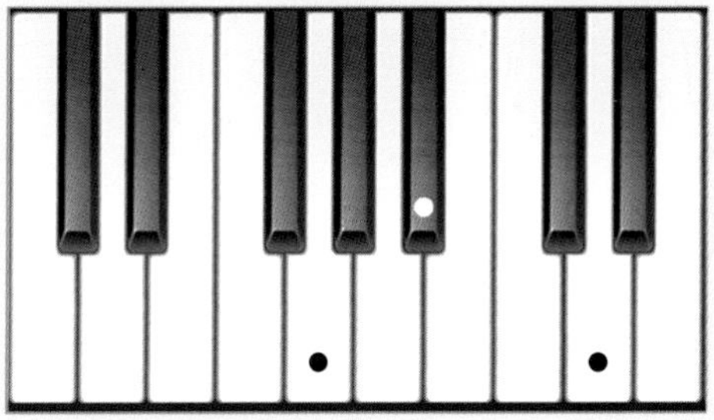

G Minor Chord

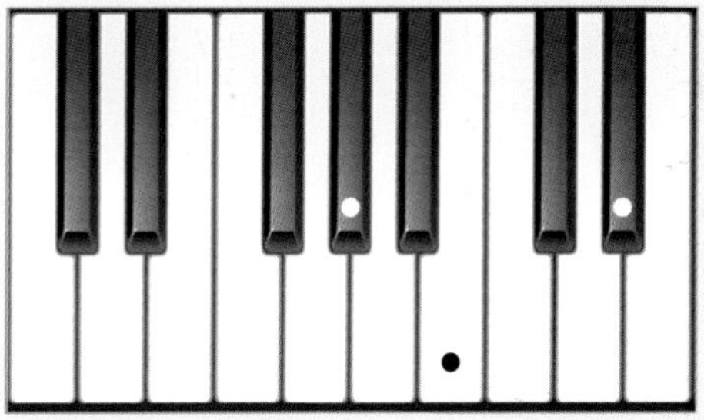

G♯ Minor Chord
Also known as A♭ Minor Chord

playing dominant 7th chords

Dominant 7th chords, which are also known simply as sevenths, are used in many styles of music. A dominant 7th chord is usually written as a letter name followed by the number 7, such as C7.

A dominant 7th chord consists of four notes—the first (root), third and fifth notes of a major scale, plus the seventh note of the scale, which has been lowered by one half step. For example, to play a C7 chord, you play the first (C), third (E), fifth (G) and lowered seventh (B♭) notes of the C major scale. A scale is a series of related notes arranged in order of pitch.

You can play a dominant 7th chord anywhere on the keyboard, using your left or right hand, since the notes that make up a chord appear in many locations. Where you play a chord depends on how high or low you want the chord to sound.

You usually use your thumb, index finger, ring finger and pinky finger to play dominant 7th chords. When using your left hand, your pinky finger plays the root note. When using your right hand, your thumb plays the root note.

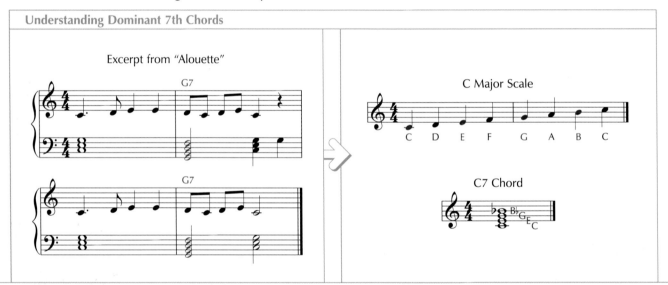

Understanding Dominant 7th Chords

Excerpt from "Alouette"

C Major Scale

C7 Chord

- A dominant 7th chord consists of four notes that you play at the same time.
- Dominant 7th chords are used in many styles of music.
- In written music, a dominant 7th chord is usually indicated as four notes stacked on top of each other on the staff.
- Dominant 7th chords are usually written as a letter name followed by the number 7, such as G7.
- A dominant 7th chord consists of the first (root), third and fifth notes of a major scale, plus the seventh note of the major scale, which has been lowered by one half step.

Note: A scale is a series of notes that you play in a specific order. For more information on major scales, see page 90.

- For example, the C7 chord consists of the first (C), third (E) and fifth (G) notes of the C major scale, plus the seventh note of the scale lowered by one half step (B♭).

Tip

Is there another way to form a dominant 7th chord?

Another way to form a dominant 7th chord is to first form the major chord and then simply add the seventh note of the major scale, except you lower the seventh note of the scale by one half step.

How can I vary the sound of a dominant 7th chord?

You have the option of leaving out the fifth note of the scale from any dominant 7th chord, which will produce a "thinner" chord sound. For example, to play the C7 chord, omit the fifth (G) note and play only the C, E and B♭ notes.

Is there an easy way to find the notes of a dominant 7th chord?

If you remember that the top (7th) note of any dominant 7th chord is one whole step below the root note, you will be able to find the notes more easily. For example, in an E7 chord, the root note is E, so the top note is D and in a G7 chord, the root note is G, so the top note is F.

Play a Dominant 7th Chord With Your Right Hand

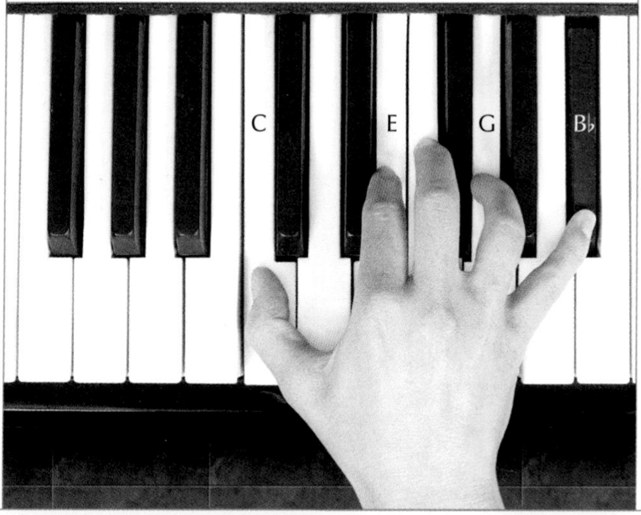

- You can play a dominant 7th chord at any location on the keyboard, since the notes that make up a chord can be found in many locations. Where you play a chord depends on how high or low you want the chord to sound.

1 To play a dominant 7th chord with your right hand, rest your thumb on the key for the first (root) note of the chord you want to play.

2 Rest your index finger on the key for the second note of the chord.

3 Rest your ring finger on the key for the third note of the chord.

4 Rest your pinky finger on the key for the top note of the chord.

5 Press all four keys at the same time to play the chord.

Play a Dominant 7th Chord With Your Left Hand

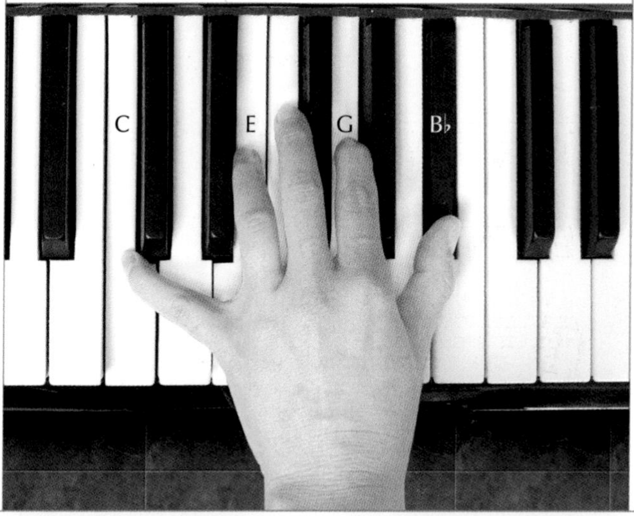

- When your right hand is playing a melody, you can play dominant 7th chords with your left hand to provide accompaniment.

1 To play a dominant 7th chord with your left hand, rest your pinky finger on the key for the first (root) note of the chord you want to play.

2 Rest your ring finger on the key for the second note of the chord.

3 Rest your index finger on the key for the third note of the chord.

4 Rest your thumb on the key for the top note of the chord.

5 Press all four keys at the same time to play the chord.

playing dominant 7th chords

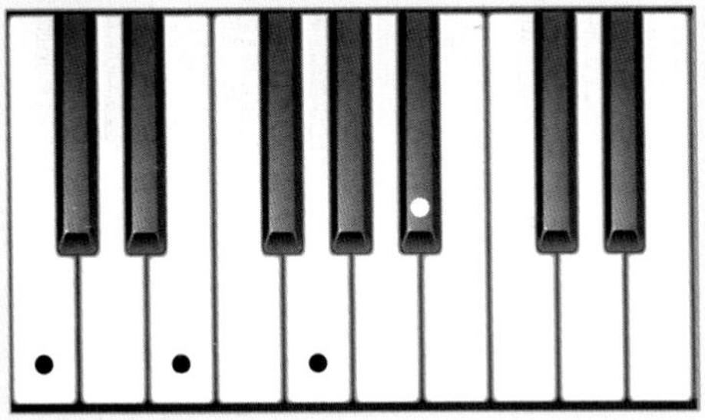

C7 Chord

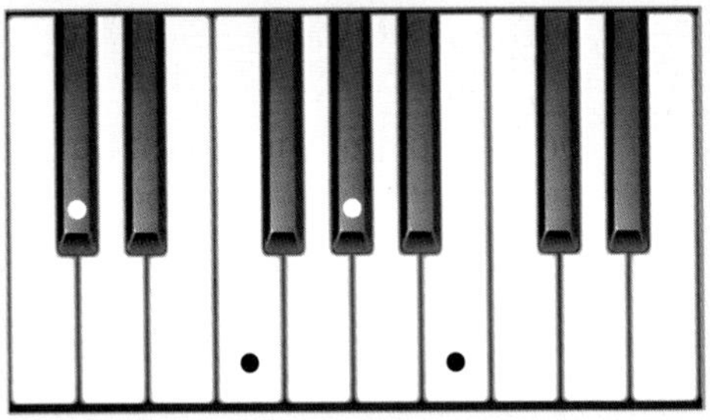

D♭7 Chord
Also known as C♯7 Chord

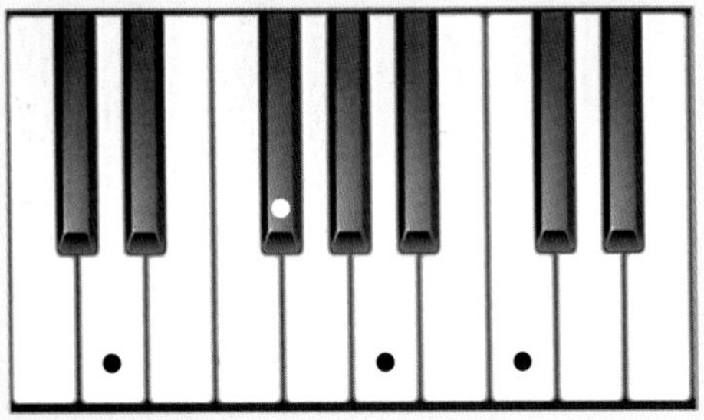

D7 Chord

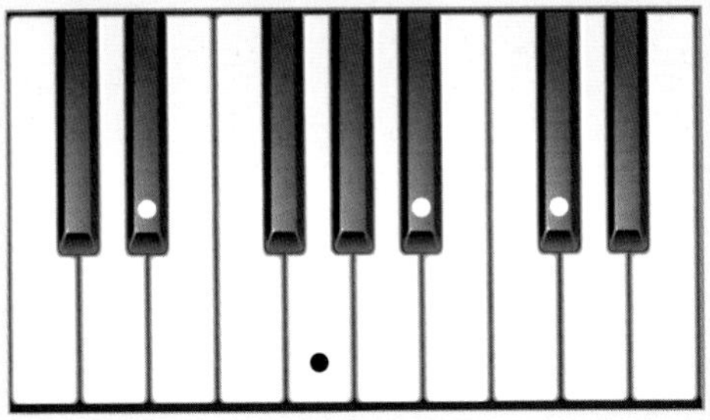

E♭7 Chord

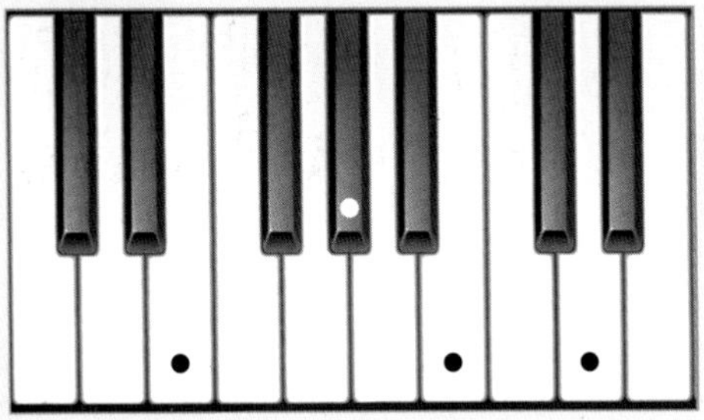

E7 Chord

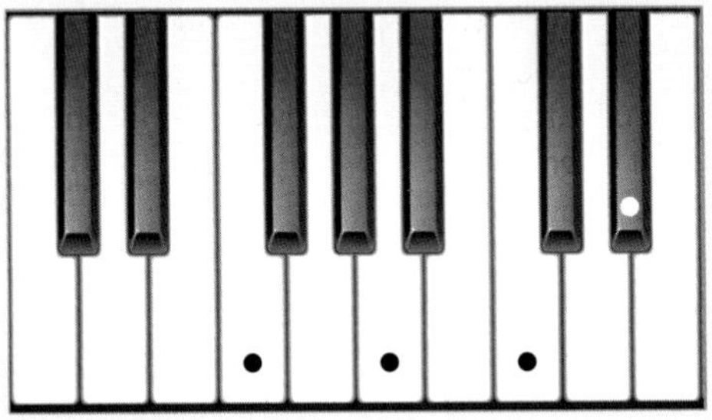

F7 Chord

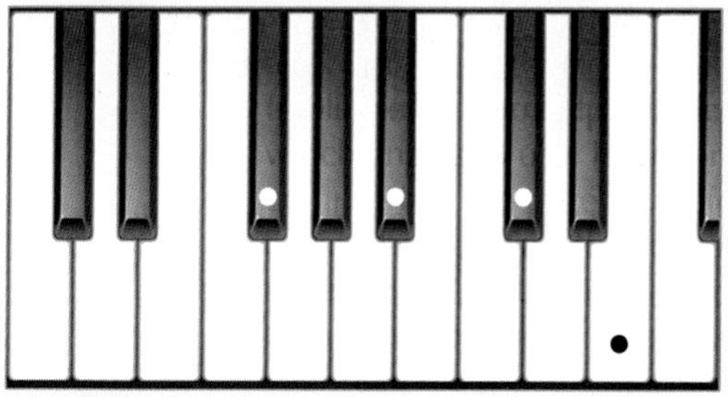

F♯7 Chord
Also known as G♭7 Chord

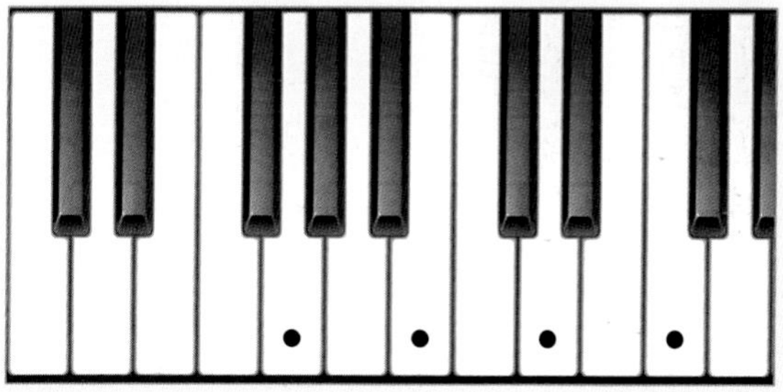

G7 Chord

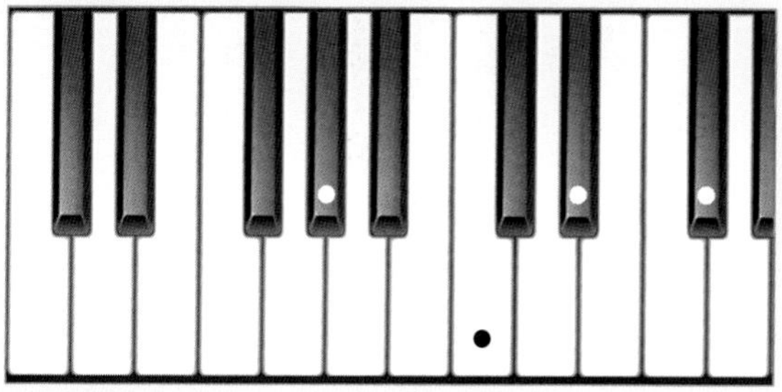

A♭7 Chord

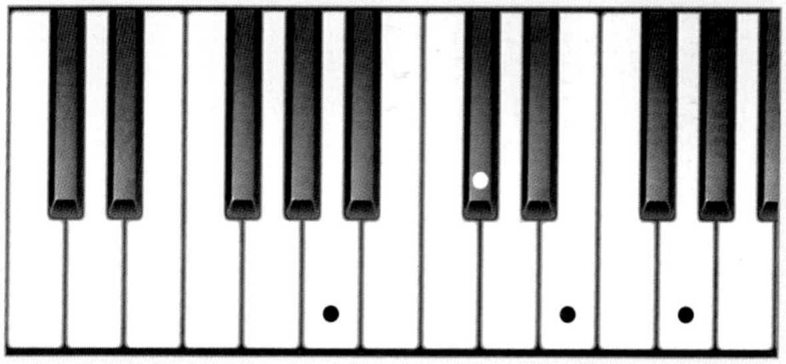

A7 Chord

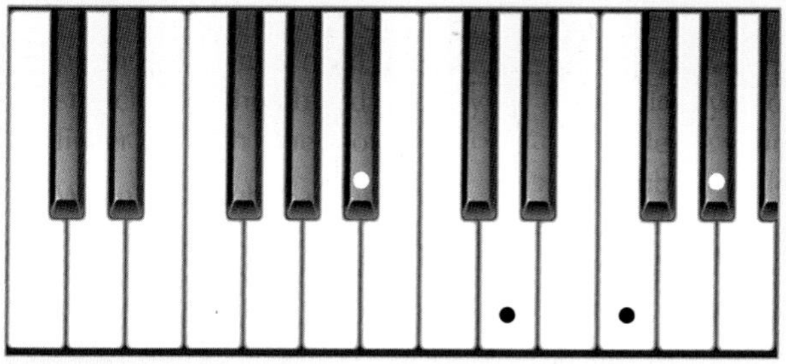

B♭7 Chord

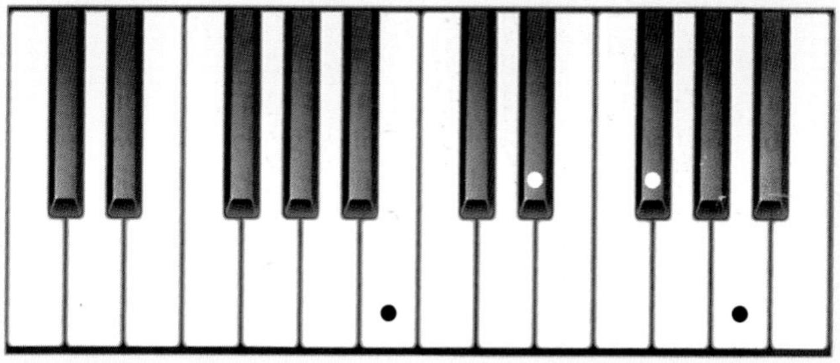

B7 Chord

playing major 7th chords

Major 7th chords are recognizable by the cheerful, jazzy sounds they produce. Major 7th chords are usually written as a letter name followed by M7, maj7 or Major 7, such as CM7, Cmaj7 or C Major 7.

A major 7th chord consists of four notes—the first (root), third, fifth and seventh notes of a major scale. A major scale is a group of related notes arranged in order of pitch. To play a major 7th chord, start with the first note of the chord's major scale and then add the third, fifth and seventh notes from the same scale. For example, to play the C Major 7th chord, you play the first (C), third (E), fifth (G) and seventh (B) notes from the C major scale together.

The notes of a major 7th chord appear in many locations on the keyboard. Where you play a chord depends on how high or low you want the chord to sound.

You usually use your thumb, index finger, ring finger and pinky finger to play major 7th chords. When using your left hand, your pinky finger plays the root note. When using your right hand, your thumb plays the root note.

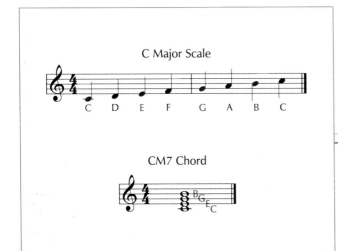

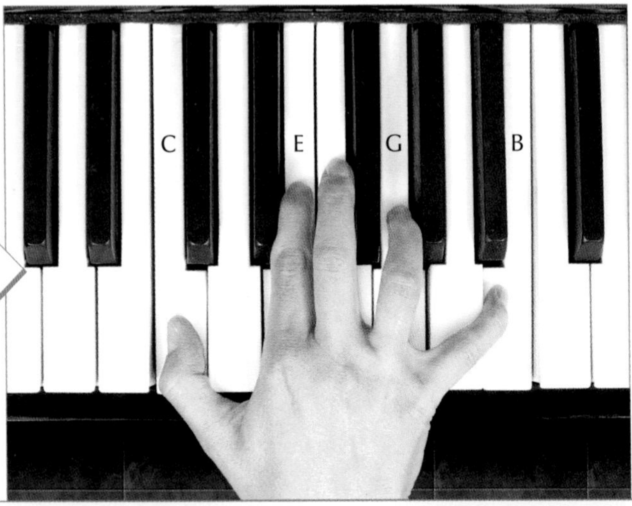

- A major 7th chord consists of four notes that you play at the same time to produce a cheerful, jazzy sound.
- Major 7th chords are usually written as a letter name followed by M7 (CM7), maj7 (Cmaj7), or Major 7 (C Major 7).
- In written music, a major 7th chord is usually indicated as four notes stacked on top of each other on the staff.
- A major 7th chord consists of the first (root), third, fifth and seventh notes of a major scale. For example, the C major 7th chord (CM7), consists of the first (C), third (E), fifth (G) and seventh (B) notes of the C major scale.

Note: For information on major scales, see page 90.

- To play a major 7th chord, use the thumb, index, ring and pinky fingers of your left or right hand to press the keys for the four notes of the chord at the same time.
- You can play a major 7th chord at any location on the keyboard, since the notes that make up a chord can be found in many locations. Where you play a chord depends on how high or low you want the chord to sound.

playing minor 7th chords

Minor 7th chords can be an effective alternative to regular minor chords to create a more textured and jazzy effect. Minor 7th chords are usually written as a letter name followed by m7, min7 or -7, such as Am7, Amin7 or A-7.

A minor 7th chord consists of four notes—the first (root), third, fifth and seventh notes of a natural minor scale. For information on natural minor scales, see page 94. To play a minor 7th chord, start with the first note of the chord's natural minor scale and then add the third, fifth and seventh notes from the same scale. For example, to play the A minor 7th chord, you play the first (A), third (C), fifth (E) and seventh (G) notes from the A natural minor scale together.

The notes of a minor 7th chord appear in many locations on the keyboard. Where you play a chord depends on how high or low you want the chord to sound.

You usually use your thumb, index finger, ring finger and pinky finger to play minor 7th chords. When using your left hand, your pinky finger plays the root note. When using your right hand, your thumb plays the root note.

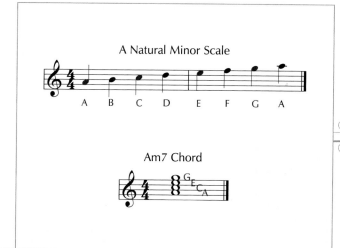

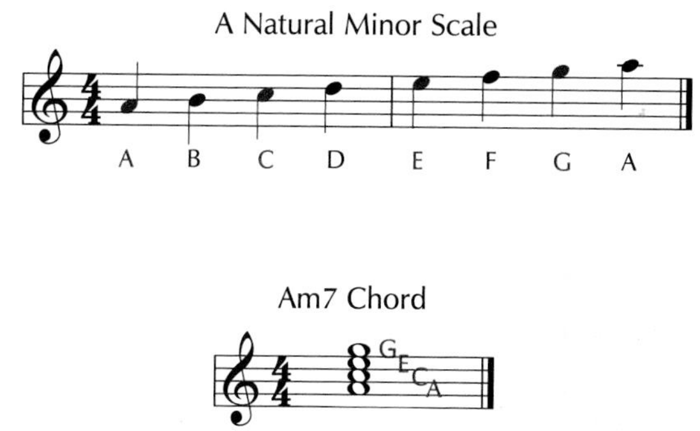

- A minor 7th chord consists of four notes that you play at the same time to produce a mellow sound.
- Minor 7th chords are usually written as a letter name followed by m7 (Am7), min7 (Amin7) or -7 (A-7).
- In written music, a minor 7th chord is usually indicated as four notes stacked on top of each other on the staff.
- A minor 7th chord consists of the first (root), third, fifth and seventh notes of a natural minor scale. For example, the A minor 7th chord (Am7), consists of the first (A), third (C), fifth (E) and seventh (G) notes of the A natural minor scale.

Note: For information on natural minor scales, see page 94.

- To play a minor 7th chord, use the thumb, index, ring and pinky fingers of your left or right hand to press the keys for the four notes of the chord at the same time.
- You can play a minor 7th chord at any location on the keyboard, since the notes that make up a chord can be found in many locations. Where you play a chord depends on how high or low you want the chord to sound.

playing 6th chords

6th chords are characterized by the full, jazzy sounds they produce and are commonly used in big band swing music. A 6th chord is usually written as a letter name followed by the number 6, such as C6. A 6th chord consists of four notes—the first, third, fifth and sixth notes of a major scale. For example, the C6 chord consists of the first (C), third (E), fifth (G) and sixth (A) notes of the C major scale. A scale is a series of related notes arranged in order of pitch.

You use your thumb, index finger, ring finger and pinky finger to play a 6th chord. You play all the notes in the chord at the same time. When you use your right hand, your thumb plays the first (root) note and your pinky finger plays the top note. When you use your left hand, your pinky finger plays the first (root) note and your thumb plays the top note.

The notes of a 6th chord can be found in many locations on the keyboard. Where you play the 6th chord depends on how high or low you want the chord to sound.

Understanding 6th Chords

C Major Scale

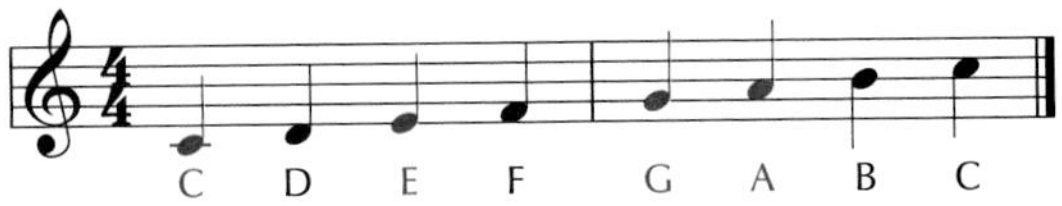

C6 Chord

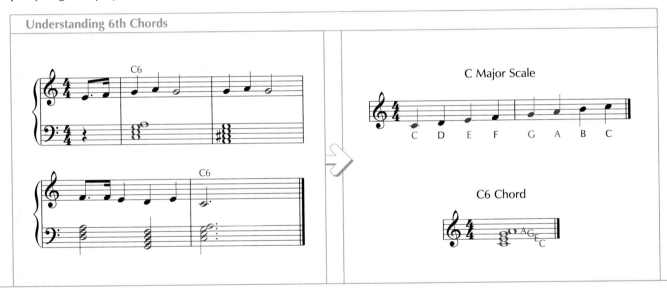

- A 6th chord consists of four notes that you play at the same time to produce a full, jazzy sound.
- In written music, a 6th chord is usually indicated as four notes stacked on top of each other on the staff.

- 6th chords are usually written as a letter name followed by the number 6, such as C6.

- A 6th chord consists of the first (root), third, fifth and sixth notes of a major scale.

Note: A scale is a series of notes that you play in a specific order. For more information on major scales, see page 90.

- For example, the C6 chord consists of the first (C), third (E), fifth (G) and sixth (A) notes of the C major scale.

Tip

How can I quickly find the top note for a 6th chord?

If you know how to play the corresponding major chord, you simply add the note that is one whole step above the top note of the major chord. For example, if you know the notes of a C major chord are C, E and G, then you can quickly create a 6th chord by adding the note one whole step above G, which is A. So, you can play C6 with the notes C, E, G and A.

Can I play a minor 6th chord?

Yes. A minor 6th chord is indicated by a letter name followed by m6, such as Cm6. To play a minor 6th chord, play the 6th chord, except lower the 3rd note of the scale on which the chord is based by a half step. For example, to play the Cm6 chord, play C, E♭, G and A, instead of C, E, G and A.

Play a 6th Chord With Your Right Hand

- You can play a 6th chord at any location on the keyboard, since the notes that make up a chord can be found in many locations. Where you play a chord depends on how high or low you want the chord to sound.

1 To play a 6th chord with your right hand, rest your thumb on the key for the first (root) note of the chord you want to play.

2 Rest your index finger on the key for the second note of the chord.

3 Rest your ring finger on the key for the third note of the chord.

4 Rest your pinky finger on the key for the top note of the chord.

5 Press all four keys at the same time to play the chord.

Play a 6th Chord With Your Left Hand

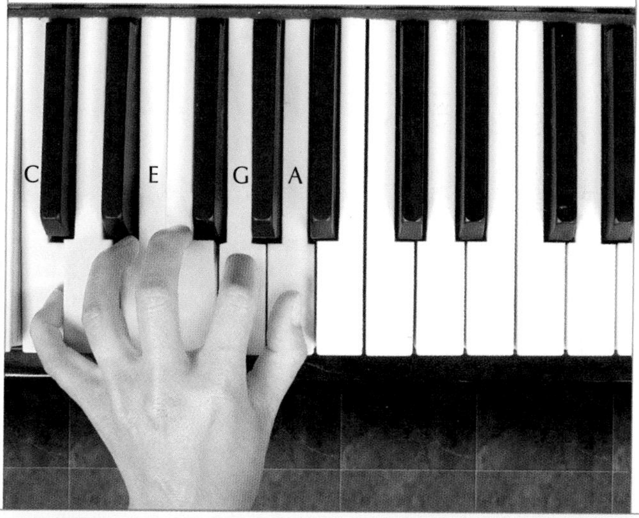

- When your right hand is playing a melody, you can play 6th chords with your left hand to provide accompaniment.

1 To play a 6th chord with your left hand, rest your pinky finger on the key for the first (root) note of the chord you want to play.

2 Rest your ring finger on the key for the second note of the chord.

3 Rest your index finger on the key for the third note of the chord.

4 Rest your thumb on the key for the top note of the chord.

5 Press all four keys at the same time to play the chord.

playing 6th chords

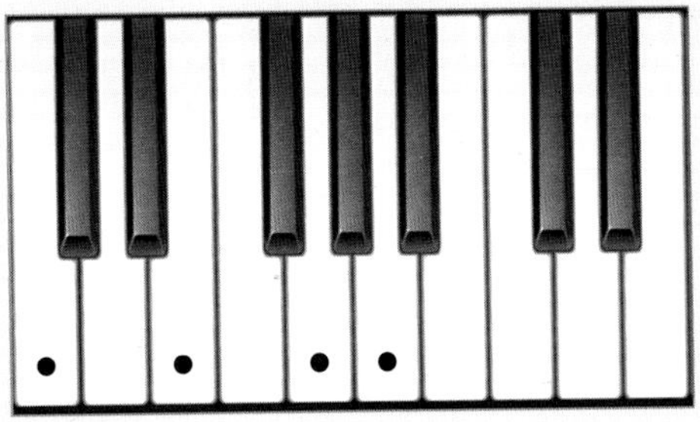

C6 Chord

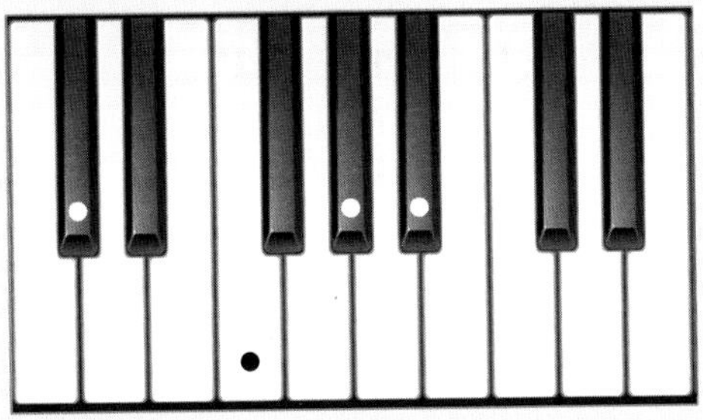

D♭6 Chord
Also known as C♯6 Chord

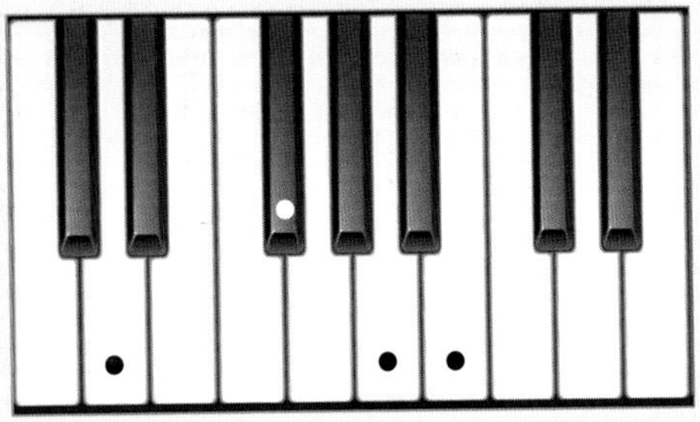

D6 Chord

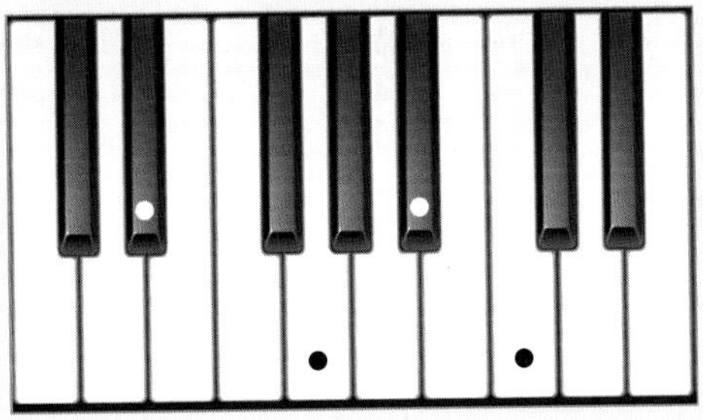

E♭6 Chord

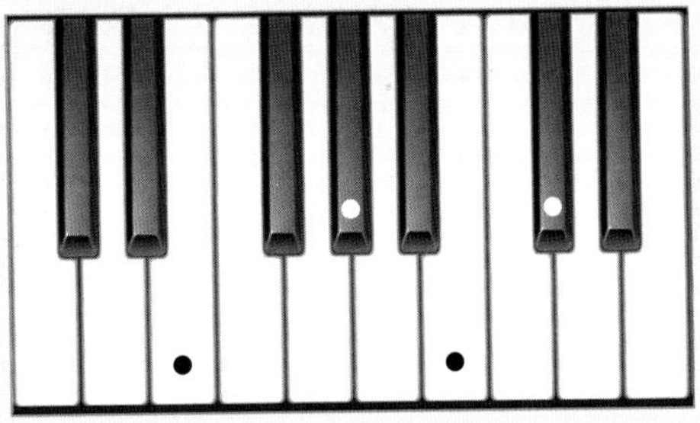

E6 Chord

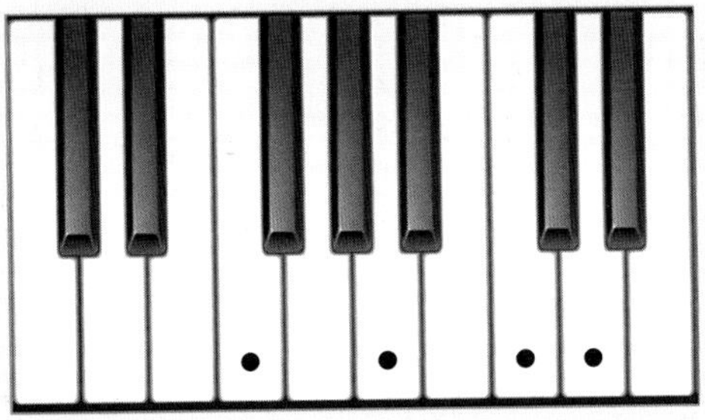

F6 Chord

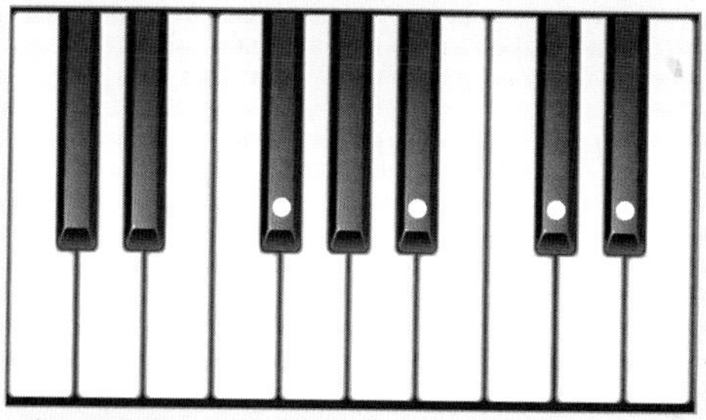

F♯6 Chord
Also known as G♭6 Chord

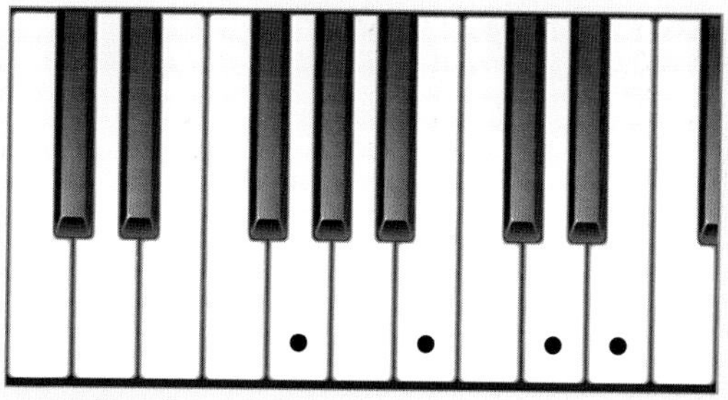

G6 Chord

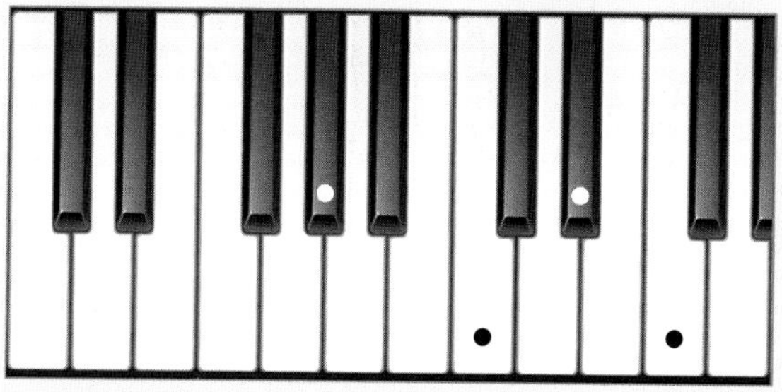

A♭6 Chord

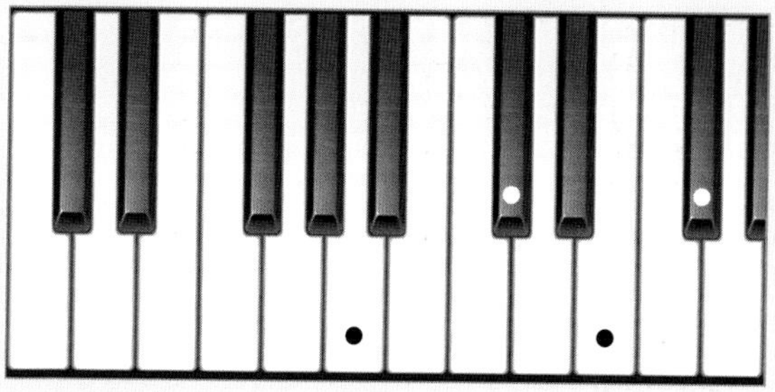

A6 Chord

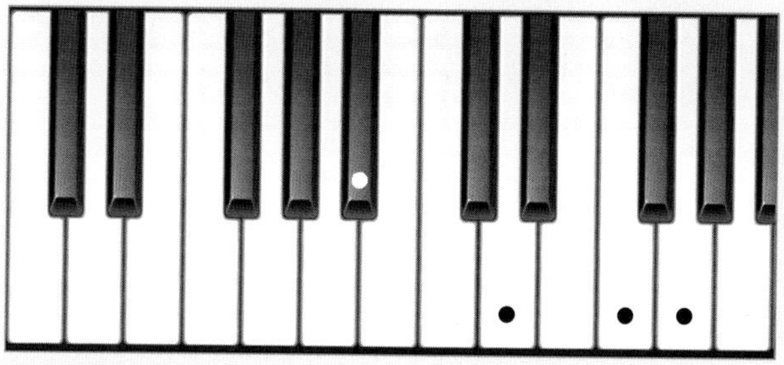

B♭6 Chord

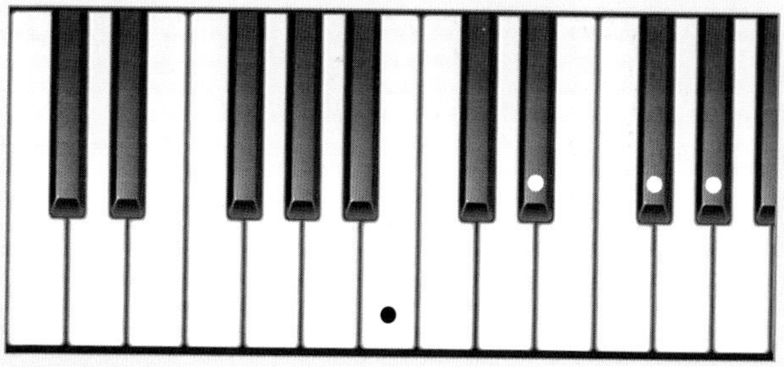

B6 Chord

playing 9th chords

A 9th chord produces a textured sound that is found in many jazz and pop songs. A 9th chord is usually written as a letter name followed by the number 9, such as C9.

A 9th chord consists of five notes—the first (root), third, fifth, seventh and ninth notes of a major scale which is played over two octaves. The seventh note of the major scale is lowered by one half step. For example, to play the C9 chord, you play the first (C), third (E), fifth (G), lowered seventh (B♭) and ninth (D) notes of the C major scale together.

A major scale is a series of notes played in a specific order. An octave refers to the distance between two notes with the same letter name on the keyboard.

Many people find it awkward to play all five notes of the chord with one hand, so often one note is played with one hand and the rest of the notes are played with the other. You will usually see 9th chords written with four notes stacked in one clef and the fifth note in the other clef, indicating which hand you use to play each note.

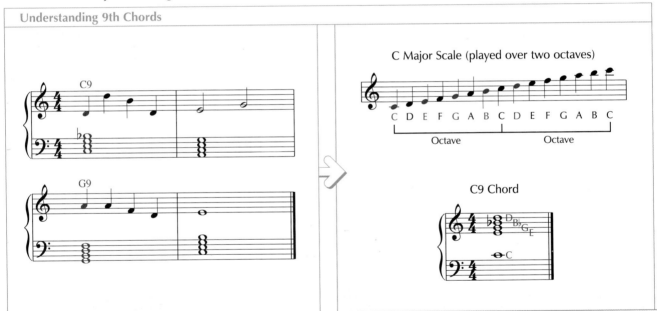

Understanding 9th Chords

C Major Scale (played over two octaves)

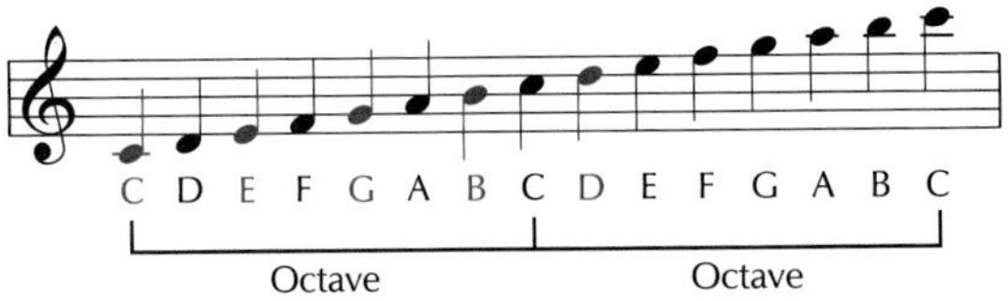

C9 Chord

- A 9th chord consists of five notes that you play at the same time, usually with both hands. 9th chords are often found in jazz and pop music.
- 9th chords are usually labeled as a letter name followed by the number 9, such as C9.
- In written music, a 9th chord is usually indicated as four notes stacked on top of each other on one staff, with a fifth note appearing on the other staff.
- A 9th chord consists of the first (root), third, fifth, seventh and ninth notes of a major scale which is played over two octaves. The seventh note of the major scale is lowered by one half step.

Note: A scale is a series of notes that you play in a specific order. For more information on major scales, see page 90.

- For example, the C9 chord consists of the first (C), third (E), fifth (G), seventh (B) and ninth (D) notes of the C major scale, except the seventh note (B) is lowered by one half step (B♭).

Tip

Is there a variation of the 9th chord?

Yes. You can play a major 9th chord, which is labeled as a letter name followed by maj9, such as Cmaj9. To play a major 9th chord, play the 9th chord, but do not lower the fourth note of the chord by one half step. For example, the notes in a Cmaj9 chord are C, E, G, B and D.

Is there a minor 9th chord?

Yes. Minor 9th chords are labeled as a letter name followed by m9, such as Cm9. To play a minor 9th chord, play the 9th chord, but lower the second note of the chord by one half step. For example, the notes in a Cm9 chord are C, E♭, G, B♭ and D.

Is there an easier way to play 9th chords?

If you find it difficult to play the 9th chord, you can play the top (9th) note at the next lower location on the keyboard. For example, when playing a C9 chord, you can lower the top note (D) and play the notes as C, D, E, G and B♭ instead of C, E, G, B♭ and D. This produces the same sound, but requires your hand to stretch less.

Play a 9th Chord Mostly With Your Right Hand

- When playing a 9th chord, you will need to use both hands since it would be difficult to reach all the notes of a chord with the fingers of one hand.

1 To play a 9th chord mostly with your right hand, rest your left thumb on the key for the first (root) note of the chord you want to play.

2 Rest your right thumb, index, ring and pinky fingers on the keys for the second, third, fourth and fifth notes of the chord.

3 Press all five keys at the same time to play the chord.

Play a 9th Chord Mostly With Your Left Hand

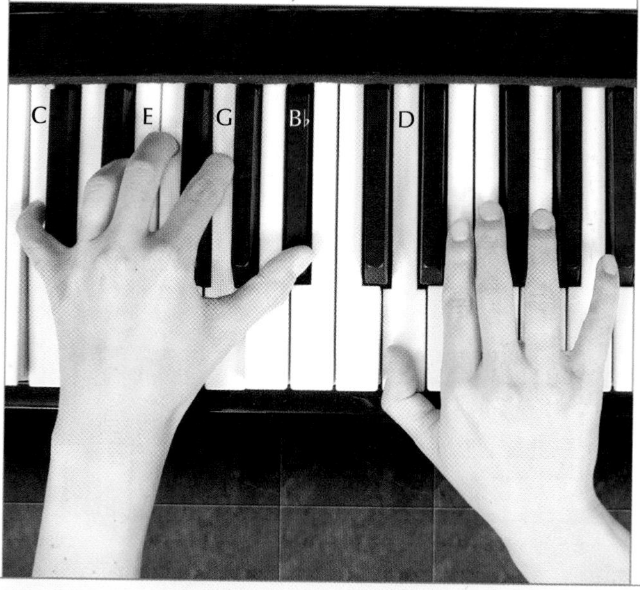

1 To play a 9th chord mostly with your left hand, rest your left pinky, ring and index fingers on the keys for the first (root), second and third notes of the chord you want to play.

2 Rest your left thumb on the key for the fourth note of the chord.

3 Rest your right thumb on the key for the fifth note of the chord.

4 Press all five keys at the same time to play the chord.

playing 9th chords

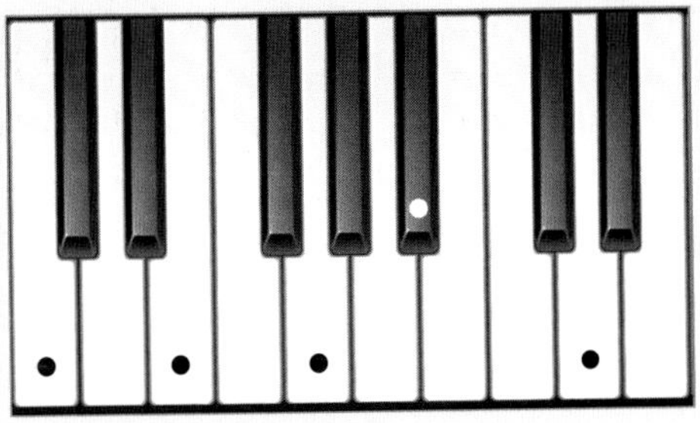

C9 Chord

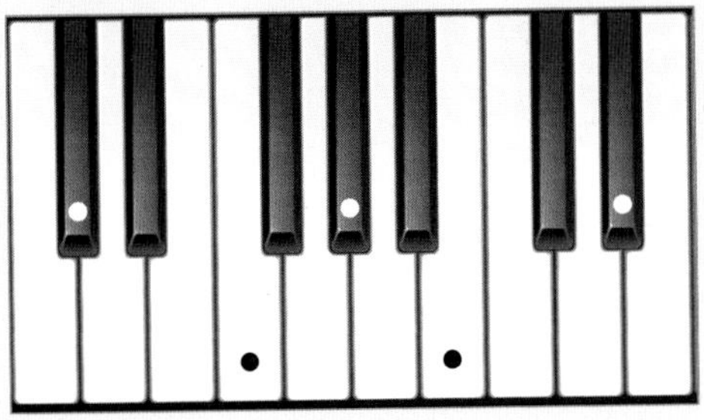

D♭9 Chord
Also known as C♯9 Chord

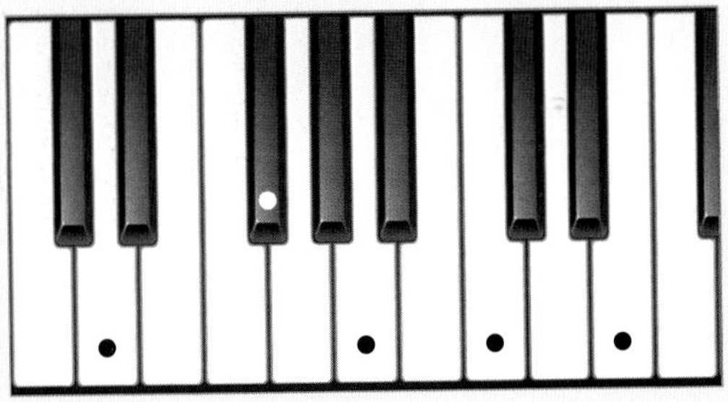

D9 Chord

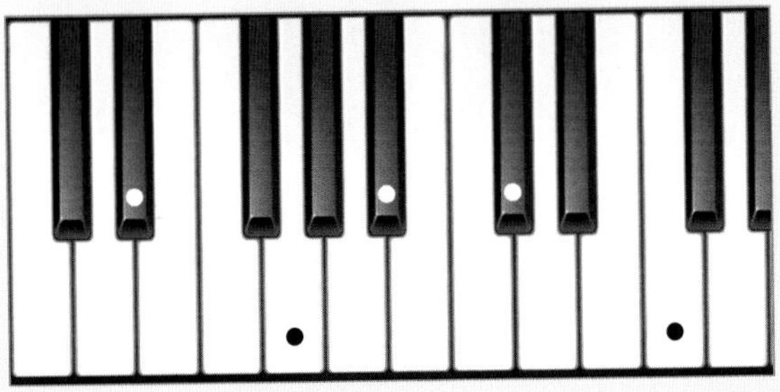

E♭9 Chord

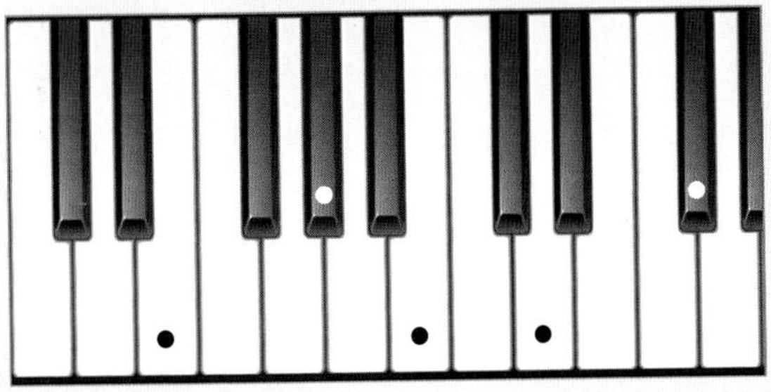

E9 Chord

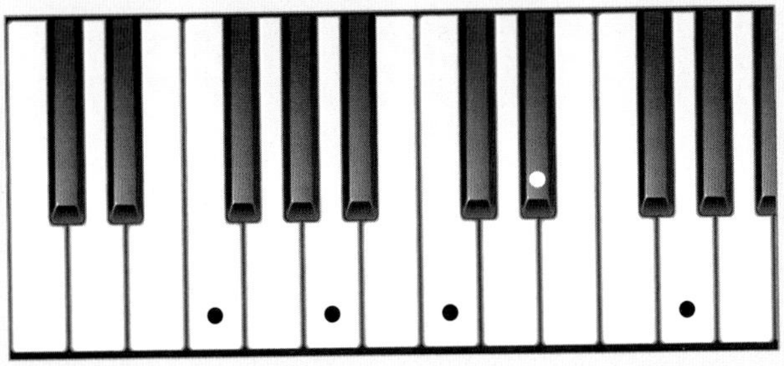

F9 Chord

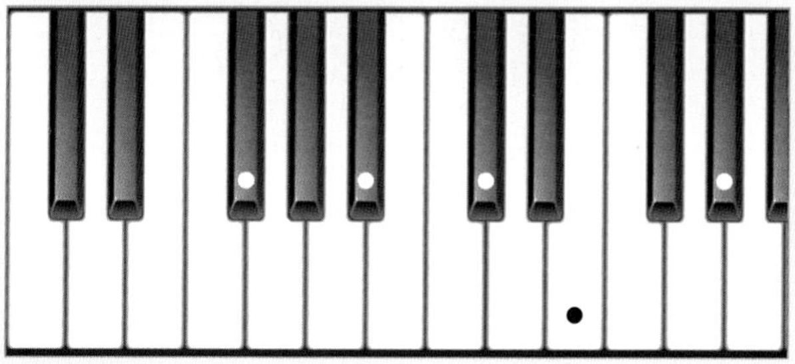

F♯9 Chord
Also known as G♭9 Chord

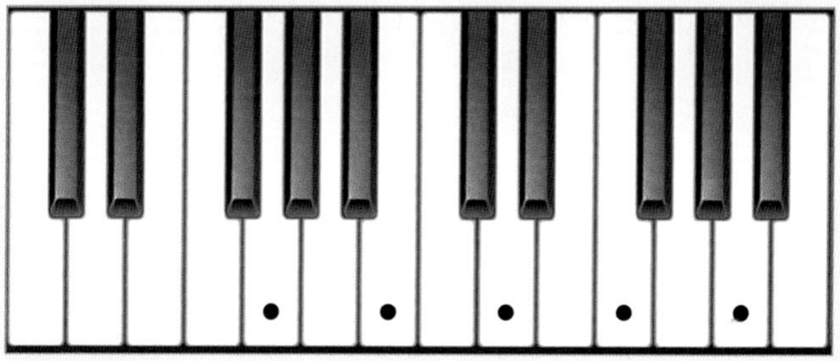

G9 Chord

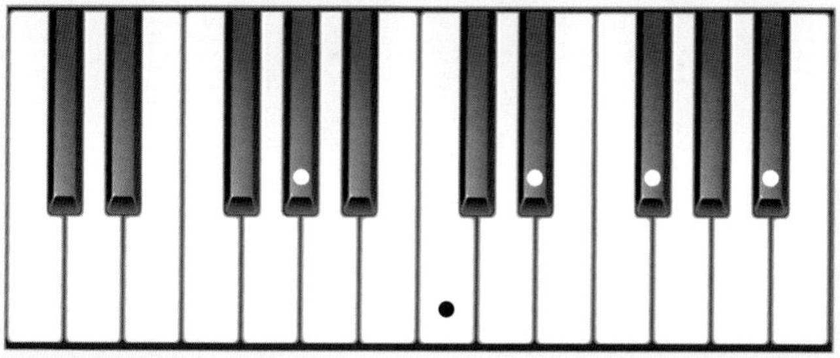

A♭9 Chord

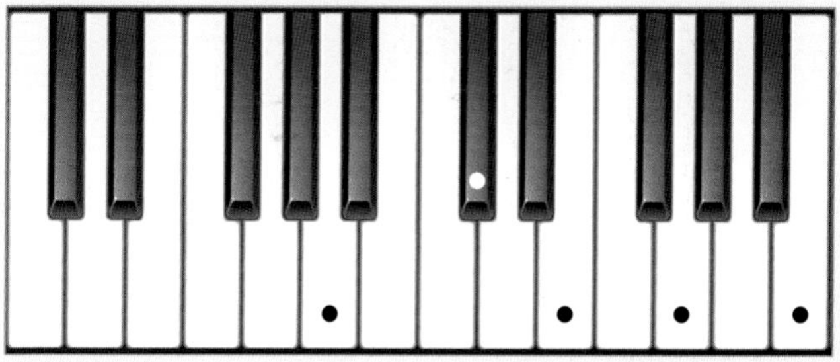

A9 Chord

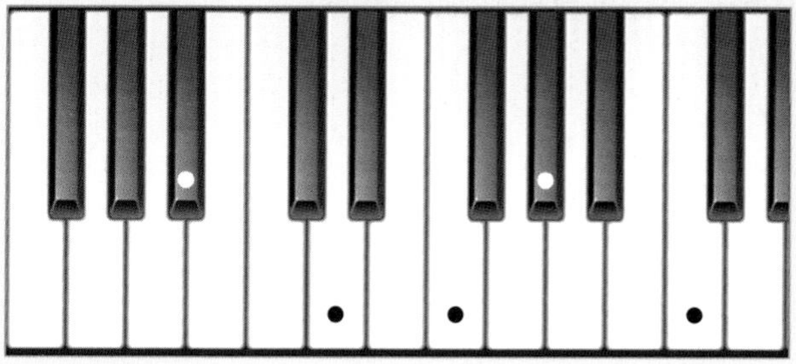

B♭9 Chord

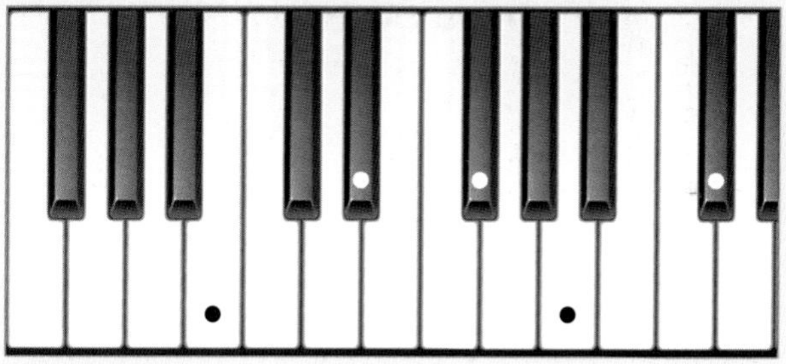

B9 Chord

playing augmented chords

An augmented chord is a variation of a major chord that produces a harsh, or jarring, sound. Augmented chords can be used to create an uneasy or unsettled feeling in music.

An augmented chord consists of the first (root) and third notes of a major scale, plus the fifth note of the major scale, which has been raised by a half step. For example, the C augmented chord consists of the first (C) and third (E) notes of the C major scale, plus the fifth note of the scale raised by a half step (G♯).

Therefore, playing an augmented chord is the same as playing the corresponding major chord, except that you raise the top note of the chord by a half step. An augmented chord is usually written as a letter name followed by a plus sign (C+), aug (Caug) or ♯5 (C♯5).

The notes of an augmented chord can be found in many locations on the keyboard. Where you play an augmented chord depends on how high or low you want the chord to sound.

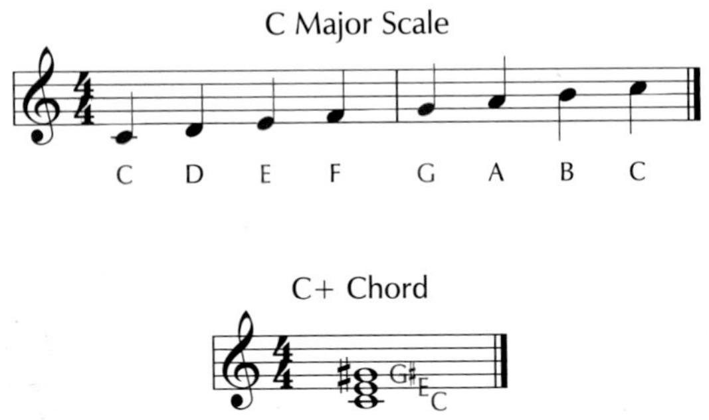

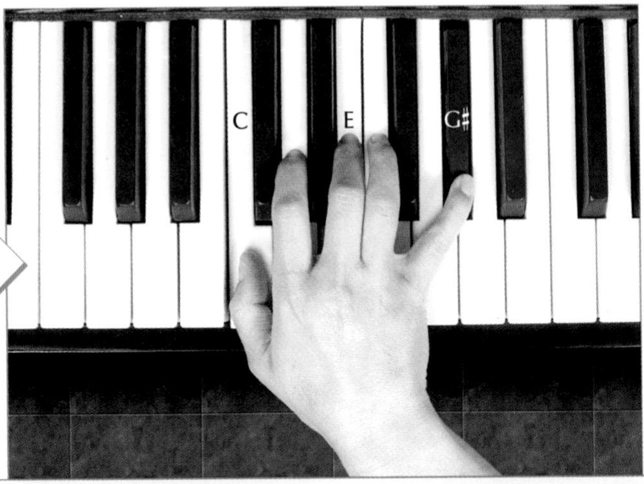

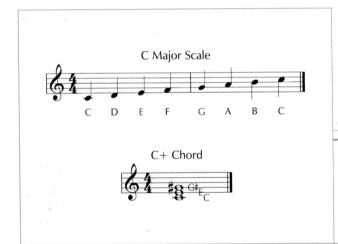

- An augmented chord consists of three notes that you play at the same time to produce a harsh, or jarring, sound.
- Augmented chords are usually written as a letter name followed by a plus sign (C+), aug (Caug) or ♯5 (C♯5).
- In written music, an augmented chord is usually indicated as three notes stacked on top of each other on the staff.
- An augmented chord consists of the first (root) and third notes of a major scale, plus the fifth note of the major scale, which has been raised by one half step. For example, the C augmented chord consists of the first (C) and third (E) notes of the C major scale, plus the fifth note of the scale raised by one half step (G♯).

Note: For information on major scales, see page 90.

- To play an augmented chord, use the thumb, middle and pinky fingers of your right or left hand to press the keys for the three notes of the chord at the same time.
- You can play an augmented chord at any location on the keyboard, since the notes that make up a chord can be found in many locations. Where you play a chord depends on how high or low you want the chord to sound.

playing diminished chords

A diminished chord is a variation of a minor chord that produces a harsh, or jarring, sound. Diminished chords are often used to create a feeling of tension or uneasiness in music. Just think of the music played in the background of a scary movie.

A diminished chord is usually written as a letter name followed by "dim" or by the degree symbol (A°). A diminished chord consists of three notes—the first (root), third and fifth notes of a minor scale, with the fifth note of the scale lowered by a half step. For example, Adim consists of the first (A) and third (C) notes of the A minor scale, plus the fifth note of the scale lowered by a half step (E♭). Therefore, playing a diminished chord is the same as playing the corresponding minor chord, except that you lower the top note of the chord by a half step.

When playing a diminished chord with your right hand, you use your thumb, middle finger and pinky finger. When playing a diminished chord with your left hand, you use your pinky finger, middle finger and thumb.

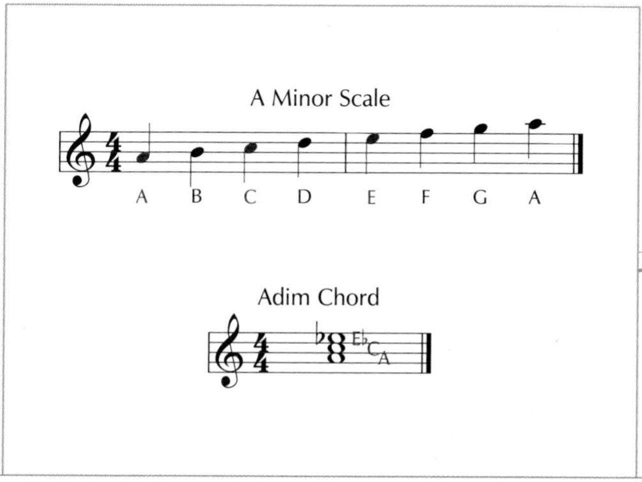

- A diminished chord consists of three notes that you play at the same time to produce a harsh, or jarring, sound.
- Diminished chords are usually labelled as a letter name followed by "dim" (Adim) or the degree symbol (A°).
- In written music, a diminished chord is usually indicated as three notes stacked on top of each other on the staff.

- A diminished chord consists of the first (root) and third notes of a minor scale, plus the fifth note of the minor scale, which has been lowered by one half step. For example, the A diminished chord consists of the first (A) and third (C) notes of the A minor scale, plus the fifth note of the scale lowered by one half step (E♭).

Note: For information on minor scales, see page 94.

- To play a diminished chord, use the thumb, middle and pinky fingers of your right hand or the pinky finger, middle finger and thumb of your left hand to press the keys for the three notes of the chord at the same time.

- You can play a diminished chord at any location on the keyboard, since the notes that make up a chord can be found in many locations. Where you play a chord depends on how high or low you want the chord to sound.

playing suspended chords

Suspended chords, which are popular in rock, jazz and blues music, create an unresolved sound that leaves you waiting for the notes or chords that follow. Two basic types of suspended chords are suspended two chords and suspended four chords. Suspended two chords are usually written as a letter name followed by sus2 or 2, such as Csus2 or C2.

A suspended two chord consists of three notes—the first (root), second and fifth notes of a major or minor scale. For example, to play a Csus2 chord, you play the first (C), second (D) and fifth (G) notes of the C major or C minor scale. A scale is a series of notes that you play in a specific order.

You can play suspended two chords anywhere on the keyboard, since the notes that make up a chord appear in many locations. Where you play a chord depends on how high or low you want the chord to sound.

When playing suspended two chords with your right hand, use your thumb, index finger and pinky finger to press the keys. When playing suspended two chords with your left hand, use your pinky finger, ring finger and thumb to press the keys.

C Major Scale

C Minor Scale

C Suspended Two (Csus2) Chord

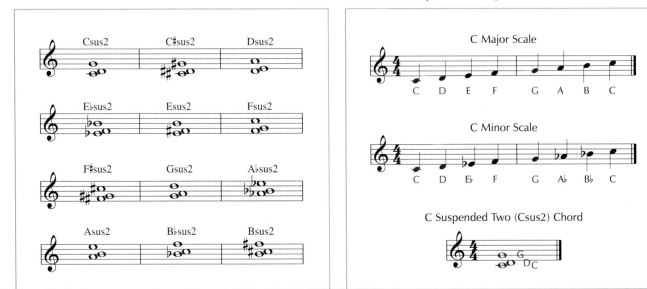

Understanding Suspended Chords

- A suspended chord usually consists of three notes that you play at the same time to produce a harsh sound. Suspended chords are also called sus chords.
- In written music, a suspended chord is usually indicated as three notes stacked on top of each other on the staff.
- There are two basic types of suspended chords—suspended two (sus2) chords and suspended four (sus4) chords. This example shows the 12 suspended two chords.

Suspended Two (sus2) Chords

- Suspended two chords are usually written as a letter name followed by sus2 or 2, such as Csus2 or C2.
- A suspended two chord consists of the first (root), second and fifth notes of a major or minor scale.

Note: A scale is a series of notes that you play in a specific order. For more information on major and minor scales, see pages 90 and 94.

- For example, the C suspended two (Csus2) chord consists of the first (C), second (D) and fifth (G) notes of the C major or C minor scale.

Tip

Is there another way that I can determine the notes in a suspended two chord?

Yes. A suspended two chord consists of the same notes as a major chord, except the middle note of the major chord is lowered by one whole step. A suspended two chord also consists of the same notes as a minor chord, except the middle note of the minor chord is lowered by one half step. For information on whole steps and half steps, see page 89.

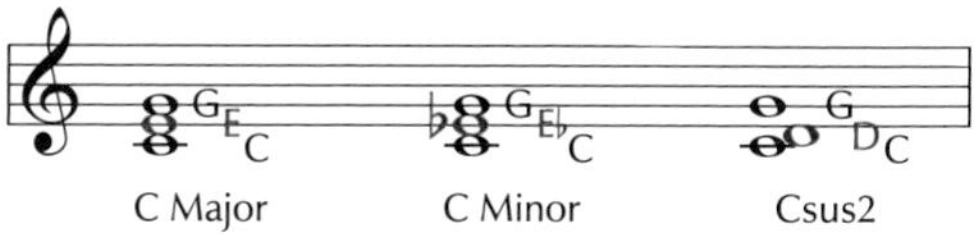

Are there different ways to play suspended chords?

Yes. You can play suspended chords as solid chords or broken chords. To play a solid suspended chord, you play all the notes in a suspended chord at the same time. To play a broken suspended chord, you play each note in a suspended chord separately, one after the other.

- You can play a suspended two chord at any location on the keyboard since the notes that make up a suspended two chord can be found in many locations. Where you play a suspended two chord depends on how high or low you want the chord to sound.

- To play a suspended two chord with your right hand, use your thumb, index finger and pinky finger to press the keys for the three notes of the chord at the same time.

- To play a suspended two chord with your left hand, use your pinky finger, ring finger and thumb to press the keys for the three notes of the chord at the same time.

- In this example of written music, play the notes as shown to practice playing suspended two chords.

- In music, you will commonly switch between a suspended two chord and a major or minor chord. For example, a musical piece may switch between the C suspended two (Csus2) chord and the C major or C minor chord.

CONTINUED...

playing suspended chords *(continued)*

Suspended four chords, which produce harsh sounds, are usually written as a letter name followed by sus4 or sus, such as Csus4 or Csus.

Suspended four chords consist of three notes—the first (root), fourth and fifth notes of a major or minor scale. For example, to play a Csus4 chord, you play the first (C), fourth (F) and fifth (G) notes of the C major or C minor scale. A scale is a series of notes that you play in a specific order.

You can play suspended four chords anywhere on the keyboard, since the notes that make up a chord appear in many locations. Where you play a chord depends on how high or low you want the chord to sound.

When playing suspended four chords with your right hand, use your thumb, ring finger and pinky finger to press the keys. When playing suspended four chords with your left hand, use your pinky finger, index finger and thumb to press the keys.

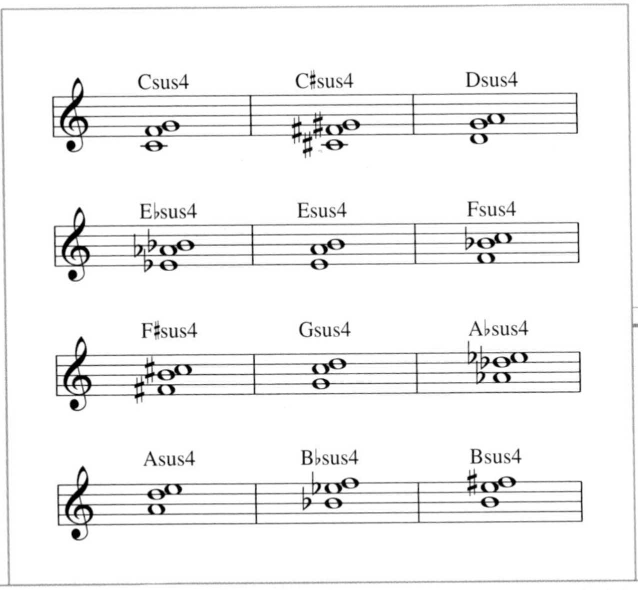

Suspended Four (sus4) Chords

- A suspended four chord usually consists of three notes that you play at the same time to produce a harsh sound.
- In written music, a suspended four chord is usually indicated as three notes stacked on top of each other on the staff. This example shows the 12 suspended four chords.
- Suspended four chords are usually written as a letter name followed by sus4 or sus, such as Csus4 or Csus.
- A suspended four chord consists of the first (root), fourth and fifth notes of a major or minor scale.

Note: A scale is a series of notes that you play in a specific order. For more information on major and minor scales, see pages 90 and 94.

- For example, the C suspended four (Csus4) chord consists of the first (C), fourth (F) and fifth (G) notes of the C major or C minor scale.

Tip

Is there another way to determine the notes in a suspended four chord?

Yes. A suspended four chord contains the same notes as a major chord, except the middle note of the major chord is raised one half step. A suspended four chord also contains the same notes as a minor chord, except the middle note of the minor chord is raised one whole step. For information on whole steps and half steps, see page 89.

C Major C Minor Csus4

Can I change 7th chords to suspended chords?

Yes. A 7th suspended (7sus) chord contains the same notes as a dominant 7th chord, except the second note of the dominant 7th chord is raised one half step. A 7th suspended chord also contains the same notes as a minor 7th chord, except the second note of the minor 7th chord is raised one whole step.

C Dominant 7th C Minor 7th C7sus

- You can play a suspended four chord at any location on the keyboard since the notes that make up a suspended four chord can be found in many locations. Where you play a suspended four chord depends on how high or low you want the chord to sound.

1 To play a suspended four chord with your right hand, use your thumb, ring finger and pinky finger to press the keys for the three notes of the chord at the same time.

2 To play a suspended four chord with your left hand, use your pinky finger, index finger and thumb to press the keys for the three notes of the chord at the same time.

- In this example, play the notes as shown to practice playing suspended four chords.

- In music, you will commonly switch between a suspended four chord and a major or minor chord. For example, a musical piece may switch between the C suspended four (Csus4) chord and the C major or C minor chord.

playing broken chords

Chords are often played as solid, or block chords, which means you play all the notes of the chord at the same time. However, you can choose to play each note of the chord separately in any order. This is called a broken chord.

There are many different ways to play broken chords. You can play one note at a time or play combinations of some of the notes in the chords. For example, you can play the root note of a chord separately and then play the top notes together. Playing broken chords by combining some of the notes is useful for creating rhythmic patterns in your music and enhancing music with distinctive rhythms, such as waltzes or polkas.

Broken chords are commonly played with the left hand as accompaniment while the right hand plays melody. When playing broken chords, you use the same fingers to play the notes as you would use to play all the notes of the chord together.

Play All Notes Separately

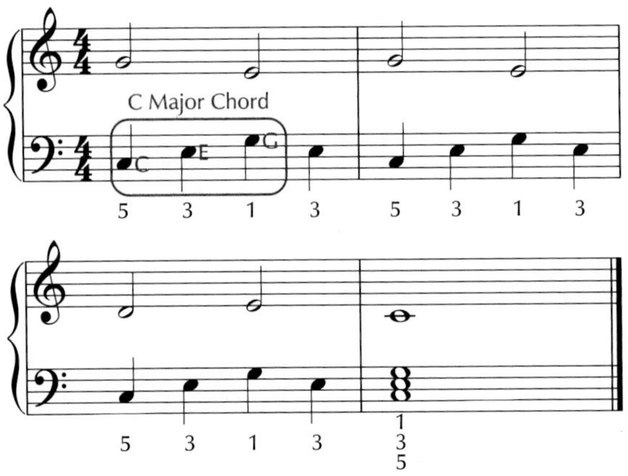

Play Some Notes Separately

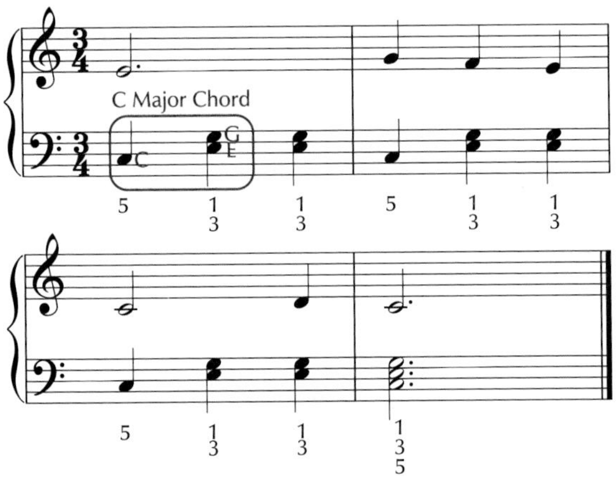

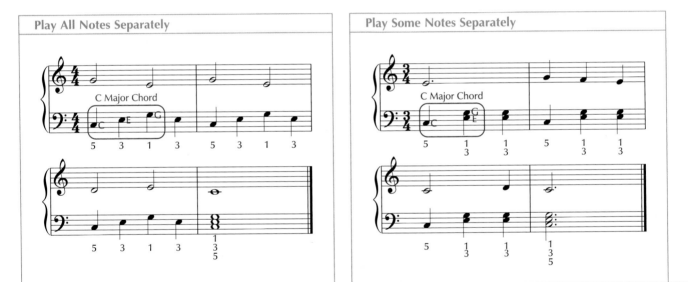

- You can play each note of a chord separately, which is known as playing a broken chord. For example, to play the C major chord, you can press the C key, then press the E key and then press the G key.
- In written music, the composer will indicate which order you should play the notes.
- In this example of written music, play the notes as shown to practice playing broken chords.
- Make sure you observe the numbers above or below the notes to help you determine which finger to use for each note. Your fingers are numbered from 1 to 5—thumb (1), index (2), middle (3), ring (4) and pinky (5) finger.
- When playing a broken chord, you can play some of the notes of the chord together. For example, to play the C major chord, you can press the C key and then press the E and G keys at the same time.
- In this example of written music, play the notes as shown to practice playing broken chords that combine some of the notes of each chord.
- Make sure you observe the numbers above or below the notes to help you determine which finger to use for each note. Your fingers are numbered from 1 to 5—thumb (1), index (2), middle (3), ring (4) and pinky (5) finger.

playing arpeggios

Chords can be played in a solid form, which means you play all the notes of a chord at the same time, or in a broken form, which means you can play each note of a chord separately. To create an interesting effect based on the broken chord, you can play a chord as an arpeggio.

To play a chord as an arpeggio, you play each note of the chord separately, from lowest to highest or highest to lowest. Then play some or all of the notes again in the same order at the next higher or lower location on the keyboard.

Arpeggios are commonly played with the left hand as accompaniment while the right hand plays melody. Learning to play arpeggios gives you more chord playing options when you are using a lead sheet to play a song. A lead sheet will often not provide written music to accompany the melody, only the name of the chord that should be played. For more information on lead sheets, see page 26.

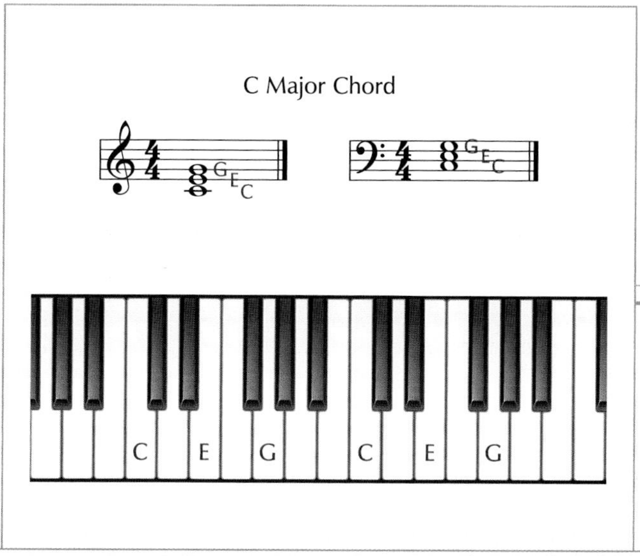

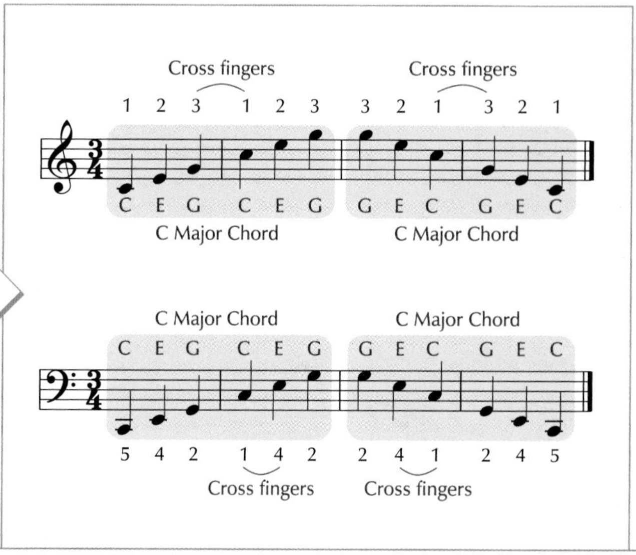

- To play a chord as an arpeggio, you play each note of the chord separately, from lowest to highest. You then play some or all of the same notes in the same order at the next higher location on the keyboard.
- For example, to play the C major chord as an arpeggio, press the C, E, then G keys. Then press the same keys in the same order at the next higher location on the keyboard.
- You can also play an arpeggio by playing the notes from highest to lowest and then playing some or all of the same notes again at the next lower location on the keyboard.
- In these examples of written music, play the notes as shown to practice playing a chord as an arpeggio. Cross your fingers over or under when needed.
- In the first example, use your right hand to play the notes of the chord from lowest to highest, then highest to lowest.
- In the second example, use your left hand to play the notes of the chord from lowest to highest, then highest to lowest.
- Make sure you observe the numbers above or below the notes to help you determine which finger to use for each note. Your fingers are numbered from 1 to 5—thumb (1), index (2), middle (3), ring (4) and pinky (5) finger.

playing three-note chord inversions

Chord inversions involve rearranging the notes of a chord. Playing the notes of a chord in different orders allows you to minimize the distance your hand has to move from one chord to the next on the keyboard.

The number of ways you can play a chord depends on the number of notes in the chord. For example, three-note chords, such as major chords, have three possible positions—root position, first inversion and second inversion.

A three-note chord in root position has the root note of the chord as the bottom (lowest) note. For example, the notes of the C major chord are C, E and G in root position.

In first inversion, the chord's original middle note becomes the bottom note. For example, the notes of the C major chord are E, G and C in first inversion.

In second inversion, the chord's original top note becomes the bottom note. For example, the notes of the C major chord are G, C and E in second inversion.

For all of the three-note chords you have learned, you should practice the different positions with your left and right hand until you are comfortable playing them smoothly.

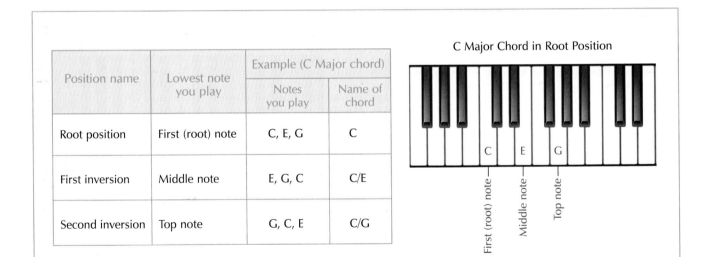

Position name	Lowest note you play	Example (C Major chord)	
		Notes you play	Name of chord
Root position	First (root) note	C, E, G	C
First inversion	Middle note	E, G, C	C/E
Second inversion	Top note	G, C, E	C/G

C Major Chord in Root Position

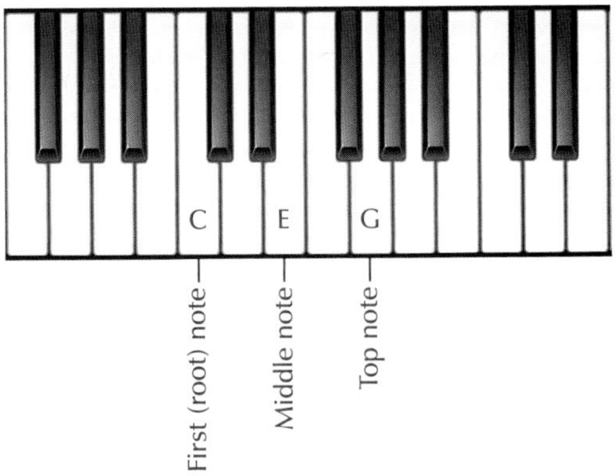

- When a chord consists of three notes, you can play the notes of the chord in three different orders, which include the root position, first inversion and second inversion.

  Note: Three-note chords include major, minor, augmented, diminished and suspended chords.

- Changing the order of the notes in a chord allows you to move easily from one chord to another without moving your hand far along the keyboard.

- In written music, a specific chord inversion is often indicated by a chord name followed by a slash (/). For example, C/E indicates that you play the C major chord with E as the lowest note.

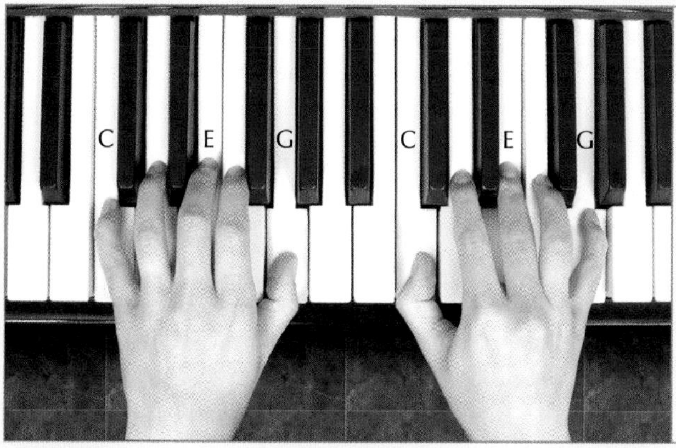

Root Position

1 To play a three-note chord in root position with your left or right hand, use your thumb, middle finger and pinky finger to press the keys for the notes of the chord.

- In this example, we play the C major chord in root position, which includes the C, E and G keys.

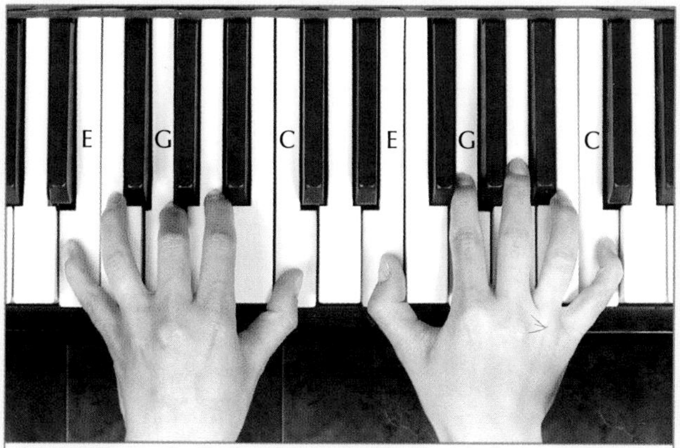

First Inversion

1 To play a three-note chord in first inversion with your left hand, use your pinky finger, middle finger and thumb to press the keys for the notes of the chord.

2 To play a three-note chord in first inversion with your right hand, use your thumb, index finger and pinky finger to press the keys for the notes of the chord.

- In this example, we play the C major chord in first inversion, which includes the E, G and C keys.

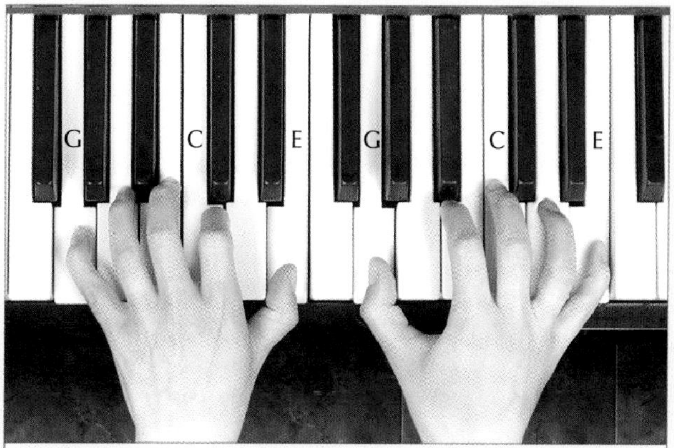

Second Inversion

1 To play a three-note chord in second inversion with your left hand, use your pinky finger, index finger and thumb to press the keys for the notes of the chord.

2 To play a three-note chord in second inversion with your right hand, use your thumb, middle finger and pinky finger to press the keys for the notes of the chord.

- In this example, we play the C major chord in second inversion, which includes the G, C and E keys.

playing four-note chord inversions

Four-note chord inversions involve rearranging the notes in chords that have four notes. Inversions allow you to play chords closer together so you can easily move from one chord to another without having to move your hand far along the keyboard.

Four-note chords include major and minor 6th chords as well as dominant, major and minor 7th chords. Although 9th chords are five-note chords, they follow the same inversion rules as four-note chords because you play one note of a 9th chord with one hand and the other four notes with the other hand. You can invert the four notes for the 9th chord that you play with one hand.

The number of possible inversions for a chord depends on the number of notes in the chord. For four-note chords, there are four possible arrangements—root position, first inversion, second inversion and third inversion. To be able to play chord inversions easily, you should practice all the positions for all the four-note chords until you become comfortable playing the chords.

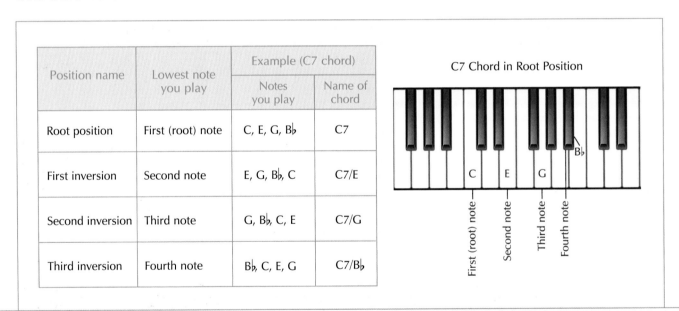

Position name	Lowest note you play	Example (C7 chord)	
		Notes you play	Name of chord
Root position	First (root) note	C, E, G, B♭	C7
First inversion	Second note	E, G, B♭, C	C7/E
Second inversion	Third note	G, B♭, C, E	C7/G
Third inversion	Fourth note	B♭, C, E, G	C7/B♭

C7 Chord in Root Position

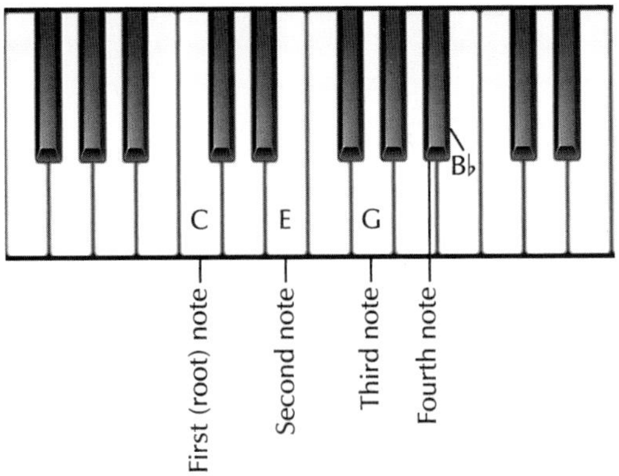

- When a chord consists of four notes, you can play the notes of the chord in four different orders, which include the root position, first inversion, second inversion and third inversion.

  Note: Four-note chords include dominant, major and minor 7th chords as well as major and minor 6th chords.

- Changing the order of the notes in a chord allows you to move easily from one chord to another without moving your hand far along the keyboard.

- In written music, a specific chord inversion is often indicated by a chord name followed by a slash (/) and the lowest note you play for the chord. For example, C7/E indicates that you play the C7 chord, with E as the lowest note.

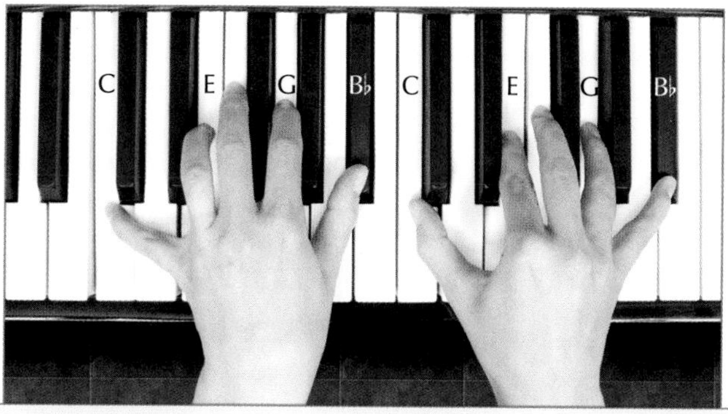

Root Position

1 To play a four-note chord in root position with your left or right hand, use your thumb, index finger, ring finger and pinky finger to press the keys for the notes of the chord.

- In this example, we play the C7 chord in root position, which includes the C, E, G and B♭ keys.

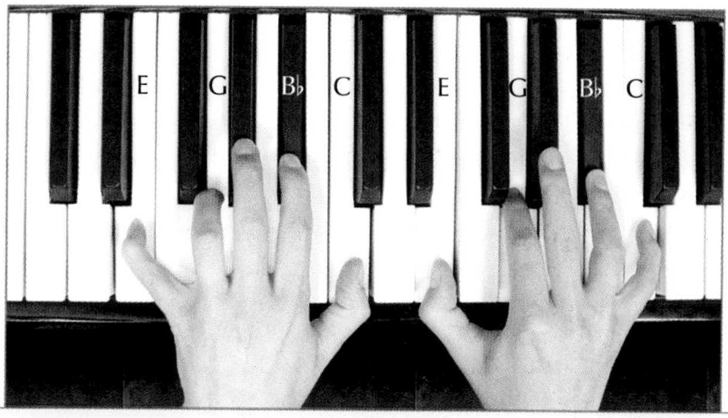

First Inversion

1 To play a four-note chord in first inversion with your left or right hand, use your thumb, index finger, ring finger and pinky finger to press the keys for the notes of the chord.

- In this example, we play the C7 chord in first inversion, which includes the E, G, B♭ and C keys.

Note: When playing a major or minor 6th chord in first inversion, use your middle finger instead of your ring finger.

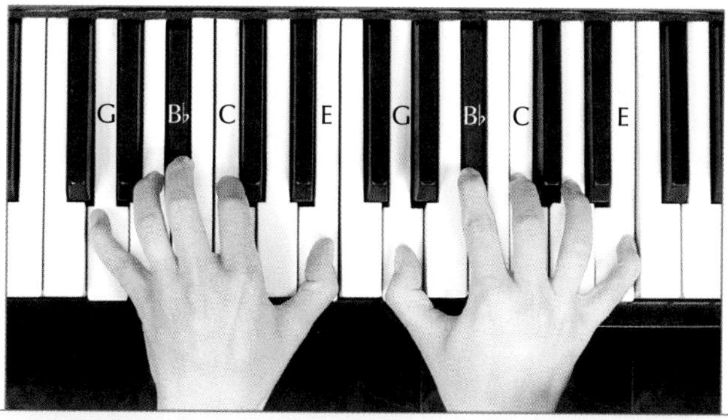

Second Inversion

1 To play a four-note chord in second inversion with your left or right hand, use your thumb, index finger, middle finger and pinky finger to press the keys for the notes of the chord.

- In this example, we play the C7 chord in second inversion, which includes the G, B♭, C and E keys.

Note: When playing a major or minor 6th chord in second inversion, use your ring finger instead of your middle finger.

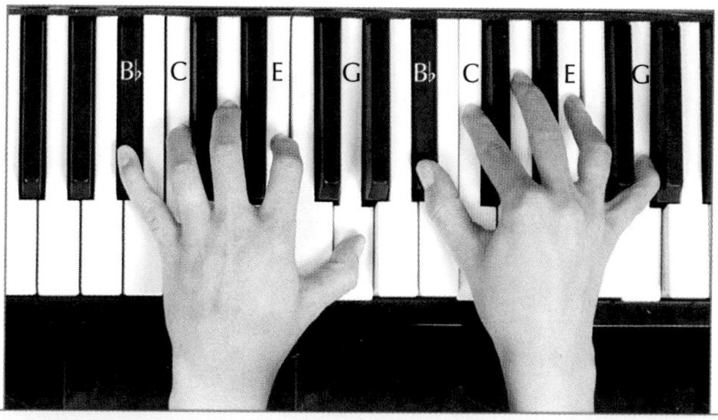

Third Inversion

1 To play a four-note chord in third inversion with your left or right hand, use your thumb, index finger, ring finger and pinky finger to press the keys for the notes of the chord.

- In this example, we play the C7 chord in third inversion, which includes the B♭, C, E and G keys.

Changing chords

When playing music using a lead sheet, you must determine the best way to play each chord. Unlike written music, which indicates the exact notes for each chord in the piece, lead sheets provide only an outline of a song, so it is up to you to decide the best way to play each chord.

Your goal should be to find a way to play the chords in a musical piece so your hand moves as little as possible as you change from one chord to another. The less you have to move your hand, the less likely you will be to hit a wrong note.

To change from one chord to another, called a chord progression, you must first determine which notes the two chords have in common and then decide which order to play the notes in the chords. When changing the order of notes in a chord, known as a chord inversion, listen to the way the chord sounds, as changing the order of the notes can subtly change the sound of a chord. Make sure you arrange the notes in a chord so the chord is easy to play, but also so the sound of the chord fits with the music you are playing.

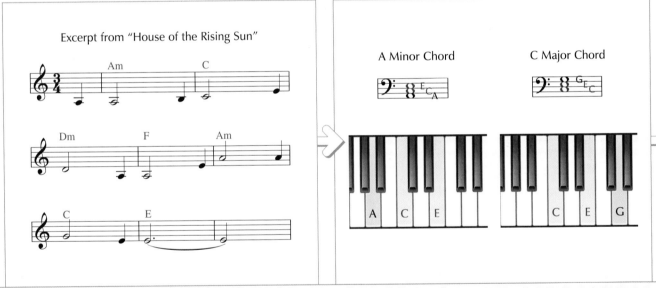

Excerpt from "House of the Rising Sun"

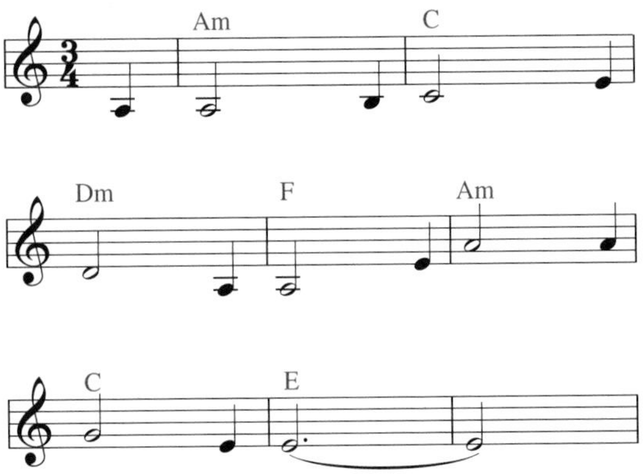

A Minor Chord

C Major Chord

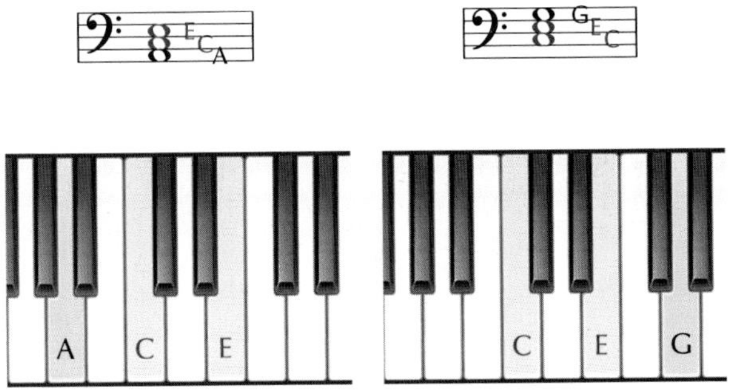

- When changing from one chord to another in a musical piece, you may need to determine the best way to play each chord so your hand moves as little as possible. Moving your hand as little as possible is less tiring for you and may help prevent errors in your playing.
- Determining the best way to play each chord is very important when using a lead sheet. A lead sheet is a piece of written music that provides an outline of a song and is commonly used when improvising. A melody, or tune, is written on a treble clef (𝄞) staff and the names of the chords you play appear above the staff.

1 To determine the best way to change from one chord to the next chord when playing music from a lead sheet, you first need to determine which notes the two chords have in common.

- For example, if you need to change from the A minor chord (A, C, E) to the C major chord (C, E, G), you first need to determine which notes the two chords have in common. In this example, the two chords have the C and E notes in common.

What if two consecutive chords do not have any notes in common?

Even if two consecutive chords do not have any notes in common, you should still determine which order to play the notes in each chord, so your hands move as little as possible. For example, when moving from C major (C, E, G) to B minor (B, D, F♯), you may want to play the notes of both chords with the root, or first, note as the lowest note, so that each finger only needs to move down one note on the keyboard.

What should I know about chords before I play music using a lead sheet?

To use a lead sheet, you should be very familiar with the notes that make up chords, as well as the differences between types of chords. For example, you need to know the difference between a major chord and a minor chord and the difference between a dominant 7th chord and a major 7th chord. With practice, you will become familiar with the notes that make up chords and the differences between types of chords. You will then be ready to play a musical piece with a variety of chords using a lead sheet.

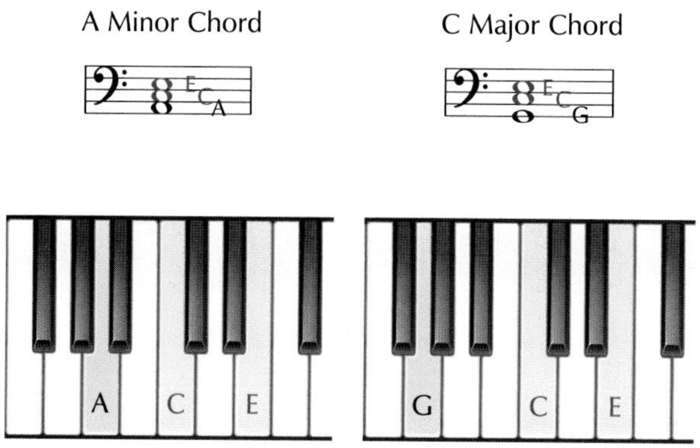

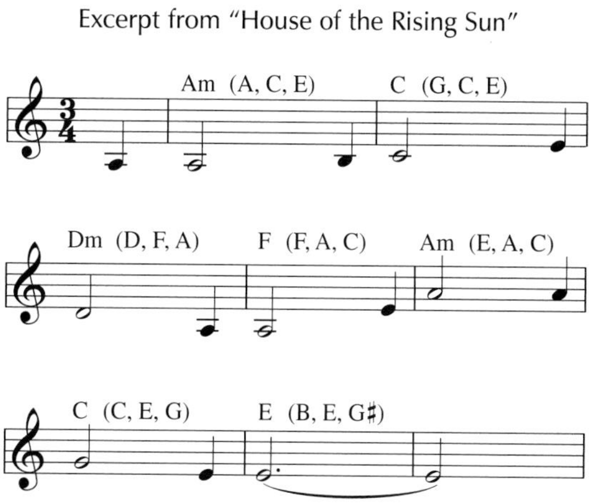

2 Determine which order to play the notes within each chord so your hands move as little as possible.

- Changing the order of the notes in a chord is called a chord inversion. For information on chord inversions, see pages 154 to 157.

- For example, to change from the A minor chord to the C major chord, change the order of the notes in the C major chord from C, E, G to G, C, E. Now, when you change from the A minor chord to the C major chord, the fingers playing the C and E keys remain in the same place.

- You can play this example of written music to practice changing between chords.

- You will need to change between the A minor (A, C, E), C major (C, E, G), D minor (D, F, A), F major (F, A, C) and E major (E, G♯, B) chords.

We Three Kings

♩ = 144 Moderately Fast

J. Hopkins

Largo
♩ = 50 Very Slow
G. F. Handel
G
Am7 D7 Am
G
C D7 C
D
C
G
D7
G
Am7 Bm
C
G A7
D
G
Am D7
G

Prelude in C Major

abridged version

Down to the Wire

♩ = 100 Moderately Slow

Frank Horvat

Toreador Song

From the Opera "Carmen"

♩ = 108 Moderately

Bizet

Mellowing Out

♩ = 60 Slow

Frank Horvat

Chapter 6

In this chapter, we move beyond the basics and learn about musical symbols and markings found in written music that add personality and expression to your piano playing. You will learn how to accentuate notes to make them stand out, how to read speed and volume markings, how to decorate notes using mordents, turns and trills and much more.

Beyond the Basics of Reading Music

In this Chapter...

- Slurs
- Staccatos
- Accents
- Tenutos
- Speed Markings
- Volume Markings
- Expression Markings
- Play Notes an Octave Higher or Lower
- Triplets
- Syncopated Notes
- Fermatas
- Grace Notes
- Trills
- Mordents
- Turns
- Glissandos
- Tremolos
- How Music is Divided into Phrases
- All About Keys
- Determining the Key of a Musical Piece
- *"Minuet in G Major"*
- *"The Skaters Waltz"*
- *"Amazing Grace"*
- *"Musette"*
- *"Maple Leaf Rag"*

slurs

A slur, or phrase marking, indicates that you should play a group of notes smoothly, so the notes do not sound detached or choppy. On the staff, a slur is marked by a curved line connecting two or more different notes. A slur can be small or large, containing just two notes or as many as 10 notes.

To play a slur, you press the key for the first note, then start pressing the key for the second note as you slowly release the first note. Simultaneously releasing the first note while pressing the second note ensures that there is no break in the sound. If two slurs appear side by side, which is quite common, you should make sure there is a break in the sound where one slur ends and the other begins.

If all the notes in a section of music are to be played smoothly, you may see "legato," in the written music instead of slur markings. "Legato," which means "smoothly" in Italian, can appear at any point in a piece where the composer wants you to start playing all the notes smoothly.

Excerpt from "Lullaby"
by Brahms

- In written music, a slur is a curved line that connects two or more different notes on the staff. Slurs are also known as phrase markings.
- When playing a slur, you play all the notes covered by the slur smoothly, making sure to hold each note until you play the next note.
- If a composer wants you to play all the notes in a piece smoothly, you will see the Italian word "legato" (smoothly) in the music. You may see "legato" at the beginning of a piece or anywhere the composer wants you to start playing all the notes smoothly.
- In this example of written music, play the notes as shown, making sure to play the notes covered by a slur smoothly.
- To play notes smoothly, press the first key and as you release the key, start pressing the next key at the same time.
- When playing notes covered by a slur, you should not hear moments of silence between any of the notes.
- When two slurs appear side by side, make sure there is a break in the sound when one slur ends and the next slur begins.

Staccatos

A staccato is a note that is played short and detached from the adjacent notes. This is an articulation technique that produces a sound similar to the plucked strings of an instrument, such as a harp or violin. Staccato is used in all types of music to add a light, textured sound to a piece.

You should play staccato notes short and light, using the same loose, bouncy wrist motion you would use when bouncing a ball. A staccato symbol can be a dot (·) or a wedge (▾). Notes with a wedge are played shorter than notes with a dot.

Although staccato notes are played more quickly, staccato notes get the same number of beats as normal notes. For example, when you play a staccato quarter note (♩), you play the note quickly, but the note still gets one beat. Make sure you do not play the note that follows a staccato too soon. The music should keep the same rhythm. Staccatos are never used for whole notes and rarely used for half notes.

- In written music, a dot (·) or wedge (▾) above or below a note indicates that you should play the note short and detached from the adjacent notes. Notes with a wedge are played even shorter than notes with a dot.
- Composers use staccato notes to add a light sound to their music.
- Staccato notes get the same number of beats as normal notes. For example, when you play a staccato quarter note (♩), you play the note quickly, but the note still gets one beat. Make sure you do not play the next note too soon.
- In this example of written music, play the notes as shown, making sure to play the staccato notes short and detached from the adjacent notes.
- When playing staccato notes, make sure you have a loose and bouncy wrist. You play staccato notes with the same wrist motion you would use when bouncing a ball.

accents

An accent is a symbol that appears above or below a note to indicate that you should play the note louder and with more force than you usually would. Accents are found in all types of music and can be used to emphasize any type of note.

When playing an accented note, try to avoid banging on the key by slamming your hand down. Instead, place your finger on the key and then use a firm downward motion of your wrist and finger to press the key, lifting your hand up slightly after pressing the key.

To make an accented note in your music really stand out, you should play the surrounding notes softer than normal so the accented note will sound louder.

An accented note can have different variations. The appearance of the accent symbol indicates how to play the note. For example, the >̣ symbol indicates that you should play the note as a normal accented note, except you should release the note quickly, as you would for a staccato note. For more information on staccato notes, see page 169.

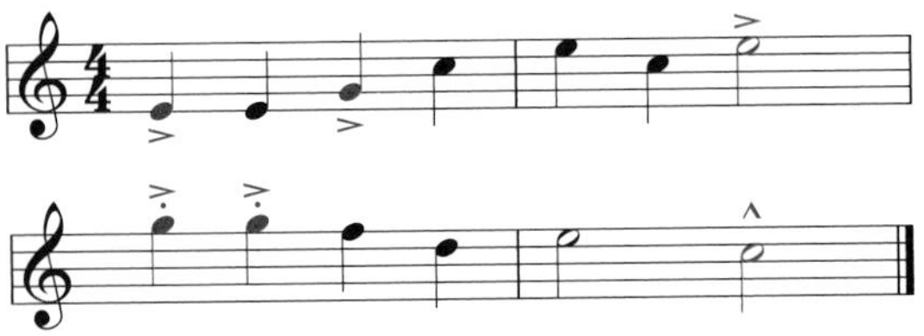

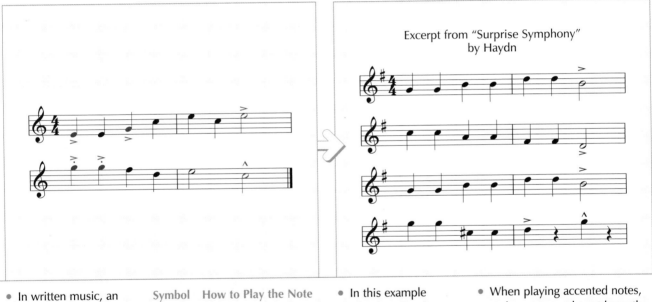

Excerpt from "Surprise Symphony"
by Haydn

- In written music, an accent is a symbol that appears above or below a note to indicate that you should play the note harder than you normally would.
- When accented notes are played, the notes sound louder, which emphasizes the notes in the music.

Symbol	How to Play the Note
>	Press the note hard.
^	Press the note very hard.
>̣	Press the note hard and release the note quickly, as you would for a staccato note.

- In this example of written music, play the notes as shown, making sure to press harder on the accented notes.

- When playing accented notes, make sure you do not bang the keys. With your fingers resting on the surface of the keys, use a strong downward motion of your wrist and fingers to play accented notes, lifting your hand up slightly after making contact with the keys.
- To make accented notes sound louder, you should play the notes surrounding the accented notes softer than normal.

tenutos

You can hold a note for its full value, but detached from adjacent notes to create a choppy sound in a piece. This technique is called tenuto.

A tenuto is a cross between a staccato and a slur. A staccato is a note that is played short and detached from the adjacent notes. A slur is two or more notes that are played without a break between the notes. Tenutos often appear on non-staccato notes in a section of music that contains many staccato notes.

While both tenuto and staccato notes are played detached from adjacent notes, unlike staccatos, each tenuto note is played for its full note value.

You play tenuto notes the same way you would play staccato notes, but the hand movement is slower. Staccato notes are played short and light, using a loose, bouncy wrist motion. When playing tenuto notes, the wrist movement is not as abrupt and quick as when playing staccatos.

Excerpt from "Waltz of the Flowers"
by Tchaikovsky

- In written music, a tenuto (–) is a symbol that appears above or below a note to indicate that you should play the note for its full value, such as 1 beat for a quarter note (♩), but the note should be detached from adjacent notes.

- Tenuto notes often appear in a section of music that contains many staccato notes, which display a dot (·). You also play staccato notes detached from adjacent notes, but staccato notes are not played for their full value. For more information on staccato notes, see page 169.

- In this example of written music, play the notes as shown, making sure to play the notes with a tenuto symbol (–) for their full value, but detached from adjacent notes.

- When playing notes with a tenuto symbol, the notes will have a choppy or detached sound.

speed markings

A speed marking usually appears at the beginning of a musical piece to indicate how fast or slow you should play the piece. You may also find speed markings in the middle of a piece to indicate that the speed should change. The speed at which a musical piece is played is referred to as the tempo of the piece.

A speed marking for a musical piece may appear as a metronome marking. A metronome is a device that makes a clicking sound to help you play at the correct speed. A metronome marking displays "M.M." followed by a quarter note and a number to signify the number of beats per minute (bpm) in a musical piece. For example, M.M. ♩=120 means that you play 120 quarter notes, or beats, per minute. Metronome markings are usually between 50 and 132 beats per minute. The more beats per minute, the faster the tempo. If you have a metronome, set the metronome at the speed specified by the metronome marking.

A speed marking may also appear as an Italian word written above the staff. For example, you may see "allegro" to indicate a fast tempo or "ritardando" to indicate that you should gradually slow down.

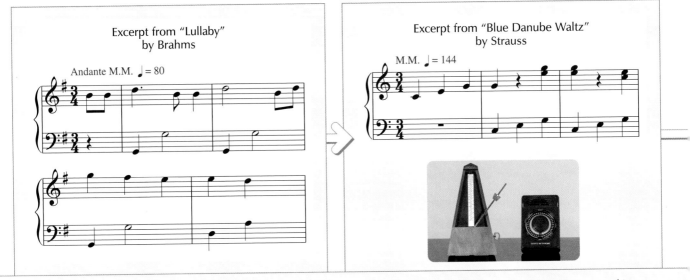

Excerpt from "Lullaby"
by Brahms

Excerpt from "Blue Danube Waltz"
by Strauss

Speed Markings in Written Music

- At the beginning of written music, you will usually find a marking that indicates the speed for playing the music. The speed at which you play music is known as the tempo.
- A musical piece can maintain the same speed throughout or change several times within the piece. When a composer wants you to change the speed, a new speed marking will appear in the music.

Metronome Marking

- A metronome is a device that you can adjust to make a clicking sound a certain number of beats per minute.
- A metronome marking is often shown at the beginning of music to indicate an exact speed for the music. You may also see a metronome marking in the middle of a musical piece to indicate a change in speed.
- A metronome marking displays "M.M." followed by a quarter note (♩) and then a number. The number indicates the number of beats per minute (bpm). For example, M.M. ♩=144 means you play 144 quarter notes, or beats, per minute. Sometimes, the M.M. is left out.

Note: The lower the number, the slower the speed.

Can a metronome marking display a note other than a quarter note?

Usually a metronome marking will display a quarter note (♩), but occasionally you may see a different note, such as an eighth note (♪), used to mark the speed of a musical piece. The note used in a metronome marking depends on the time signature of the piece and how fast or slow the piece is. For information on time signatures, see page 54.

Will I see speed markings in languages other than Italian?

Yes. Speed markings are often written in Italian, but sometimes you may find speed markings written in English, especially in pop music. French terms, such as *lentement* for slow, *modéré* for moderately and *vite* for fast, and German terms, such as *langsam* for slow, *mässig* for moderately and *schnell* for fast, are also used to indicate the speed of a musical piece.

I cannot play a musical piece as fast as the music specifies. What should I do?

Even when a fast speed is specified for a piece, you should begin practicing the piece at a slow and steady pace. Then gradually work up to playing the piece at the specified tempo.

Italian Word	Explanation
largo	very slow
adagio or lento	slow
andante	moderately slow
moderato	moderate speed
allegro	fast
presto	very fast

Italian Word	Explanation
piu mosso	Speed up
accelerando (accel.)	Gradually speed up
meno mosso	Slow down
rallentando (rall.)	Slowing down
ritardando (rit.)	Gradually slow down
poco à poco	Little by little
à tempo	Return to the original speed

General Speed Markings

- At the beginning of written music, you will often see an Italian word to indicate the speed at which you should play the music. You may also see an Italian word in the middle of a musical piece to indicate a change in speed.
- The above list shows the most common general speed markings you will see, from slowest to fastest.

Changes in Speed Markings

- In the middle of a musical piece, you may see an Italian word to indicate a change in speed. The above list shows the Italian words you may see.
- When you see "poco à poco" before "accelerando," "rallentando" or "ritardando" in written music, you should gradually speed up or slow down over a longer period of time.
- When you see "à tempo" in written music, you should return to the original speed of the music.

volume markings

Volume, or dynamic, markings are written as abbreviations of Italian terms and indicate how softly or loudly you play a musical piece.

When you see a volume marking, you play the music at the specified volume and continue playing at that volume until you see a new marking indicating you should play at a different volume. To change the volume, you press harder or softer on the keys.

If a volume marking appears above the treble clef staff, the marking is only for the right hand. If a marking appears below the bass clef staff, it applies only to the left hand. A marking that appears between the bass and treble staves applies to both hands.

You may see volume markings in written music that tell you to play softly, loudly or at a volume in between. Volume markings can also indicate that you should gradually increase or decrease the volume.

Abbreviation or Symbol	Italian Word	Explanation
ppp	*pianississimo*	extremely soft
pp	*pianissimo*	very soft
p	*piano*	soft
mp	*mezzo piano*	not too soft
mf	*mezzo forte*	not too loud
f	*forte*	loud
ff	*fortissimo*	very loud
fff	*fortississimo*	extremely loud
cresc. or <	*crescendo*	gradually play louder
decresc. or >	*decrescendo*	gradually play softer
dim.	*diminuendo*	gradually play softer
poco à poco	*poco à poco*	little by little

- In written music, how softly or loudly you should play, known as dynamics, is indicated by abbreviations of Italian words and symbols.
- Volume markings can tell you to play softly, loudly or somewhere in between. Volume markings can also tell you to gradually play softer or louder.
- You may see a combination of volume markings in written music. For example, when poco à poco appears before cresc., decresc. or dim., you should gradually play softer or louder, over a longer period of time.
- This example of written music contains volume markings. When you see a volume marking, play the music at the specified volume until you see a new volume marking.
- When you see the < or > symbol, gradually play louder or softer until you reach the end of the symbol and then continue playing at the new volume until you see a new volume marking.
- A volume marking that appears above the treble clef staff (𝄞) refers to the right hand only. A volume marking that appears below the bass clef staff (𝄢) refers to the left hand only. A volume marking that appears between the staves refers to both hands.

expression markings

Expression markings describe the feel of a piece of music or the type of emotion the music is meant to evoke. These markings aid a performer in establishing the mood of a piece.

Expression markings can appear at the beginning of piece, to set the initial mood of the piece. The markings can also indicate a change of mood in the middle of a piece.

In written music, expression markings to describe the emotion of a piece are written using Italian terms.

For example, the song Jingle Bells would be "Vivace" (lively and brisk), Silent Night "Tranquillo" (quiet and tranquil) and the American Anthem "Maestoso" (majestic). In some music, especially pop music, you may see expression markings in English. English expression markings include terms such as "lively," "sweet," "majestic" and "tranquil."

You may want to listen to various styles of music to see how different pianists express emotion in their music.

Italian Word	Explanation
Cantabile	in a singing style
Con brio	with vigor and spirit
Dolce	sweet and gentle
Espressivo	with expression
Giocoso	humorous
Grave	slow and solemn
Grazioso	graceful
Maestoso	majestic
Tranquillo	quiet and tranquil
Vivace	lively and brisk

Excerpt from "Canon in D"
by Pachelbel

- At the beginning of written music, you may see an expression marking written in Italian to indicate the emotion you should express when playing the music. You may also see an expression marking in the middle of a musical piece to indicate a change in emotion.
- The above list shows the most common expression markings you will see in written music.
- This example of written music contains expression markings. When you see an expression marking, express the emotion when playing until you see a new marking indicating a new emotion you should express.

play notes an octave higher or lower

Composers use the symbol 8va to represent notes that would otherwise be written above or below the lines of the staff. Rather than writing notes on ledger lines (—), composers keep these higher or lower notes on the staff and mark them with the 8va symbol. This helps pianists quickly read music since they are familiar with reading the notes on the staff.

When positioned above a note in written music, the 8va symbol means you play the same note one octave higher. When positioned below a note in written music, the 8va symbol means you play the same note one octave lower. An octave refers to the distance between a note and the next note with the same letter name on the keyboard.

The 8va symbol, which stands for ottava, the Italian word for octave, may not be the only symbol you see. Below notes, you may see 8vb, which stands for ottava bassa, and indicates you play the note one octave lower.

If you play an electronic keyboard, you may not be able to play some notes an octave higher or lower as indicated since some electronic keyboards contain fewer keys than pianos.

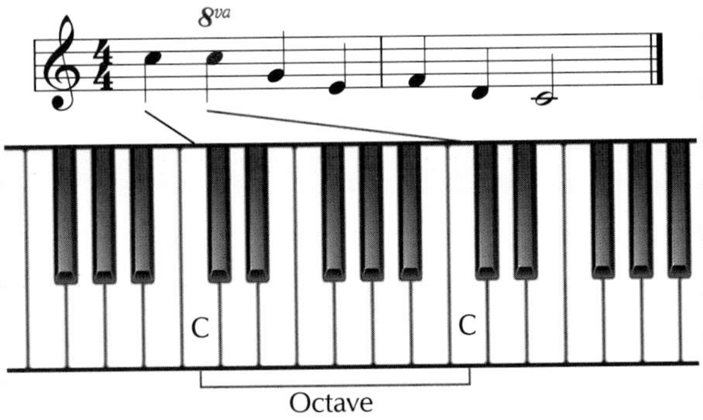

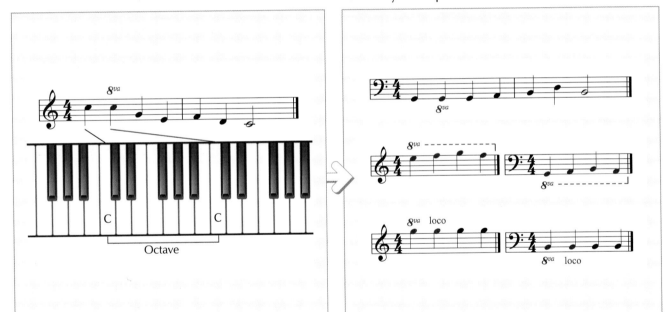

- The symbol 8va is used to indicate notes that would otherwise be written above or below the five lines on the staff.

- When you see 8va above a note in written music, play the same note one octave higher. For example, if you see 8va above a C note, play the next higher C note on the keyboard.

Note: An octave refers to the distance between a note and the next note with the same letter name on the keyboard.

- When you see 8va below notes in written music, play the same notes one octave lower. For example, if you see 8va below a C note, play the next lower C note on the keyboard.

- If a dashed line appears after 8va, play all the notes between 8va and the end of the dashed line one octave higher or lower.

- If "loco" appears after 8va, play all the notes between 8va and "loco" one octave higher or lower.

Note: Instead of 8va, you may see 8vb below notes to indicate that you play the notes one octave lower.

triplets

A triplet consists of a single beat divided into three parts. Triplets help create a special rhythm in a piece of music and are commonly found in marches, blues music, jazz music and 1950s rock ballads.

In written music, a triplet is indicated by three notes grouped with a beam, bracket or curved line and with a "3" marked above or below. To play a triplet, you play all three notes of the triplet in the amount of time it would take to play two notes of the same value.

A triplet can contain any type of note. The eighth note triplet is the most common triplet. In an eighth note triplet, each eighth note gets 1/3 of a beat instead of 1/2 of a beat. The second most common triplet is a quarter note triplet.

To practice counting the beats of the notes, you can clap your hands or tap your foot as you count the beats out loud.

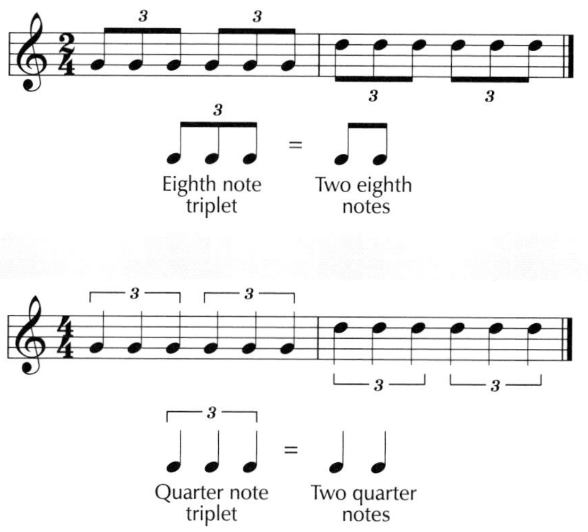

Excerpt from "Amazing Grace"
by Newton

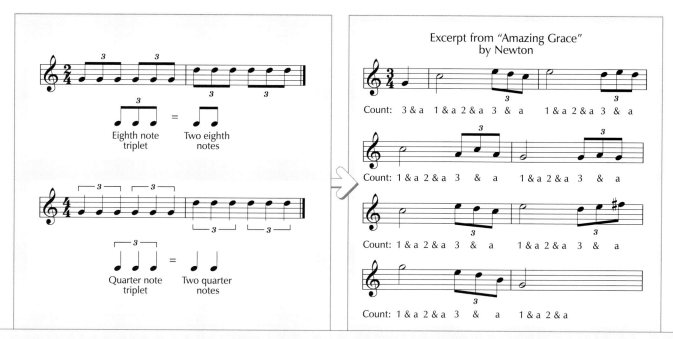

- In written music, a triplet is three notes grouped with a beam, bracket or curved line and marked with the number 3.
- A triplet has a special rhythm. The three notes in a triplet are played in the same amount of time as two notes of the same value.
- The most common triplet is the eighth note triplet. In an eighth note triplet, each eighth note gets 1/3 of a beat rather than 1/2 of a beat.
- The second most common triplet is the quarter note triplet.
- This example of written music contains triplets. To practice counting the beats of the notes, clap your hands or tap your foot as you count the beats out loud. Clap or tap only once for each note.

syncopated notes

Syncopated notes are notes that are played between the main beats in a measure and held through the next beat. Commonly used in rock, jazz, blues and latin music, syncopated notes alter the rhythm of a musical piece. This rhythm is known as syncopation. Syncopated notes can appear in particular sections of a musical piece or throughout an entire piece.

To play syncopated notes, you must become comfortable playing notes on the off beats in a piece. When you count "1 and 2 and 3 and 4 and" in a measure, the word "and" represents the off beats where you play syncopated notes. Music that contains syncopated notes is challenging for beginners to play since beginners are used to playing notes on the main beats. To make playing syncopated notes a little easier, remember to carefully count the beats in a piece of music. You may want to write the beats under the notes to help you when playing the piece.

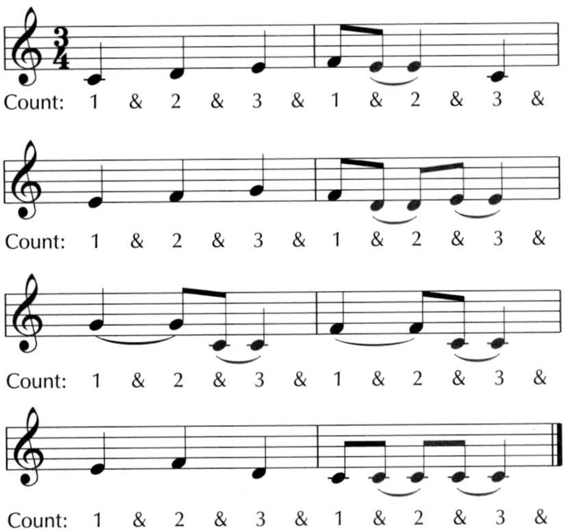

Excerpt from "The Entertainer"
by Joplin

- Syncopated notes are notes that are played between the main beats in a measure and held through the next beat. Syncopated notes are commonly used in jazz, blues, rock and latin music.

  Note: A measure is a section of music between two vertical lines on the staff.

- For example, when you count "1 and 2 and 3 and 4 and" in a measure, the numbers 1, 2, 3 and 4 are the main beats. A syncopated note is a note you play when you say "and," which you hold through the next beat.

- In this example of written music, play the notes as shown to hear the unique rhythm that syncopated notes produce.

- Syncopated notes are often tied notes. Tied notes are shown in written music as two identical notes that are joined by a curved line. You play only the first tied note and hold the note for the combined value of both notes. For more information on tied notes, see page 53.

fermatas

In written music, a fermata symbol (𝄐) appears above or below a note when the composer wants you to play a note longer than its normal value. When you see a note with a fermata, the number of beats you hold the note for is up to you. For example, if you see a fermata sign over a quarter note, you can hold the quarter note for two beats or three beats, rather than one beat. Fermatas can appear above or below any note.

Composers use fermatas to temporarily ignore the rules of the time signature, which determines the number of beats per measure. For information on time signatures, see page 54. Fermatas allow composers to add more beats to a measure than it is supposed to have. For example, if the time signature is 4/4 and there are four quarter notes in a measure, but one note has a fermata over it, that measure will have more than four beats. This effect is useful for accentuating a dramatic moment in a piece of music.

Note Symbol	Note Name	In 4/4 time, play the note longer than:
𝅝	whole note	4 beats
𝅗𝅥	half note	2 beats
♩	quarter note	1 beat
♪	eighth note	1/2 of a beat
𝅘𝅥𝅯	sixteenth note	1/4 of a beat

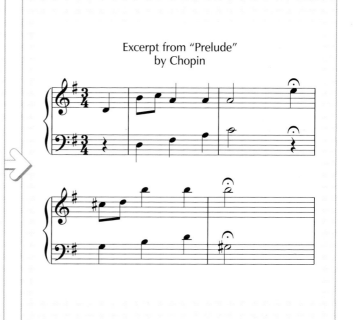

Excerpt from "Prelude"
by Chopin

- In written music, a fermata (𝄐) is a symbol that appears above or below a note to indicate that you should play the note longer than you normally would.

- For example, when you see a quarter note (♩) with a fermata, you can hold the note for more than one beat. You can hold the note as long as you feel is necessary.

- In this example of written music, play the notes as shown, making sure to play the notes marked with a fermata symbol (𝄐) longer than normal.

- Since every measure in a musical piece must have the same number of beats, composers can use fermatas to bend the rules and add more beats to a specific measure.

  Note: A measure is a section of music between two vertical lines on the staff.

grace notes

A grace note is a note that is used to decorate another note. You can think of grace notes as musical ornaments that add complexity and a more interesting sound to a piece of music. When several grace notes appear together in a row, they create a roll-like effect that leads into the next note. Since grace notes exist only to enhance the sound of a piece of music, they do not count as beats in a measure.

Grace notes, which are used in all styles of music, including rock, jazz and classical, usually appear very close on the keyboard to the notes that follow them. Playing a grace note consists of flicking the key with your finger before you play the note that follows the grace note. Grace notes, which can be found anywhere from beginner to advanced music, are very challenging for beginners to play at first. With practice, you should be able to increase the speed at which you can play grace notes.

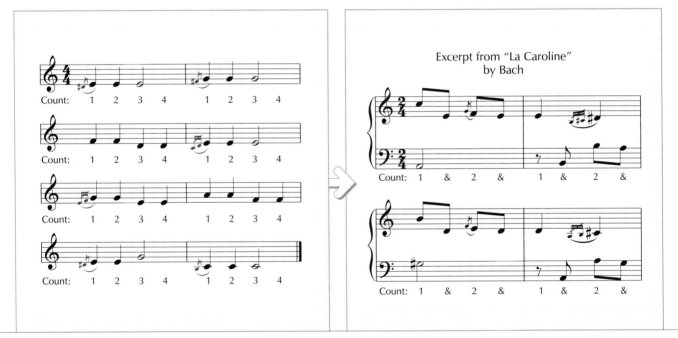

Excerpt from "La Caroline"
by Bach

- Grace notes are one or more notes that you play quickly before a note to decorate the note.
- In written music, grace notes are shown as tiny notes before a note. A curved line (◡), also known as a slur, connects grace notes with the next note.
- A single grace note looks like a tiny eighth note with a slash through its stem (♪). Two or more grace notes in a row look like tiny sixteenth notes joined with a beam (♬). When two or more grace notes appear in a row, a slash (♬) may appear through the notes.
- In this example of written music, play the notes as shown. When you see grace notes, play the grace notes quickly before the next note.
- When a measure contains grace notes, do not count the grace notes as beats in the measure.

Note: A measure is a section of music between two vertical lines on the staff.

trills

Trills are used to add texture and complexity to the melody, or tune, of a musical piece. Usually found in intermediate to advanced music, trills are especially common in Baroque, Classical and Romantic music.

Playing a trill involves alternating quickly between two notes—the written note and the next higher note on the keyboard. You usually start a trill by playing the next higher note above the written note first. When playing trills, keep your wrist at the correct height, your hand relaxed and your fingers curved and close to the keys. You should also try not to play trills too quickly or you may not be able to hear the individual notes of the trills.

In written music, a trill symbol (∿ or ***tr***) is used rather than writing out the notes of a trill. Trill symbols reduce clutter and respect the tradition of past composers who did not write out trills, since trills were improvised, or made up, by performers. In some written music, trills are marked with a reference letter that corresponds to a note at the bottom of the page, indicating exactly which notes should be played for the trills.

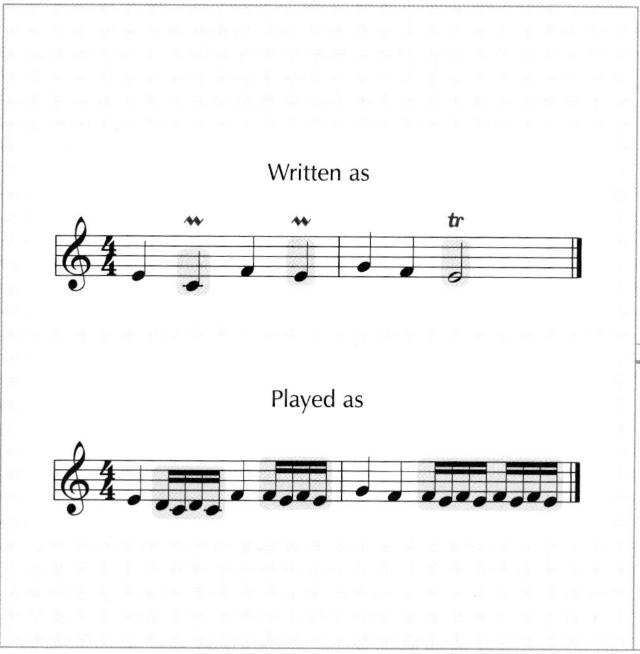

- Trills decorate the notes in a musical piece.
- In written music, a trilled note usually displays the ∿ or ***tr*** symbol above the note. When you see a trilled note in written music, you alternate your fingers very quickly between the written note and the next higher note on the keyboard.
- When you perform a trill, you usually start the trill with the next higher note above the written note. For example, if you see a trilled C note, you would alternate your fingers very quickly between the C and D notes, starting with the D note.
- When you see the ***tr*** symbol above a note, alternate between the notes for the entire note value. For example, if a trilled C note is a half note (𝅗𝅥), alternate between the D and C notes for the entire duration of the half note.
- When you see the ∿ symbol above a note, alternate between the notes twice and then hold the written note for the remaining duration of the note value. For example, if a trilled C note is a half note (𝅗𝅥), play D, C, D, C and hold the last C note for the remaining duration of the half note.

mordents

A mordent is a type of musical ornament that decorates a note, resulting in a fancier, more complex sound. Mordents are usually found in intermediate to advanced music and are common in Baroque, Classical and Romantic music.

When you play a mordent, you alternate quickly between three notes—the written note, the next lower note on the keyboard and the written note again. When playing mordents, keep your wrist at the correct height, your hand relaxed and your fingers curved and close to the keys. To ensure you can hear the individual notes of the mordents, avoid playing mordents too quickly.

Rather than writing out the notes of a mordent, composers use a mordent symbol (⁓) to reduce clutter in written music. Mordent symbols are also used to respect the tradition of past composers who did not write out mordents, since mordents were improvised, or made up, by the performer. In some written music, mordents are marked with a reference letter that corresponds to information at the bottom of the page, indicating exactly which notes should be played for the mordents.

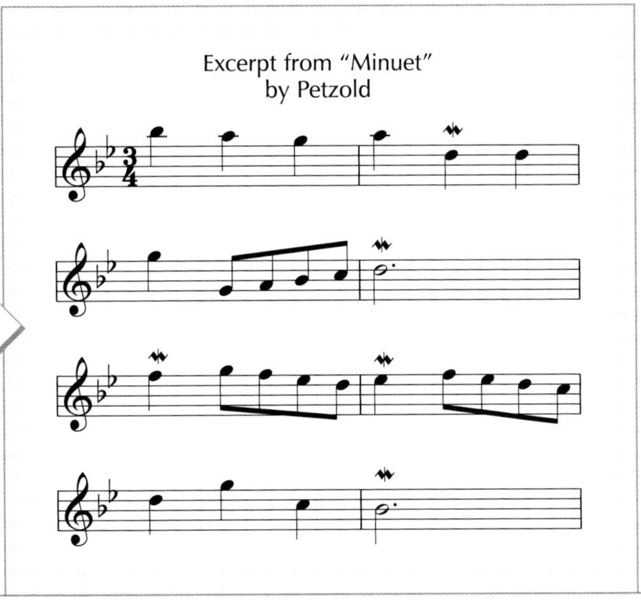

- Mordents decorate the notes in a musical piece.
- When a mordent symbol (⁓) appears above a note in written music, you very quickly play the written note, the next lower note and then play the written note again.
- For example, if a mordent symbol (⁓) appears above a C note, you would very quickly play the C, B, then C notes.
- In this example of written music, play the notes as shown.
- When a mordent symbol (⁓) appears above a note, quickly play the three notes and then hold the written note for the remaining duration of the note value. For example, if a mordent symbol appears above a C note, quickly play the C, B, C notes and then hold the last C note for the remaining duration of the note value.

turns

Turns are decorative touches that create a fancy sound. Commonly found in Baroque, Classical and Romantic music, turns are often used in intermediate to advanced music.

To play a turn, you alternate quickly between five notes—the written note, the next higher or lower note, the written note, the next lower or higher note and then the written note again. When playing turns, keep your wrist at the correct height, your hand relaxed and your fingers curved and close to the keys. You should also try not to play the notes of a turn too quickly or you may not be able to hear the individual notes.

Turn symbols (∾ or ∽) are used, rather than writing out the notes of a turn, to reduce clutter in written music and to respect the tradition of past composers who did not write out turns, since turns were improvised, or made up, by the performer. In some written music, turns are marked with a reference letter that corresponds to a note at the bottom of the page, indicating exactly which notes should be played for the turns.

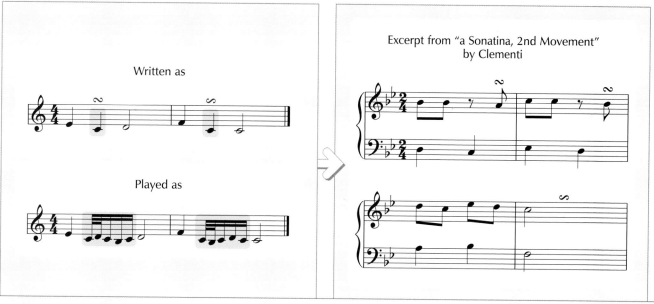

Excerpt from "a Sonatina, 2nd Movement"
by Clementi

- Turns decorate the notes in a musical piece.
- When the ∾ turn symbol appears above a note in written music, very quickly play the written note, the next higher note, the written note, the next lower note and then the written note again. For example, if ∾ appears above a C note, very quickly play the C, D, C, B, C notes.
- When the ∽ turn symbol appears above a note in written music, very quickly play the written note, the next lower note, the written note, the next higher note and then the written note again. For example, if ∽ appears above a C note, very quickly play the C, B, C, D, C notes.
- In this example of written music, play the notes as shown. When a turn symbol (∾ or ∽) appears above a note, quickly play the five notes of the turn.
- The location of a turn symbol (∾ or ∽) above a note indicates when you perform the turn. For example, if a turn symbol appears halfway between a C half note (𝅗𝅥) and the next written note, play the C note for half the duration of the note value, quickly play the five notes of the turn and then hold the last C note of the turn for the remaining duration of the half note.

glissandos

Glissandos are often used to create a dramatic, swooping sound in piano music. Most often found in intermediate and advanced pieces, glissandos appear in many styles of music, including rock, blues and classical music.

To play a glissando, you slide your thumb or fingers quickly across the keyboard, from one note to another note. Whether you use your thumb or fingers to play a glissando depends on whether the glissando moves up or down the keyboard and which hand you are using to play the glissando.

When playing a glissando, you should use the top part of your fingers—from your top knuckles to your fingertips, including your fingernails. Do not use your fingernails alone as you can break your nails. You should also remember not to press the keys too hard or you may injure your fingers. Press the keys just hard enough to make the keys sound.

Glissandos are often played with the damper pedal, which makes the notes you play continue to sound after you lift your fingers off the keys. Using the damper pedal creates a richer, fuller and amplified sound, so you do not have to press the keys as hard. This reduces the stress on your fingers when playing a glissando.

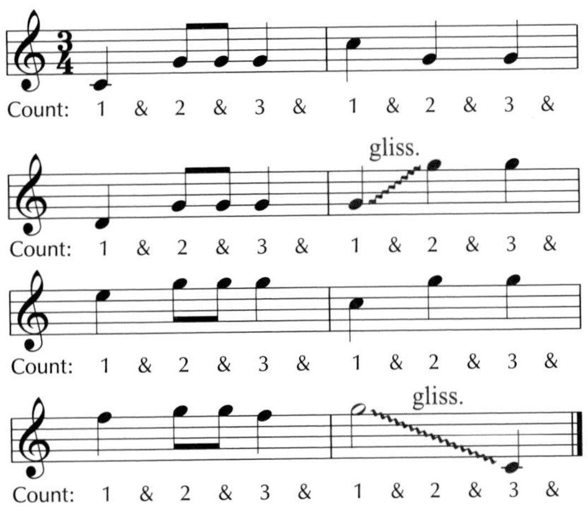

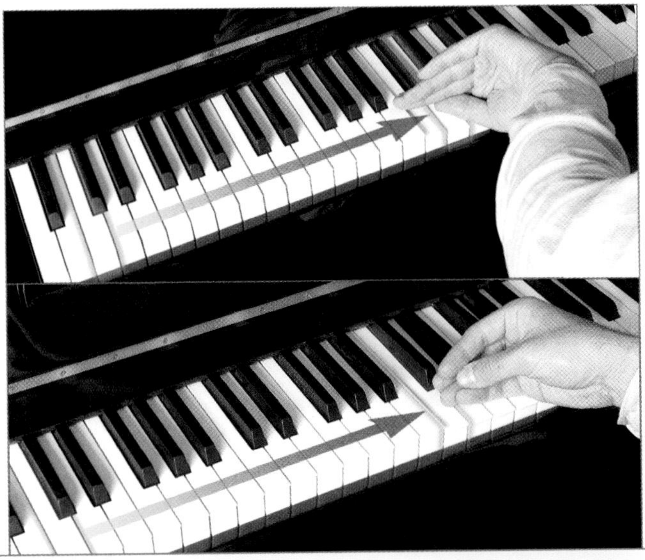

- When you play a glissando, also known as a gliss., you slide your thumb or fingers quickly across the keyboard, from one note to another note. Glissandos create a dramatic touch in a musical piece.
- In written music, a glissando appears as a diagonal wavy line between the notes you begin and end the glissando with. The word gliss. or glissando may appear above the wavy line.
- The value of the beginning note of the glissando tells you how many beats you have to reach the ending note of the glissando. For example, if the beginning note is a quarter note (♩), you have one beat to reach the ending note of the glissando.
- When you play a glissando, the top of your hand should always face the direction you are moving your hand on the keyboard.
- To play a glissando moving up the keyboard with your left hand or down the keyboard with your right hand, use the top part of your thumb to slide on the keys.
- To play a glissando moving up the keyboard with your right hand or down the keyboard with your left hand, use the top part of your middle finger with some help from the top part of your ring finger to slide on the keys. Keep all your fingers together to make your fingers stronger when sliding on the keys.

tremolos

Tremolos are often used to create tension or excitement in piano music. You will find tremolos in all styles of music, including rock, jazz and classical music.

To play a tremolo, you alternate between two single notes or two sets of notes quickly. Tremolos can contain notes that alternate between the fingers of one hand or between the fingers of both hands. A tremolo can also consist of notes of a chord, which have been broken into two parts that you can alternate quickly between.

The most common tremolo is called an octave tremolo. Octave tremolos, most often played with your left hand, involve alternating quickly between the same note at two different locations on the keyboard. For example, you can play an octave tremolo by alternating quickly between one C key and the next higher C key on the keyboard.

Tremolos are often played with the damper pedal pressed down to create a shimmering sound effect. When you press the damper pedal, all the notes you play will continue to sound even after you lift your fingers off the keys. In beginner music, you will often see brackets below the staff to indicate when you should use the damper pedal.

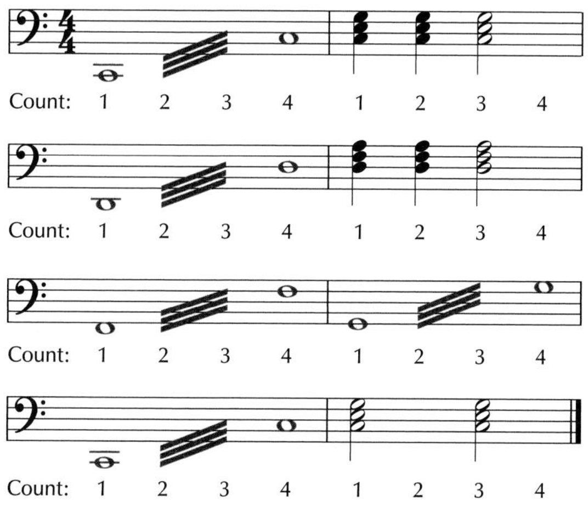

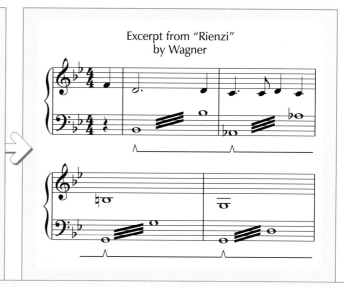

Excerpt from "Rienzi"
by Wagner

- When you play a tremolo, you alternate between playing two single notes or two sets of notes as quickly as you can. Tremolos create tension or excitement in a musical piece.
- In written music, a tremolo is shown as three thick lines between the notes you need to alternate between. The notes of a tremolo have the same note value. For example, the notes of a tremolo may be whole notes (o).
- When you play a tremolo, you alternate between playing two notes for the duration of only the first note. You then ignore the second note of the tremolo before playing the next note after the tremolo.
- In this example of written music, play the notes as shown. When you see a tremolo, alternate between the notes as quickly as you can for the duration of the first note of the tremolo.
- Tremolos are often played with the damper, or right, pedal pressed down to create a shimmering sound effect. In beginner music, you will often see brackets below the staff to indicate when you should use the damper pedal. For more information on the damper pedal, see page 206.

how music is divided into phrases

A phrase is a part of a musical piece, normally about four measures long, that expresses a complete musical idea. A measure is a section of music between two vertical lines on the staff. Composers use phrases to express ideas and add structure to a musical piece the same way writers use sentences to express ideas and add structure to a story.

In written music, you may find phrases indicated by slurs, or curved lines, above each phrase. A slur is most commonly used to indicate a phrase when the melody, or tune, of the phrase should be played smoothly. The end of a phrase may also be indicated by a comma (›) above the staff. If no phrase markings appear in a musical piece, you can look for held notes or moments of silence in the form of rests, such as the 𝄽 or 𝄼 symbols, to indicate the end of a phrase.

When you play a piece that does not include speed or volume markings, you can enhance the piece by changing the speed or volume based on where each phrase begins and ends. For example, you can slow down at the end of a phrase, which is common in popular ballads.

- Composers usually divide music into phrases to add structure to the music. Each phrase expresses a musical idea and often consists of four measures.

  Note: A measure is a section of music between two vertical lines on the staff.

- The phrases in a musical piece can be marked in two different ways. You may see a curved line, known as a slur, above each phrase or you may see a comma (›) above the staff at the end of each phrase. Some music does not contain any phrase markings.

- If you are having trouble playing a certain section of a piece, determine where the phrase containing the difficult section begins and ends. You can then repeatedly practice the entire phrase to play the entire musical idea from beginning to end.

- If speed or volume markings do not appear in a musical piece, you can change the speed or volume based on where each phrase begins and ends. For example, you can enhance many musical pieces by gradually playing louder at the beginning of a phrase and gradually playing softer at the end of a phrase.

all about keys

The key of a musical piece provides you with useful information about the piece, such as which scale the piece is based on and which notes you should play as sharps and flats.

Knowing which scale a piece is based on helps you determine which notes commonly appear throughout the piece and helps you play the piece since you will be familiar with the finger patterns used to play the notes of the scale.

When you modify music as you play, known as improvising, the key of a musical piece allows you to determine which notes will complement the notes in the piece.

The key signature, which consists of one to seven sharp (♯) or flat (♭) symbols at the beginning of the staff, indicates which notes you must play as sharps and flats and helps you determine the key of a piece. The number of sharps or flats in a key signature indicates one major key and one corresponding minor key for the musical piece.

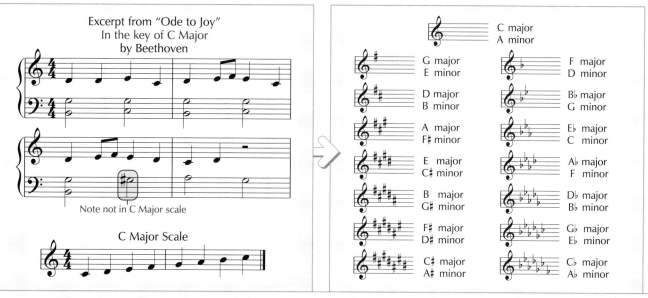

- Most musical pieces are written in a major or minor key, which corresponds to a specific major or minor scale.

  Note: A scale is a series of notes that you play in a specific order. For information on major and minor scales, see pages 90 and 94.

- A musical piece written in a specific major or minor key uses notes primarily from the corresponding major or minor scale. For example, a piece written in the key of C major uses the notes primarily from the C major scale.

- To add variety to a musical piece, a composer may include notes that do not belong to the corresponding scale.

- The key signature, which appears as sharps (♯) or flats (♭) at the beginning of a staff, indicates the notes in a musical piece that you need to play as sharps or flats. The key signature also helps you determine the key of a piece.

- Each key signature indicates one major key and one minor key. For example, the key signature containing one sharp (♯) indicates both the G major and E minor keys.

- Major and minor keys that share the same key signature are known as being relative to each other. For example, the G major key is the relative major of the E minor key. The E minor key is the relative minor of the G major key.

determining the key of a musical piece

When determining the key of a musical piece, you must first look at the key signature of the piece. The key signature appears as sharps (♯) or flats (♭) at the beginning of a staff. The key signature will indicate one major key and one minor key.

Once you have the key of the musical piece narrowed down to one major key and one minor key, you must examine the music to determine which of the two keys the piece is written in.

STEP 1: Determine the possible major and minor key of a musical piece

If the key signature contains sharps (♯)...

G major
E minor

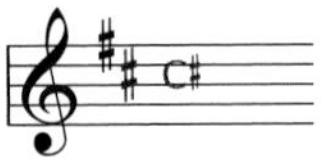

D major
B minor

A major
F♯ minor

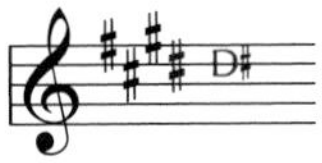

E major
C♯ minor

B major
G♯ minor

F♯ major
D♯ minor

C♯ major
A♯ minor

1 To determine the possible major key of a musical piece, name the last sharp (♯) in the key signature. Then raise the note by one half step to determine the possible major key of the piece.

Note: When you raise a note by one half step, you name the note directly to the right on the keyboard.

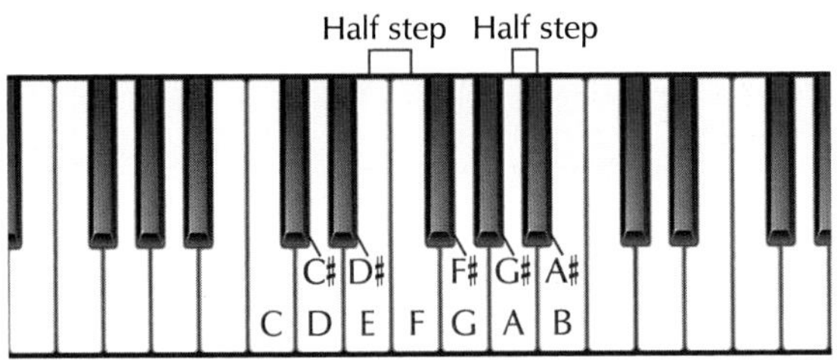

- For example, if a key signature contains four sharps (♯), the last sharp is D-sharp. One half step up from D-sharp is E, so the piece may be in the key of E major.

2 To determine the possible minor key of a musical piece, lower the name of the major key by three half steps. For example, if the possible major key is E, three half steps below E is C-sharp, so the piece may be in the key of C-sharp minor.

STEP 1: Continued

If the key signature contains flats (♭)...

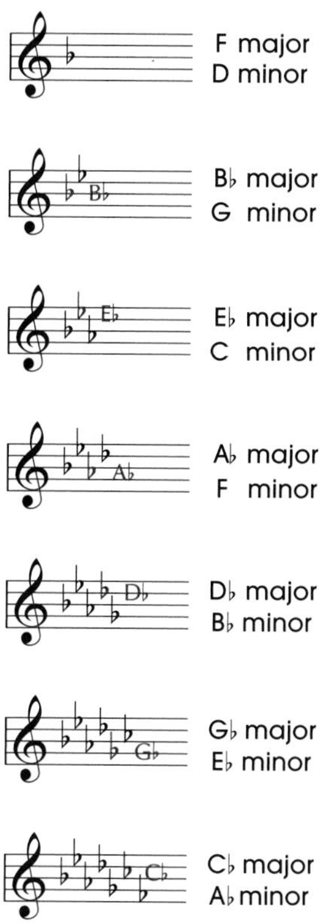

1 To determine the possible major key of a musical piece, name the second last flat (♭) in the key signature. The note you name is the possible major key of the piece.

- For example, if a key signature contains four flats (♭), the second last flat is A-flat, so the piece may be in the key of A-flat major.

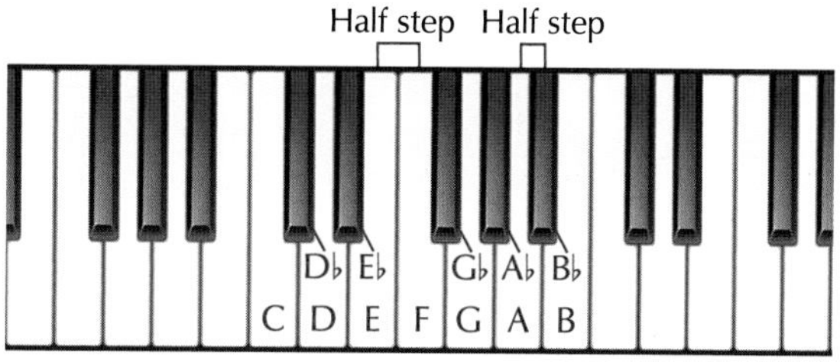

2 To determine the possible minor key of a musical piece, lower the name of the major key by three half steps. For example, if the possible major key is A-flat, three half steps below A-flat is F, so the piece may be in the key of F minor.

- When a key signature has only one flat (♭), you will need to memorize that this key signature indicates the piece is in the key of F major or D minor.

If the key signature contains no sharps (♯) or flats (♭)...

1 If the key signature contains no sharps (♯) or flats (♭), the musical piece will be in the key of C major or A minor. The C major and A minor keys are the easiest keys to identify because they share a key signature that contains no sharps (♯) or flats (♭).

CONTINUED...

determining the key of a musical piece *(continued)*

STEP 2: Determine the exact key of a musical piece

- Once you have narrowed down your choices to one major key and one minor key for a musical piece, there are three things you can do to determine which key the piece is written in.

1 Each major and minor key corresponds to a specific major or minor scale. At the beginning and end of a musical piece, look for the first and/or fifth notes in the corresponding scales.

- For example, to confirm that a musical piece is in the key of C major or A minor, look for the first and/or fifth notes in the C major (C, G) or A minor (A, E) scale at the beginning and end of a piece.

2 At the beginning and end of a musical piece, look for a major or minor chord with the same name as the major or minor key.

- For example, to confirm that a musical piece is in the key of C major or A minor, look for the C major or A minor chord at the beginning and end of a piece.

3 Look for a sharp (♯) or a natural sign (♮) before notes in the music. If a sharpened or natural note is one half step lower than the name of the minor key, the piece is most likely in the minor key.

- For example, to confirm that a musical piece is in the key of A minor, look for G-sharps in the piece.

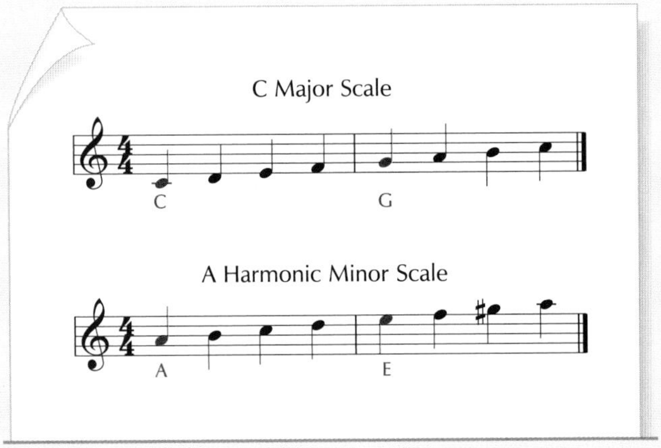

Minuet in G Major

The Skaters Waltz

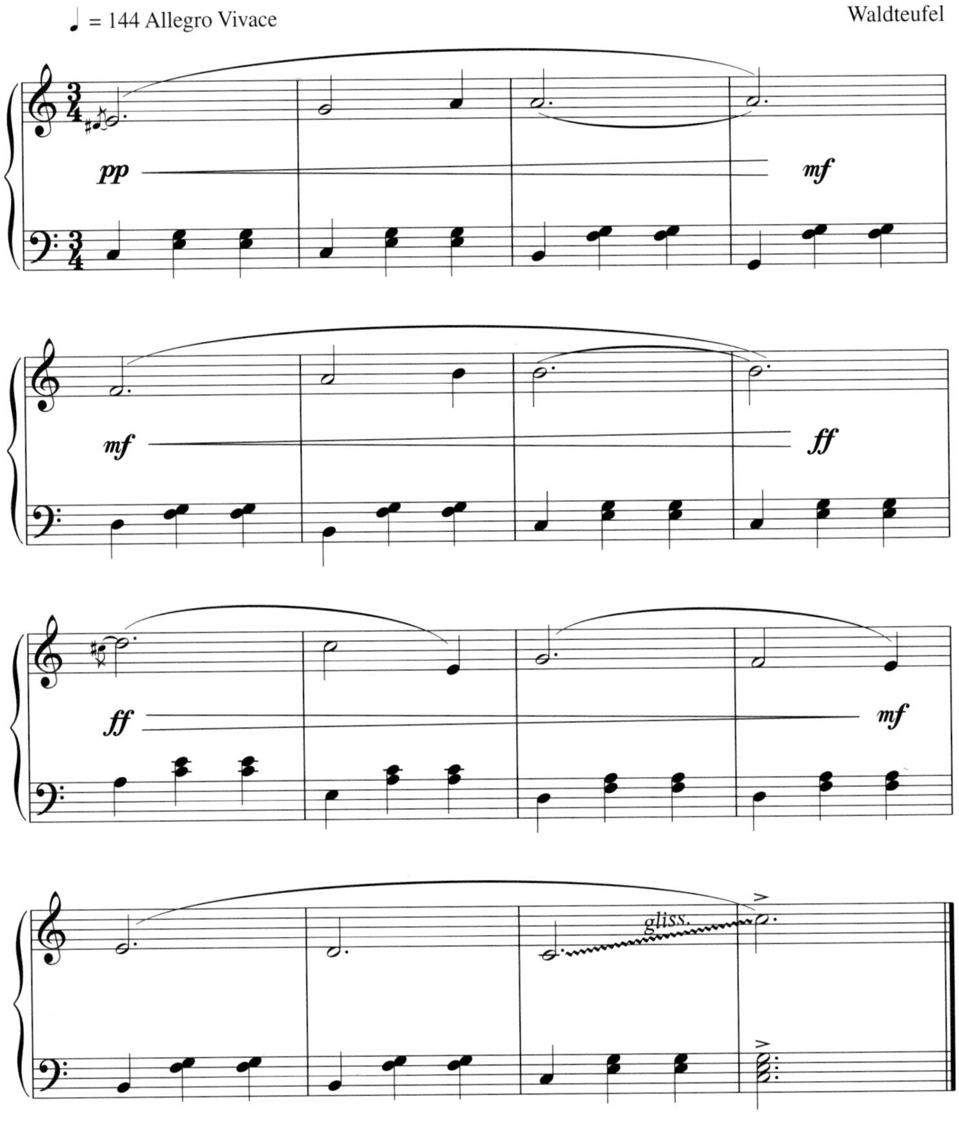

Amazing Grace

♩ = 50 Adagio, Expressive

John Newton

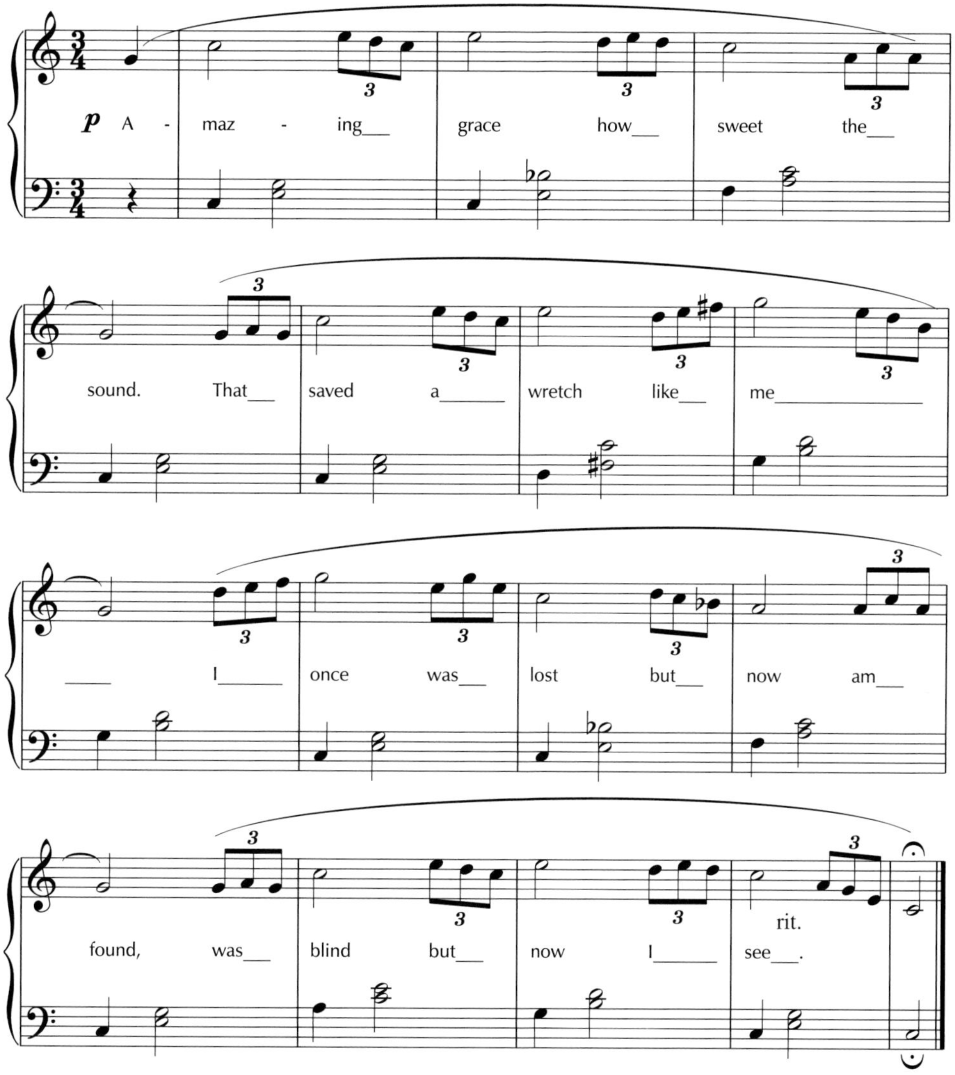

Musette

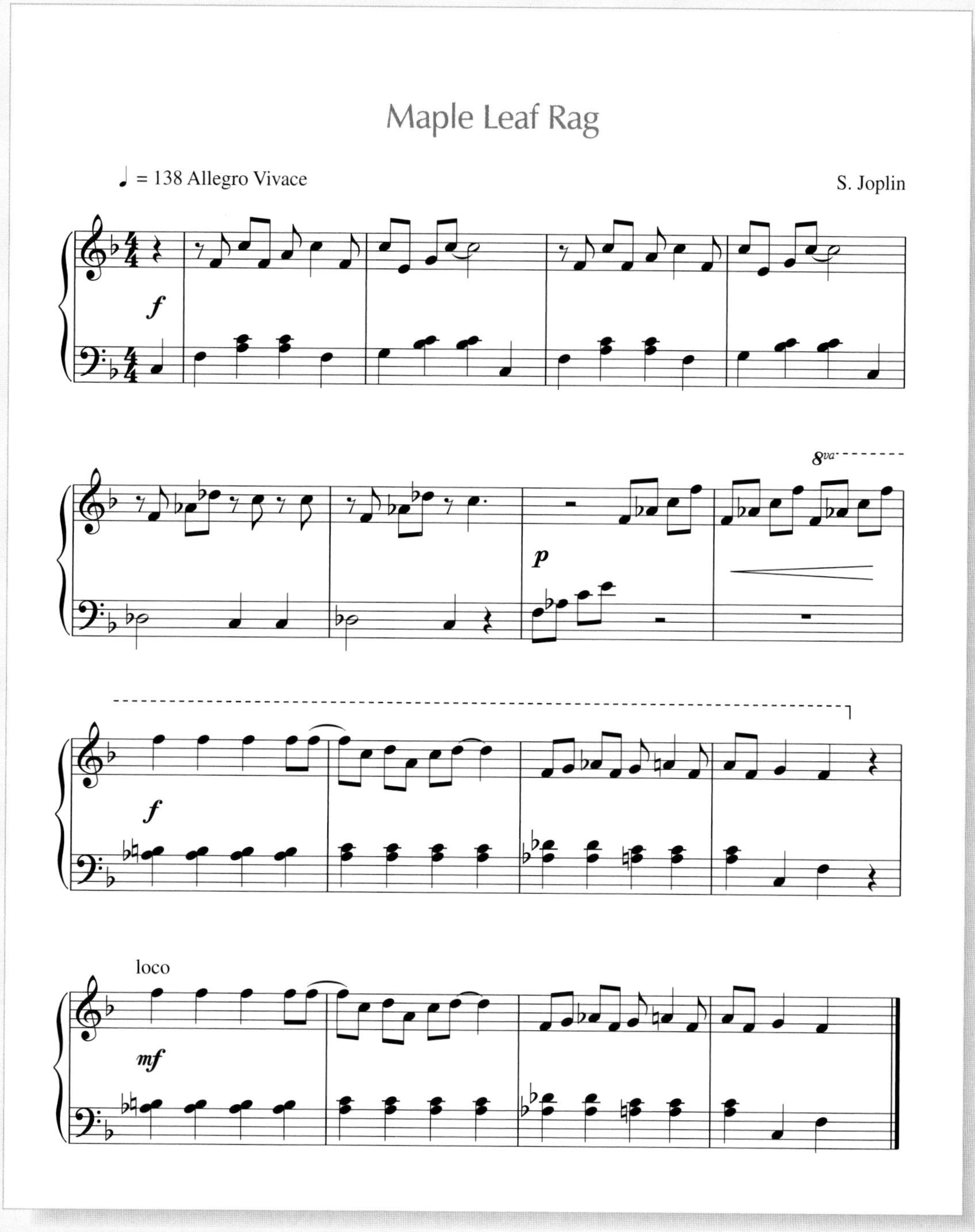
Maple Leaf Rag
♩ = 138 Allegro Vivace
S. Joplin
f
8va
p
f
loco
mf

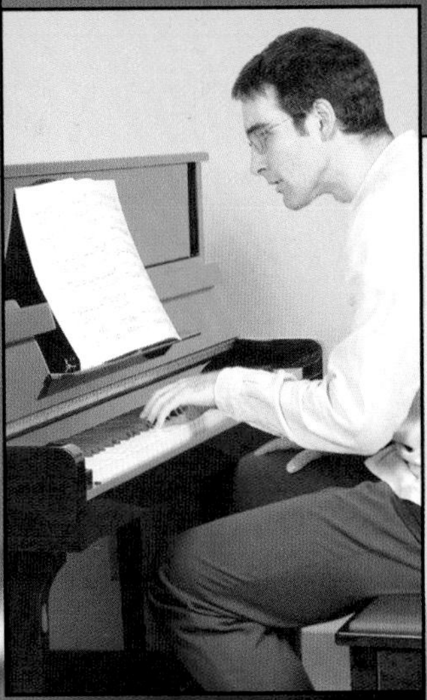

Chapter 7

This chapter includes information on ways you can improve your piano playing. You will find handy tips on what to do when you play a musical piece for the first time and how to look for a piano teacher to help you continue your musical education. This chapter also provides useful advice and information to help you efficiently use your time when practicing.

Tips to Improve Your Playing

In this Chapter...

- Playing a Piece for the First Time
- How to Practice
- Find a Piano Teacher

playing a piece for the first time

When playing a musical piece for the first time, there are several things you should keep in mind.

First, look closely at the beginning of the staff for two important parts of the written music—the key signature and the time signature. The key signature shows you which notes to play as sharps (♯) or flats (♭) throughout the piece. The time signature, consisting of two numbers, provides you with information about the beat patterns of the piece.

Second, ensure that your hands start in the correct position on the keyboard. Beginner music often helps you determine which fingers to use by including finger numbers above or below the notes. Before you start playing, you should position the correct fingers on the first notes of the piece.

Next, start by playing the notes written for your left hand and your right hand separately. When you can play the notes for each hand well, you can progress to playing the piece with both hands at the same time.

Finally, play at a slow and steady speed. You can gradually work toward playing at the correct speed as you become more comfortable with the piece.

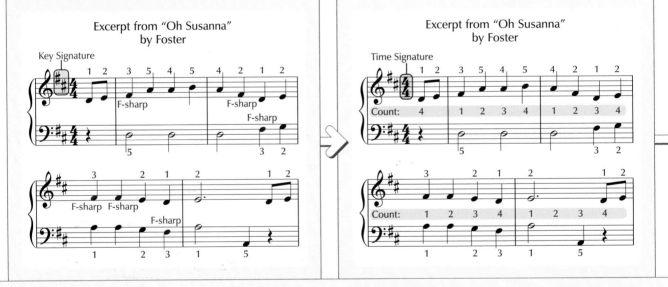

Excerpt from "Oh Susanna"
by Foster

Excerpt from "Oh Susanna"
by Foster

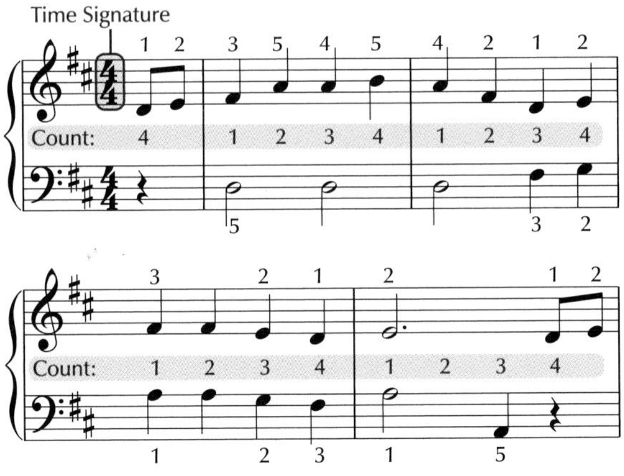

Examine the Key Signature

- Look at the key signature to determine which notes in the musical piece you need to play as sharps or flats. The key signature is displayed as sharps (♯) or flats (♭) at the beginning of the staff.

- In this example, the key signature contains an F-sharp and a C-sharp, which means you must play every F and C note as F-sharp and C-sharp throughout the entire musical piece.

Note: For more information on key signatures, see page 58.

Examine the Time Signature

- The time signature appears at the beginning of the staff and consists of two numbers. The top number indicates the number of beats in each measure and the bottom number indicates the type of note that counts as one beat.

Note: A measure is a section of music between two vertical lines on the staff.

- In this example, the time signature is 4/4, which specifies that each measure has 4 beats and each quarter note (♩) counts as one beat.

Note: For more information on time signatures, see page 54.

Tip

What else should I consider when playing a musical piece for the first time?

- You should try to look at the written music, not down at the keyboard. Most pianists only glance at the keyboard when absolutely necessary, such as when executing large finger shifts. Forcing yourself to play without looking at the keyboard trains you to navigate the keyboard intuitively, not by sight.
- If you are learning a longer piece, break it down into sections and play each section several times before moving on to the next section.
- Look at the note patterns. Knowing the relationship between consecutive notes will help you determine the distance between the keys you need to play and will help you navigate the keyboard more efficiently. For example, identifying a note as one whole step below the previous note will help you find the note quicker than identifying the note by its individual letter name.

Start with the Correct Hand Position

- Before you begin playing a musical piece, make sure your hands start in the correct position on the keyboard.
- Beginner music often includes the finger numbers above or below the notes to help you determine which fingers to use. Look at the finger numbers indicated for the first notes in the piece and position the correct fingers on those notes.

Note: Your fingers are numbered from 1 to 5—thumb (1), index (2), middle (3), ring (4) and pinky (5) finger.

Play Both Hands Separately

- Before trying to play a musical piece with both hands, play the left and right hand parts separately. When both hands can play the notes well, play the musical piece with both hands at the same time.

Play at a Slow and Steady Speed

- Start playing a musical piece at a slow and steady speed. As you become comfortable with playing the piece, gradually work toward playing at the correct speed.
- As you play, count the beats in the music to help ensure you play at a steady speed.

how to practice

All piano players, regardless of skill level, should practice playing the piano regularly. Piano practice, with its repetitive motions, not only allows you to train and strengthen your hands and fingers, it helps improve your hand-eye coordination. Developing strength and coordination will allow you to form chords and play scales more comfortably. With practice, you will eventually be able to shift your focus from simply playing notes to conveying emotion in the music you play.

To ensure you practice regularly, you should create a realistic practice schedule and stick to it as best you can. When creating a schedule, remember that how often you practice is more important than how long your practice sessions last. For example, practicing for 15 minutes every day is better than practicing for an hour one day and then not practicing for the next three days.

When practicing a piece, if you hesitate or have to stop the beat, you are playing too fast. You should play slow enough that you can keep up with the beat. If your practice session is an hour or more, you should also remember to take a break every 20 minutes so you can stand up, stretch and rest your arms and hands.

Your Practice Session

- You should spend approximately 25 percent of your practice session on warm-up exercises.
- Warm-up exercises include playing scales and playing chords.

Note: For information on playing scales and playing chords, see chapters 4 and 5.

- Warm-ups help develop your finger coordination, help stretch your fingers and help build your finger strength.

- You should spend approximately 75 percent of your practice session playing musical pieces.
- When you begin practicing a musical piece, play the left and right hand parts separately. When your left and right hands can play the notes well, you are ready to play the piece with both hands together.

- You should break down a musical piece into small portions and spend extra time repeating the parts you have trouble with. Do not rush through your practice sessions.

How will I know if a piece is appropriate for my skill level?

If you have good practice habits but a musical piece is not getting easier after practicing for about two weeks, the piece may be beyond your skill level. Put the piece away for a while and try it again when your technique and coordination has improved.

Are there other warm-up exercises I can perform?

There are several books available that provide ideas for finger exercises; however, you should not perform exercises that seem far beyond your skill level. When searching for finger exercises, some choices you have include books written by Hanon and Schmitt.

What should I do after I can play a musical piece smoothly all the way through?

When you can play an entire musical piece without hesitation, try recording yourself so you can listen to your playing objectively. Use the recording to find areas where you can improve and judge whether your playing sounds confident, without mistakes or pauses. To record your music, use a tape recorder or your keyboard's built-in sequencer.

Practice Session Duration

- Keep a consistent practice schedule. Practicing for 15 minutes every day is better than practicing for an hour one day and not practicing for the next three days.
- Beginner piano players should practice from 15 to 30 minutes every day. As you progress, the amount of time you practice will increase. Many intermediate to advanced piano players practice from 1 to 2 hours per day.
- When practicing, take breaks every 20 minutes to help rest your muscles and help avoid rushing through your practice session.

Tips for Practicing

- Keep your fingers, wrists, arms and shoulders relaxed while you practice. When you find parts of your body tensing up, shake out your arms and hands and try to relax the tense areas.
- Use a metronome to ensure you keep a steady beat.
- Play slowly at first and increase your speed only when you are able to play all the notes without hesitation.
- Set goals for yourself, such as aiming to play a musical piece 10 times in a row without any mistakes.

find a piano teacher

When looking for a piano teacher, start by asking your piano tuner and your friends for recommendations. Other good resources include piano stores, churches and community centers. When you find a potential teacher, ask for names of existing students so you can check the teacher's references. The following discusses several factors you should consider before hiring a piano teacher.

Private Teacher vs. Music School

You can hire a private piano teacher or attend lessons at a music school or academy. Private piano teachers working from their home can offer a comfortable atmosphere that may help put students at ease. However, music schools may offer piano rental options if you are unable to purchase your own piano. A music school may also provide a wider variety of options for participating in group activities, such as playing in an ensemble.

Teacher's Education

Look for a teacher whose educational background includes focused study in piano. To make sure a teacher has a degree or diploma from a recognized institution, check with your local music teacher's association. Located throughout the U.S. and Canada, these professional associations make sure their members have a certain level of education and experience.

Personality

An important part of finding the right teacher is finding someone you get along with. If you and your teacher like one another, you are likely to get more out of your classes. Conduct your piano teacher search as if you were interviewing candidates for a job.

Teaching Experience

Find out how long the teacher has been a piano instructor and how many students the teacher currently has. Also, make sure the teacher has experience teaching your age group or your children's age group, if you are looking for a teacher for your kids.

Performance Possibilities

Performing in a recital with other students is a good way to gauge your piano playing progress. Find out what kind of performance opportunities are available to students of your prospective teachers. Attending recitals before you hire a teacher is a great way to evaluate your candidates. At a recital, you can find out the ages and skill levels among your prospective teacher's students. You also can meet students—and parents of students, if you are considering teachers for your children—and observe how the teacher interacts with the students.

Teaching Methods and Philosophy

What instructional materials and methods do your potential teachers use? Do their lessons include information on improvising, playing by ear and composing? How is the lesson time divided up among elements such as good practice habits, music theory and music history? By asking these questions, you will find a teacher whose teaching methods and philosophy match the instruction you are interested in.

Fees and Scheduling

Fees can vary for piano lessons depending on the credentials and experience of a teacher. The more qualifications and experience a teacher has, the higher the rate the teacher is likely to charge. When interviewing prospective teachers, find out what your lesson fees cover and what additional fees may be required. For example, participating in auditions and exams usually costs extra. Unless your teacher loans music to students, you may have to buy your own music. You should also look for a teacher whose teaching schedule coincides with yours and find out what the teacher's policies are for cancelled and made-up lessons.

Studio Environment

Where your lessons will take place is an important consideration when choosing a teacher. Some teachers offer lessons in your home, which may be more convenient for you. Others provide lessons in their own home or studio. Wherever your lessons are, they should take place in a bright, friendly and inviting environment, preferably without a lot of noise restrictions or distractions.

Chapter 8

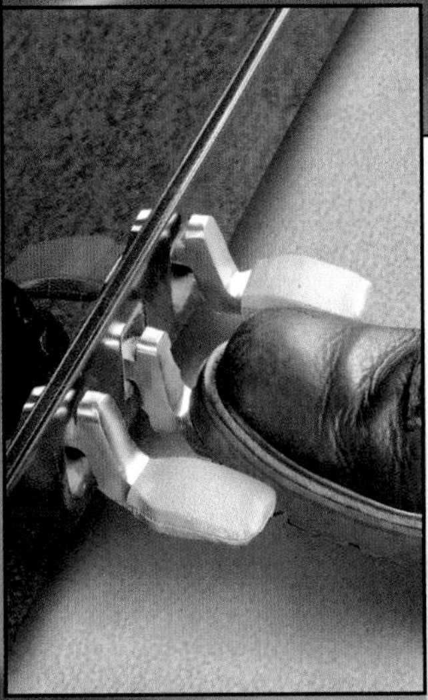

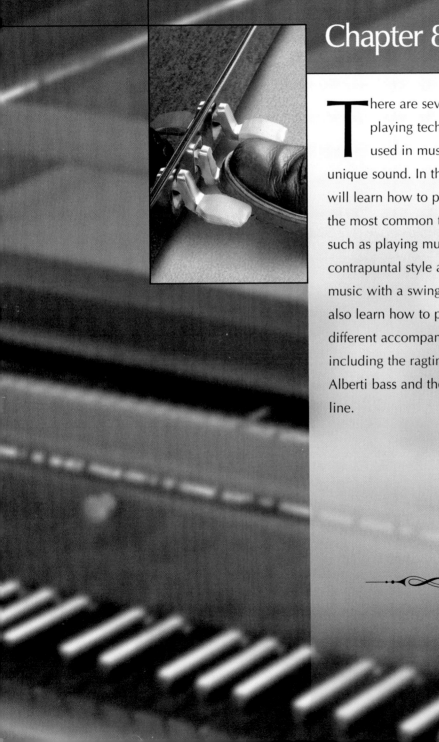

There are several special playing techniques that are used in music to create a unique sound. In this chapter, you will learn how to perform some of the most common techniques, such as playing music in the contrapuntal style and playing music with a swing beat. You will also learn how to play several different accompaniment patterns, including the ragtime pattern, the Alberti bass and the walking bass line.

Special Playing Techniques

In this Chapter...

Using the Piano Pedals

Emphasize the Melody

Play with a Swing Beat

Play Music in the Contrapuntal Style

Play the Alberti Bass

Play the Ragtime Accompaniment

Play the Walking Bass Line

Play the 12-Bar Blues

"Carefree"

"Sarabande"

"Sonatina in C Major"

"The Entertainer"

"A Walk in the Park"

"Down Home Blues"

using the piano pedals

You can use the pedals at your feet to achieve different effects when playing the piano. The motion of pressing a piano pedal is similar to pressing the gas pedal on a car. Before using the pedals, you should practice a musical piece first without the pedals. You can then add the pedals when you are comfortable playing the piece.

The number of pedals included on different types of pianos varies. All grand and upright pianos include two pedals, but many have three. Electronic pianos usually come with one or two pedals, while some come with three. Electronic keyboards usually do not include pedals, although you may be able to purchase them separately.

A damper pedal, the most commonly used pedal, is included on all upright and grand pianos and most electronic pianos. When you press the damper pedal, all the notes you play will continue to sound even after you lift your fingers off the keys, giving your music a richer, fuller sound.

When playing beginner pieces, written music will usually show you where you should use the damper pedal. However, intermediate and advanced pieces will often not include this information.

The Damper Pedal (the right pedal)

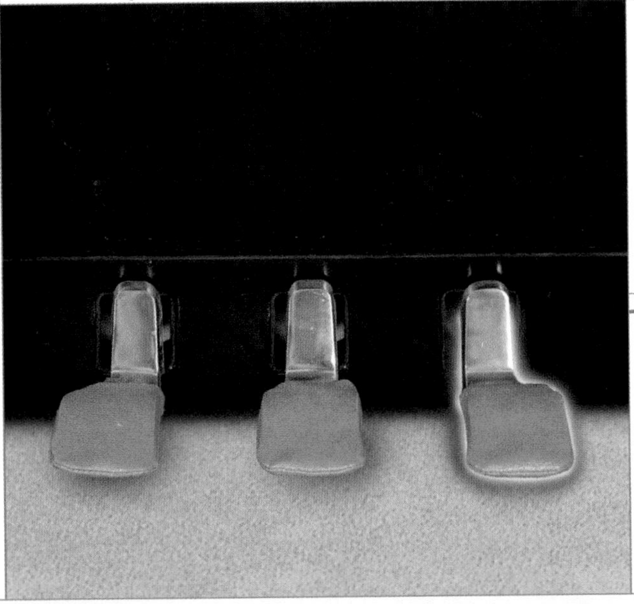

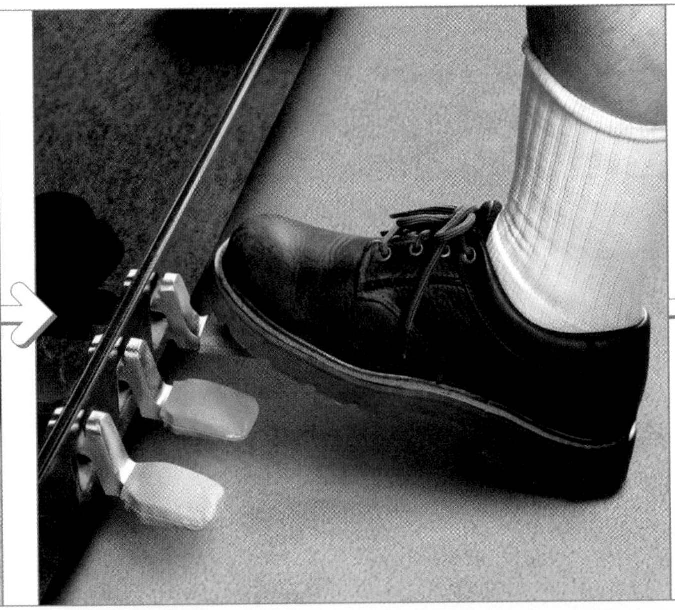

- All upright and grand pianos and most electronic pianos have a damper pedal. The damper pedal is the most commonly used pedal.

- When you press the damper pedal, all the notes you play will continue to sound even after you lift your fingers off the keys. When you release the pedal, all the notes you play will no longer continue to sound.
- The damper pedal gives your music a richer, fuller sound.

- To use the damper pedal, place the heel of your right foot on the floor in front of the pedal and place the top part of your foot on the pedal. When you press and release the pedal, keep your heel on the floor.

- If a musical piece requires you to use the damper pedal frequently, rest the top of your foot lightly on the pedal. If a piece does not require you to use the damper pedal for a significant amount of time, you can rest your entire foot flat on the floor beside the pedal until you need to use the pedal.

Tip

What should I do if a pedal is too high off the floor?

If a pedal is uncomfortably high off the floor, you can place a book underneath the pedal so the heel of your foot rests on the book. You can also try pushing the bench slightly away from the piano. Children who have trouble reaching the pedals can lean, similar to a standing position, when they need to use the pedals rather than sitting on the front of the bench.

What should I keep in mind when using the damper pedal?

When using the damper pedal, make sure you press and release the pedal in the correct locations in the piece. Some people release the pedal too early, too late or forget to press or release the pedal altogether. You will require good coordination to keep your fingers moving while pressing your foot down on the pedal, so be patient and play slowly when learning.

Also, do not use the pedal when the piece does not require the use of the pedal. Using the pedal unnecessarily results in the notes blending together and makes the music sound muddy.

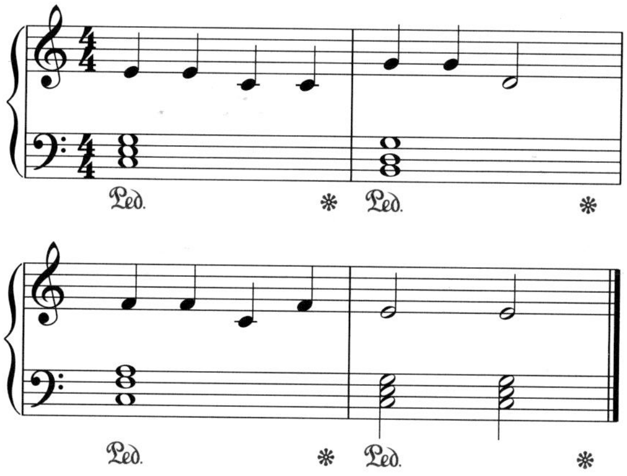

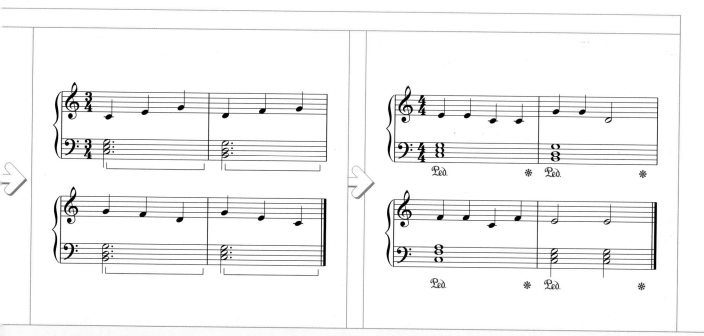

- In beginner music, you will often see brackets below the staff to indicate when you should use the damper pedal. When the bracket begins, press the pedal. You should continue to press the pedal until the bracket ends and then immediately release the pedal.

- In this example of written music, play the notes as shown, making sure to press and release the damper pedal when indicated.

- In all levels of music, you may see Ped. below the staff to indicate when you should use the damper pedal. When you see Ped., press the pedal. You should continue to press the pedal until you see ✻ and then immediately release the pedal.

- In this example of written music, play the notes as shown, making sure to press and release the damper pedal when indicated.

CONTINUED...

using the piano pedals (continued)

In addition to the right pedal, your piano may have one or two other pedals you can use to achieve different effects.

You will find a soft pedal on all upright and grand pianos and some electronic pianos. The soft pedal is useful when you want to play a section of a piece very softly. When you use the soft pedal, you should also press the keys more gently with your fingers. The soft pedal, which is the pedal farthest to the left, should be played using your left foot. A piece of music can use both the right (damper) and left (soft) pedal separately or at the same time.

The middle pedal, between the soft and damper pedals, can serve one of two possible functions—mute or sustain. You use your right foot to play the mute or sustain pedal. The mute pedal makes the notes you play sound significantly softer and muffled and is useful for practicing the piano without disturbing your family or neighbors. The sustain pedal is used in advanced music. With the sustain pedal, only the notes you play at the same time as you press the pedal will continue to sound after you lift your fingers off the keys.

Soft Pedal (the left pedal)

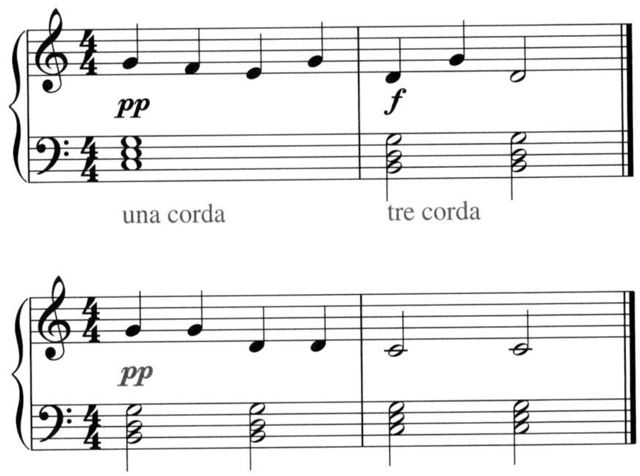

- All upright and grand pianos and some electronic pianos have a soft pedal.
- When you press the soft pedal, all the notes you play will sound slightly softer. When you release the pedal, all the notes you play will once again sound at the normal volume.
- The soft pedal helps you play more quietly. When you use the soft pedal, you should also press the keys more gently with your fingers.
- You use your left foot to press the soft pedal just as you use your right foot to press the damper pedal.
- In written music, you may see "una corda" below the staff to indicate when you should use the soft pedal. When you see these words, press the pedal. You should continue to press the pedal until you see "tre corda" and then immediately release the pedal.

Note: Una corda is the Italian term for "one string." Tre corda is the Italian term for "three strings."

- In written music, composers use the pp (very soft) and ppp (extremely soft) volume markings to indicate when you should play softly. When you see the pp or ppp volume markings, you can use the soft pedal to help you play more softly.

Tip

Can I add pedals to my electronic keyboard?

Although electronic keyboards do not usually come with pedals, you may be able to purchase pedals separately that you can plug into your keyboard. Electronic keyboards normally allow you to add one or two pedals. Pedals for electronic keyboards often perform more than one function. For example, a pedal may act as a damper pedal and allow you to change programs, such as starting or stopping a drum beat. To determine if you can add pedals to your keyboard, check your keyboard's manual.

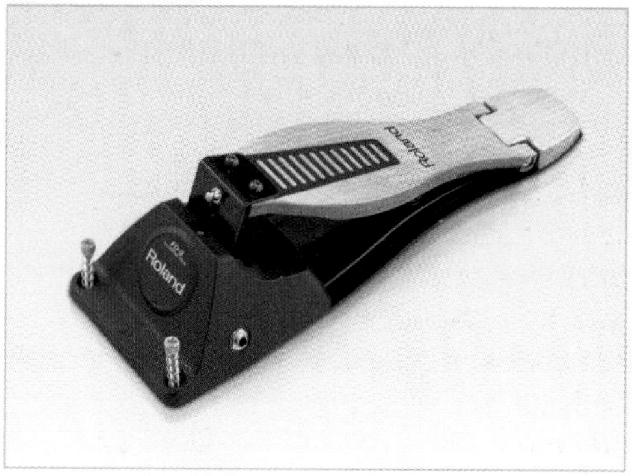

Mute Pedal (the middle pedal)

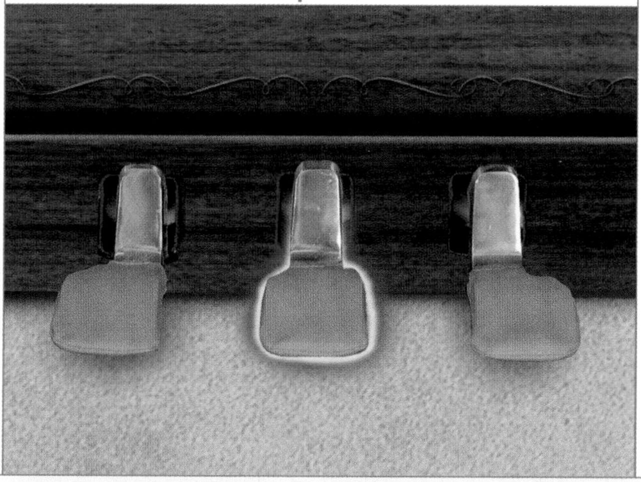

- Some upright pianos have a mute pedal.
- You use your right foot to press the mute pedal. When you press down the mute pedal and lock the pedal into position, all the notes you play will sound significantly softer and muffled. When you release the pedal, all the notes you play will once again sound at the normal volume.
- The mute pedal allows you to practice piano without disturbing your family or neighbors.

Sustain Pedal (the middle pedal)

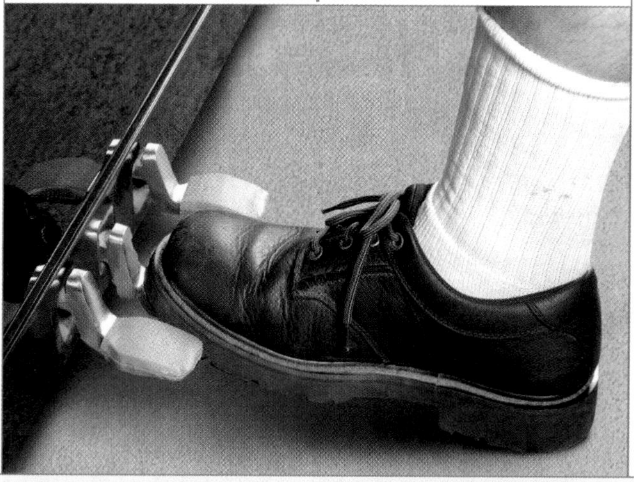

- Some upright and many grand pianos have a sustain, or sostenuto, pedal. The sustain pedal is used only in advanced music.
- When you press the sustain pedal, only the notes you play at the same time as you press the pedal will continue to sound after you lift your fingers off the keys. When you release the pedal, those notes will no longer continue to sound.
- Written music does not indicate when you should use the sustain pedal. However, the sustain pedal can free up your hands to play other notes that you cannot reach while holding down the notes you want to continue to sound.
- You use your right foot to press the sustain pedal just as you use your right foot to press the damper pedal.

emphasize the melody

To ensure that the melody of a musical piece can be heard over the accompaniment, you should emphasize the melody by playing the melody louder than the accompaniment.

Although written music does not often instruct you to play the melody louder than the accompaniment, it is important to do so, since the accompaniment can easily drown out the melody. The accompaniment usually involves playing more notes at once than the melody and often consists of lower-sounding notes. These lower notes will be louder than the higher notes of the melody, even when the melody is played at the same volume as the accompaniment.

As you play, the hand playing the melody should feel heavier and more forceful than the hand playing the accompaniment, which should play more gently. You usually play the melody with your right hand and the accompaniment with your left hand.

When learning to play the piano, you should begin playing the melody louder than the accompaniment as early as possible, as this will help you develop coordination and help you emphasize the melody when you play more difficult pieces.

Excerpt from "Polka From 'Orpheus'"
by Offenbach

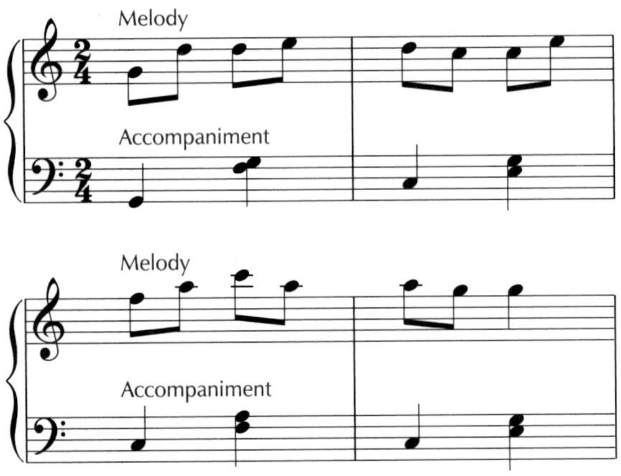

- When playing a musical piece, you should usually play the melody, or tune, louder than the accompaniment to ensure the melody is clearly heard.
- The melody is usually played by the right hand. The accompaniment, which provides a musical background for the melody, is usually played by the left hand.
- Inexperienced piano players tend to play the accompaniment louder than the melody. Playing the melody louder than the accompaniment can be challenging.
- When you begin playing a musical piece, start by playing the left and right hand parts separately before playing both hands at the same time. The hand playing the melody should press the keys with more force than the hand playing the accompaniment.
- When playing the accompaniment, pay attention to how hard you press the keys with your thumb. Your thumb is less coordinated than your fingers and can easily make an unintentionally loud sound.

play with a swing beat

A swing beat, often used in jazz, blues and country music, produces a distinctive, uneven rhythm.

Playing a swing beat involves slightly modifying the duration of beats in a musical piece. For example, when counting a beat such as "1 and 2 and 3 and 4 and," each number (1, 2, 3, 4) should last slightly longer than normal while each "and" should last slightly shorter than normal.

When playing music with a swing beat, you often play pairs of notes, with the first note of the pair receiving a slightly longer beat than the second note. For example, you may play a dotted eighth note with a sixteenth note (♪. 𝅘𝅥𝅯). Before you play a swing beat, you should carefully count the beats in the piece. You may even want to write the beats under the notes to help you when playing.

Songs that should be played with a swing beat include the phrase "swing rhythm," "swing beat" or "swing feel" at the beginning of the piece. Alternatively, if a composer thinks that people may play a certain song with a swing beat when a swing beat should not be used, the composer may include the phrase "straight beat" at the beginning of the piece.

Excerpt from "Oh Susanna"
by Foster

- Jazz, blues and country music often use a swing beat. A swing beat is a unique, uneven rhythm created by playing pairs of slightly longer beats followed by slightly shorter beats.
- When a musical piece should be played with a swing beat, the phrase "swing rhythm", "swing beat" or "swing feel" often appears at the beginning of the music.
- The pairs of notes that appear in music with a swing beat can be shown in different ways, such as two eighth notes (♫), a dotted eighth note and sixteenth note (♪. 𝅘𝅥𝅯) or a dotted quarter note and eighth note (♩. ♪).
- In this example of written music, play the notes with a swing beat.
- When counting the beats for music with a swing beat, such as "1 and 2 and 3 and 4 and," count each number (1, 2, 3, 4) slightly longer than usual and each "and" slightly shorter than usual.

play music in the contrapuntal style

Music written in the contrapuntal style involves playing separate melodies, or tunes, with the left and right hands at the same time. Playing melodies with both hands at the same time is different from many popular styles of music, such as rock and jazz, in which the right hand plays the melody while the left hand plays the accompaniment, often in the form of chords.

When playing a piece in the contrapuntal style, both hands may play the same melody but start at different times or they may play completely different tunes. Both hands may also play different rhythms or volumes throughout the piece.

The contrapuntal style, also known as counterpoint, is most commonly found in Baroque music. Some Classical and Romantic music also incorporates the contrapuntal style.

You should try to include some music written in the contrapuntal style into your practice sessions. Practicing pieces in the contrapuntal style helps you develop coordination and your ability to play piano equally well with both hands.

Excerpt from "German Dance"
by Haydn

Excerpt from "Sarabande"
by Corelli

- When you play a musical piece written in the contrapuntal style, the right and left hands both play a melody, or tune, at the same time. Both hands can play the same melody starting at different times in the piece or play entirely different melodies.
- In addition to playing separate melodies, both hands can also use different playing techniques, such as different rhythms and volume levels. For example, the right hand could play at a soft volume while the left hand plays at a louder volume.
- When you start playing a musical piece written in the contrapuntal style, start by playing the left and right hand parts separately. When both hands can play the notes well, you are ready to play the musical piece with both hands at the same time.
- You should also start playing the musical piece slowly and at a steady speed. Make sure you play notes that appear above or below each other on the staff at the same time.

play the alberti bass

The Alberti bass accompaniment pattern is often used in Classical music to provide a background for the melody, or tune, of a musical piece. The Alberti bass pattern is named after Domenico Alberti, an Italian composer who often incorporated the pattern into his music.

During the Classical period, which lasted from approximately the 1750s to the 1820s, music such as sonatas and sonatinas frequently used the Alberti bass accompaniment pattern. Sonatas and sonatinas are musical compositions made up of two to four pieces, with each piece usually played at a different speed. A sonatina is a shorter version of a sonata. The three most popular composers of the Classical period, Beethoven, Haydn and Mozart, often used the Alberti bass pattern in their music.

The Alberti bass accompaniment pattern involves using your left hand to play the notes of a chord individually, in a specific order. To ensure that the accompaniment pattern does not drown out the melody, keep your fingers on the surface of the keys to avoid pressing the keys too hard and generating too much sound with your left hand.

Excerpt from "Sonata in C Major, 1st Movement" by Mozart

- Classical music often uses the Alberti bass accompaniment pattern, which is played by the left hand.
- The Alberti bass pattern consists of playing each note in a chord individually in a specific order—the low, high, middle, then high note. You then repeat the same notes over and over.
- For example, for the C chord, you would play the C, G, E, G notes over and over.
- The notes in the Alberti bass pattern are played with a steady beat, which usually consists entirely of eighth (♪) or sixteenth (♬) notes.
- When playing the Alberti bass pattern, make sure the notes played by your left hand are played more softly than notes played by your right hand to ensure the melody will be clearly heard.
- When you begin playing a musical piece that uses the Alberti bass pattern, start by playing the left and right hand parts separately before playing both hands at the same time. You should also start playing the piece slowly and at a steady speed.

play the ragtime accompaniment

Ragtime music often uses the ragtime accompaniment pattern to provide a musical background for the melody, or tune. The ragtime style was popular in the late 19th century and was the precursor to jazz music. The ragtime accompaniment pattern, nicknamed the "oom-pah" pattern, is also commonly used in polkas and marches.

An accompaniment pattern is usually played with the left hand, while the right hand plays the melody. The ragtime accompaniment pattern consists of using your left hand to steadily alternate between a low sounding note and a chord approximately one octave higher. An octave refers to the distance between two notes with the same letter name on the keyboard. When playing this accompaniment pattern, you usually play a major or minor chord; however, a dominant 7th or diminished chord may also be played.

The ragtime accompaniment pattern is challenging to play since you must be able to jump quickly from a single note to a chord with one hand. You may need to glance at your fingers on the keyboard to make sure you hit the correct notes, but with practice, you will no longer need to look at the keyboard.

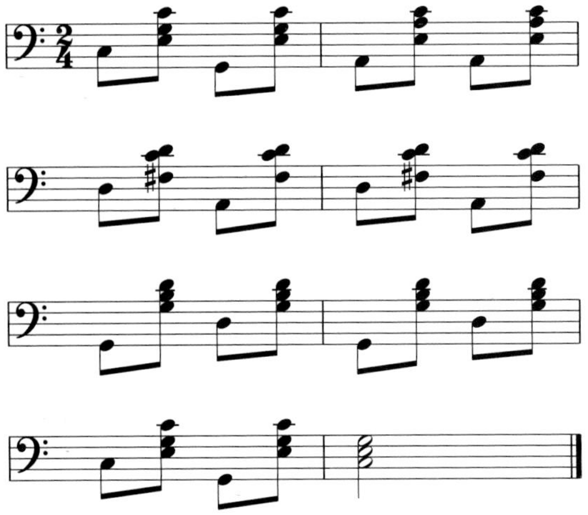

Excerpt from "The Entertainer"
by Joplin

- Ragtime music, which has a light, happy sound, often uses a special accompaniment pattern played by the left hand.

- The accompaniment pattern often used in ragtime music consists of alternating between a low sounding note and a chord about one octave higher. You alternate between a single note and chord in a steady rhythm, which usually consists of eighth notes (♪).

  Note: An octave refers to the distance between two notes with the same letter name on the keyboard.

- When you start playing a musical piece that uses the ragtime accompaniment pattern, start by playing the left and right hand parts separately. When both hands can play the notes well, you are ready to play the musical piece with both hands at the same time.

- You should also start playing the musical piece slowly and at a steady speed.

play the walking bass line

The walking bass line is an accompaniment pattern that you play with your left hand. An accompaniment pattern provides a musical background for the melody, or tune, which is usually played by the right hand.

Often found in blues, jazz and rock music, the walking bass line is commonly used when improvising, especially when playing on your own. Pianists who improvise while playing in a band do not normally play the walking bass line since a bass guitar would usually fill this role. When improvising, you commonly read music from a lead sheet—an outline of a song that gives pianists the freedom to modify the music as they play.

To play the walking bass line, you must be very familiar with the notes that make up chords since the walking bass line includes notes that belong to chords. When playing the walking bass line, at least half of the notes in a measure should be the notes that belong to the chord played in the measure.

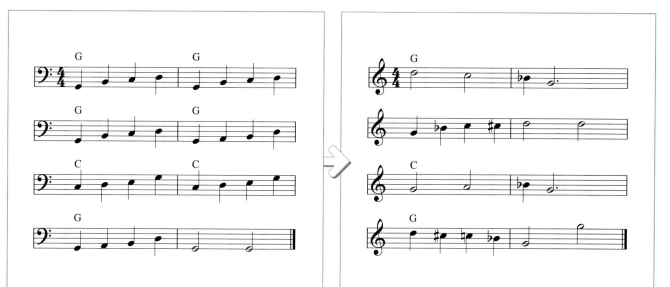

- Blues, jazz and rock music often use the walking bass line, which is a special accompaniment pattern played by the left hand.
- To play the walking bass line, you play some or all of the notes in a chord as well as one or two notes between or close to the notes of a chord. The notes are played individually and are usually played in order, moving up or down the keyboard.
- For example, for the G chord, which consists of the G, B and D notes, you could play G, B, C, D or G, A, B, D.
- You usually play the walking bass line between the first and second C notes below middle C.
- The walking bass line is commonly used when making up music as you play, which is known as improvising. When improvising, you will commonly use a lead sheet.
- On a lead sheet, you can look at the chord names displayed above the staff to determine which notes to play for your walking bass line.
- For example, if you see the C chord name, play the notes in the C chord as your walking bass line.
- Each time you see a new chord name above the staff on a lead sheet, play the notes in the new chord as your walking bass line.

Note: For information on lead sheets, see page 26.

play the 12-bar blues

The 12-bar blues is an accompaniment pattern that provides a musical background for the melody, or tune, of a musical piece.

Playing the 12-bar blues involves playing a specific pattern of three chords for 12 measures. Once you learn the pattern of chords, you can apply the pattern to any scale to play the 12-bar blues in any key.

You will often use the 12-bar blues when making up music as you play, which is known as improvising. When improvising using the 12-bar blues, you must determine which chords to play. This requires you to be familiar with scales and chords. However, you will not always need to determine which chords to play, as some written music indicates the chords you need to play.

When playing chords in the 12-bar blues, you may want to rearrange the order of the notes in a chord, known as a chord inversion, to minimize the distance your hand has to move between chords. For example, you can minimize the distance your hand moves from the C chord (C, E, G) to the F chord (F, A, C) by playing the F chord as C, F, A. For more information on chord inversions, see page 154.

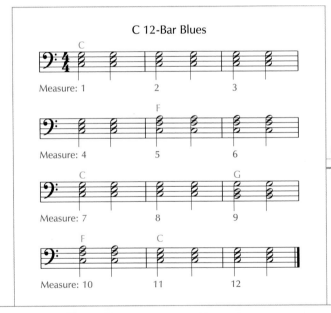

C 12-Bar Blues

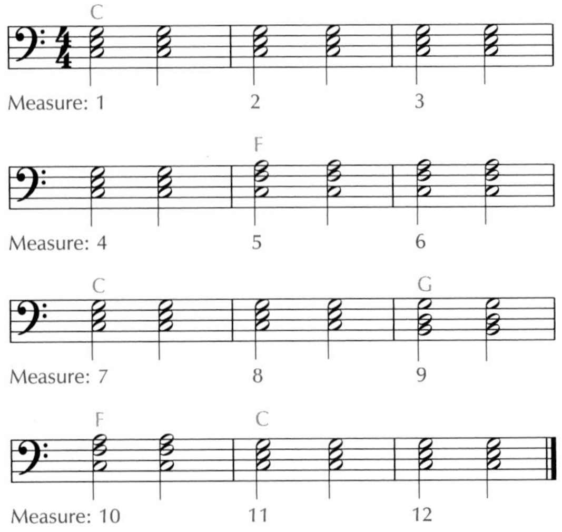

- The 12-bar blues is an accompaniment pattern which is played by the left, right or both hands. Blues music and some jazz and rock music use the 12-bar blues.
- The 12-bar blues is often used when making up music as you play, which is known as improvising.
- The 12-bar blues consists of 12 measures in which you play a specific combination of three chords. The same 12 measures are usually repeated over and over in a musical piece.

Note: A measure is a section of music between two vertical lines on the staff.

1 To determine which chords you will play in your 12-bar blues when improvising, you must first decide which major key you will play the music in. The key determines how low or high the notes in the music will sound.

Note: When playing the 12-bar blues, you will most commonly play music in a major key.

- If you are playing on your own, you can choose any major key. If you are playing with a singer or other musicians, the singer or all the musicians as a group will decide which major key to use.

Tip

To play the 12-bar blues, which chords do I play for each key?

You can use this chart to help you determine the three major chords you play, based on the first, fourth and fifth notes of the major scale that corresponds to the key you are playing the music in. For information on major chords, see page 124.

Major Key	Major Chords You Play
A	A, D, E
A♭	A♭, D♭, E♭
B	B, E, F♯
B♭	B♭, E♭, F
C	C, F, G
C♯	C♯, F♯, G♯
D	D, G, A
E	E, A, B
E♭	E♭, A♭, B♭
F	F, B♭, C
F♯	F♯, B, C♯
G	G, C, D

When playing the 12-bar blues, can I play dominant 7th chords?

Yes. Dominant 7th chords, which produce more of a blues sound than major chords, are commonly used when playing the 12-bar blues. To play the 12-bar blues using dominant 7th chords, convert the major chords to dominant 7th chords. For example, when playing a musical piece in the key of C major, instead of playing the C, F and G chords, play the C7, F7 and G7 chords. For information on dominant 7th chords, see page 132.

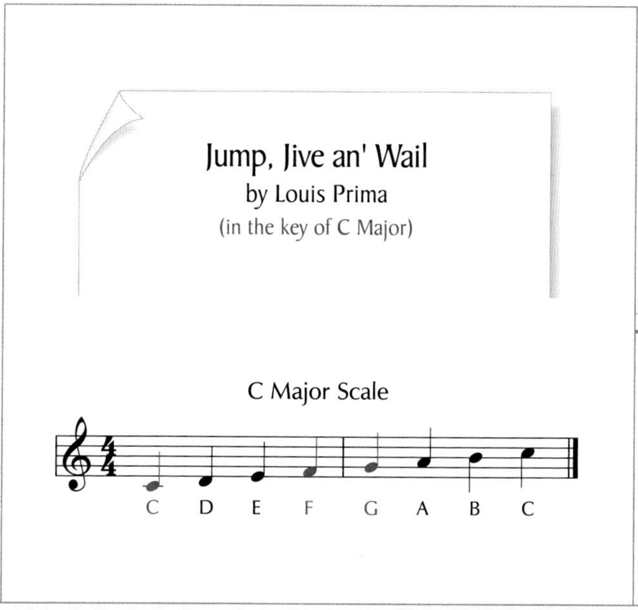

The 12 Measures in the 12-Bar Blues		
Number of measures	**Play major chord based on this note in the major scale**	**Example: key of C major**
4	First note	4 measures of the C major chord (C, E, G)
2	Fourth note	2 measures of the F major chord (F, A, C)
2	First note	2 measures of the C major chord (C, E, G)
1	Fifth note	1 measure of the G major chord (G, B, D)
1	Fourth note	1 measure of the F major chord (F, A, C)
2	First note	2 measures of the C major chord (C, E, G)

2 You next need to determine the major scale that corresponds to the major key you chose to play the music in. Each major key corresponds to a major scale with the same letter name. For example, the key of C major corresponds to the C major scale.

Note: A scale is a series of notes that you play in a specific order. For information on major scales, see page 90.

3 To play the 12-bar blues, the three major chords you play are based on the first, fourth and fifth notes of the corresponding major scale.

- For example, to play the 12-bar blues in the key of C major, you play major chords based on the first (C), fourth (F) and fifth (G) notes in the C major scale—the C, F and G major chords.

- To play the 12-bar blues, play each chord for the number of measures indicated in the above chart.

Carefree
♩ = 80 With a Swing Beat
Frank Horvat
mf
p
f
p
mf

Sarabande

♩ = 76

Corelli

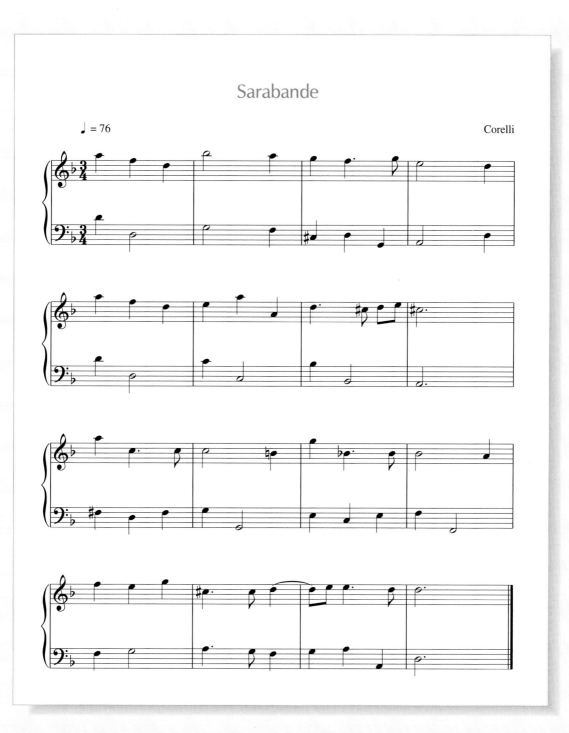

Sonatina in C Major

2nd Movement

The Entertainer
♩ = 112
S. Joplin
p
Left Hand Staccato
f

A Walk in the Park

♩ = 100 Swing Feel

Frank Horvat

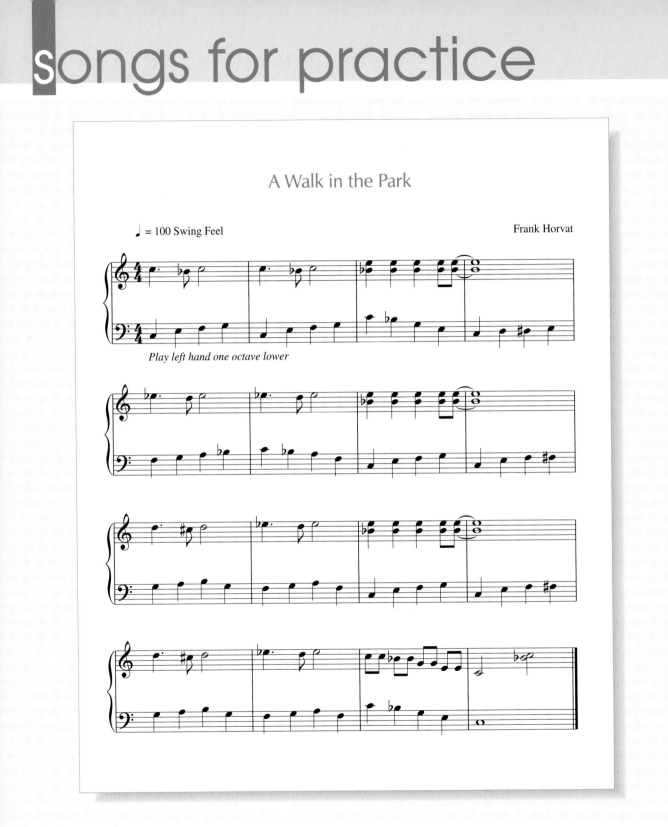

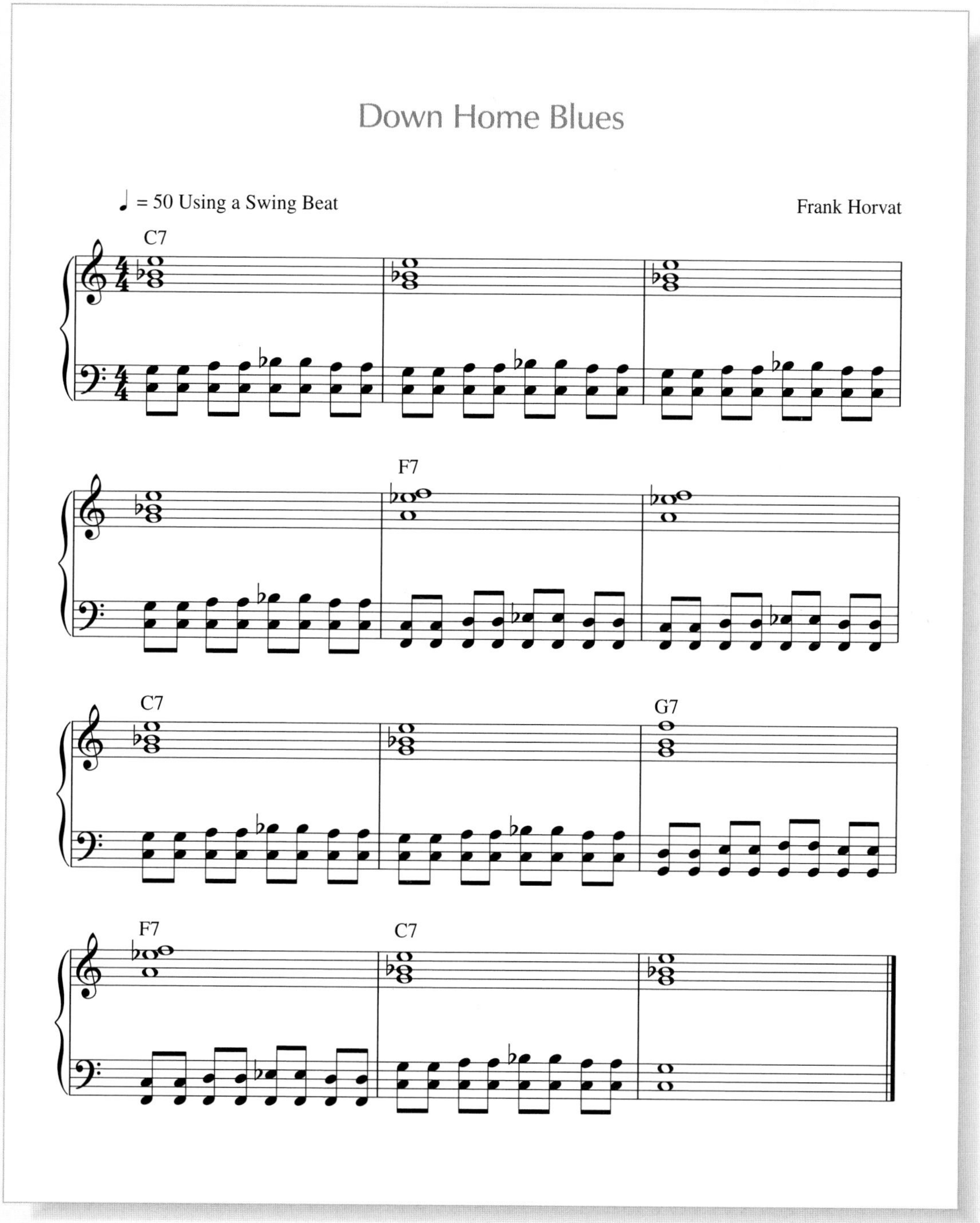
Down Home Blues
♩ = 50 Using a Swing Beat
Frank Horvat
C7
F7
C7
G7
F7
C7

Chapter 9

Improvising, or making up music as you play, allows you to add your own personal touch to music. In this chapter, you will learn how to improvise the melody, or tune, of a piece as well as the accompaniment, or musical background of a piece. You will also find helpful information about how to play with a singer and with other musicians.

Improvising and Playing with Others

In this Chapter...

improvising music

When pianists make up or modify music as they play, they are said to be improvising music. Improvising, which is common in jazz, blues, pop and rock music, allows performers to express their creativity since they spontaneously contribute their own melody and/or accompaniment to an existing piece of music.

Performers often use chords or scales as the basis for an improvised melody. The chords or scales used in a musical piece provide you with a set of notes that you can rearrange in any way you like. For example, when improvising a melody for a piece based on the C blues scale, you may want to use the notes of the C blues scale for your melody.

When improvising, you will often take your cues from a lead sheet, which is a piece of written music that provides an outline of a song—the melody written on a treble clef (𝄞) staff, with the accompaniment provided as chord names above the melody. To improvise, you elaborate on the outline the lead sheet provides.

What is Improvising?

- When you improvise, you make up or modify a musical piece as you play the piece.
- You can improvise all or part of the melody, or tune, of a piece. You can also improvise all or part of the accompaniment, or musical background, of a piece.
- You will usually use your right hand to play the melody and your left hand to play the accompaniment. If you are playing with other musicians, you may use both hands to play the accompaniment.
- When improvising, you will often use a lead sheet as a starting point for your improvisation. A lead sheet is a piece of written music that provides only an outline of a song.
- A lead sheet provides the melody written on a treble clef (𝄞) staff, with the accompaniment provided as chord names written above the melody.

Note: For more information on lead sheets, see page 26.

Tip

How else can I improvise a melody?

You can improvise a melody by simply shifting the whole melody up or down one octave and playing the melody in the new octave. An octave refers to the distance between two notes with the same letter name on the keyboard. Similarly, you can play every note in the original melody while simultaneously playing the same notes one octave higher. You can also experiment with the rhythms and note lengths in the original melody. For example, if you have a measure of four quarter notes (♩), try substituting the first quarter note with two eighth notes (♫).

Can my electronic keyboard help me improvise music?

Often, electronic keyboards can provide a background beat for various music styles, such as rock and disco. This steady background beat allows you to easily play along and improvise your own melody without having to play an accompaniment.

Improvising the Melody

Original Music

Improvised Melody (using notes of chords)

Original Music (Key of C Major)

Improvised Melody (using notes from scale)

C Major Scale

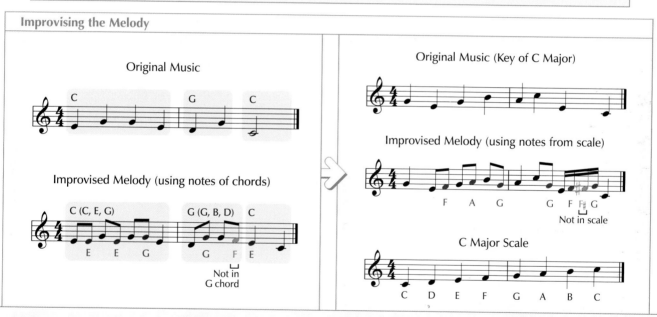

- You can improvise the melody for part or all of a musical piece by adding notes to the existing melody or creating your own melody.
- To improvise the melody, you can experiment with the notes being played in the chords of the accompaniment in the piece.
- For example, while a C major chord is being played in the accompaniment, you can improvise the melody by playing the notes in the C major chord (C, E, G). You can also include other notes that do not belong to the C major chord to add variety.
- When improvising the melody, you can also use notes based on the key of the piece.

Note: The key of a piece corresponds to a specific major or minor scale. The piece will use notes primarily from the corresponding major or minor scale. For information on keys and major and minor scales, see pages 187, 90 and 94.

- For example, if you are playing a piece in the key of C major, you can improvise the melody by playing notes from the C major scale. You can also include other notes that do not belong to the C major scale to add variety.

CONTINUED...

When you improvise, or make up, the accompaniment for a musical piece, you will usually play the chords that are written for the piece, but you customize the music by playing the chords in different ways.

You will often use a lead sheet as a basis for improvising the accompaniment. Lead sheets show you which chords to play, but you can elaborate on what is written on the lead sheets and decide how you want to play the chords. For example, you can play broken chords, arpeggios or rolled chords instead of just playing solid chords.

Improvising the accompaniment can also involve making up rhythms. For example, instead of simply holding down all the notes of a chord together, play the chord in a rhythmic pattern. Playing chords in a rhythmic pattern, known as comping, is how piano players in rock, jazz and blues bands often play chords.

When improvising, be as creative as you can, but remember to keep a steady beat with no pauses. You should also keep the mood of the piece in mind. For example, do not play a quick and exciting chord pattern if the mood of the piece is solemn and somber.

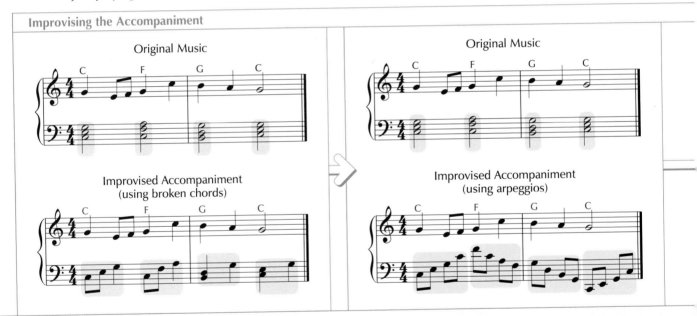

Improvising the Accompaniment

Original Music

Improvised Accompaniment (using broken chords)

- You can improvise the accompaniment for part or all of a musical piece. When improvising, you will usually play the chords that are written for the piece, but you can play the chords in different ways to alter the music.

Play Broken Chords

- When improvising the accompaniment, you can play broken chords by playing each note of a chord separately or playing only some of the notes of the chord separately.

Note: For more information on broken chords, see page 152.

Original Music

Improvised Accompaniment (using arpeggios)

Play Chords as Arpeggios

- When improvising the accompaniment, you can also play each chord as an arpeggio.

- To play a chord as an arpeggio, play the notes of the chord separately from lowest to highest or highest to lowest. Then play some or all of the same notes in the same order at the next higher or lower location on the keyboard.

Note: For more information on arpeggios, see page 153.

Tip

Are there any accompaniment patterns that can help me when I am improvising?

It is helpful to know how to play different accompaniment patterns when improvising. For example, knowing how to play the ragtime accompaniment pattern (page 214) or the walking bass line (page 215) may be useful when improvising a jazz song.

Is there a style of music that makes it easy to improvise both the melody and accompaniment?

You can easily improvise both the melody and accompaniment for a blues piece. To improvise the melody, you can use the notes of a blues scale. To improvise the accompaniment, use the chords that belong to the scale's corresponding 12-bar blues accompaniment pattern. For example, try playing the chords of the C 12-bar blues accompaniment pattern with your left hand. At the same time, experiment with the notes of the C blues scale with your right hand. For information on the blues scale, see page 111. For information on the 12-bar blues, see page 216.

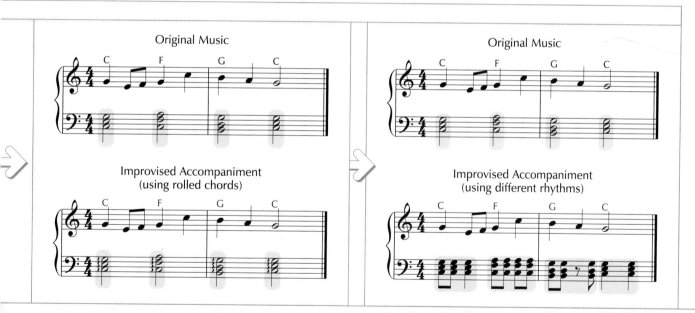

Original Music

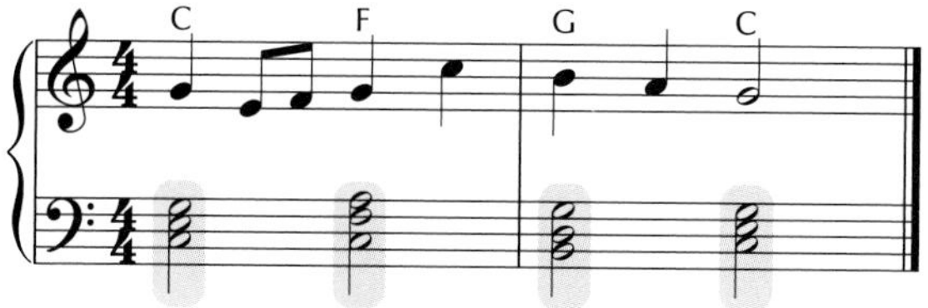

Improvised Accompaniment
(using rolled chords)

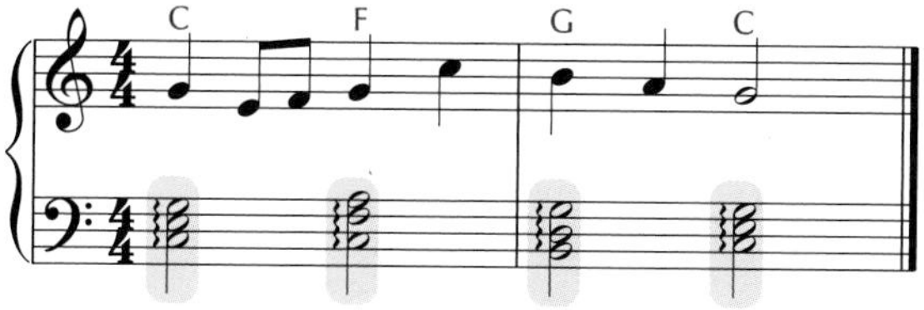

Original Music

Improvised Accompaniment
(using different rhythms)

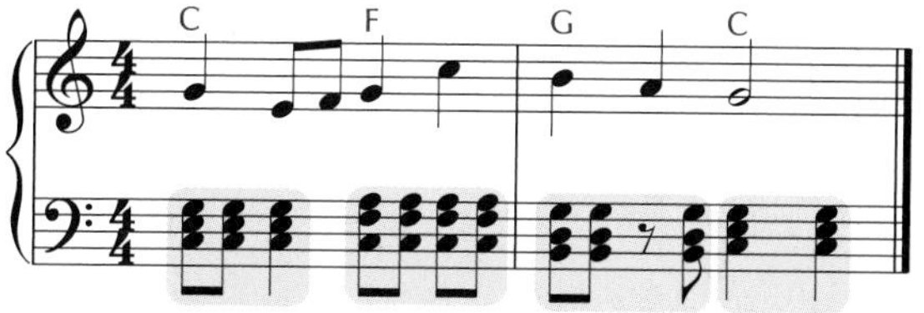

Play Rolled Chords

- Playing rolled chords is another way of improvising the accompaniment for a musical piece.
- To play a rolled chord, press and hold down the first note of the chord and then quickly play the other notes of the chord one by one, until you are holding down all the notes of the chord.

Note: The ⦚ symbol indicates to play a chord as a rolled chord.

Change the Rhythm of Chords

- You can also improvise the accompaniment by changing the rhythm of the chords you play. For example, you could hold a chord for two beats or play the chord several times during two beats.
- You can repeat the same rhythm over and over or change the rhythm throughout the piece.
- Playing chords in a more rhythmically-active pattern is called comping and is often used in rock, jazz and blues bands.

CONTINUED...

improvising music (continued)

When playing in front of an audience, you can improvise, or make up, music to begin or end a musical piece in an interesting way. For example, you can play a few extra measures at the beginning or end of a musical piece to introduce or complete the piece. Improvised beginnings and endings only need to be long enough to signal the beginning or end of the piece. They can be as short as one to four measures.

In order to effectively improvise beginnings and endings, you must know the piece well so you can decide whether you want your beginning or ending to blend or contrast with the rest of the piece. For example, you may want to improvise a loud beginning that uses many solid chords to contrast with a piece that is very soft and gentle.

The type of beginning or ending you play depends on the type of effect you want to create. For example, to get your audience's attention when you start a piece, play a loud beginning with a fast tempo. If you want to leave the audience with a quiet, peaceful feeling at the end of a piece, play a soft, gradually slowing ending.

Improvise Before a Musical Piece Begins

Clementine Introduction (played one octave higher)

Clementine Introduction (using special effects)

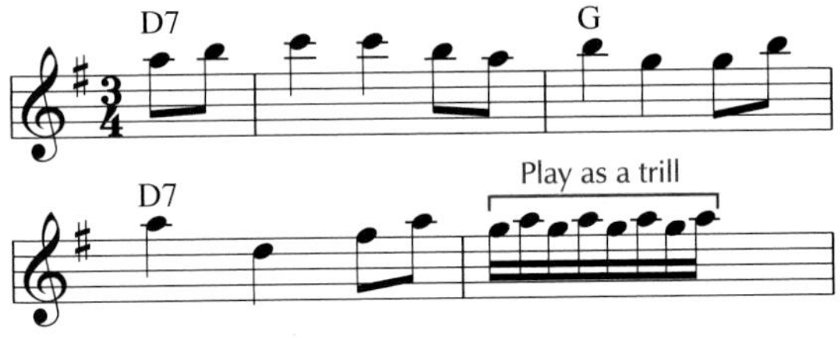

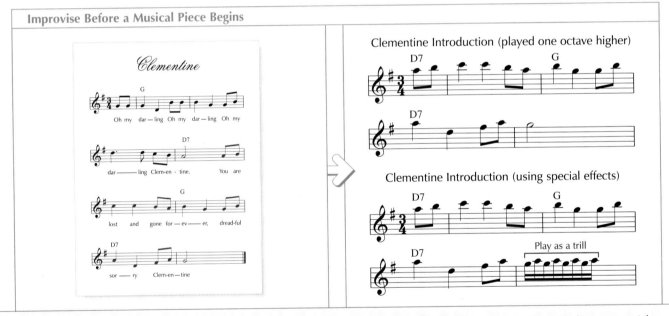

- Before you begin playing a musical piece for an audience, you can make up, or improvise, a short introduction for the piece, which announces to the audience that the piece is starting.

- When improvising an introduction for a musical piece, a common method is to find two to four familiar measures of music within the piece and play the measures at the beginning of the piece.

Note: A measure is a section of music between two vertical lines on the staff.

- When improvising the introduction by playing familiar measures of music within the piece, you can play the notes one octave higher to give the introduction a unique sound.

Note: When you play notes one octave higher, you play the notes at the next higher location on the keyboard.

- You can also use special effects, such as trills, to decorate the notes in the melody of the introduction.

Note: When you perform a trill, you alternate very quickly between a note in the melody and the next higher note on the keyboard. For information on trills, see page 181.

Tip

Can I use volume changes to improvise an ending?

To create a unique ending for a musical piece, you can repeat the last one to four measures of the piece and gradually increase or decrease the volume. Gradually increasing the volume, called a crescendo, creates a sense of excitement at the end of a piece. Gradually decreasing the volume, called a decrescendo, creates a delicate, solemn effect at the end of a piece.

Are there any other ways to improvise an ending?

Playing a cadence—playing two specific chords, one after the other—is a popular way to improvise an ending. To determine which chords you need to play, you must first determine the key of the piece. For information on keys, see pages 187 to 189. To play the cadence, you play the chord based on the fifth note of the key's corresponding scale, followed by the chord based on the first note of the key's corresponding scale. For example, to play a cadence for a piece in the key of C major, you play the chord based on the fifth (G) note of the C major scale, followed by the chord based on the first (C) note of the C major scale.

Improvise at the End of a Musical Piece

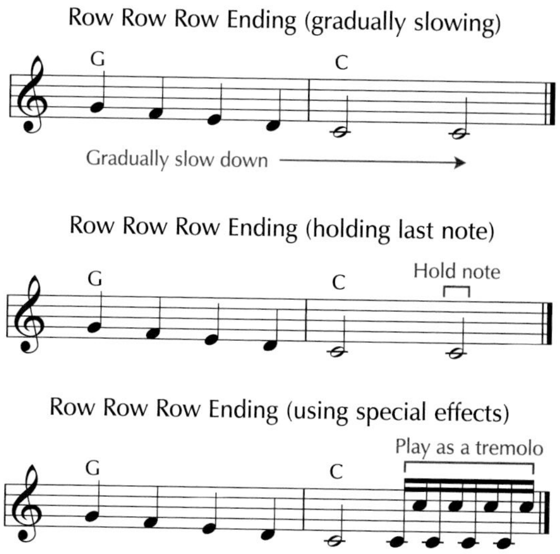

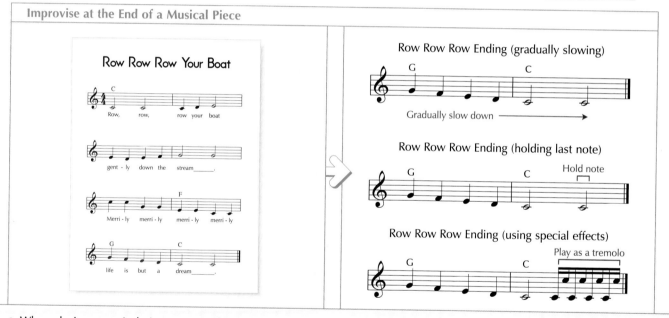

- When playing a musical piece for an audience, you can make up, or improvise, a short ending for the piece which announces to the audience that the piece is ending.
- When improvising an ending for a musical piece, a common method is to repeat the last one to four measures of the musical piece at the end of the piece.
- When improvising the ending by repeating measures, you can play the notes one octave higher to give the ending a unique sound.

Note: When you play notes one octave higher, you play the notes at the next higher location on the keyboard.

- When improvising the ending by repeating measures, you may want to gradually play the music more slowly or hold the last note of the ending longer than normal to add drama to the ending.
- You may also want to use special effects, such as tremolos, to add tension to the ending.

Note: When you play a tremolo, you alternate between two notes very quickly. For information on tremolos, see page 185.

playing with a singer

When playing with, or accompanying, a singer, a pianist often plays part of a musical piece, consisting mostly of chords and rhythmic patterns that serve as a background to the singing part.

When playing with a singer, you may use different types of written music. You may use written music that shows a grand staff, indicating the exact notes you should play, as well as an additional staff that shows the notes and lyrics a singer would sing. You may also use a lead sheet, which provides an outline of a musical piece, allowing you to improvise, or modify, the music as you play. A lead sheet also often provides the lyrics for a singer.

As you play, make sure you are not drowning out the singer. If you cannot hear the singer, you must adjust the volume of your playing. Also, listen to the singer to determine the speed you should play. If the singer speeds up or slows down during the musical piece, you must also speed up or slow down.

- You can play accompaniment on the piano to provide a musical background for a singer.
- When playing with a singer, you may use written piano music that includes an additional staff showing the notes and lyrics that a singer would sing.
- If you want to modify the music as you play, known as improvising, you can use a lead sheet. A lead sheet is written music that provides only an outline of a song.

Note: For information on the types of written music, see page 26. For information on improvising, see page 226.

- When playing with a singer, make sure you can hear the singer at all times. If you cannot hear the singer, play more softly.
- When playing a grand piano and accompanying a singer, close the lid of the piano to help soften the piano's sound.
- Listen to the singer and follow the singer through the piece. If the singer speeds up or slows down, you must also speed up or slow down your playing to stay in time with the singer.

playing with other musicians

Pianists can play any type of music with other musicians. For example, piano players can play classical music as part of an orchestra or a smaller group such as a duet, trio, quartet or quintet. Pianists can also play jazz, blues, rock or pop music as part of a band.

When playing with other musicians, the pianist often provides the accompaniment, which consists mostly of chords and rhythmic patterns that work as a background to the parts played by other musicians.

When you play classical music with other musicians, you use written music and play the notes as indicated. When you play jazz, blues, rock or pop music with other musicians in a band, you may use a lead sheet, which is a piece of written music that provides an outline of a song. Lead sheets allow you to make up, or improvise, the music as you play.

When playing with other musicians, you must always listen to the other musicians to ensure that your piano part blends with the overall sound and does not overshadow any of the other instruments.

- Classical music is often played by groups of two (duet), three (trio), four (quartet) or five (quintet) musicians. The flute, violin, viola and cello complement the piano well. You can also play a duet with another piano player.

- If you want to play jazz, blues, rock or pop music with other musicians in a band, most bands include a singer and a piano, guitar, bass guitar and drum.

- When playing with a group of musicians, one person must be the leader. You must listen to and follow the leader at all times. For example, if the leader speeds up or slows down, you must also speed up or slow down.

- When playing with other musicians, you should also make sure you can hear the other musicians at all times. If you cannot hear the other musicians, play more softly.

Changing the key of a musical piece

Changing the key of a musical piece, which is known as transposing music, involves shifting notes higher or lower in pitch. When you transpose a piece, the distance between each note remains the same, so the structure of the piece does not change.

In order to change the key of a piece, you must be very familiar with the pattern of whole steps and half steps that separate notes on the keyboard. Two keys that are separated by another key, whether white or black, are a whole step apart. Two keys that appear side by side, whether white or black, are a half step apart. For example, to change the key from C major to E major, first you must recognize that there are four half steps from C major to E major, since that is the distance between the key names. Then you shift every note in the piece up by four half steps.

When changing the music, remember that the key of a musical piece corresponds to a specific major or minor scale. A musical piece written in a specific major or minor key uses notes primarily from the corresponding major or minor scale. For information on major and minor scales, see pages 90 and 94.

Reasons for Changing the Key

- Changing the key of a musical piece changes how low or high the notes of the piece sound.

Note: The key of a piece determines which scale the music will primarily use notes from. For information on keys, see page 187.

- Changing the key of a musical piece is useful when you are accompanying a singer. If a singer cannot sing as low or high as a piece is written, you can change the piece to a key that better suits the singer's vocal range.
- Changing the key of a piece is also useful when you are playing in a band and want to change a piece to a key that will suit every instrument. For example, many guitar players are most comfortable playing in the key of E major.

How to Change the Key of a Piece

1 To change the key of a piece, you must first determine the current key of the piece you want to change. To determine the key of a piece, see page 188.

Is there another way to change the key of a musical piece?

Yes. You can simply change the notes or chords as you play by mentally moving each written note up or down by the appropriate number of whole or half steps before you play the note. This method of changing the key is quicker than rewriting the piece, but it is much more challenging.

Can I have the key of a piece changed for me?

Yes. Some electronic keyboards can automatically change the music you play. You can program the electronic keyboard to shift all the notes up or down by a particular number of whole or half steps and then simply play the notes as written. The notes will sound higher or lower, depending on how you programmed the electronic keyboard.

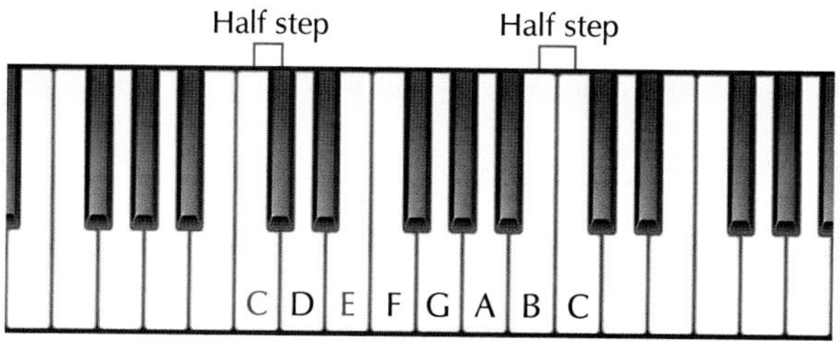

2 Determine the number of half steps between the name of the current key of the musical piece and the key you want to change the piece to.

- For example, when changing a piece from the key of C major to the key of E major, count the number of half steps between C and E. In this case, the number of half steps is four.

Note: A half step is the distance between two keys, whether white or black, that are side by side on the keyboard.

3 After determining the number of half steps between the key names, shift all the notes in the musical piece up or down by the same number of half steps.

Note: The distance between each note in the piece stays the same, but all the notes are played either higher or lower on the keyboard.

4 Change the key signature of the musical piece to reflect the new key. Each key has its own key signature which indicates the sharps and flats you need to play.

- In this example, the piece was changed to the key of E major.

Scarborough Fair

♩ = 138
Dm C Dm
Are you going to Scar - bor - ough Fair___
Dm G Dm
___? Pars - ley, sage, rose - mar - y and thyme___
Dm F
___. Re - mem - ber me to one who lives
C Dm C
there___. She was once a
C Dm
true love of mine___. She was
C Dm
once a true love of mine___.

For He's a Jolly Good Fellow

Chapter 10

When playing the piano, there are many different styles of music that you can choose from. This chapter provides you with an overview of the most popular musical styles, from the Baroque period, which started in the early 1600s, to current styles, such as rock, jazz and pop music.

Styles of Music

In this Chapter...

baroque music

The Baroque period lasted from the early 1600s to about the 1750s. During this period, the church and the aristocracy, or royalty, controlled the arts. As a result, the music, art and architecture created during the Baroque period was very extravagant, ornate and complicated. The term Baroque comes from the Portuguese word for "a pearl of irregular shape"—like the music of the time, a pearl is also extravagant and ornate.

The piano had not yet been invented in the Baroque period, so keyboard music of the time was written for the harpsichord, which was the predecessor of the piano. Although the music was not written for the piano, the music is often played on the piano when performed today.

Important Composers

There are many well-known composers from the Baroque period. Three of the most important composers of musical pieces in the Baroque style are Johann Sebastian Bach, George Frideric Handel and Antonio Vivaldi.

Characteristics of Baroque Music

- Baroque music is often played in the contrapuntal style, which means the right and left hands both play a melody, or tune, at the same time.
- The rhythms of Baroque music consist of many notes played in a short period of time. Baroque rhythms are also often very repetitive. For example, the same note values, such as eighth notes, may be played over and over.
- The music of the Baroque period uses notes from the major and minor scales and chords. Major and minor scales became more popular during the Baroque period.
- Chords in Baroque music often have extra notes added to them to give the chords a harsh sound.
- Notes in Baroque music are often decorated using trills, turns and mordents, in which two or more notes are played very quickly around notes in the music.
- Due to the volume limitations of the harpsichord, Baroque music often includes abrupt changes in volume, referred to as "terraced dynamics."
- Baroque music often uses a narrow range of notes because the harpsichord offered fewer keys than the piano.
- Today, notes with longer values, such as quarter notes and half notes, are played detached from adjacent notes to respect the fact that Baroque music was written for the harpsichord, which could not play notes smoothly.

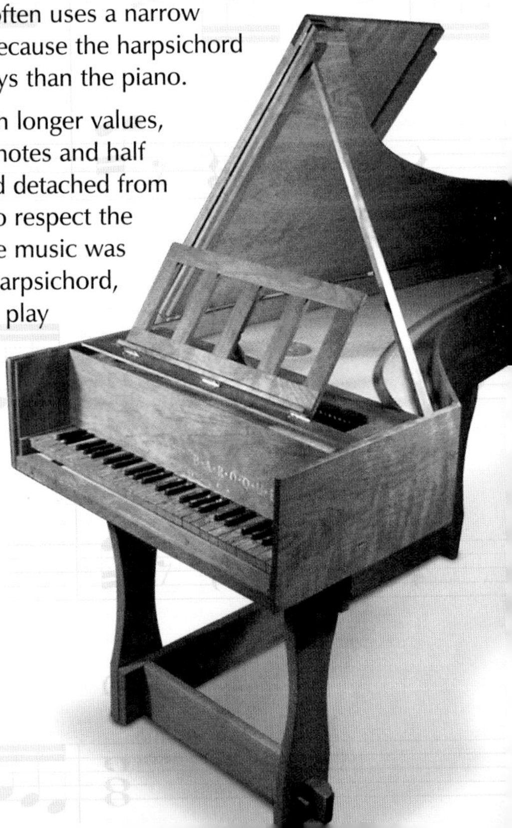

Classical music

The Classical period lasted from about the 1750s to the 1820s. The composers and artists of the Classical period were influenced by the symmetry, balance and precision of ancient Greek and Roman art and architecture. At the same time, order and properness were highly valued. As a result, Classical music is based on reason, order, rules and restraint.

Important Composers

Ludwig van Beethoven, Franz Joseph Haydn and Wolfgang Amadeus Mozart were three well-known composers in the Classical period. These composers were known as the "Viennese school" and brought new ideas and ways of composing to the music of the time.

Sonatas and Sonatinas

Sonatas and sonatinas were the preferred type of piano composition during the Classical period. Sonatas and sonatinas are musical compositions made up of two to four pieces, known as movements, with each piece usually played at a different speed. A sonatina is a shorter version of a sonata.

Characteristics of Classical Music

- Classical music is very structured. Musical phrases, or ideas, are typically four measures long.
- Classical music often uses gradual volume changes to enhance the phrases, or musical ideas, in a piece.
- The beat of Classical music is very steady.
- Classical music does not attempt to evoke a specific emotion. Listeners must interpret for themselves how the music makes them feel.
- The music of the Classical period tends to use notes from the major and minor scales and chords.
- Melodies, or tunes, in Classical music tend to be very memorable.
- Notes in Classical music are often decorated using trills, in which the pianist alternates very quickly between two notes.
- The accompaniment, or musical background, often includes quickly played notes, repeated notes, chords in which some or all of the notes are played separately and the Alberti bass pattern, in which each note in each chord is played individually in a specific order.

romantic music

The Romantic period was sparked by the French Revolution and lasted for most of the 1800s. The Romantic period was a time of revolt and revolution. Composers revolted against the structure and formality of the earlier Classical period and music became much more emotional, adventurous and passionate than ever before. Romantic composers also looked to folk music and music from far-off lands for inspiration for their music. The Romantic period was also the age of the virtuoso—a musician who entertains by showing off his or her extraordinary musical talents and artistry.

Important Composers

There are many well-known composers from the Romantic period. Some of these composers include Johannes Brahms, Frédéric Chopin, Franz Liszt, Felix Mendelssohn, Robert Schumann, Piotr Tchaikovsky, Guiseppe Verdi and Richard Wagner.

Characteristics of Romantic Music

- Romantic music commonly uses expression markings, such as dolce, which means "sweet and gentle," to indicate the emotion that should be expressed when playing the music.
- Musical pieces written in the Romantic style commonly include a wide range of volume markings within one piece. The contrast between playing one section very loudly and another section very softly helps to enhance the dramatic quality of the music.
- Many Romantic pieces use rubato, which means "in robbed time." Rubato gives the pianist the freedom to subtly speed up and slow down throughout the piece to make the piece more expressive.
- Romantic music commonly includes very high notes and very low notes because the pianos of the time offered more keys than earlier instruments.
- The music of the Romantic period commonly uses notes from the major and minor scales and chords.
- Melodies, or tunes, in Romantic music tend to be very singable.
- Glissandos, in which the thumb or fingers are quickly slid across the keyboard, are sometimes used to create a dramatic touch in Romantic pieces. Tremolos, in which the pianist quickly alternates between two or more notes, are also sometimes included to create tension or excitement.
- In Romantic music, accents, staccatos and grace notes are commonly used. Accented notes are played with more force to emphasize the notes, while staccato notes are played shorter and detached from adjacent notes. Grace notes are notes played quickly before a note to decorate the note.

Impressionist music

The Impressionist style of music grew popular in France in the 1880s and 1890s and was an influence on many musical styles throughout the 20th century.

Just as the Romantic period was a revolt against the structure and rules of the earlier Classical period, the Impressionist period was a rebellion against the emotions and drama of the Romantic period.

Impressionist composers attempted to evoke images rather than express emotions through their work and themes of the serenity of everyday life were popular in their music.

Shorter composition types, such as preludes, nocturnes and arabesques become very popular during the Impressionist period.

Important Composers

There are many important composers of the Impressionist period. Some of these composers include Claude Debussy, Maurice Ravel, Gabriel Fauré and Erik Satie.

Characteristics of Impressionist Music

- Impressionist composers were influenced by foreign music, such as the rhythms of Spanish music.
- In addition to the major and minor scales, Impressionist music also uses modes, which are an ancient form of scales, pentatonic scales and foreign scales, such as those found in Indian and Asian music.
- Impressionist music frequently uses chords moving in parallel motion. This means that when both hands are playing chords, both hands move in the same direction along the keyboard instead of moving away from each other, as was done in previous styles of music.
- Impressionist music often includes chords with many notes that usually require both hands to play, such as 9th chords.
- In Impressionist pieces, a harsh sounding chord is not necessarily followed by a more pleasing sounding chord. Composers would use as many harsh sounding chords as they required to evoke an image for the listener.
- Impressionist music often has no regular beat but uses floating rhythms instead. These floating rhythms help to enhance the dreamlike qualities of the music.
- Softer volume levels are frequently used to represent a more calm, relaxed state in the music.

contemporary music

Contemporary music is abstract, complex, technical music composed throughout the 20th century. The Contemporary period began to take shape in the years leading up to the start of World War I. Many composers of this time were rebelling against the lyrical, emotional qualities of previous musical periods. Contemporary music can often be harsh sounding and include themes of ugliness and horror.

Important Composers

Some of the important Contemporary composers of the 20th century include Igor Stravinsky, Arnold Schoenberg, Béla Bartók, John Cage, Pierre Boulez, Philip Glass and Arvo Pärt.

Characteristics of Contemporary Music

- The beat in Contemporary music may constantly change throughout a musical piece. Composers may also use odd numbers of beats per measure, such as 5, 7 or 11.
- Contemporary music may have two different rhythms playing at the same time to create a sense of chaos or aggressiveness.
- Composers often create harshness in a musical piece by using two opposite chords, such as C major and F-sharp minor, played at the same time.
- Contemporary composers often have the right hand playing in one key, such as C major, while the left hand plays in a different key, such as F minor.
- Contemporary melodies are not easily singable and often include large leaps from one note to the next.
- In some Contemporary pieces, all the notes on the keyboard are given equal importance, referred to as atonality. This style of music is not based on the major and minor scales.

Styles of Contemporary Music

There are many styles of music within the category of Contemporary music, including:

- Neoclassicism—composers revert back to the ideals of Baroque and Classical music.
- Atonality—all the notes on the keyboard are given equal importance.
- Electronic music—uses electronic instruments to produce sounds that acoustic instruments cannot.
- Chance music—written with only a set of guidelines to guide the performers.
- Post-modernism—composers combine different musical styles and techniques that were popular in the past.

rock music

Rock music started in the early 1950s and combined blues and country music with fast, intense rhythms and loud, often harsh sounds. Although rock music was originally based on youth rebellion, the music has developed into a style that can be appreciated by a wide variety of people.

Famous Performers

There are several pianists who have performed rock music in a unique and interesting way. These performers include Jerry Lee Lewis, Little Richard and Stevie Wonder.

TOP 20 ROCK SONGS

	Title	Artist
1	Stairway to Heaven	Led Zeppelin
2	Satisfaction	The Rolling Stones
3	Layla	Derek and the Dominoes
4	A Day in the Life	The Beatles
5	Won't Get Fooled Again	The Who
6	Light My Fire	The Doors
7	Comfortably Numb	Pink Floyd
8	Hotel California	The Eagles
9	Born to Run	Bruce Springsteen
10	Imagine	John Lennon
11	Rock and Roll	Led Zeppelin
12	Baba O'Riley	The Who
13	It's Only Rock 'n Roll	The Rolling Stones
14	White Room	Cream
15	Yesterday	The Beatles
16	Purple Haze	Jimi Hendrix
17	Bohemian Rhapsody	Queen
18	Truckin'	The Grateful Dead
19	Money	Pink Floyd
20	Like a Rolling Stone	Bob Dylan

Characteristics of Rock Music

- Rock songs tend to be relatively short, only lasting about three to five minutes.
- In rock music, the melody is often repeated, with a different set of lyrics, or verse, for each repetition.
- Rock songs can express very different moods and each mood is played differently. For example, in a slow ballad, the notes are played smoothly, while in a fast song, the notes are played short and detached.
- Rock music can be very rhythmically active, with many quick notes played in a short amount of time.
- Fast, repeated chords and very high notes are often used in rock songs.

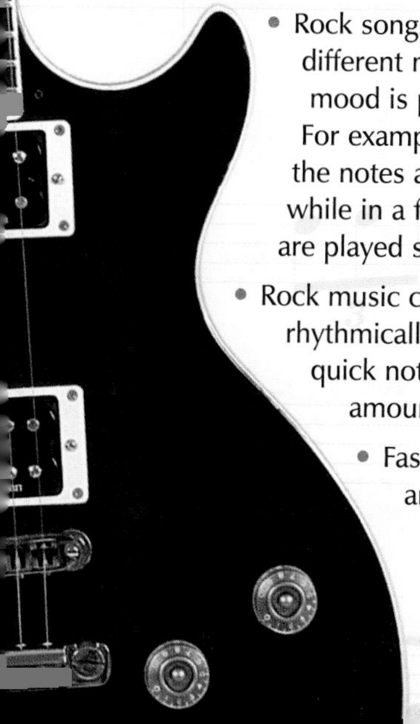

- Major and minor chords, suspended chords and 7th chords are commonly used.
- Glissandos, in which the thumb or fingers are quickly slid across the keyboard, and tremolos, in which the pianist quickly alternates between two or more notes, are commonly used in rock music for dramatic effect.
- Rock music is often less formal than other styles of music. Players often will not use traditional piano music, but instead will use lead sheets, which provide only an outline for songs.
- Rock music is often improvised. When improvising rock music, notes from the blues, pentatonic, major and minor scales as well as notes from ancient scales called modes are frequently used.
- Rock music is often played by a band. When playing the piano in a rock band, you will often only play accompaniment, which uses chords to provide a musical background for the melody, or tune.

jazz and blues music

Jazz and blues music first surfaced in the early 1900s in New Orleans. Jazz music evolved from ragtime, which is generally light, happy music, and can express a variety of emotions. Blues music developed from the African-American spiritual and working songs of the 1800s and usually expresses sorrow and the hardships of life.

Jazz and blues music often have prominent solo parts and rely heavily on improvising, which means the musicians make up the music as they play.

Famous Performers

Famous jazz pianists include Duke Ellington, Bill Evans, Keith Jarrett, Thelonious Monk, Jelly Roll Morton, Oscar Peterson and Fats Waller. Famous blues pianists include Ray Charles, Jack Dupree, Dr. John and Jimmy Yancey.

TOP 10 JAZZ & BLUES SONGS

JAZZ SONGS

	Title	Artist
1	Take Five	Dave Brubeck
2	So What	Miles Davis
3	Autumn Leaves	Cannonball Adderley
4	A Night in Tunisia	Dizzy Gillespie
5	All Blues	Miles Davis
6	Deep Purple	Les McCann/Groove Holmes
7	Bye Bye Blackbird	Miles Davis
8	The Girl from Ipanema	S. Getz/J. Gilberto
9	It Don't Mean a Thing...	Duke Ellington
10	My Favorite Things	John Coltrane

BLUES SONGS

	Title	Artist
1	The Thrill is Gone	BB King
2	Got My Mojo Working	Muddy Waters
3	Crossroad Blues	Robert Johnson
4	Pride & Joy	Stevie Ray Vaughan
5	Loan Me a Dime	Boz Scaggs
6	T Bone Shuffle	T Bone Walker
7	Still Got the Blues	Gary Moore
8	Juke	Little Walter
9	Stormy Monday	Allman Brothers/T Bone Walker
10	Boom Boom	John Lee Hooker

Characteristics of Jazz and Blues Music

- Jazz and blues music can be played at a variety of speeds. The music can be fast and energetic or can be very slow and expressive.
- Jazz and blues music tend to be based on blues scales, pentatonic scales and ancient scales called modes.
- Jazz and blues music often use a swing beat, which is an uneven rhythm.
- In jazz and blues music, the off beats, rather than the main beats, tend to be emphasized.
- Syncopated notes, which are notes played between the main beats and held through the next beat, are often used to create a unique rhythm in jazz and blues music.

- Jazz music uses a wide variety of chords, while blues music tends to include dominant 7th chords as well as major and minor chords.
- Jazz and blues music often use special accompaniment patterns to provide a musical background for the melody. When playing the walking bass line, you play the notes of a chord as well as one or two notes close to the chord, individually, in order, moving up or down the keyboard. Many blues pieces and some jazz pieces also use the 12-bar blues, which is a special combination of three chords played over 12 measures. Jazz music also often uses the ragtime accompaniment pattern, in which you alternate between playing a low note and a chord with your left hand.
- Jazz and blues pianists often use a technique known as comping, in which they spice up the chords in a piece by using interesting rhythms.

pop music

Pop, or popular, music is usually light-hearted and very lyrical. The words of the songs are emphasized and usually describe very simple themes, such as falling in love, losing a love or overcoming hardships. Pop music tends to be music that a lot of people can relate to.

Pop music has existed throughout the 20th century and is usually closely based on the most popular style of music at any particular time. For example, when jazz music is very popular, pop songs tend to be jazzy, but have a softer sound that appeals to more people.

Famous Performers

There are many talented singer-songwriters who perform their pop songs and play their own piano accompaniment at the same time. Some of these performers include Tori Amos, Billy Joel, Elton John, Sarah McLachlan, Ben Folds, Bruce Hornsby and Vanessa Carlton.

TOP 20 POP SONGS

	Title	Artist
1	With or Without You	U2
2	Respect	Aretha Franklin
3	I Want to Hold Your Hand	The Beatles
4	I'll Be There	The Jackson 5
5	Billie Jean	Michael Jackson
6	Like a Virgin	Madonna
7	Where Did Our Love Go	The Supremes
8	Losing My Religion	R.E.M.
9	Dream On	Aerosmith
10	You Really Got Me	The Kinks
11	The Tears of a Clown	Smokey Robinson
12	Nothing Compares 2 U	Sinead O' Connor
13	Music	Madonna
14	Jailhouse Rock	Elvis Presley
15	What's Going On	Marvin Gaye
16	Smooth	Santana/Rob Thomas
17	Go Your Own Way	Fleetwood Mac
18	Your Song	Elton John
19	I Will Remember You	Sarah McLachlan
20	Mrs. Robinson	Simon & Garfunkel

Characteristics of Pop Music

- Pop songs tend to be very short—lasting only about three to five minutes.
- Pop music usually has a very steady beat.
- In pop music, the same chords and melody, or tune, are often repeated throughout a song.
- Pop music tends to be played dramatically. Pianists may play some sections of a piece very loudly to create intensity and then play other sections of a piece very softly. Pop pianists also often use the damper pedal to make the notes of the piece linger.
- Pop music commonly includes major, minor and 9th chords, as well as 7th chords.
- Pop music uses a lot of syncopation, which means that notes are played between the main beats and held through the next beat.
- Pop music can be played in a less formal way. Players often will not use traditional piano music, but instead will use lead sheets, which provide only an outline for songs. Players may also simply listen to pop songs on the radio or CD and then play the songs by ear.

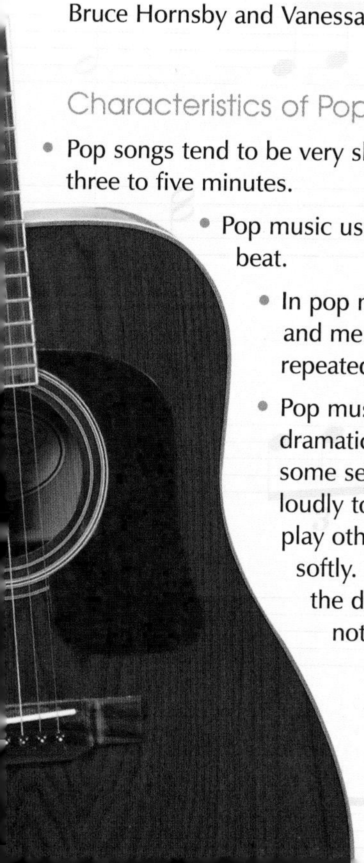

Canon in D
abridged version

♩ = 66

Pachelbel

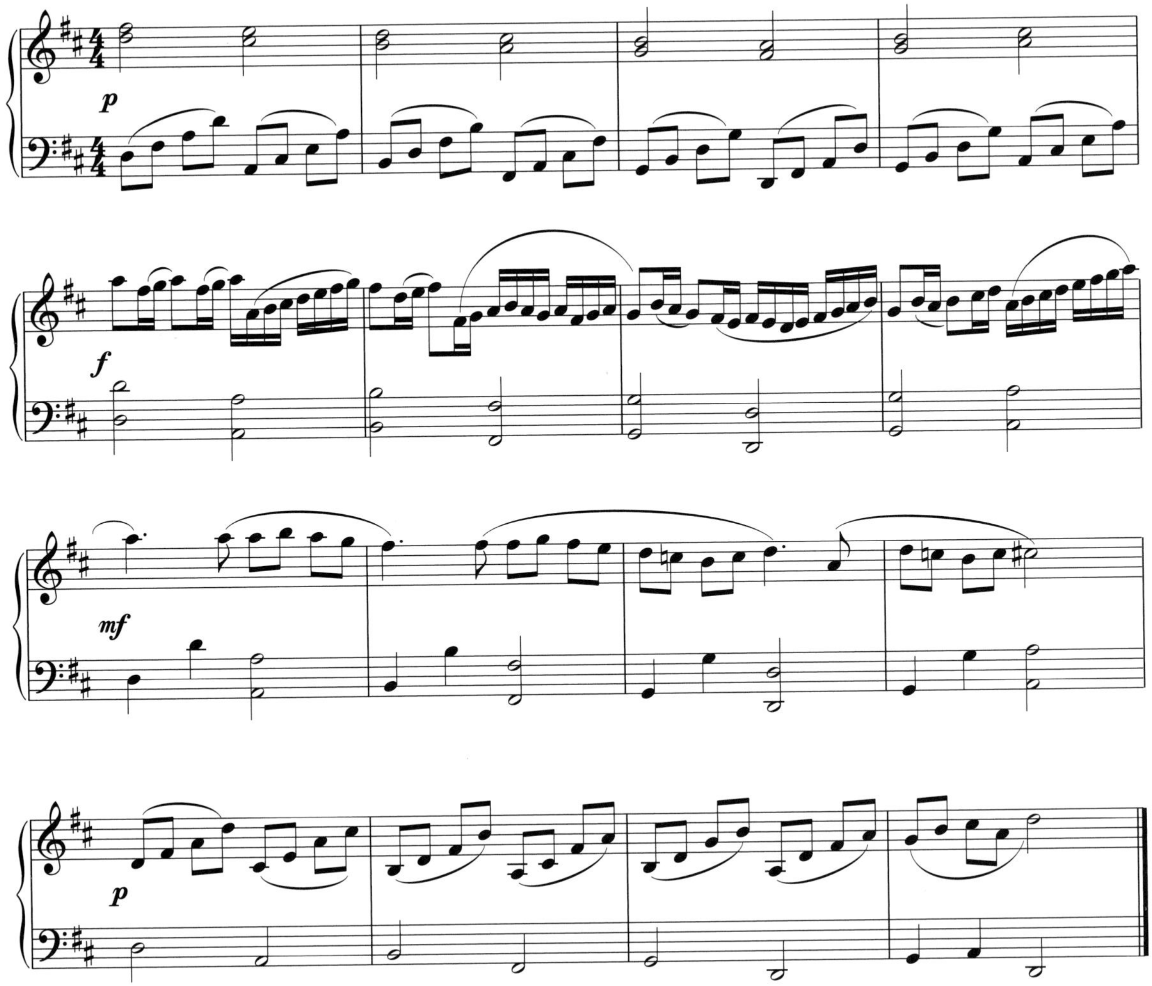

Für Elise
abridged version

♩ = 132

Beethoven

Prelude #15
abridged version

Chopin

Gymnopédie #1
abridged version

songs for practice

Rock On!

Frank Horvat

Got Your Letter

♩ = 80 With a Swing Beat

Frank Horvat

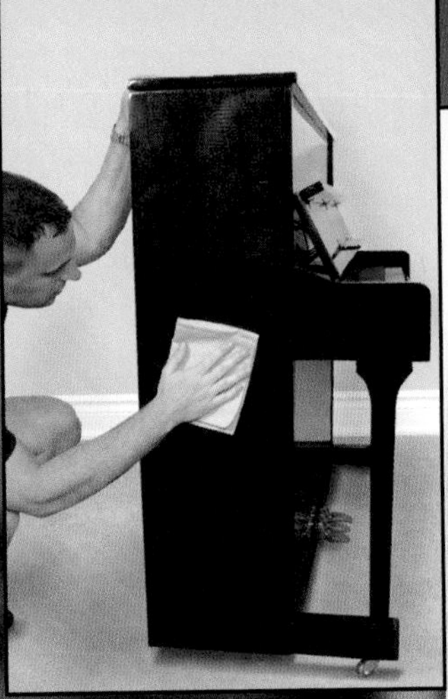

Chapter 11

In this chapter, you will find information that will help you when purchasing a piano of your own, including upright and grand pianos as well as electronic keyboards and pianos. You will also find helpful information on buying a piano bench, a metronome and many other accessories. This chapter also helps you determine the best location for a piano in your home and provides tips on how to clean your piano and having the instrument tuned.

Buying and Caring for Your Piano

In this Chapter...

- Introduction to Buying a Piano
- Buying an Upright or Grand Piano
- Buying an Electronic Keyboard
- Buying an Electronic Piano
- Examining a Piano
- Buying a Piano Bench
- Buying a Metronome
- Accessories for Acoustic Pianos
- Accessories for Electronic Keyboards and Pianos
- Find the Best Location for Your Piano
- Clean Your Piano
- Getting Your Piano Tuned

introduction to buying a piano

When buying a piano, take your time, shop around and research your options.

The most important decision you will need to make is whether you want to buy an acoustic piano or an electronic piano or keyboard. The main difference between these instruments is how each creates sound.

Acoustic pianos, including upright and grand pianos, contain strings that vibrate to produce sound. Electronic pianos and keyboards store prerecorded sound samples on memory chips to simulate the sounds of acoustic pianos.

The type of piano you choose will depend largely on how much you can afford to spend. Acoustic pianos are generally more expensive. You should also consider how much space you have and the environment where you plan to store the piano. Acoustic pianos require more space and are sensitive to temperature and humidity changes.

Avoid choosing a piano based on its appearance. An attractive piano will not necessarily produce the best sound. You should try different pianos to see how each one sounds and feels.

Acoustic Pianos

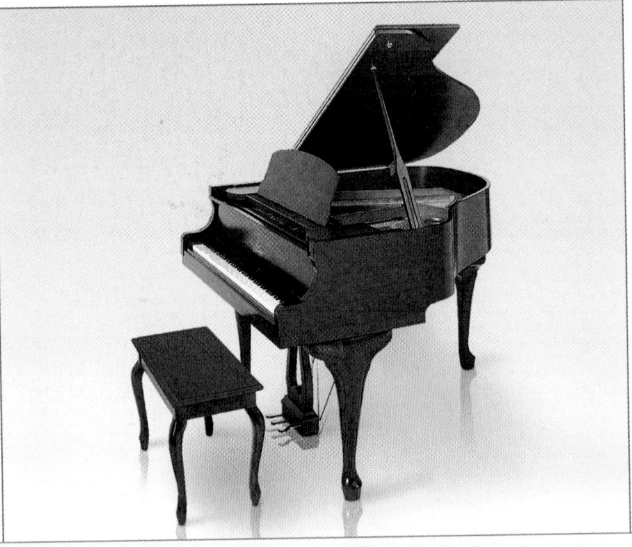

Advantages

- Better sound quality.
- More unique or interesting appearance.
- Weighted keys, which give acoustic pianos a unique feel when played.

Disadvantages

- More expensive.
- Require more space.
- Require regular tunings.
- Heavy and difficult to move.
- Sensitive to the environment, such as very hot, cold, wet or dry locations.

Electronic Pianos and Keyboards

Advantages

- Less expensive.
- Require less space.
- Do not require regular tunings.
- Easy to move.
- Not usually sensitive to the environment.
- Offer additional features such as the ability to imitate other instruments.

Disadvantages

- Electronic pianos have weighted keys, but the keys do not have the same genuine feel of an acoustic piano. Electronic keyboards do not have weighted keys.
- Electronic pianos may have fewer keys. Electronic keyboards usually have significantly fewer keys.

Tip

Can I rent a piano?

Yes. You can rent a piano and try it for a month or two before making a larger investment of buying a piano. You can ask local music stores if they rent pianos. Keep in mind that renting a piano for longer periods of time is not usually cost effective.

How can I research different pianos?

Before buying a piano, review consumer reports for the make and model of the piano you are interested in buying. You can also look up the manufacturer's Web site, which should provide valuable information about the manufacturer and the piano itself, such as any known mechanical issues.

When buying a piano, how can I make sure I get the best price?

When you shop around for a piano, have an idea of the maximum dollar amount you are willing to spend. As you look for the lowest price, keep in mind that you do not necessarily have to pay the sticker price—you can negotiate the price similar to buying a car. You may even be able to work incentives into the deal, such as a free bench, free delivery or a free tuning.

Where to Buy a Piano

- You can buy a piano from a piano dealer, from a private sale or at an auction.
- Buying a piano from a piano dealer offers many advantages. You will usually get expert advice, a wide selection and a warranty for the piano you purchase. You may also be able to upgrade to a better piano at a later time.
- Buying a piano from a private sale or at an auction gives you the opportunity to find a great piano at a reasonable price.

Buying a Used Piano

- If a piano is well built and kept in good condition, a piano can last for decades.
- Buying a used piano allows you to buy a piano at a lower cost. Some stores may also sell demonstration pianos, which you can also buy at a reduced cost. Demonstration pianos may be pianos in the dealer's showroom or pianos rented for special occasions, such as for a concert.
- Before buying a used piano, ask if the piano comes with a warranty.
- If you are buying a used upright or grand piano, have a piano appraiser check the piano for any problems before you buy the piano.

buying an upright or grand piano

If you decide to buy an acoustic piano, you have two options—an upright piano or a grand piano. There are several differences between upright and grand pianos that you should consider before choosing which type to buy.

Since upright pianos are usually placed up against a wall, they require less room than grand pianos, which are normally positioned away from the walls.

Upright and grand pianos also produce sounds differently. In upright pianos, the strings run perpendicular to the floor, causing the sound to travel toward the back of the piano. Placing an upright piano slightly away from a wall can make the sound less muffled. In grand pianos, however, the strings run parallel to the floor, causing the sound to travel upward. Grand pianos have a large lid on the top of the piano that you can prop open to allow the sound to fill the room. This makes the sound richer and louder than the sound produced by an upright piano. However, larger upright pianos can replicate the richness and volume of smaller grand pianos.

Upright Pianos

- Upright pianos are usually placed against a wall, so they require less room than grand pianos. Most upright pianos are also less expensive than grand pianos.

- The strings in upright pianos are perpendicular to the floor, which causes the sound to travel toward the back of the piano. Moving an upright piano slightly away from a wall can make the sound less muffled.

- Upright pianos have at least two pedals. Many upright pianos have three pedals. For more information on pedals, see page 206.

- Upright pianos are available in four different sizes, which vary mostly in height. Larger uprights can produce a louder sound.

- You can buy the following sizes of upright pianos.

Spinet	Very small
Apartment size	Small
Standard	Average
Upright grand piano	Large

Tip

What are some popular brand names of upright and grand pianos?

Popular brand names include Baldwin, Bösendorfer, Kawai, Samick, Schimmel, Steinway and Yamaha. However, you should make sure you do not buy a piano just for its name since the quality of a piano can be affected by factors out of the manufacturer's control, such as how it was maintained since it was built.

How do I know if a piano is well suited for the environment I live in?

Manufacturers build pianos with a particular environment in mind. For example, a piano's wood may have been dried out to be suitable for a wet climate. You can ask the sales representative at your local music store or consult with the manufacturer to find out if the piano you are interested in buying is designed to suit the environment you live in.

What else should I consider before purchasing an upright or grand piano?

You should read the fine print on your warranty. In order to keep your warranty intact, you may be required to have your piano tuned regularly and store your piano in a specific environment, such as a room with moderate temperature and normal levels of humidity. In addition, some stores may require you to use their piano technician to have your piano tuned.

Grand Pianos

- Grand pianos produce a richer, louder sound than upright pianos. Grand pianos also have more sensitive keys, so you have greater control over the sound volume when you press lightly or firmly on the keys.

- The strings in grand pianos are parallel to the floor, which causes the sound to travel upward. Opening the lid of a grand piano produces an even richer, louder sound and allows the sound to fill the room.
- Grand pianos have at least two pedals. Many grand pianos have three pedals. For more information on pedals, see page 206.

- Grand pianos are available in four different sizes. Grand pianos are measured from the front edge of the keyboard to the edge farthest away on the piano.
- Larger grand pianos produce a richer, louder sound.

- You can buy the following sizes of grand pianos. The sizes are approximate.

Baby grand .... 5′
Regular grand .... 5′6 to 6′2
Large grand .... 6′2 to 6′8
Concert grand ... 7 feet or larger

Note: Concert grand pianos are most often used on concert stages and are not usually appropriate for home use.

buying an electronic keyboard

Electronic keyboards, also known as digital keyboards, offer an inexpensive option for learning how to play the piano. While buying an electronic keyboard allows you to avoid making a large investment when you begin playing, you should consider upgrading to an electronic or acoustic piano once your playing advances.

The main difference between electronic keyboards and more expensive acoustic pianos is the quality of sound. Electronic keyboards, which use prerecorded samples stored on memory chips, simulate the sounds produced by acoustic pianos. As a result, the sound quality of an electronic keyboard is not as good.

Common features of electronic keyboards include items such as built-in speakers, a built-in metronome, touch-sensitive keys and a headphone jack. Most electronic keyboards can also imitate other instruments, such as organs and violins, and produce sound effects such as bells, whistles and cheering.

While you can only usually buy pianos from music stores, you can find electronic keyboards at several types of stores, including department stores, electronics stores and music stores.

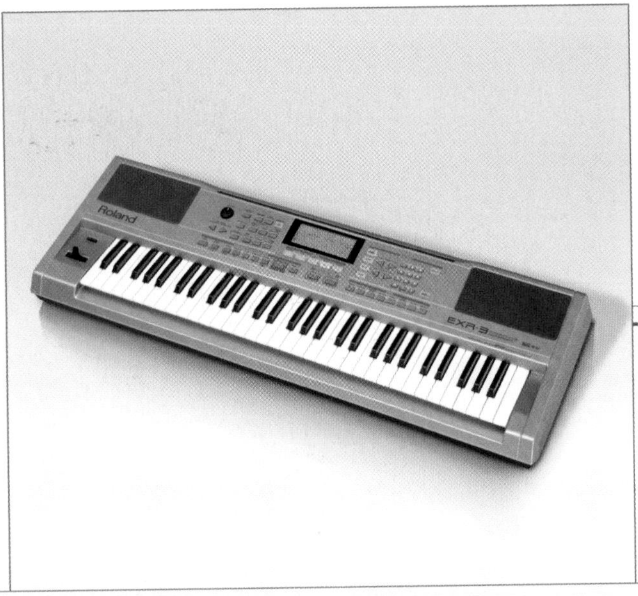

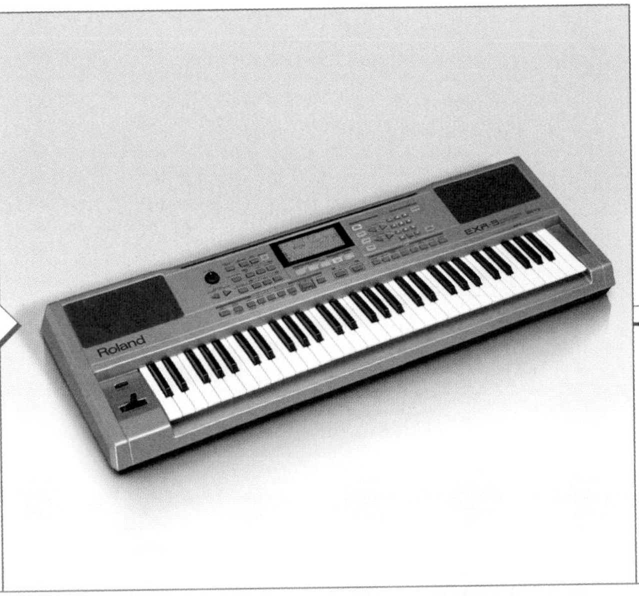

- Electronic keyboards provide an inexpensive way to begin learning how to play the piano. Once you advance in your piano playing, you should upgrade to an electronic or acoustic piano.

Advantages

- Relatively inexpensive.
- Require little space.
- Light and easy to move.

Disadvantages

- Poorer sound quality than acoustic and electronic pianos.
- Fewer keys than acoustic and electronic pianos.
- Pedals usually must be purchased separately.
- Do not have weighted keys, so the keys do not have the same feel of an acoustic piano.

Common Features

- Built-in speakers.
- Ability to imitate other instruments, such as an organ or violin.
- Provide accompaniment, which supplies a background beat for various music styles such as rock and disco.

Tip

What is the difference between synthesizers and electronic keyboards?

Synthesizers are similar to electronic keyboards except synthesizers feature more advanced capabilities, such as the ability to manipulate sounds. These advanced features help professional musicians record music and perform on stage. Synthesizers, which need to be hooked up to an amplifier since they do not have built-in speakers, produce excellent sound, but weigh more and cost more than electronic keyboards.

Is there a difference between the keys on an electronic keyboard and the keys on an electronic or acoustic piano?

Yes. The keys of an electronic keyboard are not weighted, so the keys do not have the same feel as those of an acoustic or electronic piano. As a result, keyboard players may find it difficult to play the heavier keys on pianos.

In some cases, electronic keyboards have smaller keys than acoustic and electronic pianos. Playing on an electronic keyboard with smaller keys makes the transition to a piano much more difficult, so you should try to avoid buying an electronic keyboard with smaller keys.

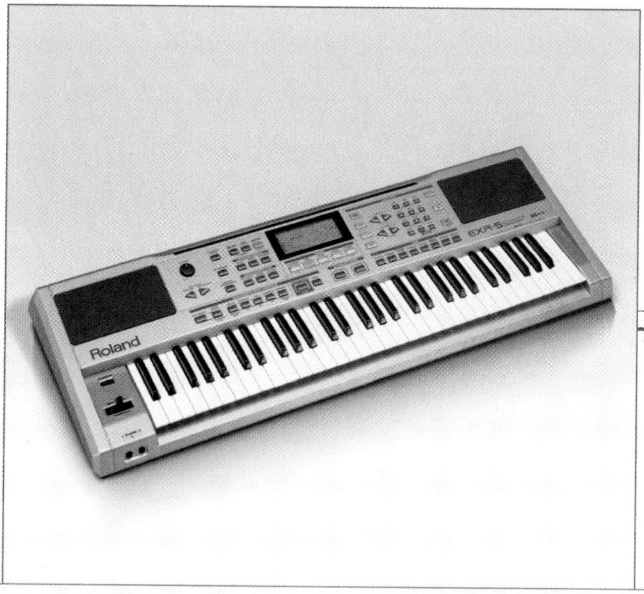

Common Features

- Sound effects, such as bells, whistles and cheering.
- Headphone jack so you can play without anyone hearing you.
- Built-in recording device, known as a sequencer, which allows you to record music you play.
- Built-in metronome, which makes a sound a certain number of beats per minute to help you play at a steady speed.
- Touch-sensitive keys, which allow you to change the volume by varying how softly or firmly you press the keys.

Less Common Features

- Ability to connect to external speakers to amplify the sound.
- MIDI (Musical Instrument Digital Interface) compatible, which allows the keyboard to interact with a computer or other MIDI-compatible instruments. For example, you can connect the keyboard to a computer so you can use music software with your keyboard.

buying an electronic piano

Electronic pianos, also known as digital pianos, simulate the sounds produced by acoustic pianos. As with any type of piano, there are several factors to consider before buying an electronic piano.

Common features of electronic pianos include items such as built-in speakers, a built-in metronome, touch-sensitive keys and a headphone jack. Most electronic pianos are compatible with MIDI (Musical Instrument Digital Interface), which allows you to connect the piano to a computer so you can use music software with your piano.

Electronic pianos are less expensive and easier to move than acoustic pianos. Unlike acoustic pianos, electronic pianos are not usually sensitive to the environment and do not require regular tunings. With more keys and better sound quality than electronic keyboards, electronic pianos are a good starting point, but once your playing advances, you should upgrade to an acoustic piano.

Popular brand names of electronic pianos include Casio, Kawai, Roland, Technics and Yamaha. Not all electronic pianos sound the same, so you should make sure that you are happy with the sound quality before you buy one.

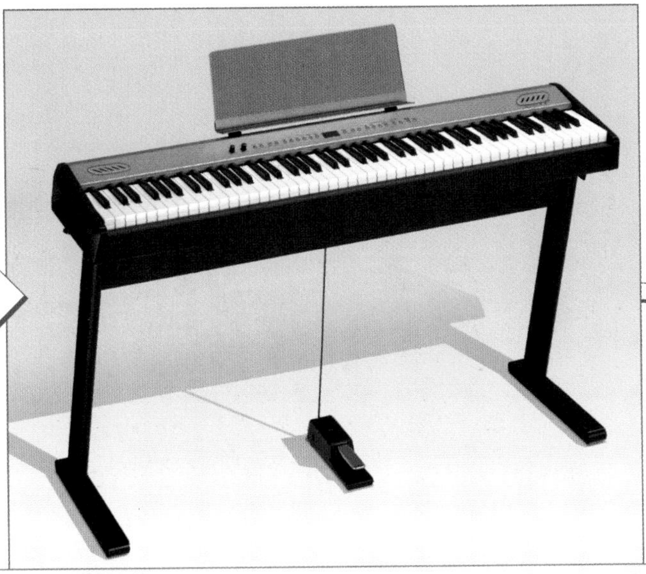

- Electronic pianos imitate the sound and feel of acoustic pianos, but are less expensive and are easier to move. Electronic pianos also do not require regular tunings and are not usually sensitive to the environment.

Advantages

- Better sound quality than electronic keyboards.
- Have weighted keys, but the keys do not have the same feel of an acoustic piano.
- Have two or three pedals.
- More keys than electronic keyboards, but may have fewer keys than acoustic pianos.

Disadvantages

- More expensive than electronic keyboards.
- Require more space than electronic keyboards.
- Heavier and more difficult to move than electronic keyboards.

Tip

How can I protect my electronic piano from changes in electrical power?

Changes in electrical power can damage your electronic piano. You can buy devices that protect your piano from brief increases (surges) or decreases (brownouts) in electricity, which can occur during lightning storms, peak electrical demands and your own household use. A surge protector protects your piano from surges and is relatively inexpensive. An uninterruptible power supply (UPS) is more expensive, but protects your piano from both surges and brownouts. A UPS contains a battery that stores electrical power, so if the power fails, the battery can run the piano for a short time.

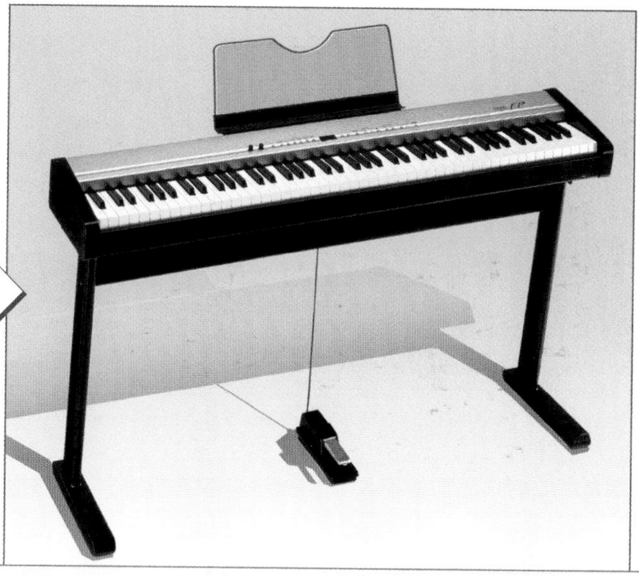

Common Features

- Built-in speakers.
- Ability to imitate other instruments, such as an organ or a group of stringed instruments.
- Headphone jack so you can play without anyone hearing you.
- Built-in metronome, which makes a sound a certain number of beats per minute to help you play at a steady speed.
- Touch-sensitive keys, which allow you to change the volume by varying how softly or firmly you press the keys.
- MIDI (Musical Instrument Digital Interface) compatible, which allows the piano to interact with a computer or other MIDI-compatible instruments. For example, you can connect the piano to a computer so you can use music software with your piano.
- Ability to connect to external speakers to amplify the sound.

Less Common Features

- Provide accompaniment, which supplies a background beat for various music styles such as rock and disco.
- Built-in recording device, known as a sequencer, which allows you to record and play back the music you play.

examining a piano

When you examine a piano that you are interested in purchasing, it is a lot like taking a car for a test drive. Similarities between the two exist, such as making sure you approve of the piano's size and appearance, working the mechanisms to listen for kinks in the sound and checking under the hood, that is, the piano lid, for signs of wear and tear.

Before you make a final decision, you should look at and try out several different makes and models of pianos. You should also examine pianos that fall within a fairly wide range of prices, which should help you recognize the sound difference between top-of-the-line pianos and those a little further down the line.

For each piano you are considering, make sure you cover the basics when examining the piano. Will it fit in your home? How does it look? Do the keys and pedals work? Does the piano's interior raise any red flags? Is the soundboard in good shape?

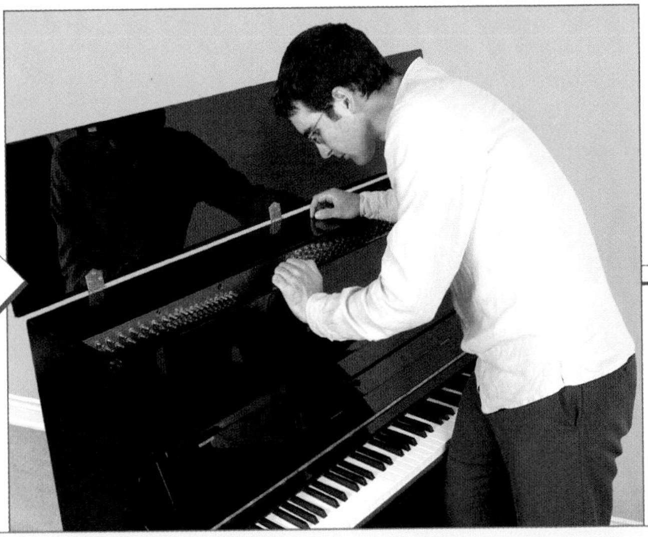

General Appearance

- Determine if you like the size, color and overall appearance of the piano.
- Look for scratches, dents and sun-faded spots on the surface of the piano.

Keyboard and Pedals

- Press every key to ensure each key produces a sound. When you release a key, make sure the key does not stay down or continue to sound.
- Make sure each key plays only one note and you do not hear a clicking sound when you press each key.
- Make sure the pedals work and move smoothly and quietly when pressed.

Inside a Piano

- Open the lid of the piano and look inside to make sure the nuts, bolts and strings are free from rust.
- Make sure all the hammers and dampers line up evenly and the felt is not worn around the hammers and dampers.

Note: Hammers strike the strings when you press keys on the keyboard. Dampers rest on the strings to stop the strings from making a sound when not in use. For more information on hammers and dampers, see page 21.

Tip

How do I compare the sounds of different pianos?

You should play the piano yourself and then ask a salesperson or friend to play the piano so you can hear what the piano sounds like from a distance. Take note of each piano's unique sound and consider which sound will work best in the space you have planned for it. Two pianos, whether acoustic or electronic, made by different manufacturers can produce different sounds. In fact, two acoustic pianos made by the same manufacturer in the same factory can produce different sounds. In the end, your decision should be based on which piano sounds the best to you.

What should I look for when examining a piano's keys?

You should take note of how the keys feel when you press them. Find out how much force is required to produce sound. The keys on each individual piano have their own feel, but most require either a light touch or a little heavier pressure to produce sound. Test each piano's keys and choose the piano that has the best feel for you.

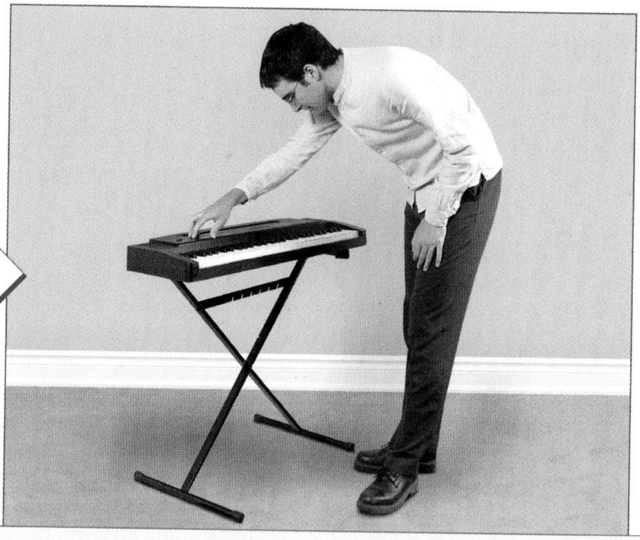

Soundboard

- Make sure the soundboard is in good condition. Check the inside and outside of the piano for cracks in the soundboard. You should not purchase a piano with a cracked soundboard since the sound quality of the piano will be drastically affected and repairing the soundboard would be difficult and expensive.

Note: The soundboard is a large piece of wood that amplifies the sound produced by the piano. On an upright piano, the soundboard is the entire piece of wood at the back of the piano. On a grand piano, the soundboard is the entire piece of wood at the bottom of the piano.

Electronic Keyboards and Pianos

- Test all the controls on an electronic keyboard or piano to ensure the controls work properly. For example, when you adjust the volume, make sure the volume changes and the speakers do not crackle.
- In stores, electronic keyboards and pianos are sometimes connected to equipment that could enhance the sound. Ask the salesperson to disconnect any equipment so you can hear how the instrument will sound on its own.
- Check the general appearance, keys and pedals of an electronic keyboard or piano the same way you would check an acoustic piano.

buying a piano bench

The best seat in the house for playing the piano is, naturally enough, the piano bench. If your piano did not come with a piano bench, you can buy one separately at a piano store.

Piano benches are designed with the piano player in mind. Most piano benches measure around 1.5 feet high, a suitable height for most piano players. For very tall or very short individuals, they may want to consider an adjustable piano bench instead. Piano benches usually measure approximately 2.5 feet across and commonly include a space under the seat to store music.

For more comfortable seating, some piano benches are padded. If your piano bench is not padded, you can add a bench cushion for more comfort. Padding on your piano bench also raises the seating position slightly, which is helpful for children who may have trouble reaching the keyboard. For information on bench cushions and other piano accessories, see page 268.

- When playing the piano, you should sit on a piano bench.

  Note: A piano bench may come with a piano you purchase. You can also buy a piano bench separately.

- Piano benches are usually made of solid wood and measure approximately 2.5 feet long by 1.5 feet high. The length of a piano bench allows two people to sit comfortably while playing the piano, which is useful when you want to play a duet.

- Many piano benches allow you to lift the seat to reveal a compartment where you can store your sheet music.
- Some piano benches also have padding to provide more comfort when playing.

- On some piano benches, you can adjust the height by turning large knobs located on the sides of the bench. These benches do not usually offer a compartment to store your sheet music and are often not as long.

buying a metronome

A metronome is a device that helps you gauge the tempo, or speed, at which you should play a musical piece. Metronome markings, such as ♩=76, are often shown in written music to indicate an exact speed for a piece. To play a musical piece at the correct speed, you set your metronome to this speed.

You can buy two types of metronomes—mechanical and electronic. Mechanical metronomes lack the bells and whistles of the electronic versions, but they are better looking, with a more traditional and classy feel, somewhat like a grandfather clock.

Mechanical metronomes must be wound up regularly and are not as durable as electronic metronomes.

Electronic metronomes are generally less expensive and include more features than their mechanical counterparts. If you buy an electronic metronome with a light that flashes for each beat, do not look at the light while playing. You should only use this light as a silent reference to become familiar with the speed of a piece before you begin to play, which is especially useful during performances.

Mechanical Metronomes

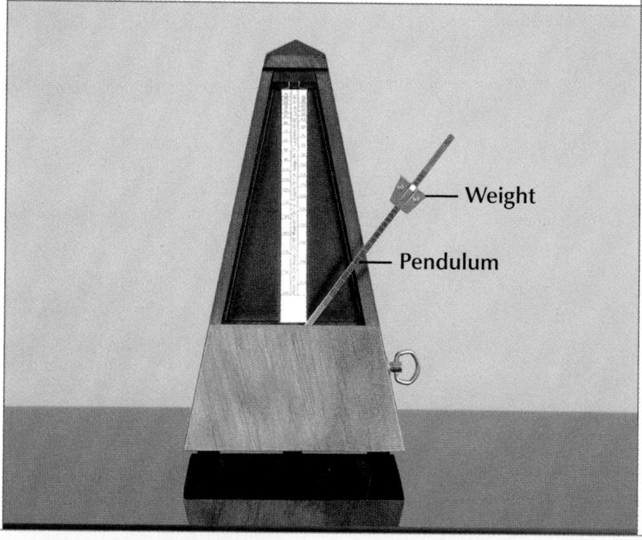

Electronic Metronomes

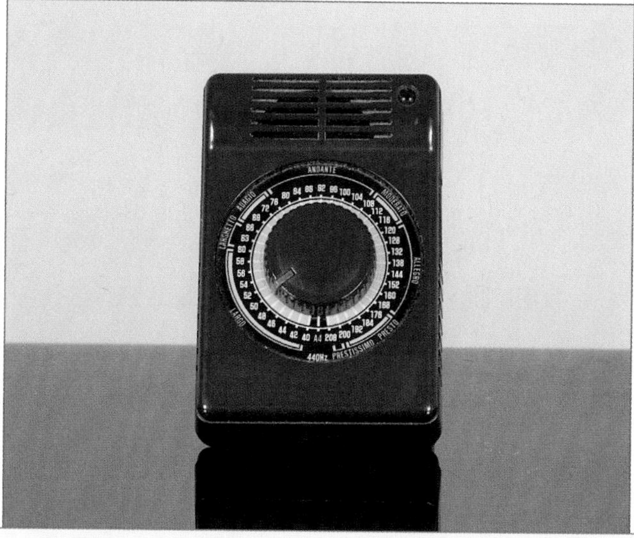

- A metronome sounds out a certain number of beats per minute to help you play at a steady speed. You can buy two types of metronomes—mechanical and electronic.
- Mechanical metronomes are more visually appealing and generally louder but must be wound up on a regular basis.
- Mechanical metronomes have a pendulum that swings back and forth. Each time the pendulum swings to one side, it makes a sound.
- The position of the weight on the pendulum determines the speed that the pendulum swings and the number of beats per minute.
- Electronic metronomes are more durable and usually less expensive.
- Electronic metronomes usually run on batteries. To set an electronic metronome, you turn a dial or press buttons to change the number of beats per minute.
- Some electronic metronomes can also provide additional features, such as a light that flashes for each beat, an earphone jack so only you can hear the sound and the ability to use a different sound to emphasize the first beat in each measure.

accessories for acoustic pianos

Acoustic pianos, which include upright and grand pianos, do not require electricity in order to work. However, they do require some additional care from you that electronic pianos do not need. These pages introduce you to some accessories that will protect your acoustic piano from elements such as dust and moisture, as well as help you play more comfortably. You should be able to find these accessories at a piano store in your area, as well as on the Web.

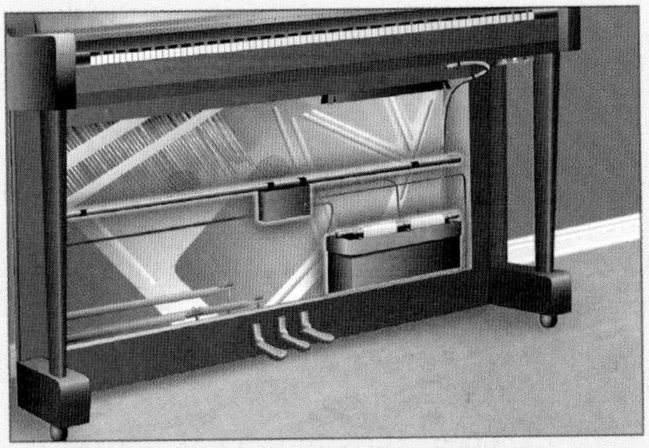

Piano Humidifiers and Dehumidifiers

If your piano is being played in a very moist or very dry environment, you can buy a humidifier and/or dehumidifier that attaches directly to your piano to help control the humidity. Moist air can cause a piano's wood to expand, while dry air can cause a piano's wood to contract. If you play a piano in either a low or high humidity environment, you may find that your piano goes out of tune more quickly than it should. You should hire a piano technician to install a piano humidifier and/or dehumidifier.

Piano Covers

A piano cover protects your piano from dust, scratches and sunlight exposure that can fade the finish of your piano's wood. Covers are available in a variety of sizes and you usually have to purchase one separately from your piano. Check with a dealer in your area for the proper way to measure for a piano cover. Available fabrics for piano covers include cotton, vinyl and quilted nylon.

Pedal Pads

Your piano may have come with pedal pads, which are pieces of fabric that slip over your piano's pedals to protect them from dust, scratches and dents. If your piano did not include pedal pads, you can purchase these accessories from a piano store or online.

Bench Cushions

After a few sessions of sitting on your piano bench, you may decide the bench needs padding or more padding needs to be added to the bench. Adding a cushion to your piano bench makes it more comfortable to sit on, allowing you to focus more on your piano playing. A bench cushion also protects the bench itself from scratches and it can elevate the sitting position for piano players who have trouble reaching the keyboard. You generally can select a fabric for your bench cushion that matches well with the decor of the room in which your piano resides.

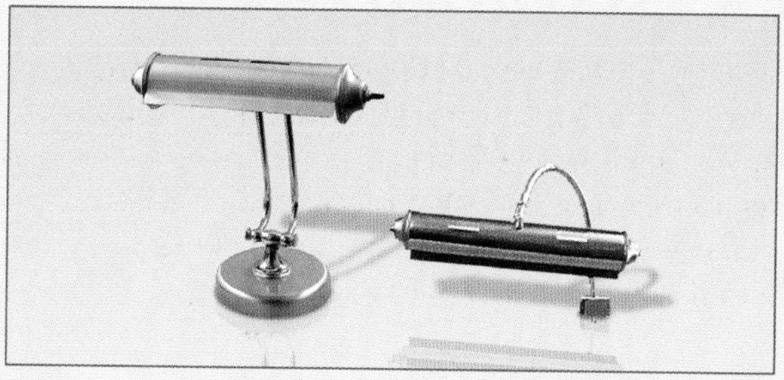

Piano Lamps

A piano lamp is a valuable accessory that provides more direct lighting to your sheet music so you can better see the music you are playing. Depending on the style of your acoustic piano, there are a couple of lamp styles to choose from. One type of lamp has a base that is usually placed on top of an upright piano, while another type of piano lamp clips onto a music stand, which is useful for grand pianos. You can also select from a variety of finishes, including brass, silver and black. Piano lamps are available at specialty lighting stores in addition to piano stores.

Piano Casters

To help move your heavy piano between different locations in your house, your piano may have casters installed that allow you to roll your piano. If you do not have casters installed on your piano, you can hire a piano technician to add them for you. Before adding casters, check with your dealer or manufacturer to make sure you can add this accessory to your piano. You should also make sure you buy the correct casters for your make and model.

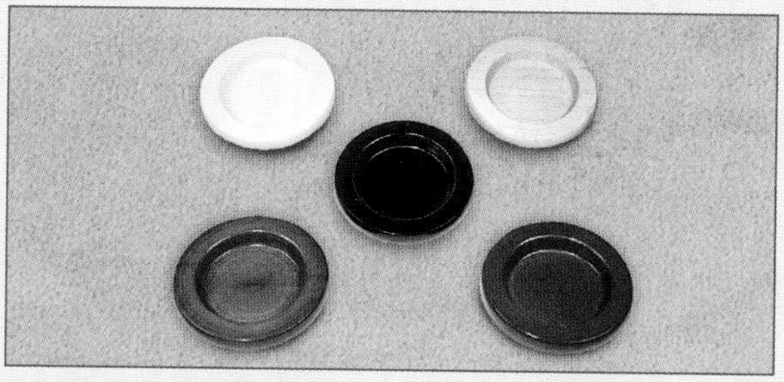

Caster Cups

After your piano is in place, you should position caster cups underneath each caster to protect your floor. Without caster cups, the weight of the piano on the casters may create indentations in your floor. Caster cups are made with materials such as wood or plastic.

accessories for electronic keyboards and pianos

You can obtain various accessories for your electronic keyboard or piano. Accessories, such as amplifiers and pedals, give you more control over the sound your electronic keyboard or piano produces, while covers, bags and cases allow you to protect and transport your instrument. Electronic keyboard and piano accessories are available at piano stores as well as on the Web.

Amplifiers

Amplifiers can connect to some electronic keyboards and most electronic pianos to produce a louder sound, which is useful if you play in a band. Amplifiers usually include built-in speakers. Before you buy an amplifier, you should check your instrument's manual to ensure your instrument can connect to an amplifier. You should also make sure that the amplifier you buy is designed for electronic keyboards or pianos and not for other instruments, such as guitars. Generally, more expensive amplifiers allow you to produce a louder and better quality sound.

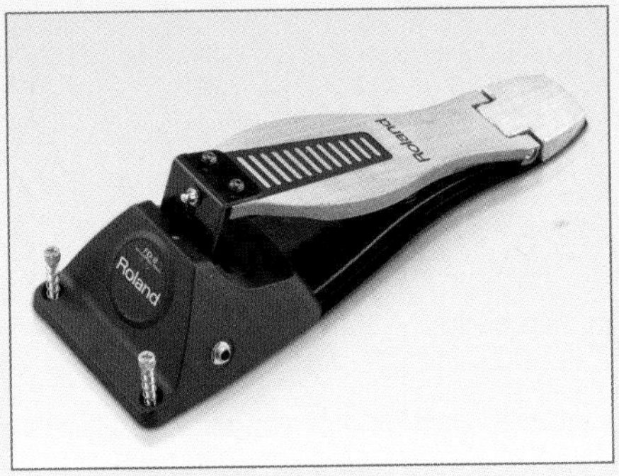

Pedals

Pedals allow you to achieve different effects when playing an electronic piano or keyboard. Electronic pianos usually come with pedals, but electronic keyboards usually do not. Electronic keyboards normally allow you to add one or two pedals, which are often capable of performing more than one function. For example, a pedal may act as a damper pedal, making notes you play continue to sound, and also allow you to change programs, such as starting or stopping a drum beat. To determine if you can add pedals to your keyboard, you should check your keyboard's manual.

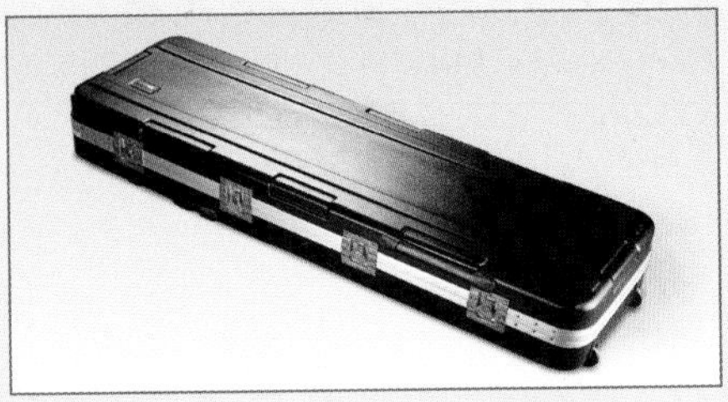

Keyboard Cases

Keyboard cases, with a hard surface and a foam-lined interior, are more expensive than keyboard bags, but are more durable. As a result, keyboard cases are usually used by people who want to protect more expensive keyboards, such as professional musicians who travel frequently. Before you buy a keyboard case, you should make sure the case is designed to suit the size of your keyboard.

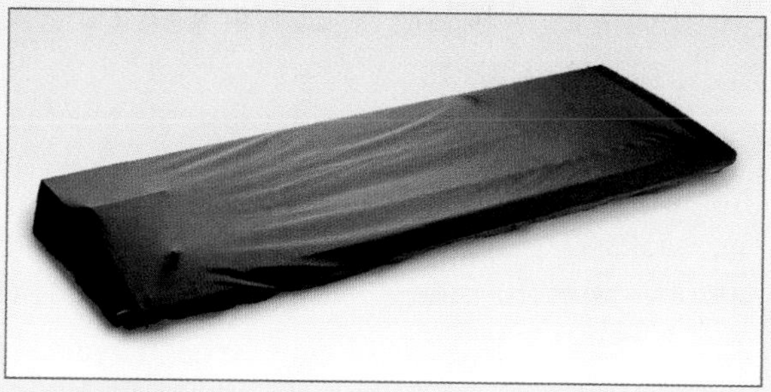

Covers

If your electronic keyboard or piano does not come with a cover, you can buy a cover to protect your instrument from dust and scratches. Unlike acoustic pianos, which include lids that close over the keyboard, all electronic keyboards and some electronic pianos do not come with these lids, so a cover is useful for protecting the keys and the rest of the instrument.

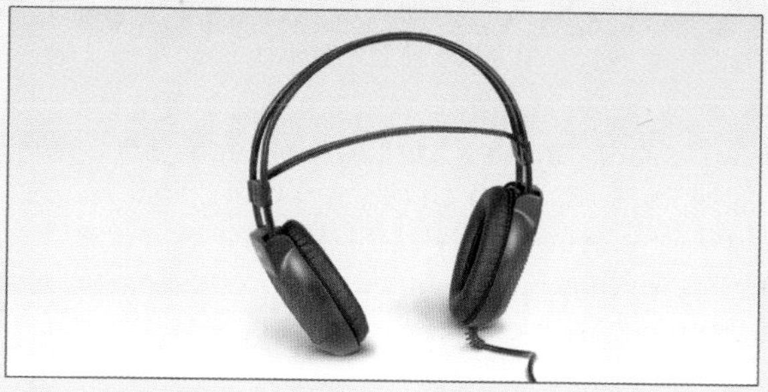

Headphones

Most electronic keyboards and pianos include a headphone jack, which allows you to connect headphones so you can play your instrument without anyone hearing you. You can buy headphones from electronic and music stores or you can use the same headphones that you use with your portable CD or MP3 player, but you may need a special adapter to connect the headphones to your keyboard or piano.

Keyboard Bags

Keyboard bags are useful for transporting your electronic keyboard to different locations. Made from a sturdy fabric, keyboard bags are lightweight, compact and easy to carry. In addition to a handle, most keyboard bags come with a shoulder strap. Keyboard bags are padded inside to provide protection for the keyboard when traveling. Some keyboard bags also have a separate storage compartment to store sheet music. If you decide to buy a keyboard bag, make sure the bag is designed to suit the size of your keyboard.

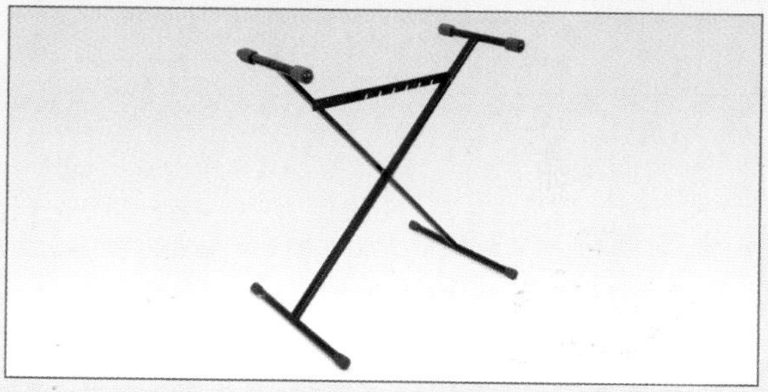

Stands

Electronic keyboards do not usually come with stands, but you can buy one separately. Keyboard stands are usually made of metal with rubber on the top so the keyboard will not slide around. Most keyboard stands also have adjustable heights, so you can raise or lower the stand to the height you need. More expensive keyboard stands are generally more stable so they will not shake when you play the keyboard.

find the best location for your piano

Finding the best location for your piano will help maintain its appearance and sound quality over time.

Since pianos are sensitive to temperature, the best location for your piano is a place where the temperature is consistently moderate. Fluctuations in temperature can cause the piano's wood to crack, swell or warp and affect the piano's performance.

You should also place your piano in a location where the humidity level, or level of moisture in the air, is moderate. Moist air can cause the piano's wooden body to expand, while dry air can cause the piano's wooden body to contract.

If you must place your piano in a dry or moist room, you can buy a humidifier or dehumidifier to help control the humidity. Humidifiers add moisture to the air and are helpful in the winter when the air is dry. Dehumidifiers remove moisture from the air and are helpful in the summer when the air is moist. You can have a piano technician install a piano humidifier and/or dehumidifier that attaches directly to the piano.

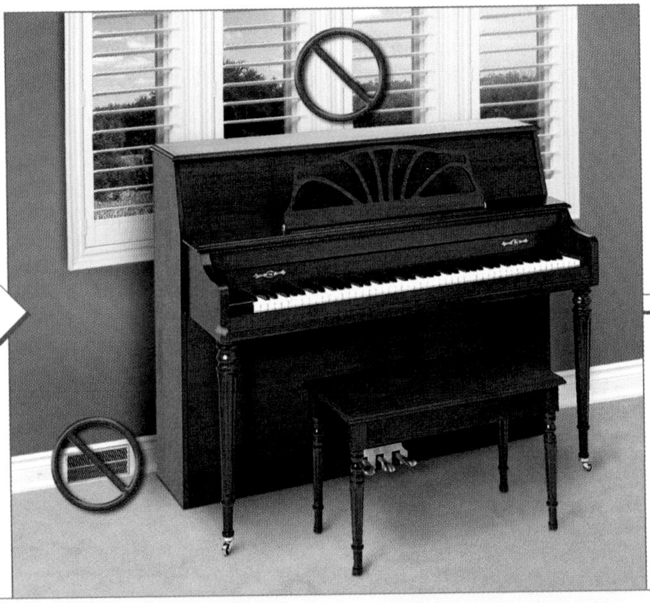

- Finding the best location for your piano will help maintain its appearance and sound quality over time. You should focus on finding the best location for your piano rather than where the piano will look the best in your home.
- You should place your piano in a location where the temperature is moderate and there will be very little fluctuations in temperature. Very cold or very hot temperatures can cause the wood in a piano to crack, swell or warp and affect the piano's performance.
- To protect your piano from high temperatures, you should keep your piano away from direct sunlight, such as near a window. Direct sunlight can fade and damage the wood of your piano.
- To protect your piano from changing temperatures, you should avoid placing your piano near a vent or in locations that have a draft, such as near a door.

Tip

How can I tell if the temperature or humidity is affecting the performance of my piano?

The easiest way to tell if your piano is being affected by temperature or humidity changes is if your piano quickly goes out of tune. If this happens, your piano may be in an environment that is too hot, too cold, too moist or too dry.

I have to put my piano near a window. What precautions should I take?

You should make sure you have window coverings that adequately block the sun. You should also avoid opening the window to keep drafts to a minimum.

How can I choose the best location for my electronic piano or keyboard?

If you have an electronic piano or keyboard, climate and humidity are not serious factors. However, you should not place your electronic piano or keyboard in an area of extreme heat, such as near a window that lets in a lot of sun.

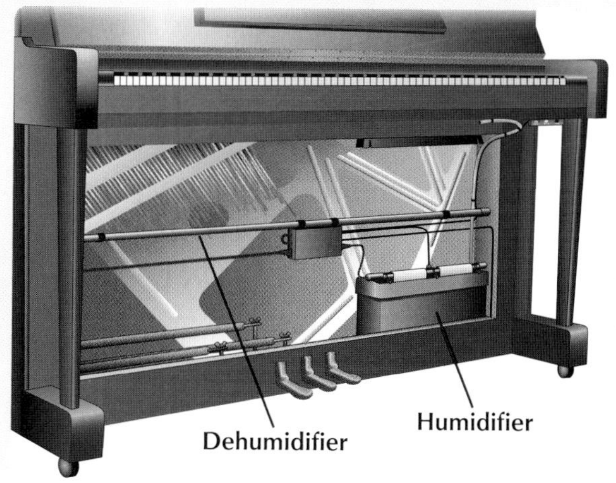

Moving Your Piano

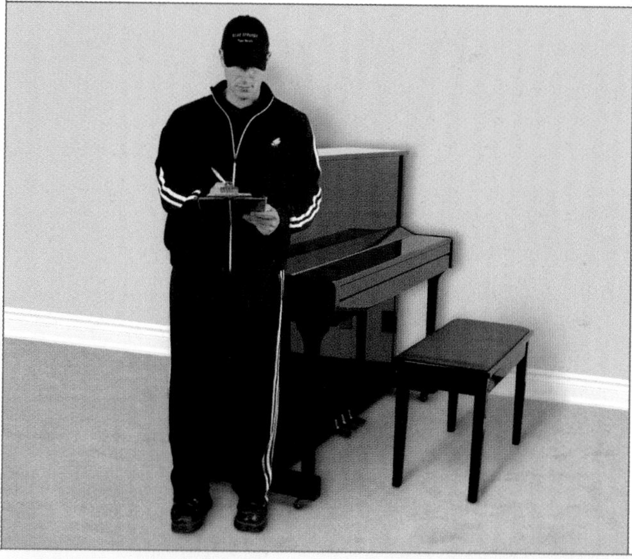

- You should place your piano in a location where the humidity level is normal.
- If you must place your piano in a dry or moist room, you can buy a humidifier or dehumidifier to help control the humidity. For better results, you can buy a piano humidifier and/or dehumidifier that attaches directly to the piano.
- Before buying any equipment to change the humidity level around your piano, consider moving your piano to a more suitable location.
- Before finding the best location for your piano, consider how you will move the piano to your home.
- When you buy a new piano, many dealers will move the piano to your home for you.
- If you need to arrange the piano move yourself, hire qualified piano movers to ensure the safety of your piano.
- To find a qualified piano mover, ask the store that sold you the piano or friends for recommendations. Most phone books have a section called "Piano Movers."

Note: Before allowing house movers to transport your piano, make sure they are qualified piano movers.

clean your piano

To maintain the appearance of your piano and avoid dust and dirt build-up, you should clean your piano regularly. How often you clean your piano depends on how dusty your home is and how often you play your piano. If you have an electronic piano or electronic keyboard, make sure you turn the power off before you clean it.

When cleaning the body of your piano, make sure you use a cleaning product that will not ruin your piano's finish. You can ask the manufacturer or the dealer who sold you the piano what products are safe to use. To clean the body of your piano, use a cloth dampened with water to wipe away dust and dirt. Immediately remove any remaining moisture from your piano with a dry cloth.

Over time, natural oils from your fingers and dirt may build up on the surface of the keys. To clean the surface of the keys, use a cloth dampened with white vinegar to wipe each key. You do not want any liquid to drip between the keys so dampen the cloth only slightly.

As a precaution, do not eat or drink around your piano. Spilling a drink on your keyboard can cause damage, potentially beyond repair.

- You should regularly clean your piano to help maintain its appearance.
- To clean the body of your piano, use a cloth dampened with water to wipe away dust and dirt. You should immediately use a dry cloth to remove any remaining moisture from your piano.
- Do not use any household cleaning products, such as furniture polish, to clean your piano without first asking the dealer who sold you the piano or manufacturer what products are safe to use. You could ruin your piano's finish.
- To clean the surface of the keys on your piano, use a cloth dampened with white vinegar to wipe each key up and down. Wiping the keys removes dust, dirt and the natural oils from your fingers and makes the keys less slippery when you play.

getting your piano tuned

Tuning a piano keeps the strings in the piano at the proper tension and ensures good sound quality. If you do not have your piano tuned regularly, the sound quality of your piano will decline gradually over time and your piano could even require major repairs.

You should have your piano tuned by a professional piano tuner unless you have received extensive training on how to tune a piano yourself. Professional piano tuners, or piano technicians, have years of education and experience and make house calls to tune pianos.

To find a good piano technician, compare prices and ask questions about how long the person has been tuning and make sure that he or she is familiar with the make and model of your piano. It is also a good idea to ask for references from customers and ask if the technician is a member of a professional organization. In addition to tuning your piano, you can check to see if the technician can perform other repairs on your piano.

Keep in mind that if your piano has not been tuned for over a year, you may need to have it tuned more than once before returning to your regular tuning schedule.

- You should have a piano tuner tune your piano regularly to ensure the best sound quality for your piano. In most cases, you should have your piano tuned twice a year.
- You should have your piano tuned at times of the year when the temperature is not too cold or not too hot, such as in the fall and spring.
- How often you play your piano and the temperature and humidity in the room where the piano is located can affect how often you should have your piano tuned. If you play your piano frequently or your piano is located in a very hot, cold, moist or dry location, you may need to have your piano tuned more often.
- To find a good piano tuner, ask your local music stores, piano dealers, music teacher or friends for recommendations.
- Many piano tuners, known as piano technicians, can also check the overall condition of your piano and perform various piano repairs, such as replacing worn or broken hardware within the piano.
- A piano tuner will require about 90 minutes to tune your piano, assuming the piano does not require other repairs.
- If you recently moved, wait a couple of months to allow the piano to adjust to the new location before having your piano tuned.

Chapter 12

This chapter is a great resource for quickly accessing information about the piano and piano music. When you need an explanation of a piano or musical term, you can refer to the comprehensive glossary in this chapter. In this chapter, you will also find an extensive list of symbols that are commonly used in written music.

Quick Reference

In this Chapter...

Common Musical Symbols

Glossary of Musical Terms

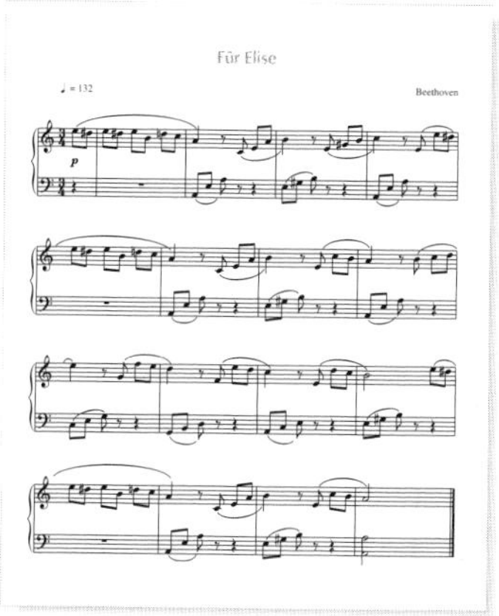

common musical symbols

Symbol	Name	Description
	Treble clef	Indicates the higher-sounding notes that you play with your right hand.
	Bass clef	Indicates the lower-sounding notes that you play with your left hand.
	Barline	Divides the music into sections of equal duration.
	Double barline	Indicates the end of a section of music.
	Double barline	Indicates the end of the music.
	Whole note	Equals 4 beats in 4/4 time.
	Half note	Equals 2 beats in 4/4 time.
	Quarter note	Equals 1 beat in 4/4 time.
	Eighth note	Equals 1/2 of a beat in 4/4 time. When two or more eighth notes appear in a row, the notes are usually joined with a beam.
	Sixteenth note	Equals 1/4 of a beat in 4/4 time. When two or more sixteenth notes appear in a row, the notes are usually joined with a beam.
	Dotted half note	Increase the amount of time you play the note by half of its original value. Equals 3 beats in 4/4 time.
	Dotted quarter note	Increase the amount of time you play the note by half of its original value. Equals 1 1/2 beats in 4/4 time.
	Dotted eighth note	Increase the amount of time you play the note by half of its original value. Equals 3/4 of a beat in 4/4 time.
	Tied notes	Play only the first note and hold the note for the combined value of both notes.
	Triplet	Play the three notes in the same number of beats as two of the notes in the triplet.
	Whole rest	Indicates a moment of silence. Do not play for 4 beats in 4/4 time.
	Half rest	Indicates a moment of silence. Do not play for 2 beats in 4/4 time.

Symbol	Name	Description
𝄽	Quarter rest	Indicates a moment of silence. Do not play for 1 beat in 4/4 time.
𝄾	Eighth rest	Indicates a moment of silence. Do not play for 1/2 of a beat in 4/4 time.
𝄿	Sixteenth rest	Indicates a moment of silence. Do not play for 1/4 of a beat in 4/4 time.
♯	Sharp	Play the black key directly to the right.
𝄪	Double-sharp	Play two keys to the right, including black and white keys.
♭	Flat	Play the black key directly to the left.
𝄫	Double-flat	Play two keys to the left, including black and white keys.
♮	Natural sign	Do not play the note as a sharp or flat.
2/2, ¢	Time signature	Describes the beats in each measure. Each measure has 2 beats and each half note counts as 1 beat.
2/4	Time signature	Describes the beats in each measure. Each measure has 2 beats and each quarter note counts as 1 beat.
3/4	Time signature	Describes the beats in each measure. Each measure has 3 beats and each quarter note counts as 1 beat.
4/4, C	Time signature	Describes the beats in each measure. Each measure has 4 beats and each quarter note counts as 1 beat.
6/8	Time signature	Describes the beats in each measure. Each measure has 6 beats and each eighth note counts as 1 beat.
𝄆 𝄇	Repetition markers	Repeat the section of music between the start repeat marker (𝄆) and the end repeat marker (𝄇). If the music does not contain a start repeat marker, return to the beginning of the music and play the music again.
1. 2.	Multiple endings	Play the first ending the first time you play the music. Return to the start repeat marker (𝄆) and play the music again, finishing with the next ending. If the music does not contain a start repeat marker, return to the beginning of the music and play the music again.

common musical symbols

Symbol	Name	Description
D.S. , 𝄋	Repetition markers	When you see D.S. , return to 𝄋 and play the music again.
D.S. al Coda , 𝄋, To Coda 𝄌, 𝄌 Coda	Repetition markers	When you see D.S. al Coda, return to 𝄋 and then play until you reach To Coda 𝄌. Then skip to the section marked 𝄌 Coda and play to the end of this section.
D.C. al Fine, Fine	Repetition markers	When you see D.C. al Fine, return to the beginning of the music, then play the music again until you reach Fine.
D.C. al Coda, To Coda 𝄌, 𝄌 Coda	Repetition markers	When you see D.C. al Coda, return to the beginning of the music and then play until you reach To Coda 𝄌. Then skip to the section marked 𝄌 Coda and play to the end of this section.
M, maj	Major chord	Indicates a major chord, such as CM or Cmaj.
m, min	Minor chord	Indicates a minor chord, such as Cm or Cmin.
7	Dominant 7th chord	Indicates a dominant 7th chord, such as C7.
M7, maj7, Major 7	Major 7th chord	Indicates a major 7th chord, such as CM7, Cmaj7 or C Major 7.
m7, min7, -7	Minor 7th chord	Indicates a minor 7th chord, such as Cm7, Cmin7 or C-7.
6	6th chord	Indicates a 6th chord, such as C6.
m6	Minor 6th chord	Indicates a minor 6th chord, such as Cm6.
9	9th chord	Indicates a 9th chord, such as C9.
maj9	Major 9th chord	Indicates a major 9th chord, such as Cmaj9.
m9	Minor 9th chord	Indicates a minor 9th chord, such as Cm9.
+, aug, ♯5	Augmented chord	Indicates an augmented chord, such as C+, Caug or C♯5.
dim, °	Diminished chord	Indicates a diminished chord, such as Cdim or C°.
sus2, 2	Suspended two chord	Indicates a suspended two chord, such as Csus2 or C2.
sus4, sus	Suspended four chord	Indicates a suspended four chord, such as Csus4 or Csus.
	Rolled chord	Press and hold down the first note of the chord and then quickly play the other notes of the chord one by one, until you are holding down all the notes of the chord.

Symbol	Name	Description
♩ = 144	Metronome Marking	Indicates the number of beats you should play per minute. Set your metronome at this speed.
largo	Speed marking	Play the music very slowly.
adagio, lento	Speed marking	Play the music slowly.
andante	Speed marking	Play the music moderately slowly.
moderato	Speed marking	Play the music at a moderate speed.
allegro	Speed marking	Play the music quickly.
presto	Speed marking	Play the music very quickly.
piu mosso	Speed marking	Play the music more quickly.
accelerando (accel.)	Speed marking	Gradually play the music more quickly.
meno mosso	Speed marking	Play the music more slowly.
rallentando (rall.)	Speed marking	Slowing down the music.
ritardando (rit.)	Speed marking	Gradually play the music more slowly.
poco à poco		Little by little.
à tempo	Speed marking	Return to the original speed of the music.
ppp	Volume marking	Play the music extremely softly.
pp	Volume marking	Play the music very softly.
p	Volume marking	Play the music softly.
mp	Volume marking	Play the music not too softly.
mf	Volume marking	Play the music not too loudly.
f	Volume marking	Play the music loudly.
ff	Volume marking	Play the music very loudly.
fff	Volume marking	Play the music extremely loudly.

common musical symbols

Symbol	Name	Description
cresc., <	Volume marking	Gradually play the music more loudly.
decresc., >, *dim.*	Volume marking	Gradually play the music more softly.
cantabile	Expression marking	Play the music in a singing style.
con brio	Expression marking	Play the music with vigor and spirit.
dolce	Expression marking	Play the music sweetly and gently.
espressivo	Expression marking	Play the music with expression.
giocoso	Expression marking	Play the music humorously.
grave	Expression marking	Play the music slowly and solemnly.
grazioso	Expression marking	Play the music gracefully.
maestoso	Expression marking	Play the music majestically.
tranquillo	Expression marking	Play the music quietly and peacefully.
vivace	Expression marking	Play the music lively and briskly.
>	Accent	Press the note hard.
^	Accent	Press the note very hard.
>.	Accent	Press the note hard and release the note quickly as you would for a staccato note.
𝄐	Fermata	Play the note longer than you normally would.
	Glissando	Slide your fingers quickly across the keyboard.
	Grace note(s)	Play note(s) quickly before the following note.
legato		Play all the notes in the music smoothly.
	Mordent	Very quickly play the note, the next lower note and then play the note again.
⌒	Slur	Play all the notes covered by the slur smoothly.

Symbol	Name	Description
·	Staccato	Play the note short and detached from adjacent notes.
▼	Staccato	Play the note very short and detached from adjacent notes.
–	Tenuto	Play the note for its full value, but detached from adjacent notes.
////	Tremolo	Alternate between playing two or more notes as quickly as you can.
tr	Trill	Alternate your fingers very quickly between the note and the next higher note on the keyboard for the entire note value.
𝆗	Trill	Alternate your fingers very quickly between the note and the next higher note on the keyboard twice and then hold the note for the remaining duration of the note value.
∾	Turn	Very quickly play the note, the next higher note, the note, the next lower note and then the note again.
∽	Turn	Very quickly play the note, the next lower note, the note, the next higher note and then the note again.
,	End of phrase marking	Indicates the end of a phrase, which expresses a musical idea.
8va, 8vb	Octave higher or lower	When you see 8va above notes, play the notes at the next higher location on the keyboard. When you see 8va or 8vb below notes, play the notes at the next lower location on the keyboard.
8va - - ┐, 8vb - - ┐	Octave higher or lower	Play all the notes from 8va or 8vb at the next higher or lower location on the keyboard until you reach the end of the line.
8va loco, 8vb loco	Octave higher or lower	Play all the notes from 8va or 8vb at the next higher or lower location on the keyboard until you reach loco.
└────┘	Damper pedal	Press and hold down the damper pedal, or right pedal, until the bracket ends.
𝆮, 𝆯	Damper pedal	Press and hold down the damper pedal, or right pedal, when you see 𝆮. Release the pedal when you see 𝆯.
una corda, *tre corda*	Soft pedal	Press and hold down the soft pedal, or left pedal, when you see *una corda*. Release the pedal when you see *tre corda*.

glossary of musical terms

6th Chord A chord consisting of four different notes, which produces a full, jazzy sound and is commonly used in big band swing music. There are two common types of 6th chords—6th and minor 6th chords. The names of 6th and minor 6th chords are commonly written with a "6" and "m6" respectively, such as C6 and Cm6.

7th Chord A chord consisting of four different notes, which is commonly used in blues and jazz music. There are three common types of 7th chords—dominant 7th, major 7th and minor 7th chords. The names of dominant 7th, major 7th and minor 7th chords are commonly written with a "7," "M7" and "m7" respectively, such as C7, CM7 and Cm7.

9th Chord A chord consisting of five different notes, which produces a textured sound and is commonly used in jazz and pop music. There are three common types of 9th chords—9th, major 9th and minor 9th chords. The names of 9th, major 9th and minor 9th chords are commonly written with a "9," "maj9" and "m9" respectively, such as C9, Cmaj9 and Cm9.

12-Bar Blues An accompaniment pattern consisting of twelve measures in which you play a specific combination of three chords. The 12-bar blues is often used in blues music.

A

Accent A symbol (> or ∧) that appears above or below a note to indicate that you should play the note harder than you normally would.

Accidental Refers to a sharp (♯), flat (♭) or natural sign (♮) that appears before a note that affects the pitch of the note.

Accompaniment Part of a musical piece that provides a musical background for the melody, or tune. In piano music, the left hand often plays the accompaniment.

Acoustic Refers to an instrument that does not require electricity to produce sound. Acoustic pianos include upright and grand pianos.

Action Refers to all the moving parts inside a piano that work together to produce a sound when you press a key. Also refers to how the keys on a piano feel, which can be a light or heavy weight.

Alberti Bass An accompaniment pattern played with a steady beat, which consists of each note in each chord played individually in a specific order—the low, high, middle, then high note. Classical music often uses Alberti bass.

Arpeggio Each note of a chord is played separately, from lowest to highest or highest to lowest, and then the same notes are played in the same order at the next higher or lower location on the keyboard.

Augmented Chord A chord consisting of three different notes, which produces a harsh sound and is often used to create an unsettled feeling in music. The name of an augmented chord is usually written with "aug," such as Caug.

B

Barline A single vertical line (|) on the staff that divides music into sections of equal duration, called measures.

Baroque Music Music written during the Baroque period, which lasted from approximately 1600 to 1750. Baroque music is complex, dramatic and ornate. The term Baroque comes from the Portuguese word for a pearl of irregular shape.

Bass Clef A symbol (𝄢) that appears at the beginning of a staff to indicate the lower-sounding notes that you play with your left hand. Bass is pronounced "base." Also called the F clef.

Beat A unit of time in music which indicates the pulse of the music.

Blues Scale A scale that consists of six different notes. Blues scales are sad sounding scales often used in jazz, blues, rock and country music.

Broken Chord Some or all of the notes in a chord are played separately.

C

Chord Three or more notes played together.

Chord Progression Moving from one chord to another within a musical piece.

Chromatic Scale A scale that consists of twelve different notes, including all the white and black keys from one key to the same key at the next higher location on the keyboard.

Classical Music Music written during the Classical period, which lasted from approximately 1750 to 1820. Classical music is based on reason, structure and objectivity.

Clef A symbol (𝄞 or 𝄢) that appears at the beginning of a staff to indicate which hand you use to play the notes on the staff.

Comping Playing chords with an interesting rhythm. Comping is often used by piano players when playing rock, jazz and blues music.

Contrapuntal Style Refers to music in which the right and left hands both play a melody, or tune, at the same time. Music written in the contrapuntal style is most commonly found in Baroque music. Also called counterpoint.

D

Damper A piece of wood with a felt pad that lifts off the strings inside a piano when you press a key, allowing the strings to vibrate and make a sound.

Damper Pedal The right pedal on a piano. When you press the damper pedal, all the notes you play continue to sound even after you lift your fingers off the keys.

Diminished Chord A chord consisting of three different notes, which produces a harsh sound and is often used to create a feeling of tension in music. The name of a diminished chord is usually written with "dim," such as Adim.

Dotted Note A note followed by a dot (·), indicating that you need to increase the amount of time you play the note by half of the note's original value. For example, a half note (𝅗𝅥) equals two beats, so a dotted half note (𝅗𝅥.) equals three beats.

Double Barline Two vertical lines on the staff that indicates the end of a section of music (‖) or the end of the music (𝄂).

Duet A musical piece for two piano players who play on either one or two pianos.

Dynamics Refers to the changes in volume in a musical piece.

E

Eighth Note A note (♪) that equals half of a beat in 4/4 time.

F

Fake Book A collection of lead sheets in a book format.

Fermata A symbol (𝄐) that appears above or below a note to indicate that you should play the note longer than you normally would.

glossary of musical terms

Fingering The way fingers are placed to play each note in a musical piece. The suggested fingering sometimes appears as numbers above or below the notes in written music, with the fingers on your left and right hands represented by the numbers one to five, starting with your thumb.

Flat A symbol (♭) that appears before a note to indicate that you should play the black key directly to the left of the corresponding white key.

Folio A collection of musical pieces in a book format.

G

Glissando Sliding your fingers quickly across the keyboard, from one note to another note. A glissando appears as a wavy line (〰) between the notes you begin and end the glissando with. Also called a gliss.

Grace Note A note played quickly before another note. A grace note is shown as a tiny note (♪) before another note.

Grand Staff Consists of a treble clef and a bass clef joined together with a brace. The grand staff allows you to read the notes for both hands at the same time.

H

Half Note A note (𝅗𝅥) that equals two beats in 4/4 time.

Half Step The distance between two keys that are side by side on the keyboard, whether the keys are white or black. Also called a semi-tone.

Hammer A piece of wood covered with felt that strikes the strings inside a piano when you press a key, causing the strings to vibrate and make a sound. Each key is connected to a hammer.

I

Improvising Making up or modifying a musical piece as you play the piece. You can improvise all or part of the melody or accompaniment of a piece.

Incomplete Measure A measure that does not have the complete number of beats required by the time signature. If a musical piece begins with an incomplete measure, the last measure will also usually be an incomplete measure.

Interval Refers to the distance between two notes.

Inversion Refers to rearranging the notes in a chord to help you move easily from one chord to another without moving your hand far along the keyboard. A chord inversion is often indicated by a slash (/) in the chord name. For example, C/E indicates that you play the C chord (C, E, G) with E as the lowest note.

K

Key A white or black item you press on a piano keyboard. Also indicates which major or minor scale the notes in a musical piece are based on.

Key Signature Sharps (♯) or flats (♭) at the beginning of a staff that indicate the notes in the music that you need to play as sharps or flats.

L

Lead Sheet A piece of written music that provides only an outline of a song, leaving pianists free to modify the music as they play, which is known as improvising. A lead sheet provides a melody written on a treble clef (𝄞) staff, with chord names written above the staff. Also called a music chart.

Ledger Line A short, horizontal line (—) that appears above or below the five lines of the staff to indicate a note that is too high or too low to appear on the staff. Also spelled "leger line."

M

Major Chord A chord consisting of three different notes, which produces a happy sound. A major chord is usually referred to by only its letter name, such as C.

Major Scale A scale that consists of seven different notes, which produces a happy sound.

Measure A section of music between two vertical lines, called barlines, on the staff. Each measure in a piece of music contains the same number of beats. Also called a bar.

Melody The singable tune of a musical piece.

Metronome A device that you can adjust to make a sound a certain number of beats per minute to help you play at a steady speed.

Middle C The C key closest to the middle of the keyboard.

MIDI Allows an electronic keyboard or piano to interact with a computer or other MIDI-compatible instruments. MIDI stands for Musical Instrument Digital Interface.

Minor Chord A chord consisting of three different notes, which produces a sad sound. The name of a minor chord is usually written with an "m," such as Am.

Minor Scale A scale that consists of seven different notes, which produces a sad sound. There are three types of minor scales—natural, harmonic and melodic minor scales.

Mode An ancient scale, consisting of seven different notes. The dorian, mixolydian and lydian modes are three commonly used modes in jazz and rock music.

Mordent A symbol (𝆙) that appears above a note to indicate that you should very quickly play the note, the next lower note and then play the note again.

Mute Pedal The middle pedal on some upright pianos. When you press the mute pedal, all the notes you play will sound significantly softer and muffled, which is useful when you want to play the piano without disturbing your family or neighbors.

N

Natural Sign A symbol (♮) that appears before a note to indicate that you should not play the note as a sharp or flat.

Note A symbol which represents the duration and pitch of a musical sound. Each note corresponds to a specific key on the keyboard.

O

Octave The distance between a note and the next lower or higher note with the same letter name.

P

Pentatonic Scale A scale that consists of five different notes and is commonly used in jazz, blues, rock and country music. In Western music, there are three main types of pentatonic scales—major, major (flat3) and minor pentatonic scales.

Phrase Expresses a musical idea and often consists of four measures in a musical piece. Music is usually divided into phrases to add structure to the music. Each phrase in music may be marked with a curved line, known as a slur, or a comma (’) may appear above the staff at the end of each phrase.

Pickup Note A note that appears in an incomplete measure at the beginning of a musical piece.

Pitch Refers to how high or low a note sounds.

glossary of musical terms

Q

Quarter Note A note (♩) that equals one beat in 4/4 time.

R

Rest A symbol such as 𝄽 or ▬ that indicates a moment of silence in music. Each type of rest indicates a specific number of beats that you should not play.

Rhythm The pattern of notes of a musical piece, consisting of any combination of shorter and longer note values.

Romantic Music Music written during the Romantic period, which took place in the 1800s. Romantic music is emotional, passionate and often tells a story.

Root Position Refers to the arrangement of notes in a chord so the root, or first, note of the chord is the lowest note. For example, the C major chord (C, E, G) in root position has the root note (C) as the lowest note.

S

Scale A series of notes that you play in ascending and/or descending order. The most common types of scales are the major and minor scales.

Sharp A symbol (♯) that appears before a note to indicate that you should play the black key directly to the right of the corresponding white key.

Sheet Music A piece of music printed on a few pages, which are folded or stapled together.

Sixteenth Note A note (𝅘𝅥𝅯) that equals a quarter of a beat in 4/4 time.

Slur A curved line (⌒) that connects two or more different notes, indicating that you play all the notes covered by the slur smoothly. Also called a phrase marking.

Soft Pedal The left pedal on a piano. When you press the soft pedal, all the notes you play will sound slightly softer.

Solid Chord All the notes of a chord are played at the same time. Also called a block chord.

Soundboard A large piece of wood that amplifies the sound produced by the piano. The soundboard is the entire piece of wood at the bottom of a grand piano and the back of an upright piano.

Staccato A dot (·) or wedge (▲) above or below a note to indicate that you should play the note short and detached from adjacent notes.

Staff The five horizontal lines and the four spaces between the lines on which notes are written. The plural form of staff is staves.

Suspended Chord A chord consisting of three different notes, which produces a harsh, unresolved sound and is commonly used in rock, jazz and blues music. There are two basic types of suspended chords—suspended two and suspended four chords. The names of suspended two and suspended four chords are commonly written with "sus2" and "sus4" respectively, such as Csus2 and Csus4. Also called a sus chord.

Sustain Pedal The middle pedal on a piano. When you press the sustain pedal, the notes you play at the same time as you press the pedal will continue to sound after you lift your fingers off the keys. Also called a sostenuto pedal.

Swing Beat An uneven rhythm created by playing pairs of slightly longer beats followed by slightly shorter beats. Jazz and blues music often use a swing beat.

Syncopated Notes Notes played between the main beats in a musical piece and held through the next beat. Syncopated notes are commonly used in jazz, blues and rock music.

Synthesizer An instrument that is similar to an electronic keyboard but has better sound quality and more advanced capabilities. Professional musicians often use synthesizers to record music and perform on stage.

T

Tempo The speed at which you play a musical piece.

Tenuto A short line (–) above or below a note to indicate that you should play the note for its full value but detached from adjacent notes.

Tied Notes Two identical notes joined with a curved line (‿), indicating that you play only the first note and hold the note for the combined value of both notes.

Time Signature Consists of two numbers, one on top of the other, that appear at the beginning of a staff to describe the beats in every measure. The top number indicates the number of beats in each measure. The bottom number indicates the type of note that counts as one beat.

Transposing Changing the key of a musical piece to make all the notes in the music sound higher or lower.

Treble Clef A symbol (𝄞) that appears at the beginning of a staff to indicate the higher-sounding notes that you play with your right hand. Also called the G clef.

Tremolo Alternate between playing two or more notes as quickly as you can. Tremolos create tension or excitement in a musical piece. A tremolo is shown as three thick lines (≡) between the notes you need to alternate between.

Trill Alternate very quickly between a note and the next higher note. A trill is shown as *tr* or 𝆖 above a note.

Triplet A group of three notes played in the same number of beats as two of the notes in the triplet. The notes in a triplet are grouped with a beam, bracket or curved line and marked with the number 3.

Tuning Adjusting the strings in a piano to the proper tension to ensure the best sound quality.

Turn Very quickly play a note, the next higher or lower note, the note, the next lower or higher note and then the note again. A turn is shown as 𝆗 or 𝆘 above a note.

W

Walking Bass Line An accompaniment pattern commonly used in blues, jazz and rock music. The walking bass line consists of playing some or all of the notes in a chord as well as one or two notes between or close to the notes of a chord. The notes are played individually and usually played in order, moving up or down the keyboard.

Whole Note A note (𝅝) that equals four beats in 4/4 time.

Whole Step The distance between two keys that are separated by another key on the keyboard, whether the keys are white or black. Also called a whole tone.

index

Numbers

A

B

C

D

index

E

F

G

H

I

J

index

K

L

M

index

Q

R

S

index

T

U

V

W

maran illustrated PIANO

MARAN ILLUSTRATED™ Piano is an information-packed resource for people who want to learn to play the piano, as well as current musicians looking to hone their skills. Combining full-color photographs and easy-to-follow instructions, this guide covers everything from the basics of piano playing to more advanced techniques. Not only does MARAN ILLUSTRATED™ Piano show you how to read music, play scales and chords and improvise while playing with other musicians, it also provides you with helpful information for purchasing and caring for your piano.

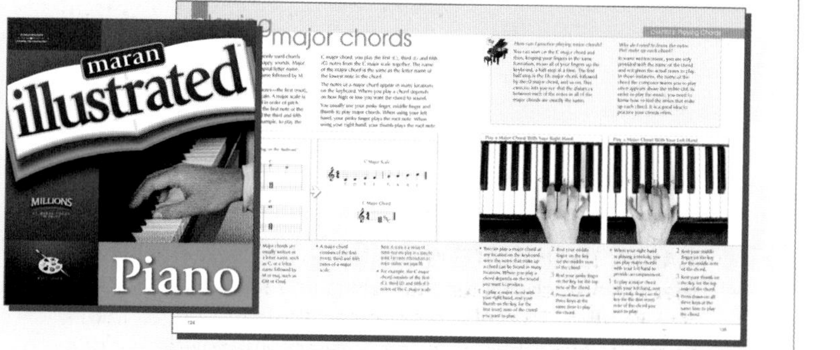

ISBN: 1-59200-864-X

Price: $24.99 US; $34.95 CDN

Page count: 304

maran illustrated DOG TRAINING

MARAN ILLUSTRATED™ Dog Training is an excellent guide for both current dog owners and people considering making a dog part of their family. Using clear, step-by-step instructions accompanied by over 400 full-color photographs, MARAN ILLUSTRATED™ Dog Training is perfect for any visual learner who prefers seeing what to do rather than reading lengthy explanations.

Beginning with insights into popular dog breeds and puppy development, this book emphasizes positive training methods to guide you through socializing, housetraining and teaching your dog many commands. You will also learn how to work with problem behaviors, such as destructive chewing.

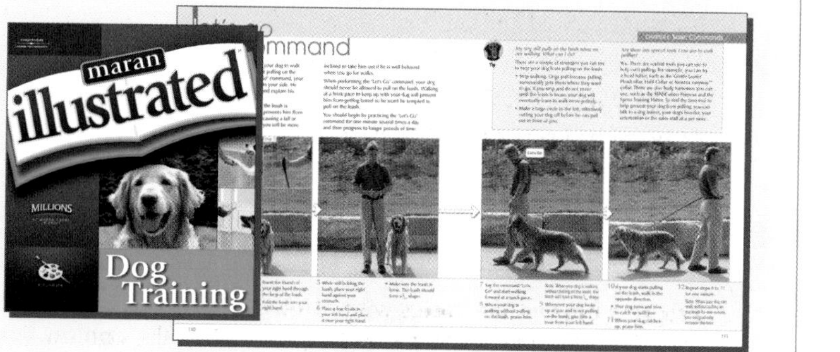

ISBN: 1-59200-858-5

Price: $19.99 US; $27.95 CDN

Page count: 256

maran illustrated KNITTING & CROCHETING

MARAN ILLUSTRATED™ Knitting & Crocheting contains a wealth of information about these two increasingly popular crafts. Whether you are just starting out or you are an experienced knitter or crocheter interested in picking up new tips and techniques, this information-packed resource will take you from the basics, such as how to hold the knitting needles or crochet hook, to more advanced skills, such as how to add decorative touches to your projects. The easy-to-follow information is communicated through clear, step-by-step instructions and accompanied by over 600 full-color photographs—perfect for any visual learner.

ISBN: 1-59200-862-3
Price: $24.99 US; $34.95 CDN
Page count: 304

maran illustrated YOGA

MARAN ILLUSTRATED™ Yoga provides a wealth of simplified, easy-to-follow information about the increasingly popular practice of Yoga. This easy-to-use guide is a must for visual learners who prefer to see and do without having to read lengthy explanations.

Using clear, step-by-step instructions accompanied by over 500 full-color photographs, this book includes all the information you need to get started with yoga or to enhance your technique if you have already made yoga a part of your life. MARAN ILLUSTRATED™ Yoga shows you how to safely and effectively perform a variety of yoga poses at various skill levels, how to breathe more efficiently and much more.

ISBN: 1-59200-868-2
Price: $24.99 US; $34.95 CDN
Page count: 320

maran illustrated WEIGHT TRAINING

MARAN ILLUSTRATED™ Weight Training is an information-packed guide that covers all the basics of weight training, as well as more advanced techniques and exercises.

MARAN ILLUSTRATED™ Weight Training contains more than 500 full-color photographs of exercises for every major muscle group, along with clear, step-by-step instructions for performing the exercises. Useful tips provide additional information and advice to help enhance your weight training experience.

MARAN ILLUSTRATED™ Weight Training provides all the information you need to start weight training or to refresh your technique if you have been weight training for some time.

ISBN: 1-59200-866-6

Price: $24.99 US; $34.95 CDN

Page count: 320

maran illustrated GUITAR

MARAN ILLUSTRATED™ Guitar is an excellent resource for people who want to learn to play the guitar, as well as for current musicians who want to fine tune their technique. This full-color guide includes over 500 photographs, accompanied by step-by-step instructions that teach you the basics of playing the guitar and reading music, as well as advanced guitar techniques. You will also learn what to look for when purchasing a guitar or accessories, how to maintain and repair your guitar, and much more.

Whether you want to learn to strum your favorite tunes or play professionally, MARAN ILLUSTRATED™ Guitar provides all the information you need to become a proficient guitarist.

BOOK BONUS!

Visit www.maran.com/guitar to download MP3 files you can listen to and play along with for all the chords, scales, exercises and practice pieces in the book.

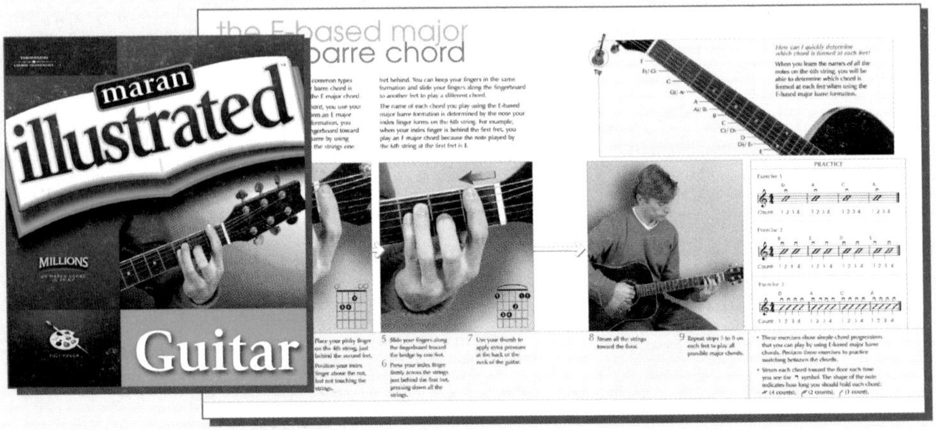

ISBN: 1-59200-860-7
Price: $24.99 US; $34.95 CDN
Page count: 320